The Voice as Something More

NEW
MATERIAL
HISTORIES
of
MUSIC

---

a series edited by
James Q. Davies *and*
Nicholas Mathew

ALSO PUBLISHED IN THIS SERIES

Musical Vitalities: Ventures in a Biotic Aesthetic of Music
Holly Watkins

Sex, Death, and Minuets: Anna Magdalena Bach and Her Musical Notebooks
David Yearsley

The Voice as Something More

Essays toward Materiality

EDITED BY
MARTHA FELDMAN AND
JUDITH T. ZEITLIN

With an Afterword by
Mladen Dolar

The University of Chicago Press
Chicago and London

The University of Chicago Press, Chicago 60637
The University of Chicago Press, Ltd., London

Published 2019
Printed in the United States of America

28 27 26 25 24 23 22 21 20 19   1 2 3 4 5

ISBN-13: 978-0-226-65639-7 (cloth)
ISBN-13: 978-0-226-64717-3 (paper)
ISBN-13: 978-0-226-65642-7 (e-book)
DOI: https://doi.org/10.7208/chicago/9780226656427.001.0001

Library of Congress Cataloging-in-Publication Data

Names: International Conference "A Voice as Something More" (2015 : Chicago, Ill.) | Feldman, Martha, editor. | Zeitlin, Judith T., 1958– editor. | Dolar, Mladen, writer of afterword.
Title: The voice as something more : essays toward materiality / edited by Martha Feldman and Judith T. Zeitlin ; with an afterword by Mladen Dolar.
Other titles: New material histories of music.
Description: Chicago : The University of Chicago Press, 2019. | Series: New material histories of music | Essays based on papers of the international conference "A Voice as Something More," held at the University of Chicago in November 2015. | Includes bibliographical references and index.
Identifiers: LCCN 2019005340 | ISBN 9780226656397 (cloth : alk. paper) | ISBN 9780226647173 (pbk. : alk. paper) | ISBN 9780226656427 (ebook)
Subjects: LCSH: Singing. | Voice (Philosophy) | Voice. | Music—Philosophy and aesthetics.
Classification: LCC ML3877 .168 2015 | DDC 783—dc23
LC record available at https://lccn.loc.gov/2019005340

♾ This paper meets the requirements of ANSI/NISO Z39.48-1992 (Permanence of Paper).

For PB and WH

Contents

Preface

The enigmatic photograph on the cover of this book is the work of the Chinese photographer and engineer Jin Shisheng (1910–2000). Entitled "Self-Portrait in Darmstadt" and taken between 1939 and 1940, it's one of a series of experimental self-portraits he made contemplating the role of the photographer and photography as "a visual technology."[1]

Here, two figures wear dark suits, white shirts, and roundish, dark-rimmed spectacles, but the man on the left holds up a camera half blocking his face. It's aimed at a man foregrounded on the right, whose mouth is stretched wide open in a wordless shout, scream, or song. Wordless to us, because as viewers we cannot hear the voice in the image, only imagine it. The photograph calls to us to fill in the empty "O" of his mouth, the conjured presence of this exaggerated voice, all the more powerful because it is elusive and ungraspable.

The disorienting composition, augmented by a second camera lying slightly out of focus on the table, also demands that we come up with a scenario that explains the unusual setup and the identity of the figures. The man holding the camera must be Jin Shisheng himself, but then he had to have taken the photograph in a mirror. Jin's oeuvre shows that he was fond of including multiple self-images and cameras in a single photograph, and at first glance the two figures do look deceptively similar. Upon closer scrutiny, however, the second man is clearly someone else. Who was he, and what were the two of them doing in Darmstadt then?

According to the photographer's son, the man with his mouth open was a German friend of his father's, who was mocking Hitler giving a speech.[2] This piece of information completely transforms our view of the photograph. The aggressive gesticulation, grimacing brow, and roaring mouth all fall into place now. The visuals suggest that photos or newsreels of Hitler would have

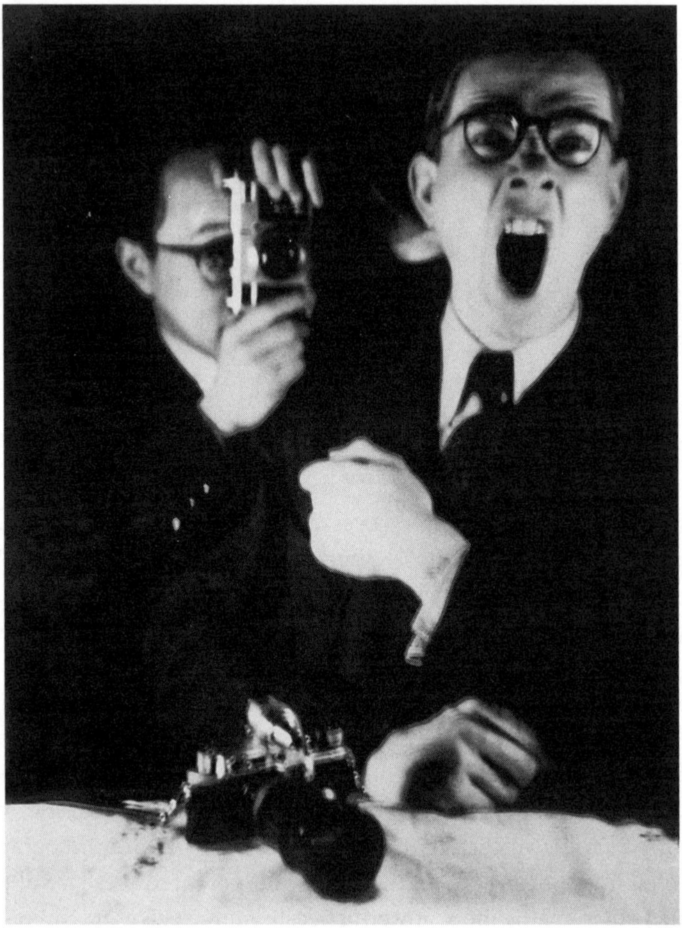

FIGURE 0.1. Jin Shisheng, "Self-Portrait in Darmstadt," 1939–1940. Courtesy of Jin Hua.

furnished a model, but for the sound of the speech, the disembodied voice of der Führer inundating the radio waves—the ghost in the machine—was terrifyingly inescapable in Darmstadt in 1939–1940.

This photograph is a fitting entry point into *The Voice as Something More* because it resonates with many of the approaches to voice explored in this book. The photo compels us to reflect on the role of technology in mediating the voice and in framing it as an "object" available for study. Yet it also exposes the limitations of both technology and the objectification of voice. It suggests the extent to which all voices can be assumed, borrowed, or ventriloquized, and points to the paradoxical status of voice as something that hovers between embodiment and disembodiment, and thus raises the uncertainty of determining to whom a voice belongs.[3] The story behind the photo and its caption reinforces the need to situate specific voices within a specific historical time and place, yet the overall puzzle of capturing voice that this visual image so cunningly stages can't be solved solely by recourse to history, biography, politics, or technology. There's always something more to the voice—a remainder, a gap, a reverb, an echo. To get at these more phantasmatic dimensions requires additional modes of inquiry, including the psychoanalytic, the literary, the mythic, and the philosophical.

This photograph also appeared on the poster and program for a three-day international conference entitled "A Voice as Something More," held at the University of Chicago in November 2015. Organized by the present editors, the conference served as a staging ground for the rethinking of voice studies that engendered this volume. Berthold Hoeckner's paper was committed elsewhere and regrettably does not appear here, but we thank him and panel chairs Jim Chandler, Jacob Smith, and Paola Iovene for contributing so much to the intellectual success and liveliness of the proceedings.

The conference in turn grew out of the Voice Project, a faculty research seminar initiated by an interdisciplinary group of faculty and sponsored by the University of Chicago's Neubauer Collegium for Culture and Society between 2013 and 2016. In addition to the three principal investigators of the Voice Project—Martha Feldman (2013–2016), David Levin (2013–2014), and Judith Zeitlin (2014–2016)—the core participants included Seth Brodsky, Daniel Callahan, Tom Gunning, Sarah Nooter, Jessica Peritz, Marcelle Pierson, Steven Rings, and Neil Verma. For two years, we met several times per term, each of us taking turns curating one of these meetings. Jim Chandler, Nicholas Harkness, and Jacob Smith also presented to the group, while Nina Sun Eidsheim and James Q. Davies gave presentations at a one-day Voice Project symposium held in spring 2014. Naturally, contributors to the present volume represent a broader range of institutions and fields.

Our book is greatly enriched by contributions from the French film scholar and composer Michel Chion and the Slovenian philosopher Mladen Dolar. Both reprise their respective roles at the 2015 conference, Chion as keynote speaker and Dolar as conference respondent. Zakir Paul's English translation, initially commissioned for use at the conference, preserves the spoken quality of Chion's lecture, with all its digressions and wit.

By happy coincidence, Dolar turned out to be teaching at the University of Chicago during the fall of 2013 when the Voice Project began meeting in earnest, and he joined our group. His presence affected the kinds of questions we were asking from the inception, and while the group moved on in other directions after his departure, we periodically returned to these questions with fresh insights. As should be clear, the title of this volume is an affectionate riposte to Dolar's field-shaping book *A Voice and Nothing More*. His latest reflections on the chapters published here appear in the form of an afterword, which offers a major commentary on his highly influential book, ten years and more after its publication, while providing a gracious and fitting conclusion to the Voice Project and this book.

A project of this duration and magnitude inevitably runs up a sizeable debt to many institutions and individuals. We gratefully acknowledge the indispensable support of the Neubauer Collegium, which sponsored not only the Voice Project but also the 2014 symposium and 2015 conference. We also thank the Franke Institute for the Humanities and the Department of Music for providing substantial additional funding for the conference. In recognition of the interdisciplinary value of voice studies, an impressive number of other entities on campus contributed further support or in-kind help: the departments of Cinema and Media Studies, Classics, Germanic Studies, and East Asian Languages and Civilizations; the Center for East Asian Studies; the Center for Theater and Performance Studies; the Film Studies Center; and the Reva and David Logan Center for the Arts.

We would also like to acknowledge with gratitude the hard work and important contributions of several other key individuals: first and foremost, the Voice Project's two graduate research interns, Marcelle Pierson (2013–2014) and Jessica Peritz (2014–2015), as well as Anne Rebull and Yiren Zheng, the graduate student coordinators for the conference, and Zhuqing (Lester) Hu, who served as rapporteur.[4] At the Neubauer, successive faculty directors David Nirenberg and Jonathan Lear, along with their then-staff Jamie Bender, Madeline McKiddy, and Matt Hess, deserve particular thanks.

We're grateful to Seth Brodsky for a canny reading of parts of the introduction to the book. For dropping everything at the last minute to help whip the manuscript into shape for submission, we wholeheartedly thank Shawn Marie Keener. To Marta Tonegutti, our editor at the University of Chicago Press, for her acumen and vision in shepherding this project from beginning to end, we express our deepest gratitude. Editorial director Alan Thomas saw the book through a crucial stage in its evolution. Editorial associates Susannah Engstrom and Tristan Bates, marketing director Levi Stahl, our designer Natalie Sowa, our copyeditor Marianne Tatom, and our production editor Tamara Ghattas all deserve thanks for their keenly intelligent contributions and enthusiastic support, along with others at the press. Finally, we thank Dean

Anne Walters Robertson and the Humanities Division at the University of Chicago for a generous publication subvention.

Notes

1. Wu Hung, *Zooming In: Histories of Photography in China* (London: Reaktion Books, 2016), 126. For this photograph, see *Zhongguo sheying: ershiji yilai* [Chinese photography: Twentieth century and beyond], ed. Rongrong (Beijing: Three Shadows Studio, 2015), 152.

2. Private communication between Judith Zeitlin, Wu Hung, and Jin Hua, November 2015.

3. It's even possible to speculate that although no radio appears in the photo, Jin's friend was lip-synching Hitler's voice as it was being broadcast.

4. For his review of the conference, see Zhuqing (Lester) Hu, "A Voice as Something More: An International Conference," *Opera Quarterly* 32, nos. 2–3 (2016): 233–37.

Illustrations

Preface

Chapter 2

Chapter 4

Chapter 7

Chapter 11

Chapter 12

Chapter 13

Chapter 15

Musical Examples (Print)

Chapter 11

Website Examples (Audiovisual)

For all audiovisual examples, go to press.uchicago.edu/sites/voice/. Captions for the examples appear below.

Chapter 1

WEBSITE EXAMPLE 1.1 An excerpt from Diana Deutsch's "Sometimes Behave So Strangely." Issued on *Phantom Words and Other Curiosities* (Philomel Records, 2003), track 21.

WEBSITE EXAMPLE 1.2 Steve Reich, *It's Gonna Rain*, opening. Issued on *Early Works* (Elektra Nonesuch, 1987), track 1.

WEBSITE EXAMPLE 1.3 Hank Williams, "Pictures from Life's Other Side," verse 1 and beginning of chorus. Issued on *Hank Williams as Luke the Drifter* (MGM, 1954), track 1.

WEBSITE EXAMPLE 1.4 Hank Williams, "Pictures from Life's Other Side," final verse. Issued on *Hank Williams as Luke the Drifter* (MGM, 1954), track 1.

WEBSITE EXAMPLE 1.5 Marvin Gaye, "Save the Children," studio recording, opening. Issued on *What's Going On* (Tamla, 1971), track 4.

WEBSITE EXAMPLE 1.6 Marvin Gaye, "Save the Children," studio recording, excerpt. Issued on *What's Going On* (Tamla, 1971), track 4.

WEBSITE EXAMPLE 1.7 Marvin Gaye, "Save the Children," performed live at the Kennedy Center, 1972, opening. Issued on *What's Going On*, Deluxe Edition (Motown, 2012), disc 2, track 8.

WEBSITE EXAMPLE 1.8	Excerpts from Bob Dylan, "Stuck inside of Mobile with the Memphis Blues Again" (*Blonde on Blonde*, Columbia, 1966, track 6); the Velvet Underground, "Sweet Jane" (*Loaded*, Cotillion, 1971, track 2); and Leonard Cohen, "Dress Rehearsal Rag" (*Songs of Love and Hate*, Columbia, 1971, track 3).
WEBSITE EXAMPLE 1.9	Patti Smith, "Land," opening. Issued on *Horses* (Arista, 1975), track 1.
WEBSITE EXAMPLE 1.10	Excerpts from Joni Mitchell, "Coyote" (*Hejira*, Asylum, 1976, track 1); and Rickie Lee Jones, "Easy Money" (*Rickie Lee Jones*, Warner Bros., 1979, track 5).
WEBSITE EXAMPLE 1.11	Laura Marling, "The Muse," opening. Issued on *A Creature I Don't Know* (Virgin, 2011), track 1.
WEBSITE EXAMPLE 1.12	Laura Marling, "Saved These Words," opening. Issued on *Once I Was an Eagle* (Virgin, 2013), track 16.
WEBSITE EXAMPLE 1.13	Laura Marling, "Saved These Words," excerpt. Issued on *Once I Was an Eagle* (Virgin, 2013), track 16.
WEBSITE EXAMPLE 1.14	Beyoncé, "Formation," opening. Issued on *Once Lemonade* (Parkwood/Columbia, 2016), track 13.
WEBSITE EXAMPLE 1.15	Kanye West, "Ultralight Beam," Chance the Rapper's verse. Issued on *The Life of Pablo* (Good/Def Jam/Roc-A-Fella, 2016), track 1.

Chapter 3

WEBSITE EXAMPLE 3.1	Luigi Nono, *Il canto sospeso*, no. 6a. Performed by the Berlin Philharmonic, with Claudio Abbado conducting (Sony Classical SK 53360, 1993).
WEBSITE EXAMPLE 3.2	Karlheinz Stockhausen, *Gesang der Jünglinge*, opening.

Chapter 4

WEBSITE EXAMPLES 4.1–4.2	Excerpt from Gregory Whitehead, "Pressures of the Unspeakable" (1991).
WEBSITE EXAMPLE 4.3	Arch Oboler, "The Dark," *Lights Out!* (ca. 1940s).
WEBSITE EXAMPLES 4.4–4.7	Excerpts from Wyllis Cooper, "The Thing on the Fourble Board," *Quiet, Please* (1948).

Chapter 7

WEBSITE EXAMPLE 7.1	Excerpt from *What Makes a Great Tenor?*, directed by Dominic Best (London: BBC Four, 2011), DVD.

Chapter 9

WEBSITE EXAMPLE 9.1	Excerpt from the end of Geminiano Giacomelli, "Sposa, son disprezzata," sung by Cecilia Bartoli on the CD *Se tu m'ami: Arie antiche* (London Records, 1990) (where it is misattributed to Vivaldi).
WEBSITE EXAMPLE 9.2	Excerpt from Dizzy Gillespie's "A Night in Tunisia," sung by Leny Andrade on the CD *Luz Neon* (Timeless Records, 1990), track 8.
WEBSITE EXAMPLE 9.3	Beginning of Patricia Barber, "Persephone," from *Mythologies* song cycle, with opening verse sung by Lawrice Flowers, live at the Museum of Contemporary Art, Chicago, IL, January 7, 2006. Filmed by I. Michael Toth.
WEBSITE EXAMPLE 9.4	Excerpt from Sandy Denny's "Who Knows Where the Time Goes?," sung by Nina Simone live at Philharmonic Hall in 1969 and issued on *Black Gold* (RCA Victor, 1970), track 5.

WEBSITE EXAMPLE 9.5 — Excerpt from Hoagy Carmichael's "I Get Along without You Very Well (Except Sometimes)," sung by Rosemary Clooney on *Rosie Solves the Swingin' Riddle!*, arranged and conducted by Nelson Riddle, 33 1/3 monaural (RCA Victor, 1961), track 3.

WEBSITE EXAMPLE 9.6 — Excerpt from Hoagy Carmichael's "I Get Along without You Very Well (Except Sometimes)," sung by Nina Simone on *Nina Simone and Piano!* (RCA Studios, 1969), track 9.

WEBSITE EXAMPLE 9.7 — Repeat of final part of website example 9.6.

Chapter 10

WEBSITE EXAMPLE 10.1 — The Dwarf as introduced by Don Estoban, the Chamberlain (James Johnson), to Ghita (Susan B. Anthony) and the maids in Zemlinsky's *Der Zwerg*, as performed by the Los Angeles Opera in a 2008 production staged by Darko Tresnjak and conducted by James Conlon, released on DVD by Arthaus Musik in 2010.

WEBSITE EXAMPLE 10.2 — The Dwarf (Rodrick Dixon) sings the song of the blood-red orange to the Infanta (Mary Dunleavy) and before the assembled court in Zemlinsky's *Der Zwerg*, as performed by the Los Angeles Opera in a 2008 production staged by Darko Tresnjak and conducted by James Conlon, released on DVD by Arthaus Musik in 2010.

Chapter 11

WEBSITE EXAMPLE 11.1 — Helmut Lachenmann, II. Streichquartett, "Reigen seliger Geister" (1989), "shadow-song." Jack Quartet, unpublished DVD.

WEBSITE EXAMPLE 11.2 — Luigi Nono, *Fragmente—Stille, an Diotima* (1980), fragment 48. Minguet Quartet, live television broadcast, Römerbad Musiktagen, Badenweiler, Germany, 2004.

WEBSITE EXAMPLE 11.3 — Alban Berg, *Lyrische Suite*, mvt. 6, “Largo desolato” (opening, with suppressed soprano voice added). Wigmore Hall Learning, Tana String Quartet with Julia Sitkovetsky.

WEBSITE EXAMPLE 11.4 — Ludwig van Beethoven, String Quartet, op. 130 (1825), mvt. 5 (Cavatina), “beklemmt” section. Artemis Quartet, 2010.

Chapter 14

WEBSITE EXAMPLE 14.1 — Burning Spear, “Slavery Days,” from the *Marcus Garvey* album (Island Records, 1975).

WEBSITE EXAMPLE 14.2 — Burning Spear, “Children of Today,” from *Living Dub: Volume 1* (Burning Spear Productions, 1982).

WEBSITE EXAMPLE 14.3 — Vybz Kartel, “Life We Living,” from *Pon di Gaza 2.0* (VP Records, 2010).

INTRODUCTION

The Clamor of Voices

MARTHA FELDMAN AND JUDITH T. ZEITLIN

This book has the contradictory aim of throwing the lights up on voice while turning them down. It does so by trying at once to identify tangible aesthetic, political, ethical, literary, and musical voices and recognizing that nothing could be more elusive than a human voice, nothing more confounding. Put that dilemma together with the fact of radical divergences in talk about voice, and you have a phenomenon that is highly refractory to analysis and dialogue. Voices nowadays are caught up in fundamentally different realms of discourse, to say nothing of practice and culture: between sounding and nonsounding voices (phonic and "aphonic"), material and nonmaterial ones, between voice as a literal phenomenon and voice as a metaphorical one. No wonder voice has become the subject of so much writing in recent years, producing a "vocal turn" to rival the linguistic and visual turns of the later twentieth century.[1]

Here we add to the conversation by recognizing the valuable contributions to these divergences that have been made by psychoanalytic theory, with its focus on interiority, at the same time as we move in a more materialist direction. What does this materialism consist of? The timbre or "grain" of the sounding voice. The flesh, membrane, mucus, and cartilage of the mechanism that produces it. The masks, veils, and scrims that hide, throw, conceal, disguise, or displace it. The vocoders, phonographs, synthesizers, and microphones that enhance, distort, or play with it. The sheer sonic pleasure voice produces but also the fears, anxieties, and tensions that set it in motion, and thus even our sonic fantasies insofar as they "stick" to our "worldly experience" and persevere "in them and through them."[2] Materiality admits of no easy boundaries, yet in its substantive guise it nevertheless erects a lithic, obdurate counterweight to the psychoanalytic voice as it's usually evoked.

In what follows, we begin by expanding on issues that produced our title and proceed to unpack the various essays between its covers. Along the way, we interrogate a variety of subjects related to the voice, which are to varying degrees explored within this introduction, particularly self and other, language, "grain," technology, music, and race.

Approaching the Voice

1

Let's begin with a rich, if simple, notion: namely, that of all the sounds made in the world, only the sound of the voice "implies a subjectivity which 'expresses itself' and itself inhabits the means of expression."[3] This is what we read in Mladen Dolar's *A Voice and Nothing More*, a book that has had a profound effect on humanistic projects over the past decade and more. Yet there is a big "but" that follows:

> But if the voice is thus the quasi-natural bearer of the production of meaning, it also proves to be strangely recalcitrant to it. If we speak in order to "make sense," to signify, to convey something, then the voice is the material support of bringing about meaning, yet it does not contribute to it itself. It is rather like the vanishing mediator (to use the term made famous by Fredric Jameson for a different purpose)—it makes the utterance possible, but it disappears in it, it goes up in smoke in the meaning being produced.

The voice may be linked to subjectivity, we're told, but it is reliably neither sense-making nor sense-reinforcing (though, unreliably, it can be both). Nor is it ever identical to either one.

That qualification haunts the relationship between voice and language in Dolar's book, much as similar qualifications haunt the relationships between voice and body and even voice and sound. To appreciate why Dolar's voice is not commensurate with language or body or sound means getting a handle on some basic Lacanian operations relevant to the subject, for the voice pursued by Dolar, here and elsewhere, is a so-called "object-voice," the voice of Lacan's *objet a* or *objet petit a* (object a or object small a)—meaning that it is not "an object" in the everyday sense of the word but rather the attempted objectification, or even inverted projection, of a constitutive lack in the subject. It is a lack inverted into a surplus. As such, it is a voice always in excess of bodies, languages, and sounds (including musical sounds), functioning as it does as an elusive (object-)cause of desire. Neither the body ("the physics of the voice") nor language ("the linguistics of the voice") nor sound can billet all its locations, meanings, and maneuvers, uttered or internal. Always left over, or on the escape, is something in the voice that cannot be accommodated or internalized, and therefore that contributes to maintaining it as a kind of other that is forever mysterious and alien to the self.[4]

In this, the Lacanian voice departs from "ordinary" meanings of voice, which see it (as Dolar stresses) as the bearer of semantic meaning or the source of aesthetic admiration (in addition to promoting such Western commonplaces as voice as a token of identity or a metaphor for individuality or sovereignty).[5] The former notion, voice as bearer of semantic meaning, would understand it rather unproblematically as that which conveys signification, carrying signs to their proper destinations where they become available for decoding. It would see a large zone of overlap between semantic meaning and phonic utterance, if not their total congruence. The latter notion, voice as source of aesthetic admiration, would see it as that which produces (or claims to produce) such feelings as delight, sorrow, or yearning, rather than understanding voice skeptically, and would perceive in it a bulwark against threats, fetishistic disavowals of castration (I attach myself passionately to this beautiful aesthetic object so as to deflect my attention from the real object that disturbs and threatens me). We return to both points below.

In delineating each of these, Dolar places voice in a position of prominence, and one that revises and virtually opposes, if somewhat orthogonally, Derrida's critique of voice. In Derrida, voice—in particular the silent inner voice of the subject—is essentially demoted from its lofty position in the metaphysics of Husserl, where it is a special token of subjective self-presence or "autoaffection" and is exposed rather as a site of difference and alterity in the subject. Dolar, like his countryman and sometime collaborator Slavoj Žižek, instead elevates voice. Far from perceiving voice as being *of a piece with* the subject or even situated alongside the subject at all, voice for Dolar and Žižek situates itself not on the side of what the subject is or produces but on the side of what the subject perceives and above all desires.[6] Voice for the Lacanian subject exists as an object. And what the subject perceives in that object is an illusory figment of desire, with desire understood as a linguistic force that voids and cuts up the subject, yet is at the same time continuous and unconscious.[7] Since the thing desired is illusory insofar as it technically does not exist, the subject can only circle around it, trying to hitch a ride with it, so to speak, to hook onto it in some way, meandering toward, around, and about it in order to find this presumed target, but forever missing it. That failed encounter, that missing of the object or object-cause (*objet a*), is something the subject fails even to experience as a "lack" or a "gap," for it is so covered over in fantasy. And yet that lack or gap, in all its negativity, is defining.[8]

What justifies this emplacement of voice in a relation of alterity and desire to the subject, rather than keeping it *within* the subject? To answer that question, we need to understand that in Lacanian accounts of early psychic development, an "object" is most often another person (classically, a parent), who, by virtue of a relationship, most often indirect, helps bring the subject to self-consciousness. Initially it is *part-objects*—not persons, but things, like breasts or, in our case, voices—in relation to which the subject develops. Crucially, the object-voice does not in and of itself act as a kind of *substitute*. On the contrary (and to go back to the ordinary meanings of voice above): anything that does act as a substitute for this object-voice—a fantasy that represses desire, more precisely—does so by repressing it as something disturbing. Hence music can have the force of a substitute, in particular when it *departs* from language, or from what Dolar calls "textual anchorage," such that even the sound of a flute or oboe or a vocal melisma might function as a disavowal of the inner psychic disturbance that the object-voice represents.[9]

What has been striking about this theory to both critics and fans is that it leads a true Lacanian to the conclusion, *faute de mieux*, that all voices are acousmatic, their source never visible or otherwise fully accessible to their bearers or hearers. The term goes back to Michel Chion's usage in *The Voice in Cinema* and before him to that of his teacher, electronic composer Pierre Schaeffer, though there the acousmatic is a particular and marked phenomenon that occurs with respect to voice, not a universal condition of it.[10] For Dolar, by contrast, there can be no such thing as what he calls "disacousmatization" (alternatively: "de-acousmatization"), the revelation of the source of the voice, since all voice is constitutively obscure and intangible to the desiring subject: in a word, acousmatic.[11]

Dolar's object-voice has prompted a series of extensions and divagations. In an ambitious and probing gloss, musicologist Freya Jarman-Ivens ventures a queering of Dolar's psychoanalytic approach, extending his sense of voice as "operator of a divide" to encompass gender within what in her treatment becomes a kind of third space. In the process, she shows how voice navigates between body and language, speaker/singer and listener, inside and outside such that there is no fixity of category, no set borders for voice, thus opening up new possibilities for understanding voice as a medium of intersubjective identification.[12] Philosopher Karmen MacKendrick explores the acousmatic dimensions of Dolar's object-voice as a starting point for thinking about disjunctions between bodies and voices—voices that are always embodied, but in no one-to-one voice/body relationship and in ways that always involve vocal borrowings from others.[13] For theater and performance studies scholar Lynne Kendrick, the object-voice inspires an inquiry into dramatic, imaginative uses of acousmatic voices that are constitutive of subjects in contemporary theater.[14] Scholar of rhetoric Jason David Myres portrays the mechanical voice of Stephen Hawking in Dolarian fashion as an *objet petit a* for Hawking's ambivalent publics, even proposing that Hawking's publics function as a collective object-voice ("Our publics . . . are never more potent than when we cannot see or hear them").[15] East Asianist Ken C. Kawashima reads in Dolar's politics of voice "a force of political organizing, especially in a state of emergency," as regards sovereignty and its relations to life and what Giorgio Agamben calls bare life (*homo sacer*), adducing the instance of Emperor Hirohito making and broadcasting his surrender speech after the bombing of Nagasaki and Hiroshima.[16] And communications scholar Joshua Gunn invokes the object-voice as a help in confronting "the now widely assumed critique of the dreaded 'metaphysics of presence' by Jacques Derrida.' "[17] If there have been detractors, they have not diminished the power of Dolar's text as a stimulus to thought across a wide range of disciplines, nor have their net effects unseated the text from its position of prominence.[18]

2

To be sure, the object-voice limned by Dolar and engaged by others is not the only voice in psychoanalytic writing, nor is it the one that dominates Dolar's own field of philosophy or its offshoot, phenomenology, much less the fields of musicology, anthropology, literary studies, gender studies, cinema studies, political theology, communication theory, or any number of others. Why then the grip of *A Voice and Nothing More* on the humanistic disciplines? First, and putting aside the wit and lure of Dolar's own writerly voice, there is something attractive about a voice that functions as an object of desire, steering a course with no real object, a course that does not really want satisfaction or cessation but only wants of itself in its endless process of not being able to reach an indefinite *it*. Dolar gives us a voice that eludes our grasp, slithering out of arm's reach in a continually recursive movement. Second, and relatedly, there is something seductive about the intermedial status that Dolar's object-voice sanctions, even if that intermedial status overlaps with a Lacanian voice without being tantamount to it. The object-voice operates not inside the mouth and throat, nor even inside the mind or ego, but in some still harder to grasp inside and outside, on an edge between both body and language. As Dolar illustrates (and as noted above), it is the middle term in a Venn diagram, the "operator of a divide."[19] Third, philosophically speaking, Dolar furnishes a more or less coherent theory of voice that is otherwise hard to come by, most especially in Lacan, a voice that reaches out in a number of different directions and gives us, from each direction, something metabolized by combining psychoanalysis and philosophy with other fields of thought. And lastly, even beyond any of the above, in telling us readers (and writers) about voice as an object of desire, Dolar has also, importantly, turned the voice itself into a kind of discursive object of desire. It might not be too much to say that that has been his greatest effect.

In assembling this volume, we make no attempt to offer a systematic assessment of Dolar's work. Many here use Dolar as a starting or ending point, while others bypass it to ask different questions about the stuff and stakes of voices, what we designate as the "something more" that our authors are after. The sounding voice, the music-producing voice, the radiophonic voice, the cinematic voice, the gendered voice, the screaming voice, the racialized voice, the recorded voice, the modernist voice, the manufactured voice, the composer's voice. The voices of mimicry, cinema, terror, politics, race, myth, media archaeology, writing, archiving, preserving. Far from being a systematic, much less philosophical or psychoanalytic confrontation with Dolar's object-voice, ours is more like an aleatory set of encounters that produces some crucial remainders. If a single propensity unifies us, it is, again, a propensity toward materiality—toward reinstating the phonic, sounding voice, thinking about the technological and cultural mediations of voice, attending to vocal listeners and producers, considering how voices are borrowed, owned, mythologized, gendered, "raced," and imitated, attending to auditors, speakers, singers, and interlocutors, testing the limits of voice, and yes, also wondering how phonic musical and literary voices might expose defects in the circuitry that mobilizes the psychoanalytic one.

3

Our concentration on materialities takes us back to what is by now an origin myth in studies of voice—the notion of "grain" as expressed in Roland Barthes's "The Grain of the Voice," which Jonathan Dunsby has aptly characterized as something of a slogan.[20] Barthes's essay is of course a trope on Julia Kristeva's notion that all signifying systems, including nonverbal ones such as music, are semiotic systems. Taking off on Kristeva's neologisms "phenotext" (coded semiotically) and "genotext" (coded socially and physiologically), and wanting to get around the persistence of the adjective ("the predicable") in approaching music,[21] Barthes proposes that in music there is "pheno-song" and "geno-song." *Pheno-song* "covers all the phenomena, all the features which belong to the structure of the language being sung, the rules of the genre, the coded form of the melisma, the composer's idiolect, the style of the interpretation. . . ."[22] More relevantly for us, *geno-song*

> is the volume of the singing and speaking voice, the space where significations germinate "from within language and in its very materiality"; it forms a signifying play having nothing to do with communication, representation (of feelings), expression; it is that apex (or that depth) of production where the melody really works at the language—not at what it says, but the voluptuousness of its sound-signifiers, of its letters—where melody explores how language works and identifies with that work. It is, in a very simple word but which must be taken seriously, the *diction* of the language.[23]

In short, *geno-song* is the grain of the voice. In the grain is "the tongue, the glottis, the teeth, the mucous membranes, the nose." In the grain is the body.

It's easy to poke holes in Barthes's theory, and many have. His evidence, consisting of a mere two singers—a French one he deeply loved and a German one he disdained, each passion seared with nationalistic ardor—makes for a case that is far too small for its claim, such that the essay ends up as an erotics of Barthes's own experience of listening with no tethering to a wider cultural world.[24] Still, no amount of quibbling with the argumentation or premises of Barthes's text has been able to significantly lower its impact. For, together with a new longing for voice and a sounding out of its ethics, there has been an urge to restore bodies to voices that modernism threatened to annihilate. In this, Barthes might be viewed as a virtual antithesis to Dolar (notwithstanding the psychoanalytic resonances in his text), inasmuch as what Barthes wants, what he longs for, is above all not just a material voice but a body *in* the voice, a phonic, envoicing body, and a voice that bodies forth.[25] Language matters not because of diction or "meaning" in their conventional senses, but because one of Barthes's avowed aims in making recourse to vocal music is "to displace the fringe of contact between music and language," and thereby open things up to voice itself and the body with it.[26] In one sense, the opening Barthes thereby allows is a narrow and confounding one, vested in the French critical tradition yet highly idiosyncratic. It has nonetheless occasioned queered and "raced" readings in the likes of Jarman-Ivens and Elias Krell, who critique its cultural and political failures but nevertheless value the support it lends embodied, identificatory practices of listening and practices of musicking (specifically "voicing") that tend to afford agency to precarious and marginalized peoples.[27]

4

Anyone concerned with the relationship between voice and language, as well as the odd crevices of social life, would do well to turn to Michel de Certeau, especially (for the former) to his essay on glossolalia (of speaking in tongues) but also his writings in *The Mystic Fable*, volume 1.[28] Certeau opens up a new strategy for exploring voice by means of the "vocal utopia" of glossolalia. For Certeau, speaking in tongues is a mere "illusion" of speech that in itself expresses nothing and signifies nothing. In this regard, glossolalia is not really as exceptional an idiom as may seem at first blush, since it "already pushes up through the cracks of ordinary conversation: bodily noises, quotations of delinquent sounds, and fragments of others' voices punctuate the order of sentences with breaks and surprises."[29] As a kind of "secondary vocalization," glossolalia, along with its kin (think of vocalise, babble, stuttering, aphasia, groaning), is opposed to what Certeau calls "the major voice," the supposed "messenger of meaning" (even though here too there is a convergence of the major and secondary voices because the former is always already compromised). Only when the major voice radically "liberates itself from its disquieting twin" (secondary vocalization) by engaging in *propositional* discourses such as the political, scholarly, or religious—discourses that largely close themselves off from the ruptures of voice—can alternative voice be suppressed and speaking circumvent dialogue. Only then can speaking defend itself from the messiness of dialogue and by the same token circumvent the Other, or at least appear to.[30] In contrast to propositional speech, what conversation does—and we will see this strongly in song—is precisely to open discourse to the noises and vexations of otherness. Conversation and dialogue challenge speech, for "as it approaches its addressee, speech becomes fragile."

As voices take possession of discourse, voodoo-like, they "trouble, break, or suspend" the autonomy of a speaker. They do so as a kind of Lacanian Other (although Certeau never calls them that)—an indefinable, ungraspable object: "Here and there, they spirit . . . [discourse] away from me, without my knowing what they are or whence they come. What other thing within me gives rise to them?" Noise or gibberish or senseless speech—"secondary vocalizations"—are thus manifestly about subject/object relations. While starting with the subject's ego, however, those relations ultimately lead to an un-Lacanian place, namely to the explicit dimensions of the social and to actual sounding voice:

> From the clamor of voices [*sabbat de voix*] overrunning and breaking up the field of statements comes a mumble that escapes the control of speakers and that violates the supposed division between speaking individuals. It fills the space between speakers with the plural and prolix act of communication and creates, mezza voce, an opera of enunciation on the stage of verbal exchange.[31]

Glossolalia, like other "mumblings," shines the spotlight on the phenomenon of speakers losing control of and violating divisions between one another. It stands in for the complex relation of language and meaning as conveyed by voice in what are largely if not purely social domains. For glossolalia and the like enable a passage between what Certeau calls "can not say" (i.e., muteness) and "can say" (i.e., speech) by introducing an illusion or fable into that passage, which organizes its receivers politically by ushering tale-telling into the symbolic order. Glossolalia can thus be thought of as a virtual stand-in for the slippery social and political effects of voice as the vehicle for verbal exchange.

In *The Mystic Fable*, volume 1, Certeau is concerned with related urges toward unsaying and the ambiguous place between saying and not saying, language and not language. The mystic experience and utterance represent for him the unstable relationship of voice to language. Mysticism gives speech license to make use of excess, directly so in theological writings, and in ways that undo the coherence of signification. As a prime example, Certeau invokes the seventeenth-century case of the mannerist Diego de Jesús, introducer of John of the Cross, the destination of whose discourse—its "addressee" or mode of address—"takes precedence over the validity of the statement" (141). However much Certeau recognizes that Diego's excess is connected to his mannerist style, he keeps his ear fixed on how the edges of language intersect with voice through extravagant troping, deviations of meaning, and "monstrous" oxymorons, comparable to the wider colonialist offenses of early modernity evinced in Ambroise Paré's monstrous bodies or Jean de Léry's "dissimilar beings."[32] Speech then becomes an excessive in-between that is akin to voice without being equivalent to it; and mystic discourse increases the number and complexity of such kinds of speech.[33]

It's tempting to think that Certeau, in calling attention to the voice/language relationship, was also broaching the notion of social performance, intersubjective communication, and attendant notions of listeners.[34] When he draws attention to Rabelais's famed fable of the "melted words"—an acousmatic specter of shipwrecked voices sunk to the ocean depths and then raised from the dead as they start to speak in the thaw of a gelid winter—he asks: "Will words that time has frozen become voices again (addressed by whom to whom?)?" The recital of those lost voices, and their urge to be heard, prompts Certeau to remind us that, according to Émile Benveniste, the circumstances of a mystic utterance are precisely those of a performance in a social domain. They are "the conversion of language into discourse."[35] Speech becomes performance.

The leap from phonic verbal performance, with its interrelational implications, to the performative preoccupations of much of the most dynamic work that's been done on voice in the past twenty-five years is not that great. We might date it to the publication of *The Queen's Throat*, when Wayne

Koestenbaum blew the lid off voice thinking with his canny and hilarious romp through the overlapping terrains of gay desire, performance, and divadom in the opera house and the living room.[36] More recently, there's been some meticulously grounded cultural work that studies the edges of performance as they relate to vocality, and shows their effects on matters of identity. These take shape in studies of queer voices by Krell, Jarman-Ivens, Judith Halberstam, and Deborah Vargas,[37] but also in a variety of ethnographic traditions. Amanda Weidman's *Singing the Classical, Voicing the Modern*, for example, analyzes the elision of voice with classicism in twentieth-century performances that map out a concertedly modern space of Indianness. In *Songs of Seoul*, Nicholas Harkness shows how clean vocalizing, especially in classical singing, becomes identified with Christianity and with the modernity of the nation in South Korean singing practices, training close attention on both their bodily and phenomenological dimensions.

5

What relationship do these various projects have to that most performative and stylized of all speech acts—music uttered through the mouth and throat, and even nonvocal musics that recall or index the voice (as with Seth Brodsky's essay in this volume)? It hardly needs saying that understanding vocal performance as the object of a fetish is not the view of an academic majority and certainly not the layman's view. Vernacularly, voice is asserted as the most revealing manifestation of a unitary self, and something that can set voice apart from language. As singer Jeff Buckley put it in a famous Paris interview:

> Your voice is your essence. Ask any singer, it's the most revealing thing you could possibly do. . . . The voice gives you information. You know how people talk in two languages, the words that they give you and the information that is really conveyed through the sound of their voice? That's how children learn to speak, that's how people know the truth.[38]

Heedless of exhortations we hear nowadays to discern in voices a multiplicity of others, Buckley—famed (ironically) for masterfully imitating but also transforming numerous styles and voices in a richly internalized brew—suggests that voice aligns with a pure interiority of the self.[39] Yet even as Buckley asserts this, he describes a voice that does not sync up perfectly with language, but often works around it in perpetuating untruths. Hence its division from language remains.[40]

That divide of sound and sense and the varied relations it animates is the subject of numerous writings on voice, many of them oriented in music and lyric voice. Aaron Fox's *Real Country*, for example, notes that "singing and vocal movements in the direction of song mark the embodied and emplaced sociality of language, which may even achieve temporary dominance over referential sense."[41] Sarah Nooter's *The Mortal Voice in the Tragedies of Aeschylus* makes this proposition a starting point for an astutely lyrical understanding of Aeschylus's sound world.[42] Bonnie Gordon wants to overturn the Rousseauian philosophical tradition that claims that words and music were fused in some originary mythic gloss by looking at how the machinic body of the castrato (whose intentionally altered voice and anatomy "brings materiality of voice to the fore") is mediated through the intervention of voice "as matter instrumentalized."[43] And the relation is paramount in Gary Tomlinson's study of Aztec song in the era of contact between Europeans and American "others," which attempts to characterize what is particular in the relation *voice : language* by expanding the Derridean dyad of speech and writing (by which the subject has long been implicated in Western metaphysics) to a triad encompassing speech, writing, and vocalization that carves out a special place for voice.

It is worth dilating on this last, precisely because for Tomlinson the addition of vocalization to the speech/writing dyad is essential to the business of listening closely to others.[44] It shapes his study and explains why he launches his narrative with an instance of the terror produced in seafaring Europeans by a sound that seemed to them to escape the semantic order—the terrifying yet all-too-human cawing of cahows, Bermudan seabirds whose screeching explorers found so demonic that it caused them to abandon the isle.[45] Other examples follow as Tomlinson listens for the cultural work that various contact-era American songs aimed to accomplish, and that European travelers readily ignored (the cosmogonic work of songs among the Inca, the sacred immanence in songs of the Aztecs, the sheer fullness and excess of Tupi songs in Brazil). Yet even as these vocal sounds and musics model something of what Certeau called, in a rather Lacanian formulation, "the insurmountable alterity from the subject's desire," the desire they mobilize arguably moves American song through, around, or alongside language and signmaking, not totally outside them.[46] Contact-era American songs thus deserve a special place in the pantheon where previously speech and writing competed for rule.[47]

If these historical and ethnographic projects attempt to think through the material relations of language, voice, and music, philosopher Adriana Cavarero, in her much-read *For More Than One Voice: Toward a Philosophy of Vocal Expression*, gives us a far more sweeping project: namely to elevate the status of voice, including the singing voice, as a way to upend the millennia-old philosophical centrality of language, logos, and the symbolic order.[48] Central to this effort is her valorization of the uniqueness of all sounding voices, what she calls a "vocal ontology," contra Aristotle, for whom only semantic utterance counts as voice, entangled as it is in his conglomerated entity "signifying voice" (*phone semantike*). Counterpoised to Aristotle here is Derrida, whose notion of voice is still sutured to logos as a site of meaning-intention—of autoaffective presence—where it remains problematically (for Cavarero) silent, speaking inwardly only to the self. In her imagining, neither *phone semantike* nor that silent voice can tell us anything about voices that sound and resound such that each is uniquely indicative of a particular person. Only a body to which a sounding voice is attached can tell us that.

Whether Cavarero's axiom of uniqueness holds water is a matter for debate. Brian Kane has disputed it for philosophical and epistemological reasons (how can the uniqueness of all voices be established?), and studies of vocal mimicry, like Laurie Stras's and Tom Gunning's in this volume and Steven Connor's on ventriloquism, would seem implicitly to challenge it on empirical ones (if voices can so easily imitate, how can they be unique?).[49] We might bracket such criticisms on grounds that Cavarero's focus on uniqueness is more ethically and politically motivated than philosophically so, and read her text as a recalibration of metaphysics carried out to shift authoritarian attention away from the semantic regime and toward the body, including the musicking body. If we're right in doing so, then we could say that music in Cavarero overturns the centrality of language all told by introducing a voice that hums and sings, allowing in her work what Ryan Dohoney calls "a space of contestation between voice and signification."[50] For Cavarero, a lifelong feminist, this antimetaphysical music also introduces pleasure into the body/language nexus as part of a feminine logic, as against the masculine logic of logos/semantics.[51] Music is commensurate with unique souls interacting within an "interrelational plurality," which in turn constitutes a utopian feminist space that accommodates difference.

6

Does music do all these things for voice? And does voice do something that cannot be comprehended under the auspices of sound alone? Recent tendencies in the academy push us toward rethinking music as a subset of the larger category of sound and away from our past focus on music as a unique, exalted domain preternaturally bent on edging out others by colonizing them or representing them as noisy (non-Western) alterities.[52] Yet in considering voice some find reason to preserve a bit of music qua music. For Nina Sun

Eidsheim, the argument—turning the anticolonialist one on its head—is ethical, drawing its case from the realm of experimental vocal music to think against the "figure of sound" as static, symbolizing, and thus essentializing and in favor of a "principle of vibration" as the basis for voice and music as flexible, relational, and listener-oriented.[53] By what other name would we call the organized, expressive vocality of Neanderthals, which in Gary Tomlinson's account precedes the symbolic by as much as 250,000 years?[54]

The most sustained arguments on questions of music and voice in the American and continental critical traditions have come from Carolyn Abbate in work that now spans nearly three decades.[55] At the outset, Abbate mapped out a peculiarly personal view of voice, not as vocal performance per se but as "certain isolated and rare gestures in music, whether vocal or nonvocal, that may not be perceived as modes of subjects' enunciations" (the wordless coloratura in Lakmé's "Bell Song" or the melismas in the Queen of the Night's arias, for example).[56] At the same time, Abbate's "voice" has also generally been a "voice-object," hence something the search for which is persistent and which the presence of a performing body can actually impede. Indeed, what makes the voice/body/music relationship operative for Abbate is that the music-oriented object-voice tends to generate the uncanny—a condition that emerges when music is in the mix but its partner language is destroyed and the performer thus terrifyingly dehumanized, affecting onlookers much like the inscrutable cahows of Tomlinson's Bermudan narrative.[57]

Music of course has a curious part in all this. In nineteenth-century Europe, philosophers wanted it to be voiceless and better yet textless in order to be pure and transcendent. Yet Abbate shows that while music may escape language, it has a privileged relationship with voice, and even did then. *In Search of Opera* clarifies and deepens our sense of that relationship by reorienting our thinking about European opera around a range of transhuman and largely material (if sometimes intangible) media: vessels, mediums, ghosts, inanimate objects.[58] Think of the Commendatore in *Don Giovanni* or the mother Antonia in the last act of *Les Contes d'Hoffmann*, characters that "amplify" (an Abbatean concept) our sense of things by offering themselves as phantasmic, incorporeal presences, and in ways that are at once epistemological (because omniscient), psychological (because persuasive), and imaginary (because loud). Both music and voice carry the danger that what lies behind the trickery is something that is made to *seem* human but isn't: a mere ghost in the machine.[59] Engendering the uncanny, those ghosts are also manifest in technologies of vocality.

Abbate's disembodied voice, musical and non, almost always suggests chicanery, power, and authority in the guise of a bedeviling apparatus. So it is with Dolar, whose opening gambit is a foray into automata the phenomenal effects of which, like the circuitry of Lacanian desire, belie their cause. But notions of disembodied voice that are bound up with media have also gone beyond the Lacanian gloss. In "Sound Object Lessons" (2016), Abbate thinks in unpredictable ways about technological affordances, especially the microphone as used in film, in relation to voice and sound. "Amplification" remains a grounding trope, but now in the form of the "sound close-up," auditory equivalent to the cinematic (visual) close-up whereby experience of the enlarged thing might do something to the relevant sense but will not do it unidirectionally (thing working on sense), but multidirectionally (things, bodies, notions working on senses and senses on things, bodies, notions). The cash-out is not a single argument but a series of insights, privileging something like Deleuzian flatness over argumentational hierarchy in a way that is amenable to the very object that voice is.

7

Media and the apparatus have similarly preoccupied writers on ventriloquism, including Kane and Connor, as well as writers on the posthuman voice—the voice transmitted through prostheses or manipulated by other technological means—which in turn has ended up foregrounding questions about race and voice.[60] How did this happen? An early instance comes from Alexander Weheliye's now indispensable critique of N. Katherine Hayles's *How We Became Posthuman* (1999), a critique that says that the subject of Hayles's "posthuman body," far from being a human subject in all its infinite variety, is in fact the liberal enlightened white subject of the later eighteenth century.[61] For Weheliye, as for others working in the vein of critical race theory, the body of the black subject is a different matter, and it is most spectacularly manifested in formations of blackness produced in technologically leveraged modes of music-making and in any number of technologically driven genres tied to black creativity, from rap and hip-hop to dub, zook, funk, house, afropop, and so on. In this, the black body, he asserts, is not fully given (or "a given"), but conjured, most compellingly by such now-classic black writers of the last century as W. E. B. DuBois, Ralph Ellison, Richard Wright, Lorraine Hansberry, and James Baldwin, all of whom worked to discover a new black subject that has been brutally owned, commoditized, circulated, stolen, slain, and generally laid low.[62] Blackness is never simply and already *in* the voice and body that materialize that subject (though in part it is); rather, for Weheliye and others, black voice and body also insinuate themselves into different discourses and techniques: writing, phonography, and machinic technologies of recording, sampling, and special effects (cell-phone rings, vocoder effects, and so on) that rematerialize and restage those bodies and voices (cf. Andrew F. Jones's essay in this volume). Black voices in popular music here are thus like Deleuze and Guattari's "desiring machines," where desire and its object are effectively one and the same.

Technologies and bodies find their way into other writings on race and voice, if differently motivated. Josh Kun's *Audiotopia: Music, Race, and America* (2005) is mobilized by its focus on identity as the sine qua non of music as it concerns bodies, voices, and races.[63] Strikingly for our purposes, Kun tracks the technology of identity-making through Baldwin, whose memoir *The Devil Makes Work* (1975) recounts how his experiences with movie-watching start out by forcing him to watch a stranger but end up with the stranger watching him. They turn into acts of making the strange familiar inasmuch as watching the stranger makes the viewer into a stranger to himself. Baldwin's account explains for Kun the mechanism of difference, helping ground the claim that music (especially popular music) is permanently entangled with race, functioning like Foucault's "heterotopias" or Certeau's "delinquent spaces" to allow "a kind of effectively enacted utopia," an "identificatory contact zone" delineated through heard songs and voices.[64] Nowhere was that contact zone stronger for Baldwin than with the sound of a blues voice, especially the voice of Bessie Smith, mediated by the alterity of the phonograph to unlock "airless, labeled [identity] cells," queerly and racially charged.[65]

Race writings on voice are hardly reducible to any single genre or tilting. Recent ones instead find common footing in the restoration of agency to listeners and above all performers, especially vocalists of color, as witnessed in essays by Stras, Jones, Feldman, and Rings in this volume. For the voice of color, agency means above all vocal heterogeneity and difference, sounding out in what Fred Moten calls "the break," operating in the in-between.[66] Not infrequently, this involves forms of borrowing that amount to thievery, as Daphne Brooks insists in the case of Amy Winehouse (the thief) and Maureen Mahon in the case of Big Mama Thornton (the one thieved from).[67] It involves what Brooks, Malik Gaines, and Joshua Chambers-Letson all think of as using voice to resist and negate the impossible negativity of the condition of color, and what Beth Coleman thinks of as deploying vocal and other technologies as a resource for making racial agency.[68] And it comports with intersectional theories of race and gender that see in voice a new opening onto modes of agency, relationality, mobility. It would be hard to think how restitution of the body of the voice could be more urgent for our time.

The Chapters

The chapters in this volume constitute a clamor of voices in yet another sense from that sketched above. We have organized the book to highlight the eclecticism and plurality of the contributions by disrupting obvious groupings by discipline, geography, historical period, or genre. Instead, we deliberately mix it up so that a sinologist brushes up against a theorist of contemporary pop music, a media archaeologist of radio against an analyst of high modernist music, a classicist against a historian of cinema, and a historiographer of kabuki against a critic of Jamaican dancehall. The point is to make the authors converse with one another outside their comfort zones, in an effort to capture the freewheeling give-and-take of the Neubauer faculty seminar and capstone conference at the University of Chicago out of which these essays emerged.

Not minimizing or papering over gaps and breaks between the chapters is a deliberate strategy adopted in this book for several other reasons. As a concept, the "gap" has proven extraordinarily productive for theorizing about voice, particularly in the Lacanian vein developed by Dolar in his influential work. On a thematic level, the "gap" plays a recurrent structuring role throughout many of the contributions to the volume, most prominently in Martha Feldman's essay on virtuosic vocal failure, which is simply entitled "Voice Gap Crack Break." Then, too, in a new, messy field like voice studies with so many avenues still to be explored, omissions and disjunctions are inevitable, completeness or comprehensiveness neither possible nor desirable.

What all the chapters do share is a tendency to push back against the blind spots or conventional wisdom in their respective fields, to challenge certain commonplaces in thinking about voice. Each contribution in its own way also grapples with the materiality of the voice by keeping concrete, contextualized voices in the foreground, rather than allowing voice as an object of analysis to fade into pure metaphor or figurative generalization. So Robert Polito's chapter takes on that indispensable chestnut, the trope of the poet's voice, via James Merrill's monumental poem *The Changing Light at Sandover*, which incorporates large swaths of voices from beyond the grave, dictated to him through the Ouija board. Neil Verma's chapter tackles the scream not as the exemplar of voice prior to or exceeding language ("*the* voice as it screams"), but as a concrete problem of aesthetics and technology in radio horror drama ("*a* voice as it screams"). The subtlety of Seth Brodsky's arguments in dismantling another sacred cow is offset by the bluntness of his title: "There Is No Such Thing as the Composer's Voice." And James Q. Davies's chapter proudly wears its polemics on its sleeve, declaring itself in its title to be "Against the Voice Itself."

1

In the opening section, "Sound-Producing Voice," both music theorist Steven Rings and Chinese opera historian Judith Zeitlin approach the physical, sounding voice as residing on a kind of continuum. For Rings, the continuum of interest lies between speech and song, with the difference between them being one of degree, rather than of kind. Although he posits that porousness between speech and song is the norm, the two idioms nonetheless coexist in what he calls "a contextual asymmetry" so that in any given context, one of them will predominate, "setting off its other like a figure against the ground." And it is within this "other," this marked figure, that the materiality of the voice comes to the fore. In ordinary life, song is the marked term, speech the unmarked one, but within the world of Anglophone popular music, which furnishes the test case for his study, this dynamic is reversed. Here, singing becomes the norm, and speaking the marked term (with early hip-hop/rap being a notable exception). Ranging over recordings by stars from country music, punk rock, R&B, folk revival, and hip-hop, Rings pinpoints what exactly happens and what is at stake in those moments where speech emerges from within song. Far from a mere formal experiment, Rings's chapter probes how such interplay between song and speech affects the meaning of the lyrics, the persona of the singer, and modes of address to the audience, buttressing his conclusion that voice, more than any other "sonic element" in a song, matters as "a vehicle for social interactions."

Zeitlin confronts a different problem as she tries to figure out how the human voice was theorized in Chinese thought before the modern era, in a system where voice was not overladen with extensive figurative meanings and never built up into a master trope on the order of "identity," "agency," "subjectivity," and "style." She argues that linguistically and conceptually, the default in Chinese discourse has been to situate the voice on a continuum with other sounds rather than isolating it as a separate category. Her strategy therefore is to uncover certain key moments where the human voice is distinguished as something different and valorized. This leads her to trace the emergence of different models of the sounding voice from antiquity to the eighteenth century. She locates a pivotal change in court literature of the Six Dynasties (third–fifth century CE), where the voice is championed as superior to other musical instruments because more "natural." This discourse of "naturalism" produces new theorizations of the human voice: as a carnal instrument whose material substrate is flesh, thus linking it to the sensual body of an entertainer; as a conduit of communication beyond language requiring no external tool; and as the origin of music, which is inherent in the human organism through the tonal qualities of (the Chinese) language itself. She concludes with another pivotal change, this time appearing in an eighteenth-century pedagogical treatise for the voice by physician Xu Dachun during the heyday of Kun opera. This treatise, she argues, develops a kind of modern *technê* for instrumentalizing the singer's body in a utopian attempt (a defensive fantasy, we might say psychoanalytically) to invest voice with the ability to bridge the gap separating musics of the past and the present.

2

If Rings and Zeitlin track variation across a normative continuum, Marcelle Pierson and Neil Verma swing to the other extreme in the following section to offer "Limit Cases" for apprehending the voice—that of sung text in high musical modernism for Pierson, and the scream in radio for Verma. Pierson sees the status of voice as coming into conflict with the ideology of musical modernism in the work of postwar Darmstadt composers because associated with old-fashioned melody, emotion, and humanism. She reads two cases, both instances of texts set to music using serial techniques in the late 1950s, as taking diametrically different approaches to the problem of voice defined in opposition to the other: Luigi Nono's *Il canto sospeso* ("The Suspended Song") and Karlheinz Stockhausen's *Gesang der Jünglinge* ("Song of the Youth"). Although Nono's piece was written for live performance, and Stockhausen's for the recording studio, both selected texts of acute historical and emotional significance in the wake of the Second World War, and both strove to make words themselves unintelligible, dismantling and disfiguring them as a way to recuperate, however paradoxically, the viability of the human voice in their music.

In Verma's witty chapter, the scream turns the "extreme" voice, the voice "on edge," the voice beyond language, into a technical and ontological problem for radio. It's unclear from listening to recordings of live radio dramas from the 1940s, for instance, whether a given scream was made by a vocal performer or as a special effect by an engineer, whether it was made live on air or by putting in prerecorded sound. As such, Verma's examples also point to another sort of unknowable gap in the disembodied, acousmatic voice(s) of and on radio, which enhances their effect of uncanniness. At the heart of his chapter is a tour de force reading of a classic radio horror play from the 1940s called "The Thing on the Fourble Board," in which he treats the scream as a "source of critical approach to radio listening rather than a problem to be solved by one." The shocking revelation of the Thing's identity provides him with a platform to stage an allegorical reading of the "ritualized birth of a voice" hovering somewhere between audibility and inaudibility, which in turn provides him a key for excavating the buried history of radio as a medium.

3

Robert Polito's contribution initiates a new section ("Vocal Owners and Borrowed Voices"), but his chapter, no less than Pierson's and Verma's, focuses on a limit case, where, to borrow Polito's borrowing of T. J. Clark, "the pressures and capacities of a particular mode of representation . . . tend to be clearest because the capacities are pressed to the breaking point."[69] For Polito, the problem is voice in modern poetry and the limit case is James Merrill's *The Changing Light at Sandover*, published—all 560 pages of it—in 1982. By channeling composite, occult voices obtained through his séances at the Ouija board, Merrill's experiment results in what Polito describes as a "sustained dismantling of a lyric voice." *Sandover* makes manifest the language of possession, animism, and ventriloquism shadowing modern theoretical approaches to poetic voice: as something physical, given breath and sound by the poet or reader; as a metaphor for an author's distinctive style; or as a reductionist cliché equivalent to the self ("no poet has a voice, only voices," just as no poet has a self, only selves). In so doing, *Sandover* confounds any normative grasp of the voice in modern poetry while substantiating the uncanny truths on which "the chronic enigma of poetic voice" depends.

Virtuosity is a word Polito never uses, but the verbal pyrotechnics of Merrill's masterpiece, whatever the collaboration with the Ouija board, demand attention to the poet himself and his command of these voices. (Listen to Merrill read some passages aloud and you'll be struck by how seamlessly the othered words of the dead or of cloned bats dissolve into the poet's own patrician tones.) *Performance* is another word that Polito never uses, but it lies at the heart of Laurie Stras's case study of a song recorded in 1925 by blueswoman and actress Ethel Waters. Entitled "Maybe Not at All," the song showcases Ethel's virtuosity as a singer by mimicking the styles of her rivals, Bessie Smith ("Empress of the Blues") and Clara Smith ("Queen of the Moaners"). Like Polito, Stras is interested in how assuming someone else's voice destabilizes notions of voice as a marker of authenticity and subjectivity, but she reframes the issue as a measure of the versatility and self-positioning of the artist.

Stras's essay uses mimicry as her limit case for the idea of self in vocality, specifically mimicry of a celebrity voice familiar through recorded sound that is recognized as belonging to a particular person. Like a sonic signature, a famous voice may possess the capacity to verify and authenticate, and hence can be forged or illegally appropriated (an issue that, Stras notes, has been the target of recent lawsuits claiming copyright over ownership and usage). Vaudeville impressions, however, depend on the audience being in on the game, upon knowing that the voices being heard are not the "real" voice of the singer. Such imitation is therefore meant not to deceive but rather to elicit appreciation for the impressionist's prowess by exposing "the constructedness of both the model's vocality and . . . [the singer's] own." (Fast-forward to Tom Gunning's chapter for the opposite case of a vocal mimicry meant to defraud.) Stras shows how such chameleonic mastery, while troubling the idea of any fixed bonds between voice, body, and authenticity, can paradoxically end up becoming "representative of a single individual's identity" all the more.

"I Am an Essentialist," proclaims James Davies in the title of his provocative, political chapter—in quotation marks to show that he is putting on a voice, to drive home the idea, as Stras does, that any voice is to some extent "put on" and cannot simply be hailed as the free, autonomous expression of self. His principal target is the fetishization of "pure" voice—the holy grail of the voice itself—in the elite world of opera in the nineteenth and twentieth centuries. For Davies, this cult of the voice is epitomized by its sacerdotal priest Pavarotti, who even intones: "My voice is my possessor. . . . I'm the servant of my voice." Davies's counterargument is that "vocal aura is less a byproduct of voice's detachment from the world than an effect of voice's deep connection to that world." What makes voices powerful is their ability to inspire "social belief and social belonging." Whizzing us through a brief history of how the operatic voice has been imaged and imagined since the mid-nineteenth century, the essay demonstrates that "no straightforward, causal relationship" exists between "the voice" and "the body" (or even individual body parts), because our knowledge and experience of the two is never "natural" but always culturally and socially determined and therefore politically implicated and fraught. Bodies are not just "sculpted by vocal training" but "phenomenologically constructed in voice," just as the cultivation of a certain type of voice also requires cultivating a certain understanding of embodiment.

4

The four chapters in the next section, as signaled by its heading, "Myth, Gap, Wound," all confront voice, in one way or another, as fantasy in a Lacanian sense—as a defensive mechanism supporting the subject's desire by means of fantasy, which papers it over and, as Brodsky puts it, "lends the world a consistency it wouldn't otherwise have." This is the part of the volume that engages most directly with Dolar's ideas. Two of the contributors even cite the same crucial passage from his book about voice being "a structural illusion, the core of a fantasy that the singing voice might cure the wound inflicted by culture," with the concomitant disavowal of the fact that voice's "allegedly miraculous force stems from its being situated in this gap." Each of the chapters takes a concrete, material case or problem whose exposition enables the author to push Dolar's arguments in another direction so they might become "something more."

"Is the Voice a Myth?" asks Shane Butler, cleverly playing on several senses of myth in his title. These include something that is reputed to exist but does not, a core cultural narrative with legitimating and explanatory value, and classical mythology as written by Ovid in his great poem the *Metamorphoses*. Butler's complex and wide-ranging essay returns us to the problem of the poet's voice raised by Polito, but takes us down a path of many twists and turns as befits the essentially recursive nature of both voice and myth. This is why the myth of Echo and Narcissus figures so prominently in Butler's reading, with Echo rather than Narcissus revealed to be the central figure in the story. Signifying lack as a protagonist, Echo turns out to be the ventriloquized voice of Ovid himself, who calls his poem a "continuous song," and claims immortality for himself in the final lines: "I shall be read by the mouth of a people," and so, "I shall live." Echo's fate also substantiates Butler's point that "the truth of myth is revealed only in the retelling," as he revisits some of the now canonical refractions of classical myths related to voice, language, and the body in Boccaccio, Shakespeare, Freud, Lacan, Derrida, and last but not least, Dolar.

Martha Feldman's chapter reinserts a material substrate of concrete, empirical voices into the psychoanalytic discussion of the gap. But not just any voice. Her subject is the virtuoso singer's willful deployment of vocal failure, those instances where the voice cracks, strains, or seems to run out of breath at strategic instances in a song. Like Verma, then, Feldman takes on "the extreme voice," "the voice on edge," but as a musicologist, the vocal breakdowns that interest her are more subtle and supple. To work, they require a genre with a clear-cut decorum of good singing and an audience of knowledgeable listeners who will recognize—and invest in—the risk-taking and the vulnerability exposed. Accordingly, she draws her examples from classical bel canto and jazz, culminating in Nina Simone's indelible recording of an old jazz standard, "I Get Along without You Very Well (Except Sometimes)." Like Davies, Feldman refutes the idea that the virtuoso's power must be based on a perfect, autonomous voice; rather, she shows how the extreme pleasure a fan derives from flashes of masterful imperfection depends on voice being "transactional," transaction being a process in which singer and listener mutually engage in an attempt to forestall loss. Virtuosic vocal failure points to "gaps in the very status of the voice," exposing the "messy surplus" and the "in-betweenness of voice" as something exceeding both language and music, exposing the pull of desire and the impossibility of fulfilling it.

Like Feldman, David Levin is interested in exploring the role that vocal failure can play in rendering—rather than disavowing—the gap in which Dolar situates voice. Levin's chapter, however, takes a very different approach by examining the public staging of a singer's failure and its consequences within the diegetic work of opera. Or, more precisely, within two specific operas. Levin dissects a key scene of staged vocal performance from Zemlinsky's opera *Der Zwerg* (*The Dwarf*, 1919–1921), in which the Dwarf sings for the Infanta of Spain and is ridiculed by her. This scene he reads dramaturgically as a modernist reframing of the famous singing contest in Wagner's *Die Meistersinger* of 1862, in which Beckmesser is bested and humiliated by the hero Walther. Both operas present the singer as grotesque and deformed, the Dwarf physically and Beckmesser symbolically as a "Jew" figured in Wagner's terms. A key difference, Levin argues, is where the audience is located vis-à-vis the failed singer. Whereas in *Meistersinger*, the audience is primed to embrace Walther as "the Cure to the wound opened up by Beckmesser's spectacular failure" and to approve Beckmesser's aggressive expulsion, in Zemlinsky's opera, the Dwarf, as an outcast and victim, is allowed to elicit the audience's empathy and induce a modernist understanding that the human subject itself is riven. In other words, the singing voice of the Dwarf doesn't perform the act of suturing over a wound and restoring loss, but instead serves "as a testament to the inevitability of that loss and the impossibility of that restoration" within opera.

The topic (and rhetorical method) of Seth Brodsky's essay is disavowal itself. "The composer's voice is the same as nothing," he says, where "nothing" exists as an absolute value or positive essence. (Think of the Cyclops's answer "Nobody" to the question "Who blinded you?") Brodsky returns us to the challenge voice poses to the modernist composer raised earlier by Pierson, but pursues this "voice of modernism" obliquely through the string quartet rather than through sung verse. Proceeding backward through time, his four examples start from Helmut Lachenmann's Second String Quartet (1989) and Nono's *Fragmente* (1979–1980), then move to Berg's *Lyric Suite* (1926), and finally end up with Beethoven's late quartet, op. 130. Like Levin, Brodsky is interested in the composer's theatricalization of voice in music, though not as dramatized in an operatic work. Rather, his paradoxical claim is this: The modernist composer's voice is "fundamentally operatic". . . . but involves a staging of the impossibility of making something appear . . . an endeavor not simply to make nonappearance appear, but to make it "sing."

5

Michel Chion—doyen of theories of voice in cinema—takes a fresh look at the subject in the playful interlude that follows. Entitled "Vowels/Consonants: The Legend of a 'Gendered' (Sexual) Difference Told by Cinema," his chapter extends ideas originally developed in his recent book *Écrit sur L'ecran*, first published in French in 2013 and now available in Claudia Gorbman's English translation as *Words on Screen*.[70] Here he asks: What happens to voice when there is writing onscreen? Are words pronounced by a character in the film or silently sounded out by a spectator in the audience? Or are letters onscreen even vocalizable at all? Specifically, he explores diverse cases in which the screen shows words in languages based on the Latin alphabet, especially when composed of incomplete, fragmented, or scrambled letters. Taking us on a virtuosic adventure through cinematic treatments of the letters *A*, *O*, and *I*, and ending with labial clusters like *bud*, Chion finds the gendered binaries that film maps onto the distinction between vowels (woman/speech/song) and consonants (man/writing/words) to be surprisingly durable.[71] In all this, he refuses the implicit linguistic uniformity that, in his view, Derrida presumes for writing—a uniformity that occludes writing's inherent linguistic plurality, with or without its association with voice. (Indeed, Chion also acknowledges still wider linguistic differences that come with the nonalphabetic system of writing in a cinematic tradition like that of China, which lies outside his empirical domain.)

6

If it seems ironic that our final section, "Technology, Difference, and the Uncanny," should begin with Sarah Nooter's chapter on Ancient Greece, we should remember that (as many contend) there is no absolute break between the prerecorded "natural" voice and the technological voice today, no absolute disconnect that "modernity" initiates.[72] For Nooter, classical sources from Aristophanes and Pindar to Plato and Aristotle show early glimmerings of the interest in the "vocalic uncanny" that we find in recent technologies, such as Auto-Tune, Amazon's Echo, and Apple's Siri. Like Brodsky, however, she approaches the issue of voice via sound made with musical instruments, rather than voices. Her essay's most daring and controversial move is to propose substituting the term "musical prosthesis" for "musical instrument." She proposes that both of her examples, the *aulos* (an oboe-like instrument heard as mimicking the human voice) and the *salpinx* (a kind of war trumpet heard as an invulnerable weapon striking terror in the human heart), be considered prostheses in the sense of being attachments to the mouth and extensions of the breath. As physical attachments, these wind instruments "become part of the human body and adjust its contours." They can also be considered stand-ins for the voice because when playing them a musician cannot speak or sing, and because in ancient Greek, voice (*phone*) is understood as "part of the utterance that comes from the mouth but does not necessarily produce linguistic meaning." By displacing and "ventriloquizing" the voice while altering its timbre, volume, and projection, these sonic prostheses are invested with an inhuman, uncanny power. This effect is amplified when a human becomes a vocal prosthesis for a god—that is, a bodily instrument (medium) through which a divine breath is blown, whether in the guise of a priestess serving as a mouthpiece for the prophecies of Apollo, or a poet possessed by the spirit of the Muse.

Andrew Jones foregrounds the political relationship between the vocalic uncanny and sound technology in his essay on Vybz Kartel, the Jamaican dancehall music superstar convicted for murder and the self-styled "Voice of the Jamaican Ghetto." (The "duppy" in his title is a Caribbean term for "ghost.") The paradox that grips Jones isn't the familiar one of how a voice "predicated on its singularity" can "ventriloquize the speech of the multitude," but rather how the use of an electronically mediated, robotic-sounding voice affects that claim. In particular, what he's after is the "ubiquitous creative misuse" of Auto-Tune pitch-correction software to distort the voice in genres of black popular music such as dancehall and rap in acts of agency, even political agency (cf. the discussion of Weheliye in part 1 above, and Rings's point in his chapter about how Auto-Tune turns mumbled speech into song). In a manner reminiscent of Nooter's approach, Jones characterizes the Auto-Tuned voice as hovering on "the border between the organic and prosthetic, the human and not-quite human," with Auto-Tune even being "used as a second-order instrument for playing the voice." Like Feldman and like other writers on voices of color, then, he's interested in the interrelational "in-betweenness" of voice and the "transactional" spaces that techniques of deliberate vocal imperfection can open up between singers and their publics. But Jones situates the technological, sonic, and political uses of Auto-Tune within a specific sonic history of Jamaican postcolonial popular music, including earlier genres like classic reggae and dub. In his examples, culminating in Kartel's 2009 anthem "Life We Living," technically induced reverb, echoes, gaps, and distortions, combined with lyrics explicitly conjuring past slavery or social inequality in the dehumanized ghetto, turn such songs into haunted spaces and the singer into a medium, "opening channels through which other voices . . . demand to be heard." Yet within the live combative social space of dancehall, rival deejays can also put Auto-Tune to more aggressive use, wielding it against one another as "sonic armor" on "diss tracks" to "render the voice of the performer invulnerable to attack."

The uncanny, because missing, voices that concern Jonathan Zwicker belong to kabuki actors. The conundrum his chapter pursues is primarily a historiographical one: the near erasure of voice as a medium from the Japanese history and archives of prewar kabuki theater, at least until very recently. This despite the hundreds of extant SP (78 RPM) records of kabuki plays produced between 1907 and 1945 and evidence that in 1890 the earliest public demonstrations of phonography in Japan showcased a brief recording of kabuki actors. One of the actors on this earliest sound recording, superstar Ichikawa Danjūrō IX, also furnished the kabuki dance performance that is the subject of the oldest surviving Japanese film recording, made in 1899 but, as stipulated, publicly screened only after his death. Zwicker attributes the disproportionate weight that pioneering prewar Japanese theorists, historians, and preservationists gave to image and gesture in their conception of kabuki to the perspective of filmic technology—specifically to the combined absence of the actor's voice onscreen and the fantasy of the actor's presence afforded by the cinematic image, which enabled scholars and critics "to reimagine the visual record of Kabuki's past as protocinematic." The ontology of the absent voice started to be understood as a historical problem for kabuki only in the early 1930s, he argues, with the emergence of broadcast radio and talkies alongside phonography, that is, once the mechanically reproduced voice could be reconfigured as "an auditory trace" or remembrance of a moment that had already passed and was now "potentially archivable."

"To whom does a recorded voice belong, to the living or the dead?" This question, posed by Tom Gunning in his chapter on the popular mythology of the technological voice as a source of uncanny terror, is also the central riddle he finds embedded in key films by Roberto Rossellini and Fritz Lang. Gunning addresses it by showing how the rhetoric and fantasies of the technologically mediated voice reveal their role in "merging the psychological and the political, thereby generating both intimacy and terror." That merging also founds the notorious relationship between the technological voice and the ideology of fascism, with radio as the weapon of choice. For, as he argues, the disembodied, ungraspable, invulnerable voice of broadcast radio (especially once coupled with the playback capacity of sound recording) acquires the ghostly ability to breach barriers of time and space at will, to infect listeners and stealthily swap out their voices, to penetrate human bodies and possess them. Gunning traces this fantastic rhetoric backward to the historical emergence of modern technologies of communication in tandem with the nineteenth-century Spiritualist movement (which reminds us that Merrill's Ouija board is the planchette's last parlor-game remnant). Laterally, he connects this fantastic rhetoric both to its real uses of the all-powerful, all-penetrating radio voice in fascist propaganda and intimidation, and to psychotic fantasies of persecution and surveillance via the "influence machine" and "dissolution of ego boundaries" in psychoanalytic theory. Weaponizing the technological voice may have a precedent in Nooter's classical prosthetic voice and a descendant in Vybz Kartel's Auto-Tuned dancehall voice, but in Gunning's film examples, the best defense against a vocal weapon is comic debunking, when a voice is shown to be technological and nothing more.

Notes

1. The term "vocal turn" was proposed by Brian Kane, "The Voice: A Diagnosis?," *Polygraph* 25 (2015); shorter version as "The Model Voice," in Feldman et al., "Why Voice Now?," Colloquy, *Journal of the American Musicological Society* 68, no. 3 (Fall 2015): 671–77. Other recent considerations of voice include *Voice: Vocal Aesthetics in Digital Arts and Media*, ed. Norie Neumark, Ross Gibson, and Theo van Leeuwen (Cambridge, MA: MIT Press, 2010); Christian Utz, Frederick Lau, et al., *Vocal Music and Contemporary Identities: Unlimited Voices in East Asia and the West* (New York: Routledge, 2012); Amanda Weidman, "Anthropology and Voice," *Annual Review of Anthropology* 43 (2014): 37–51; Nina Sun Eidsheim and Anne Schlichter, "Introduction: Voice Matters," *Postmodern Culture* 24, no. 3 (May 2014), and their entire issue on voice; *On Voice*, ed. Walter Bernhart and Lawrence Kramer (Leiden: Brill/Rodopi, 2014); Feldman et al., "Why Voice Now?," 653–85; *Voice Studies: Critical Approaches to Process, Performance and Experience*, ed. Konstantinos Thomaidis and Ben MacPherson (New York: Routledge, 2015); "Vocal Performance: New Perspectives in the Study of Vocal Music," issue of *TRANS: Revista transcultural de música / Transcultural Music Review* 18 (2014), ed. Úrsula San Cristóbal Opazo; and "Vocal Organologies and Philologies," ed. Emily Dolan, full issue of *Opera Quarterly* 33, no. 3–4 (Summer–Autumn 2017). Important in a now-older layer of studies are *Embodied Voices: Representing Female Vocality in Western Culture*, ed. Leslie C. Dunn and Nancy A. Jones (Cambridge: Cambridge University Press, 1994); and Steven Feld, "Vocal Anthropology: From the Music of Language to the Language of Song," in *A Companion to Linguistic Anthropology*, ed. Alessandro Duranti (Oxford: Blackwell, 2004), 321–45. Finally, for the phenomenological take on voice, see Don Ihde, *Listening and Voice: Phenomenologies of Sound*, 2nd ed. (1976; Albany: State University of New York Press, 2007); and for an ambitious Lacanian gloss on the popular voice, see Richard Middleton, *Voicing the Popular: On the Subjects of Popular Music* (London: Routledge, 2006).

2. Quoted from Dolar, "Voices That Matter," in this volume, 341.

3. Mladen Dolar, *A Voice and Nothing More* (Cambridge, MA: MIT Press, 2006), 15. Kaja Silverman's feminist gloss, *The Acoustic Mirror: The Female Voice in Psychoanalysis and Cinema* (Bloomington: Indiana University Press, 1988), preceded Dolar by nearly two decades.

4. For a far fuller and more analytical appraisal of Dolar's "qualifications" (or negations) than we can muster here, see Brian Kane, *Sound Unseen: Acousmatic Sound in Theory and Practice* (New York: Oxford University Press, 2014), 206–22. Kane calls these, in philosophical terms, "reductions." We are indebted to his analysis of them without either endorsing or refuting his assertions about ethical conundrums in Dolar, the theopolitical dimensions of which are also the subject of Jodi Dean, "The Object Next Door" (review of *A Voice and Nothing More* by Mladen Dolar; *The Neighbor: Three Inquiries in Political Theology* by Slavoj Žižek, Eric L. Santner, and Kenneth Reinhard [Chicago: University of Chicago Press, 2005]; and *The Parallax View* by Slavoj Žižek), *Political Theory* 35, no. 3 (June 2007): 371–78, at 375.

5. Dolar, *A Voice*, 4 and passim.

6. For Žižek's take, see especially *Looking Awry: An Introduction to Jacques Lacan through Popular Culture* (Cambridge, MA: MIT Press, 1991), as well as many others of his books. Those new to psychoanalytic discourses on voice will want to read the engaging and lucid account of Alice Lagaay, "Sound and Silence: Voice in the History of Psychoanalysis," *e-pisteme* 1, no. 1 (2008): 53–62.

7. See Dylan Evans, "Desire," in *An Introductory Dictionary of Lacanian Psychoanalysis* (London: Routledge, 1996), 36–39. Evans's Lacanian abecedarium has an entry for "gaze" but none for "voice," which, at least for most American and continental audiences, seems to have remained something of an arcane subset of Lacan's thinking until the publication of *Gaze and Voice as Love Objects*, ed. Slavoj Žižek and Renata Salecl (Durham, NC: Duke University Press, 1996), brought out in the same year.

8. An important account of how this works in music and outside it is Seth Brodsky's *From 1989: Or European Music and the Modernist Unconscious* (Oakland: University of California Press, 2017).

9. Dolar, *A Voice*, 43, and more generally 42–52.

10. Michel Chion, *The Voice in Cinema*, trans. Claudia Gorbman (New York: Columbia University Press, 1999), originally published in French in Éditions de l'Étoile/*Cahiers du cinema* (1982); and Pierre Schaeffer, *Traité des objets musicaux* (Paris: Éditions du Seuil, 1966).

11. See also Kane, *Sound Unseen*; and Jaishikha Nautiyal, "Listening with/to Nature's Voice: An Ethical Polyphony," *International Journal of Listening* 30 (2016): 151–62.

12. Freya Jarman-Ivens, *Queer Voices: Technologies, Vocalities, and the Musical Flaw* (New York: Palgrave Macmillan, 2011), esp. introduction and chap. 1.

13. Karmen MacKendrick, *The Matter of Voice: Sensual Soundings* (New York: Fordham University Press, 2016), 6–8 and passim.

14. Lynne Kendrick, "Speaking in Theatre: A Voice and Something More," paper given at the conference "False Alarm: Aurality, Errancy, and Voice," King's College, London, June 26, 2016, now part of Kendrick's *Theatre Aurality* (London: Palgrave, 2017), chap. 3, "Voice: A Performance of Sound." Our thanks to Kendrick for sharing both texts with Feldman before *Theatre Aurality* was published.

15. Jason David Myres, "The Bit Player: Stephen Hawking and the Object Voice," *Rhetoric Society Quarterly* 46, no. 2 (2016): 156–75.

16. Ken C. Kawashima, "The Voice of Interpellation and Capitalist Crisis: Notes toward an Investigation of Postwar Japanese Ideology," *boundary 2* 42, no. 3 (2015): 63–77, at 64; and Giorgio Agamben, *Homo sacer: Sovereign Power and Bare Life*, trans. Daniel Heller-Roazen (1995; Stanford, CA: Stanford University Press, 1998).

17. Joshua Gunn, "Speech Is Dead; Long Live Speech," review-essay (of Adriana Cavarero, *For More Than One Voice: Toward a Philosophy of Vocal Expression*, trans. Paul A. Kottman

[Stanford, CA: Stanford University Press, 2005]; Dolar, *A Voice*; Clifford Nass and Scott Brave, *Wired for Speech: How Voice Activates and Advances the Human-Computer Relationship*; Walter Ong, *The Presence of the Word: Some Prolegomena for Cultural and Religious History*, reprint [New Haven, CT: Yale University Press, 2002, orig. pub. 1967]), *Quarterly Journal of Speech* 94, no. 3 (August 2008): 343–64, at 350.

18. Cf. Shane Butler, *The Ancient Phonograph* (New York: Zone Books, 2015), 17–24; Kane, *Sound Unseen*, 206–22; Devin Zane Shaw, review of Jacques Lacan, *Écrits: The Complete Text*, trans. Bruce Fink (New York: W. W. Norton and Co., 2005); Dolar, *A Voice*; *De Philosophia* 19, no. 2 (2006): 99–104, esp. 104; and David W. Samuels, "Music's Role in Language Revitalization—Some Questions from Recent Literature," *Journal of Linguistic Anthropology* 25, no. 3 (2015): 346–55, at 349.

19. Dolar, *A Voice*, 73.

20. Roland Barthes, "The Grain of the Voice," in *Image, Music, Text*, trans. Stephen Heath (New York: Noonday Press, 1977), 179–89. Barthes also riffs on Panzéra in "Music, Voice, Language," in *The Responsibility of Forms*, trans. Richard Howard (New York: Hill and Wang, 1985), 275–85. For Jonathan Dunsby's critical analysis of the Barthes/grain phenomenon, see his "Roland Barthes and the Grain of Panzéra's Voice," *Journal of the Royal Musical Association* 134, no. 1 (2009): 113–32; and see too Jarman-Ivens's *Queer Voices*, 5–7 and passim.

21. Barthes calls the predicate "the bulwark with which the subject's imaginary [always] protects itself from the loss which threatens it" (179) and calls frequent attention to jouissance.

22. Barthes, "Grain," 182.

23. Barthes, "Grain," 182–83.

24. See Jarman-Ivens, *Queer Voices*, for the last point, even though she values the notions of "grain" and "geno-song."

25. Dolar states his objection outright in his single nod to Barthes, tucked into a footnote: "Barthes—*le grain de la voix*, the grain of the voice, 'the materiality of the body speaking its mother tongue,' 'the body in the singing voice,' and so on . . . will never do. The problem is that the voice cannot be pinned to a body, or be seen as an emanation of the body, without a paradox" (*A Voice*, 197n10). The paradox is that because voice for Dolar is always necessarily acousmatic, its topology can never really be "disclosed" (*A Voice*, esp. 72–73, and see Dolar's "Voices That Matter" below).

26. Barthes, "Grain," 181.

27. See Elias Krell, "Singing Strange: Transvocality in North American Music Performance" (PhD diss., Northwestern University, 2014), 35, 44, and passim. See also Licia Fiol-Matta, *The Great Woman Singer: Gender and Voice in Puerto Rican Music* (Durham, NC: Duke University Press, 2017), esp. 139 and 230, for whom the "thinking voice" allows female Puerto Rican singers to become protagonists in situations in which they otherwise have little agency.

28. Michel de Certeau, "Vocal Utopias: Glossolalias," *Representations* 56 (Autumn 1996): 29–47, originally published in 1980; and idem, *The Mystic Fable*, vol. 1, *The Sixteenth and Seventeenth Centuries*, trans. Michael B. Smith (Chicago: University of Chicago Press, 1992), chaps. 4–6, originally published in 1982.

29. Certeau, "Vocal Utopias," 29.

30. Certeau, "Vocal Utopias," 30.

31. Certeau, "Vocal Utopias," 30; see further at 31–33.

32. See especially Certeau, *Mystic Fable*, 129–43, and 143 for references to Paré and Jean de Léry.

33. Certeau, *Mystic Fable*, 144.

34. This is not so far from Certeau's preoccupations with consumers ("users") and their modes of appropriation ("poaching") and subversion in *The Practice of Everyday Life*, trans.

Stephen Rendell (1984; Berkeley: University of California Press, 2011), originally published in French in 1980.

35. Certeau, *Mystic Fable*, 163–64.

36. *The Queen's Throat: Opera, Homosexuality, and the Mystery of Desire* (New York: Poseidon, 1993). Relatedly, a large literature exists on divadom and fandom as it relates to voice, of which see Mary Anne Doane, "The Voice in Cinema: The Articulation of Body and Space," *Yale French Studies* 60 (1980): 33–50; Terry Castle, "In Praise of Brigitte Fassbaender," in Castle's *The Apparitional Lesbian: Female Homosexuality and Modern Culture* (New York: Columbia University Press, 1993), 200–238; and Jean Ma, *Sounding the Modern Woman: The Songstress in Chinese Cinema* (Durham, NC: Duke University Press, 2015). These raise the specter of a phantasmatic dimension of voice and sound, on which see Mladen Dolar, "The Burrow of Sound," *Differences: A Journal of Feminist Cultural Studies* 22, no. 2–3 (Summer–Fall 2011): 112–39.

37. For the last two, see Judith [now Jack] Halberstam, "Queer Voices and Musical Genders," in *Oh Boy! Masculinities and Popular Music*, ed. Freya Jarman-Ivens (New York: Routledge, 2007), 183–95; and Deborah R. Vargas, *Dissonant Divas in Chicana Music: The Limits of La Onda* (Minneapolis: University of Minnesota Press, 2012).

38. Jeff Buckley, Paris interview, ca. 1994, https://www.youtube.com/watch?v=Gip77qGXWT4, accessed February 7, 2017.

39. Cf. MacKendrick, *Sensual Soundings*, and J. Q. Davies, *A Romantic Anatomy of Performance* (Berkeley: University of California Press, 2014), for two prominent recent examples.

40. To hear this in contradistinction to the psychoanalytic voice—from which Buckley's take on voice is a far cry—consider the voice portrayed by Michel Poizat, a voice that erupts as a pure instant, high and piercing like the cry of an angel. In the purity of that instant, Poizat's voice—classically that of an operatic soprano—lacks all signification, manifesting itself as sheer nothingness. It becomes the insatiable if elusive object of a fan's desire, an endlessly frustrated desire for total ecstasy. This Lacanian voice is delineated in Poizat's *Le cri de l'ange: Essai sur le jouissance de l'amateur de l'opéra* (1986), which made its way to English-language readers as *The Angel's Cry: Beyond the Pleasure Principle in Opera*, trans. Arthur Denner (Ithaca, NY: Cornell University Press, 1992). Where Poizat falters is at the meeting point of the object-voice and the subject, for far from stumbling, meandering, and never attaining the object-voice in the mode rehearsed above, Poizat's subject/fan sometimes encounters it head-on in a rush of jouissance. The fetish becomes the object attained, at least in a certain interpretation.

41. Aaron A. Fox, *Real Country: Music and Language in Working-Class Culture* (Durham, NC: Duke University Press, 2004), 272.

42. Sarah Nooter, *The Mortal Voice in the Tragedies of Aeschylus* (Cambridge: Cambridge University Press, 2017), esp. the introduction.

43. Bonnie Gordon, "It's Not about the Cut: The Castrato's Instrumentalized Song," *New Literary History* 46, no. 4 (Autumn 2015): 647–67, quote at 649. Also critical is Gordon's attention to noise in her projects on Jefferson, slavery, the Black Atlantic, and Zora Neale Hurston, especially her lecture "Feminist Noise," Committee on Women and Gender Endowed Lecture, American Musicological Society, November 2, 2018.

44. Fred Moten similarly hears a "phonocentric deafness" in Derrida; see *In the Break: The Aesthetics of the Black Radical Tradition* (Minneapolis: University of Minnesota Press, 2003), 185.

45. Gary Tomlinson, *The Singing of the New World: Indigenous Voice in the Era of European Contact* (Cambridge: Cambridge University Press, 2007), 2.

46. Michel de Certeau, "Ethno-Graphy: Speech, or the Space of the Other: Jean de Léry," in *The Writing of History*, trans. Tom Conley (New York: Columbia University Press, 1988), 212, quoted in Tomlinson, *Singing of the New World*, 46.

47. Were there any doubt about the Aztec elisions between the materiality of writing and the less material speech and vocalization, such that singing linked the Aztec directly to a world of thingly reference, as Tomlinson argues, the case of Nahuatl song would seem to obviate it. Its pictographic writing system had, in his estimation, something like a "fully material volume" that was only rendered metaphorical, hence less material, by the work of conquerors who alphabetized it in ways that he argues were deaf to its meanings (*Singing of the New World*, 30 and passim).

48. Adriana Cavarero, *For More Than One Voice: Toward a Philosophy of Vocal Expression*, trans. Paul A. Kottman (Stanford, CA: Stanford University Press, 2005), originally published in 2003.

49. See Kane, *Sound Unseen*, 152–56; and Steven Connor, *Dumbstruck: A Cultural History of Ventriloquism* (Oxford: Oxford University Press, 2000).

50. Ryan Dohoney, "An Antidote to Metaphysics: Adriana Cavarero's Vocal Philosophy," *Women and Gender: A Journal of Gender and Culture* 15 (2011): 70–85, at 78 (and see the quote of Cavarero at the beginning of Dohoney's essay, with its appeal to singing).

51. Another promusical antimetaphysician is Carolyn Abbate, whose views have been voiced in "Opera, or the Envoicing of Women," in *Musicology and Difference: Gender and Sexuality in Music Scholarship*, ed. Ruth A. Solie (Berkeley: University of California Press, 1993), 225–58; and *In Search of Opera* (Princeton, NJ: Princeton University Press, 2001). See discussion that follows.

52. Kane makes an explicit argument for this in *Sound Unseen*, 226. We cannot begin to do justice here to the now vast and growing range of sound studies literature, which intersects and overlaps with that on voice, but see, for example. *The Sound Studies Reader*, ed. Jonathan Sterne (New York: Routledge, 2012), which brings out the technological and material interface between sound and voice around which much of the conversation between sound studies and voice studies turns.

53. *Sensing Sound: Singing and Listening as Vibrational Practice* (Durham, NC: Duke University Press, 2015), introduction, esp. 17, and 11 on the objection to sound over music. For a related point, see James Q. Davies, "Voice Belongs," in Feldman et al., "Why Voice Now?," 677–81, on how voices "belong" in distinct if highly various ways.

54. *A Million Years of Music: The Emergence of Human Modernity* (Brooklyn, NY: Zone Books, 2015).

55. See Abbate, *Unsung Voices: Opera and Musical Narrative in the Nineteenth Century* (Princeton, NJ: Princeton University Press, 1991); idem, *In Search of Opera*; and idem, "Sound Object Lessons," *Journal of the American Musicological Society* 69, no. 3 (2016): 793–829, with various other entries along the way.

56. Abbate, *Unsung Voices*, ix.

57. Abbate, *Unsung Voices*, 11 and passim.

58. Abbate, *In Search of Opera*, 152 and passim.

59. Cf. Jelena Novak, *Postopera: Reinventing the Voice-Body* (Farnham, UK: Ashgate, 2015), which looks at the reinvention of the relation between voice and body in modern opera with attention to Dolar and Žižek; and Connor, *Dumbstruck*.

60. See also Joseph Auner, "'Sing It for Me': Posthuman Ventriloquism in Recent Popular Music," *Journal of the Royal Musical Association* 128 (2003): 98–122.

61. N. Katherine Hayles, *How We Became Posthuman: Virtual Bodies in Cybernetics, Literature, and Informatics* (Chicago: University of Chicago Press, 1999); and Alexander G. Weheliye,

"'Feenin': Posthuman Voices in Contemporary Black Popular Music," *Social Text* 71, vol. 20, no. 2 (Summer 2002): 21–47. We also draw here on Weheliye's important *Phonographies: Grooves in Sonic Afro-Modernity* (Durham, NC: Duke University Press, 2005).

62. See esp. "'Feenin,'" 27. Cf. also Kodwo Eshun, *More Brilliant Than the Sun: Adventures in Sonic Fiction* (London: Quartet Books, 1998); and Lindon Barrett, *Blackness and Value: Seeing Double* (Cambridge: Cambridge University Press, 1999), both critiqued in Weheliye, "'Feenin,'" 27–30.

63. Berkeley: University of California Press, 2005.

64. Kun, *Audiotopia*, 12 and chap. 3.

65. On listening in discourse around voice and race, see Kun, *Audiotopia*; Nina Sun Eidsheim, "Race and the Aesthetics of Vocal Timbre," in *Rethinking Difference in Music Scholarship*, ed. Olivia Bloechl, Melanie Lowe, and Jeffrey Kallberg (Cambridge: Cambridge University Press, 2015), 338–65; idem, "Marian Anderson and 'Sonic Blackness' in American Opera," *American Quarterly* 63, no. 3 (September 2011): 641–71; idem, *The Race of Sound: Listening, Timbre, and Vocality in African American Music* (Durham, NC: Duke University Press, 2019); and Jennifer Lynn Stoever's *The Sonic Color Line: Race and the Cultural Politics of Listening* (New York: New York University Press, 2016). The last focuses on listeners' racialization of voices, across a continuum of racialized white immigrants (mostly Italian) in the case of Jenny Lind's concertgoers in the Midwest and South, and across complex fields of production and reception in the case of the promotion of Lead Belly (chaps. 2 and 4).

66. Moten, *In the Break*. See further in Feldman, "Voice Gap Crack Break," 196 below.

67. Daphne A. Brooks, "Amy Winehouse and the (Black) Art of Appropriation," *The Nation*, September 10, 2008; idem, "'This Voice Which Is Not One': Amy Winehouse Sings the Ballad of Sonic Blue(s)face Culture," *Women & Performance: A Journal of Feminist Theory* 20, no. 1 (March 2010): 37–60; and Maureen Mahon, "Listening for Willie Mae 'Big Mama' Thornton's Voice: The Sound of Race and Gender Transgressions in Rock and Roll," *Women and Music: A Journal of Gender and Culture*, vol. 15 (2011): 1–17. Far less often, black voices are racialized as white: see Mark Burford, "Sam Cooke as Pop Album Artist—A Reinvention in Three Songs," *Journal of the American Musicological Society* 65, no. 1 (Spring 2012): 113–78.

68. Malik Gaines, *Black Performance on the Outskirts of the Left: A History of the Impossible* (New York: New York University Press, 2017); Joshua Chambers-Letson, *After the Party: A Manifesto for Queer of Color Life* (New York: New York University Press, 2018), which he kindly shared with Feldman in manuscript; Daphne A. Brooks, *Bodies in Dissent: Spectacular Performances of Race and Freedom, 1850–1910* (Durham, NC: Duke University Press, 2006); and Beth Coleman, "Race as Technology," *Camera obscura* 70, vol. 24, no. 1 (2009): 177–207.

69. T. J. Clark, *Farewell to an Idea: Episodes from a History of Modernism* (New Haven, CT: Yale University Press, 1999), 7.

70. Michel Chion, *Words on Screen*, ed. and trans. Claudia Gorman (New York: Columbia University Press, 2017).

71. Cf. Dolar, "Voices That Matter," this volume, 355n27, on Chion.

72. See also Butler, *The Ancient Phonograph*; and James Q. Davies's chapter in this volume.

PART I

Sound-Producing Voice

1

Speech and/in Song

STEVEN RINGS

In our daily world of social interactions, singing is marked, speech unmarked; in the world of song, the reverse holds.[1] Such, at least, is the commonsense view, which might tempt us to assume a difference in kind between speech and song. Yet scholars from fields as diverse as anthropology, linguistics, and cognitive science have long argued that the difference is instead one of degree—speech and singing arrayed on a continuum. Aaron Fox, for example, lends an attentive ear to the musicality of everyday speech in white, rural Texas, and explores its affiliations with country singing.[2] Fox's work intervenes in a long ethnomusicological tradition of probing the porous border between speech and song.[3] An intellectual world away, perceptual psychologist Diana Deutsch has demonstrated the ways in which repeated snippets of speech can quickly begin to sound like singing.[4] She stumbled on the phenomenon heard in **website example 1.1** which involves her own voice—by accident, while editing a recording. As one listens, the change is both gradual and immediate, a difference in degree that eventually throws off its cloak to reveal a difference in kind. Deutsch's voice seems to cross a qualitative threshold at some point, taking on a kind of material insistence. Removed from the syntagmatic chain of speech, the *musical* aspects of her voice—pitch, rhythm, timbre—are somehow vivified, brought to life and dancing before our ears. The words' propositional force, by contrast, falls away, leaving behind a phonemic husk. Sounds behaving strangely, indeed.

Though Deutsch artificially manufactures her example through a looped recording, real-world examples in which repetitive, heightened speech approaches the condition of song are not hard to find: the auctioneer, the keening mother, the charismatic preacher, the Quranic reciter. In such examples, musicality and communicative context are inseparable. But a small technological nudge can disturb the balance. Consider **website example 1.2**, the opening of Steve Reich's 1965 tape piece *It's Gonna Rain*.[5] Reich manipulates a recording of Pentecostal preacher Brother Walter delivering an apocalyptic sermon in San Francisco's Union Square in 1964. Walter's speech approaches the condition of song all on its own, an effect that Reich heightens through unnervingly tight loops.

In these examples, we hear song emerging *from within* speech, so to speak, as a kind of latent presence or potential. And when it emerges, the voice can seem to reclaim its material autonomy, *phoné* asserting itself over and against *logos*.[6] Per Aaron Fox, this material assertion is an effect of singing *in general*: "Singing heightens the aural and visceral presence of the vocalizing body in language, calling attention to the physical medium of the voice, the normally taken-for-granted channel of 'ordinary' speech."[7] But what about those contexts when "ordinary speech" is not the norm, but singing *is*? That is, what about speech in the world of song? If quotidian speech makes the materiality of the singing voice perspicuous, does song repay the debt? That is, in the world of song, does speech become *audible*?

I pose these questions not to suggest that they admit of univocal answers—there are too many traditions of speaking within song for that—but to prime our ears for the gallery of examples that I will explore in this chapter. They are drawn from diverse popular song traditions—early country to recent hip-hop—and each involves a performer who both speaks and sings. This leaves out a lot, most notably art music traditions like *Sprechstimme*, melodrama, *Singspiel*, *opéra bouffe*, and so on, as well as musical theater. Moreover, I will not consider popular music examples in which an individual speaks who is not the singer (think Vincent Price in Michael Jackson's "Thriller"). There will nevertheless be plenty to discuss. I am especially interested in the ways in which speech can emerge as a marked figure against the unmarked ground of more conventionally coded musical sound, a relationship that can focus our ears on the very sonic features that often fade into transparency (or inaudibility) in everyday talk, as Fox notes. Here, though, Fox's relationship is reversed, as it is *speech* that can seem to regain its granular opacity within song. We will also attend to the ways in which the speech-song dynamic can interact with questions of meaning, sometimes animating lyrics with a kind of heightened hermeneutic legibility, at others suggesting a dialectic of interiority and exteriority, at still others, modeling diverse modes of real-world social or performative interaction. Finally, I will explore the ways in which these performers vocally navigate the transition from song to speech or vice versa. In some examples, vocalists explicitly cordon speech off from song—the commonsense notion of a difference in kind retaining its force—while in others, performers fluidly traverse a continuum between speech and song. Strikingly, through the 1980s, vocalists of the latter type—whom we might call "continuum singers"—tend to come from largely white, northern, urban scenes lionized by a critical elite (think folk revival, punk, indie). By contrast, the more sharply demarcated examples reside on the margins of elite taste (think early country and R&B). Along the way I will venture some thoughts on this rather Bourdieuian state of affairs,[8] and also note its dissolution in the hip-hop era, which has led to an extraordinary flourishing of vocal practices, speech and song circulating ever more freely.

Hank Williams, "Pictures from Life's Other Side" (1951)

There is an entire genre of country song called the "recitation song," in which the singer either speaks throughout or alternates speaking and singing. The subject matter is often devotional or cautionary, with nods to tent revival and radio preaching traditions. As Hank Williams biographers Colin Escott, George Meritt, and William MacEwen put it, "The recitation was a little homily, usually with a strong moral undertone, narrated to musical accompaniment."[9] Recorded examples date back to the 1930s; by the 1950s, recitation songs were an old-fashioned, niche item. Hank Williams nevertheless maintained a deep fondness for the genre, despite his producer Fred Rose's resistance, and recorded some of its most celebrated examples in the final years of his life, under the name Luke the Drifter.[10] Among the most famous is "Pictures from Life's Other Side," which Williams recorded in 1951, and which became the first track on the posthumous LP *Hank Williams as Luke the Drifter*. The song consists of three spoken verses and one sung chorus. The verses narrate tragic scenes "from life's other side," while the chorus offers a capsule meditation in song. **Website example 1.3** includes the first verse and the beginning of the chorus.

The crisp distinction between vocal modalities is immediately evident. As in all of his Luke the Drifter recitations, Williams shuttles between two discrete registers: he either speaks or he sings, but he does not shade gradually from one to the other. Yet it is worth noting that the spoken portions are not everyday speech—they are heightened. Williams's intonation suggests the fervor and intensity of a radio preacher, while the prosody and rhyme scheme match the sung chorus rather than the rhythms of colloquial speech. Indeed, at times his reciting voice feels almost yoked to the musical structure, pulled ineluctably forward. This is one reason for the sense of urgency and peril that belies the folksy drawl. Another is Williams's tendency to draw out certain syllables with quivering intensity, as on the words "pictures" (pronounced "pitchers") and "love" in the third line of verse one ("There's pictures of love and of passion"). Why, then, do the verses register so unambiguously as speech? Most obvious is Williams's treatment of pitch and contour. He explicitly—and perhaps exaggeratedly—shapes each syllable with the characteristic arch of speech, sliding into and out of emphasized syllables, rather than settling on sustained pitches slotted into the discrete locations of the diatonic scale (in this case, E major).

This avoidance of sung pitch means that Williams's voice can no longer project that central element of popular song: the melody. But the melody is there, nestled into the musical accompaniment behind Williams's recitation. Note the fiddle in **website example 1.3** (played by Jerry Rivers). This is a phenomenon common to recitation songs, and indeed to songs in many genres that involve speaking: the melodic line, as though extracted from the voice, is relocated to a different part of the sonic texture. I will refer to this as melodic "ghosting." Williams's speaking voice is ghosted throughout the song: by Rivers's fiddle in verses one and three, by Don Helms's steel guitar in verse two. Tellingly, the ghosted melody disappears in the chorus, when Williams sings. Yet the logic of ghosting is not subtractive in any simple sense: the voice is not made *less* by the process. Rather, it can seem to *gain* a kind of palpable materiality, as the complex grain of speech emerges into sonic relief against the conventional code of the melody and its embedding country waltz. By making sonically explicit that parameter of the musical texture that the voice no longer possesses—melody—the ghosted line paradoxically *amplifies* the speaking voice. Ghosted melody settles unobtrusively into the accompanimental fabric, reinvesting the speaking voice with obdurate, material difference.

In country recitation songs, this crisp division between recitation and coded song indexes a shift in implied participatory musicking.[11] In the verses, Williams addresses the listener in narration; in the chorus, he solicits participation.[12] Singing, after all, affords "singing along."[13] Indeed, the musical code underwrites the social efficacy of group singing, allowing participants to anticipate pitch and rhythm, affording entrainment with the overall flow of the music (however inexact that entrainment might be in practice).[14] Everyday speech affords no such opportunities for entrainment or pitch matching. Though one perhaps *could* "speak along" to Williams's recitation in "Pictures from Life's Other Side," given its regular prosody, to do so would seem odd. The narrative explicitly suggests a direct address. Indeed, Williams enacts this address even more explicitly on other Luke the Drifter songs, beginning with locutions that evoke radio preaching, such as "You know, friends . . ." ("Help Me Understand") or "Now, friends . . ." ("I've Been down That Road

Before"). When the sung chorus or refrain arrives, one can then easily imagine an audience that had been listening attentively to the verse joining in for the chorus, much as a congregation sings a hymn after a sermon.

The interaction of speech and song in country recitations often invites hermeneutic attention. Consider **website example 1.4**, the final verse from "Pictures from Life's Other Side." Williams recites the opening of the verse as before, the quivering intensity of his voice even more in evidence, but then shifts surprisingly into song for the final two lines: "God help her, she leaps, oh there's no one to weep / It's just a picture from life's other side." The transgression is arresting. Singing now finds its way into a portion of the song that we had assumed was the domain of speech, as the narrator reacts to the suicide of the unwed mother, child in her arms. No listener or imaginary "congregant" would be prepared to sing along at this point: this is the narrator's voice, seemingly moved to spontaneous song. The undertone of moral fervor and peril now surfaces, as Williams's balanced delivery from the chorus gives way to a singing voice infused with the quiver and break of the recitation. Distanced, rueful musings on "life's other side" give way to affective shock in the present tense, as though Luke the Drifter is now in the picture itself, a helpless observer to its tragic events.

Such hermeneutic legibility in country recitations can seem to generate a kind of affective intensity in primary colors. Another vivid example is "The Green, Green Grass of Home," as recorded in 1965 by Porter Wagoner. The song begins with Wagoner singing sonorously of arriving in his "old home town," with its "green, green grass." His family and his girlfriend Mary—with "hair of gold and lips like cherries"—joyfully greet him at the train station. In the third verse, however, the Technicolor images give way to the gray of a death-row jail cell, and Wagoner switches from singing to weary recitation:

> Then I awake and look around me,
> At the four gray walls that surround me,
> And I realize, yes, I was only dreaming.
> For there's a guard and there's a sad old padre—
> Arm in arm we'll walk at daybreak. . . .

As with "Pictures from Life's Other Side," the result will strike some as pure kitsch. For others—especially cultural insiders and country connoisseurs—the effect is one of concentrated emotional intensity. Williams's Luke the Drifter songs have an especially fervent following, devoted listeners who hear in his speaking and singing genuine emotional extremity and peril, the voice as exposed nerve.[15]

Marvin Gaye, "Save the Children" (1971)

One encounters a similar bifurcation between speech and song in a vast range of R&B, soul, and funk. Spoken parts are common in seduction songs (think Barry White, Bobby Womack, Lionel Richie) as well as in more narrative songs in which the speaker interacts with a chorus of encouraging background singers (examples are legion in the girl-group repertory—for example, the Shangri-Las' "Leader of the Pack"—and in later male groups like the Chi-Lites, the O'Jays, and the Manhattans). Marvin Gaye occasionally performed within the seductive speak-singing tradition, though he also employed the technique in other contexts. On his 1971 concept album *What's Going On*—a thematically unified plea for social justice and environmental stewardship—speech and song intermix on two tracks to evoke different contexts of African American sociality: a party on the title track and the call-and-response patterns from black worship on "Save the Children." We will focus on the latter. As the excerpt in **website example 1.5** begins, note the melodic ghosting behind Gaye's spoken phrases, performed here by strings and a wordless vocal melisma from the background singers. The gulf between the speech and song in the passage is immediately obvious: Gaye's exquisite singing voice inhabits an altogether different space from his disarmingly direct speaking voice, with its expressions of helplessness and dismay, and its earnest appeals for social action. The most obvious manifestation of that gulf is register: Gaye's singing voice floats high above his speaking one, as though transposing it to a higher, aspirational frequency, and infusing it with the ethical suasion of song.

Whether we hear this as an echo, a response, or an affective amplification turns in part on whether we recognize that there are actually *two* voices singing on the track. Both voices are Gaye's, but he recorded them separately. This multitracking contributes subtly to the sense of antiphonal alternation between two voices. Such alternation loosely indexes a practice in African American worship, as well as a variety of white traditions, known as "lining out" or "hymn lining": the preacher speaks or sings a line of the hymn right before the audience is to sing it.[16] The multitrack setting arguably underwrites the illusion of lining out, but we also explicitly recognize Gaye in both voices, and at first it seems as though the alternation might be in real time, on one track. And, of course, congregations do not sing this way. This is a virtuosic solo voice, in a soul idiom. We are thus initially unsure whether this is one voice divided between speech and song, or two different voices, each with its own native mode of expression, their interaction offering a tenuous connection to a real-world sacred practice.

This sense of multiplied vocality increases later in the track, as the illusion of lining out breaks down further. Gaye's speaking and singing voices begin to overlap more and more, until they are largely simultaneous, the singing voice duplicating the speaking one rhythmically, but remaining distinct from it timbrally and registrally, oil and water. Consider **website example 1.6**, in which Gaye's two vocal parts align, and are then joined by female background singers who enter for one brief interjection. The backing singers' interjection is peculiarly stylized: one might imagine a backing choir, exhorting congregants to "live your life!" But the line is delivered in heightened speech, not gospel song, and in an odd unison.[17] Voices seem to multiply without legible reference to a real-world social context.

Nevertheless, the fact that Gaye's delivery *implies* such interactive contexts is underscored by a live performance of the song from the Kennedy Center in 1972.[18] **Website example 1.7** presents the beginning of the song in this performance, in which Gaye asks, speaking: "I just want to ask a question: Who really cares?" In the pause, a female audience member shouts out: "I care!" There is a remarkable performative doubling here: the track's technologically mediated representation of antiphonal alternation is susceptible to slippage into real-world interaction when the song is performed live, by one charismatic speaking voice in front of real bodies.

Patti Smith, "Land" (1975)

The crisp delineation of speaking and singing in early country and R&B repertories contrasts markedly with the practice of a wide range of speak-singers within the folk-rock and protopunk scenes, active at the height of Gaye's career. These are artists whose singing voices shade ever toward speech, whether as a result of vocal limitation, strategic choice, or some combination of the two. **Website example 1.8** juxtaposes three canonical examples: Bob Dylan, Lou Reed (with the Velvet Underground), and Leonard Cohen. One hardly thinks of these three singers as interchangeable, but the juxtaposition brings out clear similarities. Flatly declaimed recitations coalesce around nodal points of melodic and metric focus, only to slip away again, with nonchalant indifference to bourgeois musical decorum. Antecedents for Dylan's speech-singing style include the Beats and Woody Guthrie's talking blues. For Reed and Cohen, the most proximate antecedent is Dylan himself, avatar of countercultural cool and literary ambition. Such literary commitments are an obvious place to begin when wondering about this style of vocal delivery and its sharp divergence from country and R&B practices as regards the relationship of speech and song. The bohemian art worlds within which these singers circulated—the Chelsea

Hotel, Andy Warhol's Factory—surely also played a role, as did middle-class rejection of middle-class convention, a stance not available to most musicians in the rural, white South or the urban, African American North.

We can easily multiply our roster of hipster speak-singers as the 1970s progress: in addition to Dylan, Reed, and Cohen, think of Iggy Pop, David Byrne, Jonathan Richman, Tom Verlaine, Joey Ramone, Richard Hell. All denizens of the downtown New York scene around CBGB—and all men. We should also note that the number of women speaking in country recitations or in early R&B and soul is vanishingly small. Yet, in other genres—from classic blues to 1960s girl groups—we find female performers engaging in a rich practice of speaking and singing.[19] These gender disparities are surely overdetermined by multiple factors—cultural, racial, institutional, commercial. To explore them in depth would merit a separate study. For now, we can simply be thankful for Patti Smith, the first prominent female artist to enter the ranks of the CBGB speak-singers. A seminal figure in the nascent punk scene, Smith was a self-professed Dylan fanatic, whose fandom for the Beats and Symbolists may even have surpassed his.[20] She performs her bohemian bona fides via an extraordinary voice that ranges fluidly and sometimes violently across the speech/song spectrum, rarely settling for long at either pole.[21] Nowhere is this more in evidence than in "Land," from her 1975 debut album, the opening of which is presented in **website example 1.9**.

Smith begins with the closest thing to actual speech that we have yet heard: a spoken narrative about an attack on a boy, Johnny, based in part on William S. Burroughs's novel *The Wild Boys*. Smith speaks quietly, emphasizing her thick Jersey accent. Behind her voice we hear a flanged guitar begin to pulse on a single harmonic (generating the "rhythm" that the lyrics refer to). More strikingly, we also hear *another* recording of Smith's speaking voice, quieter and distanced by reverb, reciting similar, but not identical, words. There is no melodic ghosting here, but the vocal doubling is a conspicuous substitute, a blurry sonic emblem for the two characters. As if to confirm this, the vocal parts lock together as the two boys lock eyes (0:22). Smith's previously unmetered speech now entrains to the building groove, underscoring the sense of inevitable, growing threat. Eventually Smith begins to sing a bluesy minor third (0:48: "Suddenly, Johnny gets the feeling . . ."), in the first passage that codes clearly as "singing," though the rasp of Smith's speaking voice is never far away. The effect is of Smith "musicalizing" her voice in stages, each stage corresponding to a new dramatic development. Here, it is Johnny's "sudden" realization that he's being surrounded by "horses, horses, horses"; bass and drums enter to mark the moment. This incantatory repetition of "horses" then *brings forth a song*: "The Land of a Thousand Dances," made famous by

Wilson Pickett a decade earlier. The door to the song opens by pivoting on an outrageous pun: from horses (implying heroin) to the song's first nonsense couplet: "Do you know how to pony / Like bony maroney."

Smith's voice has now moved as far toward song as it will in this number, but that Jersey twang is still there. It reanimates the beloved R&B classic, while simultaneously insisting on its transformation: a white woman now sings and gives the song a surreal new literary-performative staging—the song seems to emerge from *within* Smith's poetry. It is tempting to hear the whole as a sort of punk-rock Rousseauian origin myth in reverse: literary speech finds its way into song, resignifying a canonical precursor text. An originary "authenticity" is thereby regained, the sturdiest rock myth of all.

Laura Marling, "Saved These Words" (2013)

If Smith helped establish a space in which later generations of punk-inspired female singers might move freely between speech and song, singer-songwriters like Joni Mitchell and Rickie Lee Jones did the same for female singers of a more folk or jazz bent—bohemians of a different stripe.[22] **Website example 1.10** includes two representative samples, from Mitchell's "Coyote" (1976) and Jones's "Easy Money" (1979). We can hear their influence in the voice of Laura Marling, a prodigiously talented young musician from the burgeoning West London folk scene. One can gain a quick sense of Marling's nimble vocal resources in **website example 1.11**, the opening of her 2011 song "The Muse." Country inflections give way to brief hints of Mitchell and even a bluesy melisma, before dissolving into the cutting spoken conclusion. The rate of vocal change is brisk; it is no surprise that a singer with this kind of elastic—almost rubbery—vocal agility will tip into speech as easily as into full-throated song. Indeed, Marling alternately performs the speech/song relation as both continuous *and* disjunct, as the situation demands.

The song "Saved These Words," which concludes her 2013 album *Once I Was an Eagle*, vividly demonstrates this vocal fluidity. The opening (**web. ex. 1.12**) is quietly meditative and close-miked, Marling's singing voice seemingly exhausted and strategically creaky. Two verses of similar cut follow, and then the affective contour angles steeply upward. If Marling's initial singing voice seemed poised on the edge of speech, she now moves to each extreme, first speaking and then singing the question "Should you choose?" The song's concluding sweep builds from there, deriving its energy from the contrast, Marling's voice passing silently over the gulf (**web. ex. 1.13**).

Spoken delivery is a natural choice in a song about words and curses. But the sung portions, marked by Marling's striking move into the upper register, energize the negative vocal space that intervenes. Hermeneutic readings are easy to come by here, and not especially interesting without Marling's physically sounding voice. But *with* that voice, the text begins to hum with energy and excess, as speech and song engage in their reciprocal amplification. Also notable are the shifting pronouns—from "you" to "he" and back—which complicate the sense of address: it is not always obvious to whom Marling is speaking. Nor does her singing invite the kind of participatory interaction we observed in Hank Williams. Rather, we listen in. The result is a vicarious affective identification, not unfamiliar in the singer-songwriter tradition, the voice limning a space of bourgeois interiority.

Beyoncé, "Formation" (2016)

In my opening gambit, I suggested that speech and song typically exhibit what we might call a *contextual asymmetry*: within a given social or aesthetic context, either speech or song will tend to predominate, setting off its other like a figure against a ground. In the examples surveyed thus far—stylistically, historically, and culturally diverse as they are—singing is clearly the unmarked norm, against which the spoken voice vividly emerges, its material otherness vividly marked.

There is good evidence, though, that in certain corners of musical mass culture this contextual asymmetry is well on its way to dissolving. In the era of hip-hop, rappers increasingly sing, and pop and R&B singers increasingly rap (or quasi-rap). In hip-hop's early days, rapping and singing were crisply divided—for example, between rapped verses and sung hooks, typically delivered by a distinct emcee and singer. But soon hip-hop artists began to emerge who were just as likely to sing as rap: Lauryn Hill, Queen Latifah, Missy Elliott, Andre 3000, and more recently Drake, Nicki Minaj, Kanye West, Frank Ocean, and many others. Moreover, in certain rap subcultures—for example, in Atlanta's trap scene—Auto-Tune has become all but ubiquitous, turning even mumbled raps into quasi-song, yet another technological nudge that transforms speech into song (recall the examples from Deutsch and Reich with which the chapter began). In this new aesthetic landscape, even mainstream pop singers like Taylor Swift can slip into quasi-rapped verses (witness "Shake It Off"), while plenty of R&B singers—Chris Brown, Brandy, Trey Songz, Beyoncé, Anderson .Paak—rap with ease.

Early February 2016 saw the release of two extraordinary songs that inhabit this new space of speech/song fluidity. Beyoncé's "Formation"—released February 6, the day before the Super Bowl—generated volumes of internet commentary. The song and its astonishing video engage powerfully with

Hurricane Katrina, the Black Lives Matter movement, gender and race across multiple axes, the New Orleans caste system, and the same city's "bounce" musical culture, with its strong LGBTQ ties. This chapter cannot possibly do these issues justice, but it can focus closely on Beyoncé's voice. **Website example 1.14** presents the song's opening. From a purely formal perspective, the vocal trajectory is remarkably similar to Patti Smith's in "Land": an initial speaking voice is "musicalized" in stages, gradually shading fully into song. But the poetic and cultural particulars could not be more distinct. In place of Smith's aestheticized punk-rock Symbolism, an elite practice on the margins of the mainstream, we have Beyoncé's celebration of marginalized identity (female, black, southern) via a song at the very center of the mass-cultural universe.

Beyoncé's speaking voice at the song's opening thus presents a paradox. It is close-miked and seemingly intimate, her delivery gravelly and creaky, encouraging one to lean in and listen closely. Yet it is a voice amplified by the megaphone of global capital, on a scale unimaginable in past decades. She performed the song for an estimated 112 million viewers at the Super Bowl—to the outrage of conservative commentators—and millions more have watched the video online. And yet a flood of internet commentary, news stories, and think pieces made it abundantly clear that many of those millions found her difficult to understand. Her lyrics and delivery were evidently most illegible to white listeners (conservative or otherwise), a fact brilliantly skewered by a *Saturday Night Live* parody.[23] In part this is due to the specificity of the references, from the cryptic nods to rumors about her and Jay-Z belonging to the Illuminati, to a mention of the chain restaurant Red Lobster as a kind of fine dining—an idea familiar to poor black southerners, but not to elite urban whites. But I suspect her vocal delivery also has something to do with the strong reaction the song has evoked—specifically, the way in which her irresistible progression from speech to song enacts the song's central theme: a triumphant claiming of personal identity that is inextricable from a broader political and social critique.

The first four lines mix black slang with a celebration of wealth and status familiar from hip-hop:

> Y'all haters corny with that Illuminati mess
> Paparazzi, catch my fly and my poppy fresh
> I'm reckless when I rock my Givenchy dress (stylin')
> I'm so possessive so I rock his Roc necklaces

Her ostensible addressees are the rumor-spreading "haters" in line one and the paparazzi in line two, both taunted with evident relish, but these pop-cultural hangers-on clearly are not the real enemy—or the song's most important audience. The stakes become clearer in the next two lines, in which Beyoncé celebrates her mixed racial heritage—her voice now defiant, edging toward song. She ends the couplet by flipping a classist and racist slur—"bama"—reclaiming it with exultant multitracked vocals.[24] Now singing full voice, she makes her point even more emphatically, defending her daughter's hairstyle, black facial features, and her country roots:

> 5 My daddy Alabama, momma Louisiana
> You mix that negro with that Creole, make a Texas bama
> 7 I like my baby heir with baby hair and afros
> I like my negro nose with Jackson Five nostrils
> 9 Earned all this money but they never take the country out me
> I got hot sauce in my bag, swag

All this makes the sudden drop to speech for the line about hot sauce that much more effective—a wry aside that some southern commentators have read as among the most authentic lines in the song.[25] Having been swept up in the progression of her voice from the song's beginning—and somatically enlisted in its program of resignification, reclamation, and pushback against respectability politics—we are once again surprised by a vocal left turn. While the steady "musicalization" of Beyoncé's voice from the creaky, spoken opening lines through the fully sung lines (numbered 7 through 9 above) has the effect of pulling the listener in and soliciting participation, the drop back to speech for one of the song's most culturally specific references (line 10) brings that participation up short, as the singer speaks her identity. As the world hangs on every vocal swerve, grasping to interpret, Beyoncé insists that identity is a matter of moment-to-moment negotiation, vocal performance as political assertion.

Kanye West, Chance the Rapper, "Ultralight Beam" (2016)

Less than a week after "Formation" dropped, Kanye West presided over a shambolic "listening party" for his latest album, *The Life of Pablo*, in Madison Square Garden. Again, commentary was wall to wall, though much of the heat came from some tawdry throwaway lines on the record and Kanye's bewildering Twitter activity. Nevertheless, the album contains some astonishing music, especially from his many, many collaborators. Chief among these is Chancelor Bennett, aka Chance the Rapper, a hip-hop phenom from Chicago's South Side, whose fame has skyrocketed since *Pablo*'s release. Though he is primarily a rapper—as his stage name cheekily asserts—his voice exhibits all of the agility of Laura Marling's, but in photonegative: where she tips effortlessly into speech, he tips effortlessly into song. (Both are also prodigies who released critically acclaimed music in their teens.)

Chance contributes a verse on the record's opener, "Ultralight Beams," a track so vocally rich that an entire paper could be devoted to it. In addition to Kanye's and Chance's voices, it includes a full gospel choir, evangelical luminary Kirk Franklin, R&B singers Kelly Price and The-Dream, and a four-year-old girl delivering a bracingly emphatic prayer.[26] But Chance is the heart of the song. **Website example 1.15** begins with the tail end of Kelly Price's verse right before Chance begins.

The gospel architecture is immediately evident: choir and solo singers precede a charismatic sermon that builds from rhythmic speech toward song, at which point choir and congregation reenter ecstatically. The dialectic of sacred and profane—Saturday night and Sunday morning—has been central to African American popular music at least since Ray Charles. But in recent years it has reemerged with a new vividness in hip-hop, due in large part to Kanye's early hit "Jesus Walks" and to Kendrick Lamar's transcendent work. Chance's Christianity and gospel allegiances are also amply in evidence in his mixtapes *Acid Rap* (2013) and *Coloring Book*, released three months after West's *Life of Pablo*.[27]

What is so striking about the present virtuosic verse is how Chance's voice navigates the many hinges between the sacred and the profane. There is one particular hinge—arguably the central one in the verse—that I would like to focus on. At the exact midpoint of his thirty-two-bar rap, Chance states, and then repeats, "This is my part, nobody else speak." The repetition serves as a pivot: his timbre changes, the dynamic drops, and his voice hovers on the cusp of song. The next line, sung tremulously, is straight from the gospel children's songbook: "This little light of mine / (I'm gonna let it shine)." This breakthrough into communal, sacred song then acts as an affective launching pad for the verse's euphoric conclusion, replete with wild reimaginings of Noah and the rainbow, "Amazing Grace," and Lot's wife turning into a pillar of salt. All of this is interwoven with ecstatic self-references and a shout-out to Chance's South Side Chicago stomping grounds—79th Street in Chicago's Chatham neighborhood.

This is a fitting place to conclude—speech and song as a sort of rapturous soteriology. For nowhere else in American culture do speaking and singing circulate so freely—and so symmetrically—as in African American worship.[28] And it is no news that religious observance across cultures yields a vast proliferation of vocal practices, speaking and singing intermixed in abundance.

Hank Williams and Marvin Gaye both tap directly into such practices. Patti Smith, by contrast, is overtly hostile to Christianity—the LP that contains "Land" begins with the line "Jesus died for somebody's sins, but not mine"—but her voice bespeaks a different kind of faith: one in the aesthetic, a commitment to its transcendent extremes. As for Laura Marling and Beyoncé, theirs is, among many other things, a vocal poetics of identity—from radically different subject positions, to be sure—in which the self is continually reconstituted through a voice calibrated to its social others.

That voice is the vehicle of such social transactions speaks to its status as "something more"; it is hard to imagine another sonic element within the world of song indexing the social so vividly. We should also note that the "evidence" for this chapter has been the sounding voice in all of its material specificity—what Nicholas Harkness has called the "voice voice."[29] While voice as a conceptual category is highly capacious—or, as Harkness puts it, "metaphorically productive"[30]—this chapter demonstrates that attentiveness to the "voice voice" is no less theoretically productive. One can go further: the examples above remind us that social and aesthetic efficacy of voice is inseparable from the moment of its empirical sounding. As such, voice studies can remind us to train our ears on that moment—when breath, vocal folds, and resonating cavities negotiate the space between speaking and singing. In all of the cases surveyed in this chapter, traffic between speech and song opens up a space in which aspirational limits can be approached asymptotically, in a form of social performance that straddles the break—not only between speech and song, but between self and other.

Notes

1. The linguistic theory of markedness denotes an asymmetrical relationship between two terms. The less common, marked term stands out as a figure against the ground of its unmarked counterpart, bearing greater informational content as a result. For a well-known application of markedness theory to music, see Robert S. Hatten, *Musical Meaning in Beethoven: Markedness, Correlation, and Interpretation* (Bloomington: Indiana University Press, 1994). Hatten draws in part on Edwin L. Battistella, *Markedness: The Evaluative Superstructure of Language* (Albany, NY: SUNY Press, 1990).

2. Aaron A. Fox, *Real Country: Music and Language in Working-Class Culture* (Durham, NC: Duke University Press, 2004).

3. See, for example, George List, "The Boundaries of Speech and Song," *Ethnomusicology* 7 (1963): 1–16. For a more recent study, which cites much of the intervening literature, see Tyler Bickford, "Music of Poetry and Poetry of Song: Expressivity and Grammar in Vocal Performance," *Ethnomusicology* 51 (2007): 439–76.

4. Diana Deutsch, Trevor Henthorn, and Rachael Lapidis, "Illusory Transformation from Speech to Song," *Journal of the Acoustical Society of America* 129 (2011): 2245–52. Website exam-

ple 1.1 is included on Deutsch's CD *Phantom Words and Other Curiosities* (La Jolla, CA: Philomel Records, 2003).

5. Reich's composition predates Deutsch's discovery of the "speech-to-song illusion," as she calls it, by thirty years. Among other experimental-music antecedents to Deutsch, one could include Brian Eno and David Byrne's 1981 album *My Life in the Bush of Ghosts*, which employs looped recordings of preachers, politicians, and an exorcist, among others.

6. On the relationship between *phoné* (voice) and *logos* (word, language, reason) in the history of Western philosophy, see Mladen Dolar, *A Voice and Nothing More* (Cambridge, MA: MIT Press, 2006); and Adriana Cavarero, *For More Than One Voice: Toward a Philosophy of Vocal Expression* (Stanford, CA: Stanford University Press, 2005). For a recent model that situates *phoné* and *logos* within a practical interpretive framework, see Brian Kane, "The Model Voice," *Journal of the American Musicological Society* 68 (2015): 671–77.

7. Fox, *Real Country*, 272.

8. Pierre Bourdieu's theories of distinction and *habitus* are both relevant here. For the former, see his *Distinction: A Social Critique of the Judgment of Taste*, trans. Richard Nice (Cambridge, MA: Harvard University Press, 1984); for the latter, see his *Outline of a Theory of Practice*, trans. Richard Nice (Cambridge: Cambridge University Press, 1977), esp. chap. 4. For a vivid and accessible discussion of both distinction and *habitus* in the context of popular music, see Carl Wilson, *Let's Talk about Love: A Journey to the End of Taste* (New York: Continuum, 2007), chap. 8.

9. Colin Escott, George Merritt, and William MacEwen, *I Saw the Light: The Story of Hank Williams* (New York: Back Bay Books, 2015), 136–37.

10. According to Escott et al., Williams adopted the pseudonym Luke the Drifter at Rose's suggestion, to avoid confusing jukebox owners who wanted to stock only Williams's "harder," honky-tonk material; *I Saw the Light*, 137. For more on the signifying energy of Williams's voice, including discussion of the Luke the Drifter recordings, see Richard Leppert and George Lipsitz, "'Everybody's Lonesome for Somebody': Age, the Body, and Experience in the Music of Hank Williams," *Popular Music* 9 (1990): 259–74.

11. On the term "musicking," see Christopher Small, *Musicking: The Meanings of Performance and Listening* (Middletown, CT: Wesleyan University Press, 1998); and—for a more recent application of Small's term—Gary Tomlinson, *A Million Years of Music: The Emergence of Human Modernity* (New York: Zone Books, 2015).

12. I am grateful to Laurie Stras for stressing this point.

13. Gino Stefani has written eloquently on melody as "music in so far as it is close at hand; it is that dimension of music which everyone can easily appropriate in many ways." See Gino Stefani, "Melody: A Popular Perspective," *Popular Music* 6 (1987): 21–35, quote on 21.

14. Justin London defines entrainment as "a synchronization of some aspect of our biological activity with regularly occurring events in the environment." Justin London, *Hearing in Time: Psychological Aspects of Musical Meter* (New York: Oxford University Press, 2004), 4. The fact that listeners often entrain to regular musical stimuli does not mean that their resulting actions (e.g., dancing, singing, foot tapping) are perfectly coordinated with others' similar actions. For a classic discussion, see Charles Keil, "Participatory Discrepancies and the Power of Music," *Cultural Anthropology* 2 (1987): 275–83.

15. A sampling of recent YouTube comments for a posting of "Pictures from Life's Other Side" is indicative. One states: "This man could just rip your heart right out and show it to you while it's still beating. . . ." Another, in all caps, evidently agrees: "IF THIS DOESN'T GIVE U

CHILLS U MAY ALREADY B ON THE OTHER SIDE! NO BETTER EMOTIONS THAN THIS HERO CAN PULL FROM YOUR VERY SOUL!!!!" https://www.youtube.com/watch?v=4M_AHB0g98E, accessed August 12, 2016.

16. On "hymn lining," see William H. Tallmadge, "Dr. Watts and Mahalia Jackson—The Development, Decline, and Survival of a Folk Style in America," *Ethnomusicology* 5 (1961): 95–99. One secular (and admittedly very white) extension of this tradition, which will be familiar to some readers, is Pete Seeger's performance practice of calling out the text of a song before each line, to encourage his audience to sing along.

17. The background singers on the record—a Motown house ensemble of female singers known as the Andantes—struggled to learn their unusual parts, and one of them, Louvain Demps, commented on their peculiarity: "He had us doing a lot of things just for texture, and that could be difficult to understand." Ben Edmonds, *What's Going On? Marvin Gaye and the Last Days of the Motown Sound* (Edinburgh: Mojo Books, 2001), 186.

18. This was in fact the only live performance Gaye ever gave of the complete album (Edmonds, *What's Going On?*, 227–28). This live concert was included with the thirtieth-anniversary, two-CD deluxe rerelease of *What's Going On* in 2001.

19. For an especially illuminating collection of essays on the music of girl groups, with a focus on questions of gender, race, and class, see Laurie Stras, ed., *She's So Fine: Reflections on Whiteness, Femininity, Adolescence, and Class in 1960s Music* (Burlington, VT: Ashgate).

20. On Smith's indebtedness to Rimbaud, see Carrie Jaurès Noland, "Rimbaud and Patti Smith: Style as Social Deviance," *Critical Inquiry* 21 (1995): 581–610.

21. For a detailed study of Smith's vocal delivery on another iconic song, see Mike Daly, "Patti Smith's 'Gloria': Intertextual Play in a Rock Vocal Performance," *Popular Music* 16 (1997): 235–53.

22. I am grateful to Sarah Boak for reminding me of Rickie Lee Jones's importance as a late-1970s bohemian speak-singer.

23. The sketch—an ad for a fictional film called "The Day Beyoncé Turned Black"—first aired on February 13, 2016: https://www.youtube.com/watch?v=ociMBfkDG1w, accessed November 1, 2016.

24. "Bama" is a slang term that originated in the DC area to denote a rural southern black (the word is shortened from "Alabama") trying to "pass" as urban and sophisticated. See the entry in UrbanDictionary.com: http://www.urbandictionary.com/define.php?term=Bama, accessed August 15, 2016.

25. See, for example, the February 7 post from blogger Red Clay Scholar, "Getting in Line: Working through Beyoncé's 'Formation' ": https://redclayscholarblog.wordpress.com/2016/02/07/getting-in-line-working-through-beyonces-formation/, accessed August 15, 2016.

26. The latter is Natalie Green, who became an internet meme through her mother's Instagram post of her prayer in a car's backseat. See http://www.complex.com/music/2016/02/kanye-west-ultralight-beam-sample-natalie-interview, accessed August 15, 2016.

27. The relative roles of gospel and hip-hop in Kanye's and Chance's 2016 releases have been much debated. See, for example, Jack Hamilton's *Slate* article, "Chance the Rapper's *Coloring Book* Is the First True Gospel-Rap Masterpiece," which also includes a sensitive discussion of Chance's vocal versatility: http://www.slate.com/articles/arts/music_box/2016/05/chance_the_rapper_s_coloring_book_reviewed.html, accessed August 15, 2016.

28. For a detailed study of the relationship between speech and song in African American preaching, including a detailed survey of the scholarly literature, see Braxton D. Shelley,

"Sermons in Song: Richard Smallwood, the Vamp, and Contemporary Gospel Performance" (PhD diss., University of Chicago, 2017), chap. 2 and idem, "Analyzing Gospel," *Journal of the American Musicological Society* 72, no. 1 (spring 2019): 181–243.

29. Nicholas Harkness, *Songs of Seoul: An Ethnography of Voice and Voicing in Christian South Korea* (Berkeley: University of California Press, 2013), 11.

30. Harkness, *Songs of Seoul.*

2

From the Natural to the Instrumental: Chinese Theories of the Sounding Voice before the Modern Era

JUDITH T. ZEITLIN

This chapter stems from a single question: How was the human voice conceptualized and theorized in China before the advent of the modern era? The simplicity of the question is deceptive because the answers are by no means self-evident or easily available. One thing is clear: a history of the voice in Chinese thought doesn't lead us in the direction of individual identity, personal agency, collective will, subjectivity, authenticity, style, or any other of the main figurative connotations we take for granted when writing about the voice in English or other European languages. To put it otherwise, in traditional Chinese discourse, voice isn't a central metaphor or keyword. That's not to say you can't find figurative associations with it, or that metaphorical formulations played no role in representations and descriptions of the voice. Rather, voice on its own is rarely a master trope or signifier. This may be one reason why there exists surprisingly little scholarship on Chinese theories of the voice, despite an abundance of studies on related theorizations of music, poetry, listening, and *qi* (in the narrowest sense, breath or air; in the broadest sense, "the omnipresent, 'basic stuff' of the phenomenal world"; and in an extended sense, the spirit or manner of a work).[1]

When we turn to the material, physical voice with which this volume is principally concerned, there is another story to tell. Here we find a rich vein of discourse that enables us to analyze a range of culturally and historically specific meanings given to the literal, sounding voice over the longue durée, particularly in the context of singing. In the Chinese case, this necessitates excavating key moments where the voice is deliberately disentangled from a broad matrix of sound and valorized. For the default maneuver in Chinese traditional writings, I argue, is to situate the human voice on a continuum with other sounds, rather than isolating it as a categorically separate phenomenon in its own right. My strategy in this chapter, therefore, is to trace the emergence of different models of the voice over time. I begin with two diametrically opposed approaches to the voice in canonical writings from early China (fifth century BCE to first century CE): an expressive model found in Confucian statements on music and poetry and a physiological model found in the volume on acupuncture in *The Yellow Emperor's Inner Canon*. I then locate a major turning point in court literature of the Six Dynasties (third to fifth centuries CE), where a model of voice as a natural musical instrument is developed in several interesting directions. These first two sections provide the basic groundwork for my third and final section, which argues that the fullest emergence of the autonomous human voice as an analytical category appears in a pedagogical treatise of the mid-eighteenth century. Written by the Qing dynasty physician Xu Dachun to promote his method for the singing of Kun opera, the treatise advocates a modern, technical approach to training the voice as an idealized vehicle for repairing a fatal rupture between the musics of the past and present.

The ordinary term for voice in spoken Mandarin and written Chinese today is *sheng-yin*, a term that broadly denotes any kind of sound or noise; it's only context that determines whether it means the human voice or not. This is already common in earlier periods. For instance, a brief Yuan dynasty work called *On Singing*, our earliest extant treatise on the subject, which dates from the fourteenth century, asserts that "people's voices (*sheng-yin*) are not equally endowed; each has its own strongpoints."[2] Or take a Ming dynasty play from the sixteenth century, where the ghost of a murdered woman knocks on her lover's door in the middle of the night and asks coyly: "Don't you recognize my voice (*sheng-yin*)?"[3] The word *sheng-yin* is a compound composed of two characters, *sheng* and *yin*, which can each be combined with other characters to create additional words. As independent characters, sometimes defined in opposition to one another, but more often used interchangeably, *sheng* or *yin* can be used alone to signify voice, but each also has a long history of denoting sound, tone, note, music, timbre, and other sonic concepts.

Etymologically, the two characters have very different derivations, however. Our earliest Chinese dictionary, the *Shuowen jiezi* (completed in 100 BCE, during the Han dynasty), links *sheng* with instrumental sound: the graph 聲 is composed of the semantic component of "ear" 耳, with the phonetic component of "stone chime" 殸. The *Shuowen* identifies *yin* 音, on the other hand, as deriving semantically and graphically from the character for speech 言, which, in turn, contains the semantic component of "mouth" 口.[4] At the time of the *Shuowen*, the graphic forms for *yin* (sound) 音 and *yan* (speech) 言 were nearly identical; some scholars believe that in even earlier forms of writing, the two shared a single graph.[5] Nonetheless, and despite the profound etymological differences between *sheng* and *yin*, the *Shuowen* defines them circularly in terms of each other, suggesting that their principal meaning as general sound, including voice, had long since converged.

The Expressive Model

There is an extensive and well-studied discourse on music and poetry in early works of the Confucian school, where music and poetry are closely related and occupy exalted positions, but there is no formulation of the voice as a specific entity on its own. That is, the voice isn't singled out, defined, or privileged, but is simply implied, subsumed within an undifferentiated model of expressive human sound and movement. Let me give some canonical examples. The earliest iteration, thought to date from around the fifth century BCE, appears in the *Classic of Documents*:

> Poetry expresses intent. Singing extends the words, and sound (*sheng*) follows that extension. The pitches make the sound (*sheng*) harmonious. When the eight timbres (*yin*) are in accord, one does not encroach upon the place of another. Thus spirits and human beings are also in perfect harmony.[6]

Poetry expresses, that is, puts into words or language, some intense thought or feeling, whatever is intently in the heart and on the mind. Singing extends those words, both by prolonging the syllables and by making the words last long so as to be transmitted to future generations. Voice is not specifically mentioned but is strongly implied, both because poetry would have been vocalized and sung aloud, and because of the contrast set up in the second half of the passage to instrumental sound—the "eight timbres," referring to the eight different kinds of instruments in the ritual court orchestra. The twelve pitches (or pitch standards—the same character *lü* can also mean "pitch pipes") were, in Kenneth DeWoskin's words, "a chromatic-pitch gamut in just intonation, believed to be absolute and invariable and related to standards of cosmic authority."[7] So, when all is right, both vocal and instrumental sound will bring human governance on earth and the cosmic realm in heaven into perfect accord.

A passage from the "Record of Music" chapter in the *Book of Rites*, probably datable to the first century BCE, further refines this model of expressive human sound but situates it within the individual:

> All musical tones (*yin*) are born in the human heart-and-mind. Feelings are stirred within and therefore take external shape as sounds (*sheng*), and when the sounds assume a pattern, they are called musical tones (*yin*).[8]

Variations on these ideas abound in Confucian texts, but two points most concern us here. The first has to do with the hierarchical distinction drawn between *sheng* (raw sound) and *yin* (patterned sound). Each of these can still refer to the voice, but not exclusively and with different valences. As Robert Ashmore explains:

> *Sheng* "is the most basic level and includes animal cries, the human voice apart from its conscious patterning, or any undifferentiated sound."
>
> *Yin* "is sound plus patterning, human song or speech, as well as the whole gamut of musical sounds. Animals have *sheng* but not *yin*."[9]

The second point involves the direction of human sound production from inside to outside. Sound is something having its origins within an individual's heart-and-mind (*xin*, the heart, is the bodily location of feeling, thought, and consciousness), but that is only aroused and released when some external stimulus triggers certain emotions. The often-noted similarity between this passage and another roughly contemporaneous passage from "The Great Preface" to *The Classic of Poetry* makes this telos of stimulus and expression even clearer, though neither *sheng* nor *yin* is used:

> Poetry is where intent goes. In the heart-and-mind it is being intent; coming forth in words, it is poetry. When feelings are stirred within, they take external shape as words. When words are inadequate, we sigh them. When sighing is inadequate, we extend them through singing. When singing is inadequate, unconsciously we dance them with our hands and beat them with our feet.[10]

Again, though not restricted to vocalization, the voice—as meaningful sound coming from within the human mind and body—furnishes the most direct inspiration for the overall paradigm of inward to outward movement to express feelings. It is worth noting, however, that in "The Great Preface," the graduated progress of the externalization emphasizes the involuntary and intensifying nature of the release, and in addition to vocal expression like speech, sighs, and song includes gesture and dance. Indeed, in classical Chinese, the character for music (*yue*, which also means "joy") encompasses not only vocal and instrumental sound, but dance as well.

The Physiological Model

By contrast, running parallel to this complex Confucian discourse where voice is placed on a continuum with other sound-making processes, a detailed account of the vocal apparatus appears in *The Yellow Emperor's Inner Canon*, the foundational text of the Chinese medical tradition, which is believed to date to the second to first centuries BCE, at least in some form. The passage occurs in *The Divine Pivot*, the volume on acupuncture, and it consists of a dialogue between the mythical Yellow Emperor and one of his teachers about how to treat sudden voice loss. Why is it, the Yellow Emperor asks, that after a sudden bout of anger or grief someone may be struck dumb? What pathways are blocked? The teacher's reply provides a precise, mechanical physiology of the voice:

> The gullet is the path taken by water and grain.
> Through the windpipe, the *qi* ascends and descends.
> The epiglottis is the gate for the sounds (*sheng*) of the voice (*yin*).
> The lips of the mouth are door-leaves for these sounds.
> The tongue is the trigger to release the sounds.
> The uvula is the pass to be crossed by the sounds.
> The posterior nostrils are the locations where the *qi* is separated before it flows out.
> The transverse bone[11] is the location where the spirit and the *qi* manage the movement of the tongue.[12]

This important passage, overlooked outside the history of Chinese medicine, establishes the normative through the pathological. Two different pathways are distinguished, one for food and drink (the esophagus) and one for *qi* in the narrow sense of breath or air (the larynx). In the broadest sense, *qi* encompassed much more. As Harper explains: "It was the air man breathed, it was the nourishment extracted from food; it was what suffused the body and made man alive; it was what connected the human organism to the larger operations of nature."[13] In *The Divine Pivot*'s model, healthy vocal production is conceptualized as a sequence that involves opening, crossing, and flowing through a series of metaphorical doors, gates, and borders to release sound through the mechanism of the tongue. The assumption that emotions stirred within can impede the ability to speak basically follows the same kind of logic governing vocal production in "The Record of Music" passage above, except that here the emotions are too sudden and too strong: the result is a total *suppression* rather than *expression* of sound. In the context of acupuncture, the key diagnostic problem is to identify precisely how and where in the chain the blockage has occurred so needle therapy can be applied to the corresponding point:

> When someone suddenly has no voice (*yin*), cold *qi* has settled at his uvula. Hence the uvula cannot open. When it opens, it will not go down again. Eventually there will be no opening or closing at all. Hence [the patient] has no voice.[14]

What I find remarkable in this exchange is how straightforwardly voice is presented. As the direct object of a verb (*wu*, to have not), a sounding voice is simply a thing that a person either lacks or, by extension, possesses. In this sense, it *is* a voice and nothing more.

Later medical treatises elaborate on "losing one's voice" (*shi yin*) as a syndrome referring to laryngitis or hoarseness; they also deal with a related syndrome called "muteness" (*yin*[a]), also discussed in *Basic Questions*, the other volume of *The Inner Canon*.[15] In an extensive entry on vocal disorders, the late Ming physician Zhang Jiebin (1563–1642), an authoritative commentator on *The Inner Canon*, provides an updated and more complex physiology of vocal production, in which he singles out the key roles played by the heart, lung, and kidney systems.[16] Still, what is striking even here is that the voice becomes discernible only when it is defective or fails. The physiological model is invoked in the Chinese context only when the voice bears signs of illness or trauma, and becomes a problem requiring attention. This is one reason why a medical approach to vocal production was not incorporated into aesthetic discourse or later programs for training the voice.

Voice as Natural Musical Instrument: Three Models

Only in the third to fifth centuries BCE, during the period of the Six Dynasties, did an autonomous voice begin to be valorized over other forms of sound. This is the key turning point in a history of Chinese theories of the voice. In the space available here, I can only point to two broader intellectual developments that are particularly relevant to this shift: one, a new valorization of the natural, in the sense of "what is naturally so" or "so-in-itself," and two, the emergence of art and aesthetics as an independent realm of inquiry beyond cosmology, moral philosophy, and statecraft.[17] What the three models I identify below all share is a concept of voice as a natural musical instrument that is therefore superior to all others.

THE CARNAL VOICE ("FLESH")

In a casual conversation purported to have taken place between a general and his aide, the general inquires: "When I'm listening to performers, stringed instruments don't sound as good as bamboo, and bamboo instruments don't sound as good as flesh. Why would that be?" The aide replies: "Because in each case you're getting closer to what's natural."[18] The general is riffing on the ancient nomenclature of the "eight timbres," in which musical instruments are classified metonymically according to the material of which they are fashioned. In this system, bells are "metal," flutes are "bamboo," zithers are "silk" (the material used for the strings), and so on. The voice never figured on the original list. Thus, the addition of a ninth timbre—"flesh"—is a *bon mot*, in keeping with the source of this anecdote, *A New Account of Tales of the World*, a fifth-century court compendium of wit and wisdom. The general's puzzlement at his own preference for "bamboo" over "silk" and "flesh" over both indicates that this is an inversion of the expected hierarchy whereby the elegant zither reigned supreme and voice was beside the point. But the real punch line belongs to his clever aide, who reveals the underlying logic behind the puzzle: the privileging of the natural.

Although it may seem self-evident that in this new hierarchy voice would come out on top, it is nonetheless worth pondering *why*. A first answer might concern craftsmanship and objects. Zithers require more varied materials (wood, metal, silk) and are more complexly made than flutes, which are just bamboo tubes with holes. The voice, of course, requires no crafted object outside itself. A second answer, a corollary of the first, might concern the relationship to the human body. String instruments use the hands alone to make music, whereas wind instruments use hands plus breath (privileged as *qi*). But the voice is an instrument of pure *qi*—pure body, pure life force. A third answer, perhaps most importantly, is that the general and his aide are not just talking about *any* voice, but the voice of an entertainer, a base musician of servile status. And not just *any* musician, but in all probability, a female entertainer belonging to the general's private household.[19] In this context, the equation of a voice with "flesh"—the whole body, not just a part of it—makes all the more sense. The repertory a woman would have sung for him as entertainment would have fallen into the loose category of "popular music"; it was certainly not the ancient ritual music or music of self-cultivation that counted as "refined music"; in this respect, no matter how skilled the singer, she would have sounded "unrefined," and perhaps in this respect, more "natural."

VOICE BEYOND LANGUAGE (WHISTLING)

Another anecdote from *A New Account of Tales of the World* posits an entirely different sort of natural voice through whistling, a technique that unleashes the transcendent power of a human voice stripped of words and is thus able to resonate with the spirits of nature.

Set in the natural world of the mountains as opposed to the social world of wealth and power, the anecdote concerns the pilgrimage of Ruan Ji (210–263 CE), a poet, musician, and philosopher, to seek the wisdom of a Daoist recluse. Ruan finds the hermit perched on the edge of a cliff and seeks to engage him in abstruse and learned discourse, but the man remains stubbornly unresponsive. Only when Ruan gives up and makes "a long whistling sound" does

FIGURE 2.1 Ruan Ji whistling. Stamped brick tile, late fourth–early fifth century CE. Photo by Wu Hung.

the man finally laugh and speak to him: "'Do it again.'" Ruan complies, but by now having lost interest, he leaves. He is already halfway down the mountain, when suddenly "he heard above him a shrillness like an orchestra of many instruments, while forests and valleys reechoed with the sound. Turning back to look, he discovered it was the whistling of the man he had just visited."[20]

Ruan's attempts to engage the hermit leave the man totally bored. Only when Ruan, out of frustration or desperation, abandons verbal communication and spontaneously whistles does the hermit perk up and laugh; and only after Ruan abruptly abandons even whistling and withdraws does the hermit truly answer him. Although Ruan is introduced at the outset of the anecdote as a master whistler, he has more than met his match in the hermit. What their whistling consisted of, other than being a high-pitched, piercing, and drawn-out sound made through puckered lips, we don't precisely know (**fig. 2.1**). It may have involved arcane breathing and vocalization techniques associated with Daoist practitioners and the quest for immortality.[21]

Ironically, the valorization of whistling as a voice beyond language receives its most expansive treatment in the rhapsody, that most epideictic of Chinese literary genres, renowned for its verbal pyrotechnics and word magic. A long "Rhapsody on Whistling," composed by the third-century poet

Chenggong Zi'an and anthologized in another fifth-century court compendium, develops the paradigm of the voice as a natural musical instrument even more explicitly than the anecdote. Making extensive use of musical terminology throughout, it includes the names of musical notes and modes, and frequently conflates whistling with singing. It is the closest we have to a rhapsody purely on voice. Here, for instance, we have an idealized protagonist in the guise of a young gentleman who has forsaken the vulgar world of "pomp and circumstance" to journey into nature and cleanse his spirit.[22]

> He emits marvelous sounds from his vermillion lips.
>
> Stirs mournful tunes from his glistening teeth.
> The sounds rise and fall, rolling within his throat;
>
> The breath (*qi*) pours forth from his mouth strong and heavy, then suddenly rises . . .
>
> This truly is a perfect natural sound,
> Which not even strings and winds can imitate.
> Thus, to make this sound one needs no instrument,
> To effect it one requires no other thing.
> He takes it near at hand from his own body,
> And does it by using his mind and controlling his breath (*qi*).
> He simply moves his lips and there is a tune,
> He opens his mouth and creates a sound.
> Moved by whatever he encounters,
> He responds in kind, sings forth accordingly.
> The sound is light but never boisterous,
> It is faint but never inaudible.
> In clarity and intensity it matches syrinx and mouth organ,
> In richness and smoothness it equals lute and zither.
>
> Its mysterious wonder is sufficient to commune with gods and awaken spirits . . .[23]

As in the exchange between the general and his aide, the voice is proclaimed superior to strings and winds because it approaches the perfection of natural sound. Entirely self-sufficient and spontaneous, the voice is naturally so in itself, requiring no external instrument and eschewing language or conscious thought. Composed entirely of the human body's resources of breath (*qi*), it is connected organically to the vital forces (*qi*) of the natural world. Just as the hermit's whistling was likened to "an orchestra of instruments," here the young noble's voice wondrously encompasses the finest sonorities of strings and winds, imbuing it with the potential "to commune with gods and waken the spirits."

Yet unlike the anecdote, which emphasized the communicative function of whistling, the rhapsody steers whistling back to an expressive model of voice, extolling the act of whistling not so much for its power to engage a listener (whether human, nature, or the divine) as for the emotional and physical relief it provides the whistler himself. Whistling thereby becomes a therapeutic practice, enabling the performer to "release the grief and anger of pent-up thoughts," ensuring that no dangerous blockage occurs, so that "although the heart is grieved, it is never harmed."[24]

VOICE AS INHERENTLY MUSICAL (LANGUAGE IS TONAL)

A different set of concerns generates the remarkable passage on the voice in *The Literary Mind and the Carving of Dragons*, the great systematic treatise on poetics, authored by Liu Xie (465–522 CE), an aspiring courtier who later became a Buddhist monk. The passage opens chapter 33, whose title can be translated as "Musicality" or "Regulation of Sound," which addresses the formal aspects of euphony in a literary work. Here, perhaps for the first time, we find an unequivocal manifesto of the voice distinguished from undifferentiated "sound" (*sheng*) through the addition of the character for "human" (*ren*):

> The origin of music is found in the human voice [*ren-sheng*], inherent in which is the scale of *gong* and *shang* [two notes on the pentatonic scale]. Musical quality of the human voice is inherent in man's very blood and physical vitality [*qi*]. On this basis, early kings created music and song. So we know that musical instruments depict the human voice: the human voice does not imitate the sounds of the instruments. Language may be the crux of literary writing and the key to the divine intelligence (imagination), but the musicality of the voice is the result of the movements of the lips and mouth only.[25]

In this radical genealogy, the origin of music lies squarely in the human voice—not in the pitch pipes, musical instruments, birds, animals, or other conventional inspirations for the mythical sage-kings of antiquity, who are credited with the invention of music and song.[26] Liu's claim is predicated on the innate presence of the pentatonic scale within the sounding voice, which in turn is created from what sustains life (blood and *qi*) within the human organism. This, then, is yet another version of the argument that the voice takes precedence over other musical instruments because it is the most natural of all instruments. But the underlying poetic stakes are new.

Liu is writing at a moment in which the recognition that Chinese is a tonal language, triggered in part through the encounter with Sanskrit, was leading to the creation and gradual adoption of specific tonal regulations (alternation of word tones in specific patterns) for euphony in poetic composition. (Poetry was understood as a written art, but poems were typically chanted aloud when composed or read.) Musicality for Liu therefore inheres in language—the pivotal mechanism for literary writing and the imagination—but only when the words are uttered aloud. He expands on this principle of physical vocalization soon thereafter when, after referring to musical laws governing the singing of specific notes, he asserts that "the difference in the movement of the throat, tongue, lips and teeth" is what makes it "possible to distinguish the different tonal qualities clearly."[27]

Liu fully recognizes that the achievement of proper sound in a literary work does not reside solely in external vocalization; it isn't simply the chanting of a verse that makes it sound harmonious, but the prior act of composition in the mind where the sound is born. To make this point, Liu draws an analogy between playing a stringed instrument and writing a poem, which seems to take him remarkably close to the idea of an "inner voice."

> When someone detects a discordant note while playing a zither, he is aware of it and will retune the string. But if there is any tonal fault in a literary composition, the writer seldom recognizes it and makes the necessary corrections. The musical notes are produced on strings, and so it is possible to achieve harmony; but one often fails to achieve concord with the sounds (*sheng*) that germinate in the mind (*xin*). Why? Because it is easy to be clever when listening to an external source but difficult to hear acutely when listening to an inner source.[28]

Liu's "sounds that germinate in the mind" is a slight variation on the canonical definition of musical tones from "The Record of Music" discussed earlier. What's new in this context is Liu's addition of the verb "to listen," which arrests the outward movement of expressive sound by positing a poetic process of "inward listening." *What* the poet is listening to inwardly and *with what* is not exactly clear, and this turns out to be the crux of the difficulty for Liu as he extends the analogy between versifying and playing an instrument. The reason it's so hard for a poet to correct a tonal fault through "inward listening," he says, is that there is no hand involved—that is, no clear division between the agent and object of the action in this "confused entanglement between the sound (*sheng*) and the mind (*xin*)."[29]

To sum up, let me review the importance of these three models of the natural voice for later developments in sung verse, opera, and singing pedagogy. The idea of the voice as a carnal instrument, fully embodied in the base but alluring persons of household entertainers, courtesans, and actors, becomes a cornerstone for understanding the social relations of singing in subsequent periods. The formula "silk doesn't sound as good as bamboo,

FIGURE 2.2 Landlady readying prosthesis for "Lion's Roar." *Kung Fu Hustle* (Stephen Chow, 2004).

FIGURE 2.3 "Lion's Roar" shattering everything in its path. *Kung Fu Hustle* (Stephen Chow, 2004).

bamboo doesn't sound as good as flesh" is repeatedly cited in discussions of singing, both to champion the superiority of voice over other musical instruments and to account for its emotional and erotic power. A conception of the voice as "enfleshed" is also apparent in terms that denote a good singing voice metonymically as "throat." As for the transcendent model of whistling, although a Tang dynasty treatise, probably dating from the eighth century, attempts to teach a would-be whistler the secret techniques in detail, the art was lost long ago. The idea survives in later tradition mainly as a literary allusion, usually as a laudatory reference to the singing or versifying practiced by literati with lofty aspirations.[30] The fantasy of a voice beyond language tapping into superhuman bodily powers through training in esoteric techniques does live on in Chinese martial arts fiction and film, most memorably in the parodic "Lion's Roar" scene in Stephen Chow's *Kung Fu Hustle* (2004), where a woman's voice, enhanced with the prosthesis of a bronze bell (**fig. 2.2**), becomes a lethal weapon shattering everything in its path (**fig. 2.3**).

Most important for subsequent developments in poetry and sung verse, however, is the model of the human voice as inherently musical because language itself is tonal. Tonal regulation, still nascent in Liu Xie's day, became codified over the next centuries in the creation of the new genres of regulated verse and song lyrics written to preexisting tune patterns. The practice of composing new verse to a set of labeled tunes became the building block of Chinese opera, which coalesced as an art form during the thirteenth century. There was no designated composer for music as we understand the term today, only poet-playwrights who wrote the words to the arias, and the singers and their accompanists who realized the music in performance. A perennial problem for Kun-style opera (which arose in the latter half of the sixteenth century to become the dominant form of elite theater in the seventeenth and eighteenth centuries) was how to facilitate the proper matching of new texts to current tune patterns, especially because Kun opera performance was stringent in requiring "the contours of the word tones" to mesh appropriately with "the contours of the melodic tones."[31] As befit its privileged status as an object of intense connoisseurship, Kun opera also generated a sizeable body of theoretical and prescriptive writings devoted to the art of singing the words to arias, culminating in the mid-eighteenth-century treatise *A Pedagogical Method for the Operatic Voice* by the physician Xu Dachun (1693–1771).

A *Technê* for the Voice

In 1743, the seventh year of the emperor Qianlong's reign, Xu's elderly mother had recently lost her sight and lacked any prospect of amusement, so he hit upon a plan: he would purchase two boys for the household and hire an old actor named Wei Tianju to teach them to sing popular arias from the Kun operas of the day. The plan worked to a point, but Xu was dissatisfied with the quality of the boys' singing: "Though they'd gotten all the music (*yin*), they had no diction." He therefore advised Wei to teach them according to the method of "the 'four vowels' and the 'five consonants,'" but to that Wei objected that their singing then wouldn't accord with the instrumental accompaniment.

> So I instructed him: "Let me try singing it this way. You play along on your flute, and let's see if doesn't fit harmoniously after all." And indeed, it worked perfectly. After that Wei was totally convinced and used this method to teach the boys. Their voices (*yin*) came out high and loud, the rhythm nice and clear: the result far surpassed any ordinary sound. I then expanded the explanations and wrote *A Pedagogical Method for the Operatic Voice (Yuefu chuansheng)*.[32]

It had long been an established practice in wealthy and educated milieus, especially Xu's home region of Suzhou, the epicenter of Kun opera, to keep boys or girls as household entertainers. Moreover, Xu came from a musical family of opera lovers, and others of his writings indicate that he also took the boys with him to perform at social gatherings outside the house.[33] The servile status of the boys is marked by the absence of their names,[34] replaced exclusively by the name of their teacher, a retired actor, presumably of some repute.

The treatise itself, published in 1748, consists of thirty-five short chapters and belongs to the category of technical literature. Stylistically, it is unusually clear and systematic, in keeping with Xu's status as a learned doctor with broad interests in different branches of scientific knowledge, including river control and geography, as well as medicine, music, divination, and natural philosophy.[35] The contents of the book show his involvement with the methods of the Qing evidential movement and its emphasis on fact-based approaches to reviving Classical learning. Thus his book was aimed not at young singers like these boys, who were usually illiterate, probably not even at professional teachers from the ranks of actors, but rather at the community of scholars and amateur musicians like himself.[36] As a practicing physician who also published influential books on medicine, including on *The Yellow Emperor's Inner Canon*, he was undoubtedly well versed in the medical literature on the vocal apparatus, but he doesn't address the problem of defective voices in his treatise on singing, and physiological models therefore receive no mention in it. Nor does it address issues of breath control or the bodily circulation of *qi*.[37] Instead, he is chiefly concerned with how to ensure the proper enunciation and vocalization of sung lyrics, advocating what he called for short "the method of the five consonants and the four vowels." This terminology, he tells us, derived from his early exposure to new currents in phonology.[38] One of the driving forces of the evidential movement, phonology sought to reconstruct the original pronunciation of the Confucian classics, especially the odes in the *Classic of Poetry*, in order to revive the lost sounds of the ancients. In this respect, Qing phonology, though the most ambitious and intellectually rigorous of these attempts, was simply the latest in a perennial quest to mitigate the irreparable loss of ancient music.

An emphasis on, even obsession with, the proper pronunciation of the lyrics is also characteristic of most earlier publications on the singing of Kun opera. This in part reflects the biases of the scholars who compiled them, but also acknowledges that in singing Kun opera, matching the tune to the words is considerably more difficult than learning the tune itself.[39] What is unusual about Xu's book in light of his predecessors is how remarkably *untextual* it is, how uninterested he is in providing annotated examples of specific lyrics or experimenting with available notational systems for scoring arias.[40] Instead, he takes a resolutely *practice*-based approach, focused on his "mouthing method." As he explains, such techniques are not like music theory and poetic verse that can be passed down and taught through books, or notated, as in musical scores for instruments. Moreover, since mouthing methods change over time, and since sound is by nature ephemeral, he argues, any attempt to try to capture the original singing style of the ancients would be futile. Hence the sung verse of the present day—Kun opera—is the book's target.

Xu's mouthing method can be best understood as an attempt to convey embodied knowledge by breaking it down into its component parts, to systematize and rationalize an unwritten set of teachings ordinarily conveyed orally from tutor to pupil. "Whenever a word is sung, there must be a release, middle turn, and conclusion to the sound, and each word must also take over from the preceding word and continue onto the following one."[41] The claim is that a singer trained to follow his method of pronouncing the words (which includes constant adjustment to smooth the transition between word tones and to fit the beat and rhyme) will be able to execute any aria properly and intelligibly. At its core, Xu's treatise takes an approach to singing pedagogy that may be called "instrumental" in two senses. Eminently practical and functional, his technique is designed to serve, instrumentally, as a means to an end. Pushed to its full implications, it also enables any vocalist to become de facto a musical instrument.

Once again, we find that a direct analogy to musical instruments underpins a theory of the human voice, but the substance of the analogy has changed. In chapter 3, Xu distinguishes between sonic entities like thunder and wind, which have no visible shape and can't be made or fixed, and sonic entities like musical instruments, which do have visible shape and can be made and fixed. For musical instruments, sound is determined by the shape of the instrument: if you want to change the sound, you have to make changes on the instrument. For instance, to produce the note scored as *che* on the flute, you must use the proper fingering; to produce the note scored as *gong*[a], you must change the fingering. "Why, even the Blind God of Music himself couldn't use the fingering for *gong*[a] and produce a *che*!"[42] He contends that it's the same for the human voice. But how to change the shape of a vocal instrument? At its most basic, the mouthing method can be reduced to correct phonation of the five consonants and the four vowels: the former by exerting force properly in the five different places in the vocal apparatus—throat, tongue, front teeth, back teeth, and lips; the latter by adhering properly to the four mouth positions of opening, leveling, bringing together, and closing the lips.

Voice is no longer on a continuum with what is naturally so and therefore superior to musical instruments, but is placed on a continuum with musical instruments as an implement that can be manufactured and regulated, opposed to the uncontrollable forces of nature. In this respect, we may understand Xu's treatise as a type of modern project to develop a *technê* for the body—that is, to mandate a craft, art, and technology for the body—which requires instrumentalizing that body.[43] Doing so also enables him to unmake the singer's carnal body as vocal object of desire and skirt the erotic danger that keeping household entertainers of either gender always posed to owners, who effectively owned their bodies as well as entertainment services. The upshot is that by instrumentalizing the body, Xu's *technê*, through its very clarity, divests the voice of its customary mystery and allure.

He therefore seeks to restore the voice's mystique and value by recourse to a loftier and more rhetorical line of argument. Fueling his highly pragmatic and technical orientation is an idealized, even utopian view of the human voice. As he declares in the introduction:

> When the ancients made music, they took the human voice (*ren-sheng*) as the root. As the *Classic of Documents* says: "Poetry expresses intent. Singing extends the words, and the voice (*sheng*) follows that extension. The pitches make the voice harmonious." If it's not possible to make out the human voice, even if you possess the pitch-pipes, how can the voice be in harmony with them? Hence if the human voice survives, then the root of music will not have perished in this world. The phrase "Transmitting the Voice" (*chuan sheng*) in my title means the ways through which the human voice is transmitted to posterity.[44]

Xu cites the canonical statement on poetry and music from the *Classic of Documents*, but for him *sheng* refers now not to undifferentiated sound, as previously, but to *ren-sheng*, the human voice. For Xu, the human voice possesses transcendental value as a living, constantly renewable link to the moral and cosmic ideals of the past, though it is still in danger of perishing if the proper methods for singing the lyrics of our own age are not followed and the words are unintelligible to listeners. While the music of the ancients is gone and cannot be transmitted to posterity, the human voice can and must be: this is the ultimate aim of his pedagogical method for the operatic voice. Or, as he puts it much more eloquently: "The Dao of music was lost long ago, but there still survives a single thread to it within the singing of opera."[45]

Because music is inherently mutable, Xu contends that his contemporaries are doomed to failure if they attempt to reconstruct the original music of the classics, wanting singers "to sing every word and every line exactly as the ancients did."[46] In his view of opera, only two things are fixed and unchangeable: not melodies and rhythms, but the system of keys and modes and the need for mouthing methods. As he contends in chapter 1, the crucial link to the ancient sage-kings is music, and the root of music is the human voice:

> If we can grasp the true essence of mouthing-methods and keys and modes, then as Mencius says: "Whether it is the music of today or the music of antiquity makes no difference."[47] . . . For the "Fundamental Pitch" (*yuan-sheng*)[48] of the universe has never been silent in the world for a single day. . . . In being born with this physical form, a human being inherently has this voice, and so also has the implement[49] through which to strike balance and harmony. But without a human being to project it, the human voice will be drowned and forgotten, for it cannot vibrate by itself.[50]

Thus, as in the case of *The Literary Mind and the Carving of Dragons*, the musicality of the voice is inherent to the human organism, but Xu's model of the voice is much more radically performative. Only by actually singing (or listening to singing) can this capacity of human beings be activated and continually renewed; only the sound-producing voice can bring the human microcosm into harmony with the order of the cosmos and human governance in harmony with the teachings of the sage-kings. And not just this. Only the *trained* operatic voice can realize this potentiality by perfecting the sounding instrument that all human beings innately possess.[51]

Notes

My deep thanks to Martha Feldman, Paola Iovene, Wu Hung, and Robert Ashmore for their comments on drafts of this essay, and to my research assistant extraordinaire, Jiayi Chen. I'm grateful to Donald Harper for his help with medical matters and to Ed Shaughnessy for his help with etymology. I acknowledge with pleasure the input of Yiren Zheng, Lester Hu, and Li Shunhua, the members of a reading group on Chinese music in spring 2015, where many of these ideas coalesced. Finally, I thank the Neubauer Voice Project gang for helping me gestate this essay in the first place.

1. Donald J. Harper, *Early Chinese Medical Literature: The Mawangdui Medical Manuscripts* (London: Kegan Paul, 1988), 77. On *qi* as a term in literary discourse, see Stephen Owen, *Readings in Chinese Literary Thought* (Cambridge, MA: Harvard Council on East Asian Studies, 1992), 584–86. For scholarship on the Chinese singing voice, see Koo Siu Sun (Gu Zhaoshen), "Ge zhi weiyan changyan ye: qu chang fasheng lilun chutan" (A preliminary investigation of vocalization theory for aria singing), *Xiju yanjiu* 7 (January 2011): 1–36; and his invaluable series *Writings on the Theory of Kun Qu Singing* (Kunqu yanchang lilun congshu), cotranslated and annotated with Diana Yue (Hong Kong: Oxford University Press, 2006).

2. *Yannan zhiyan* (pseud.), *Changlun* [On singing], in *Zhongguo gudian xiqu lunwen ji* (Zhongguo xiju chubanshe, 1982 reprint of 1959 ed.), vol. 1, 161.

3. Xu Zichang, *Shuihu ji* [Outlaws of the marsh], in *Liushi zhong qu* (Beijing: Zhonghua shuju, 1958), vol. 9, scene 31, 95.

4. Xu Shen, *Shuowen jiezi zhu*, with annotation by Duan Yucai (Shanghai: Shanghai guji chubanshe, 1981): for *sheng*, 592; *yin*, 102; *yan*, 88. For dating of this and other early works cited in my chapter, see Michael Loewe, *Early Chinese Texts: A Bibliographical Guide* (Berkeley: Society for the Study of Early China, 1993).

5. Li Pu et al., eds., *Gu wenzi gulin* (Shanghai: Shanghai jiaoyu chubanshe, 2004), vol. 9, 137–38; *Jinwen changyong zidian*, ed. Chen Chusheng et al. (Xi'an: Shaanxi renmin chubanshe, 1987), 268.

6. Based, with my modification, on DeWoskin's modification of Karlgren's translation in Kenneth J. DeWoskin, *A Song for One or Two: Music and the Concept of Art in Early China* (Ann Arbor, MI: Center for Chinese Studies, 1982), 20.

7. DeWoskin, *A Song for One or Two*, 46. See also Lothar von Falkenhausen, *Suspended Music: Chime-Bells in the Culture of Bronze Age China* (Berkeley: University of California Press, 1994), 296–98, who translates *lü* as "pitch standards."

8. Modified from von Falkenhausen's translation, *Suspended Music*, 2. See also DeWoskin, *A Song for One or Two*, 20; and Scott Cook, "'Record of Music': Introduction, Translation, Notes, and Commentary," *Asian Music* 26, no. 2 (Spring–Summer 1995): 24–26.

9. Robert Ashmore, "The Art of Discourse," in *Early Medieval China: A Sourcebook*, ed. Wendy Swartz et al. (New York: Columbia University Press, 2014), 206. On animals having (or understanding) *sheng* but not *yin*, see also Roel Sterckx, "Transforming the Beasts: Animals and Music in Early China," *T'oung Pao* 86 (2000): 1–46, esp. 5–7.

10. Modified translation partly based on Owen, *Readings in Chinese Literary Thought*, 40–41; with reference to DeWoskin, *A Song for One or Two*, 20.

11. Anatomically, it is unclear exactly what "transverse bone" (*henggu*) refers to. *Huangdi neijing cidian* [The Yellow Emperor's inner canon dictionary], ed. Guo Aichun et al. (Tianjin: Tianjin kexue jishu chubanshe, 1991), 930, defines it as "bone at the base of the tongue." Don Harper (private correspondence) suggests that "perhaps the musculature back there is thought to 'transverse' the tongue at its base and account for tongue control." Zhang Jiebin glosses it as "the cartilage (*ruangu*) in the throat, which connects at bottom to the lungs and heart, and so is utilized by the spirit and *qi*. It connects at top to the root of the tongue and so governs the tongue's mechanism for lifting and releasing." *Leijing* (The Inner Canon Classified, ca. 1624), *Siku quanshu zhenben wuji, juan* 21, 39b–41a.

12. Paul U. Unschuld, trans., *Huang Di Nei Jing Ling Shu: The Ancient Classic on Needle Therapy* (Oakland: University of California Press, 2016), chap. 69, 623–24, with slight modification.

13. Harper, *Early Chinese Medical Literature*, 77.

14. Unschuld, trans., *Huang Di Nei Jing Ling Shu*, 625. The corresponding point is not the uvula itself, but "the foot minor yin conduit," which "encloses the transverse bone and ends at the uvula."

15. On the syndrome of "voice loss" (*shi yin*), see *Zhongyi dacidian* [Dictionary of Chinese medicine], *Neike* vol. [internal medicine] (Beijing: Renmin weisheng chubanshe, 1987), 98; on "muteness" (*yin*[a]), see 401. The character for muteness 瘖 (*yin*[a]) is written by adding the illness radical to the character for voice 音 (*yin*); a variant adds the mouth radical instead (*yin*[b] 喑).

16. Zhang Jiebin, "Sheng *yin*[a]," in *Jingyue quanshu* [The complete writings of Dr. Zhang] (Shanghai: Shanghai kexue jishu chubanshe), 1984, vol. 1, 487.

17. DeWoskin, *A Song for One or Two*, 155–58.

18. Richard B. Mather, trans., *A New Account of Tales of the World* (Minneapolis: University of Minnesota Press, 1976), 205 (chap. 7, #16), romanization modified.

19. *Ji*, the character used for entertainer here, is technically gender neutral, but by the fifth century "had become the common term designating female entertainers who served in the entourages of wealthy and powerful households." See Beverley Bossler, "Vocabularies of Pleasure: Categorizing Female Entertainers in the Late Tang Dynasty," *Harvard Journal of Asiatic Studies* 72, no. 1 (June 2012): 73–74.

20. Mather, trans., *A New Account of Tales of the World*, 331 (chap. 18, #1), romanization modified.

21. See E. D. Edwards, "'Principles of Whistling': Hsiao Chih—*Anonymous*," *Bulletin of the School of Oriental and African Studies* 20, no. 1/3 (1957): 217–29. See also Yiren Zheng, "Sounding the Ineffable: On Third-Century Chinese Whistling as an Alternative Voice" (unpublished essay).

22. Chenggong Zi'an (3rd c. CE), "Rhapsody on Whistling," trans. David Knechtges, *Wen xuan or Selections of Refined Literature* (Princeton, NJ: Princeton University Press, 1996), vol. 3, 317. This piece was classified under "Music" and bears many similarities to the rhapsodies on different musical instruments in this section of the anthology. Only a few fragments of the "Rhapsody on Singing" (*ge fu*) survive.

23. Knechtges, *Wen xuan*, 317.

24. Knechtges, *Wen xuan*, 321 and 319.

25. Victor Yu-chung Shih, trans., *The Literary Mind and the Carving of Dragons* (Hong Kong: Chinese University of Hong Kong Press, 1983), 353, modified. Parentheses are in the original translation; italics in brackets are my glosses.

26. For myths on the origin of music, see DeWoskin, *A Song for One or Two*, 56–63; and Sterckx, "Transforming the Beasts," 8–10.

27. Shih, *The Literary Mind and the Carving of Dragons*, 353.

28. Shih, *The Literary Mind and the Carving of Dragons*, 353, with my heavy modifications.

29. This is not an easy passage. I think the point is that inward listening is hard because mind and sound are still separate entities. Shih translates this line very differently: "When we listen to the inner voice, we often confuse the sounds with other mental activities."

30. See Edwards, "'Principles of Whistling.'" For "whistling" as an epithet of praise for literati singing style during the late Ming, see Peng Xu, "Courtesan vs. Literatus: Gendered Soundscapes and Aesthetics in Late-Ming Singing Culture," *T'oung Pao* 100, no. 4–5 (2014): 417–22.

31. Isabel Wong, "Kunqu," in *The Garland Encyclopedia of World Music: East Asia*, ed. Robert C. Provine et al. (New York: Routledge, 2002), 293.

32. Xu Dachun, "Huxi fu jun zixu" [An autobiographical self-introduction], in *Wujiang Xu shi zongpu* [Genealogical records of the Xu clan from Wujiang] (Beijing: Xianzhuang shu ju, 2002), 3.55a–b. The best study and translation of Xu's treatise *Yuefu chuansheng* is Koo Siu Sun and Diana Yue, *Xu Dachun: The Tradition of Sung Poetry* (Hong Kong: Oxford University Press, 2006). The Chinese page numbers I give for *Yuefu chuansheng* are keyed to the edition in *Zhongguo gudian xiqu lunzhu jicheng* (Beijing: Zhongguo xiju chubanshe, 1982 reprint of 1959 ed.), vol. 7.

33. On his family involvement in opera and music-making, see Huang Ying, "Quxue jia Xu Dachun yanjiu" [A study of the opera scholar Xu Dachun], MA thesis (Suzhou University, 2008), chap. 1. For more on Xu's singing boys, see his collection of sung verse *Huixi daoqing* [Xu Dachun's *daoqing* songs], in Ren Zhongmin, ed., *Sanqu congkan* [Independent aria series] (Taipei: Zhonghua shuju, 1964).

34. Literati writers sometimes do provide the names of their household entertainers, but these tend to be casual first names or nicknames; full names with proper surnames are rarely, if ever, given.

35. On Xu Dachun's medical writings and thought, see Paul U. Unschuld, *Forgotten Traditions of Ancient Chinese Medicine* (Brookline, MA: Paradigm Publications, 1990); and *Xu Lingtai yanjiu wenji*, ed. Xu Jingpan et al. (Shanghai: Shanghai kexue jishu chubanshe, 2001). Xu became so famous as a doctor that he was several times summoned to court in Beijing by imperial degree. See Arthur W. Hummel, *Eminent Chinese of the Ch'ing Period* (Taipei: SMC Publishing, 1991), reprint of 1943 ed., 322–24.

36. Xu harbored still higher aspirations for the audience and impact of the book. His "Autobiographical Self-Introduction," 55, mentions that on the basis of this book, the Minister of Revenue wanted to recommend him for an appointment to a newly established imperial court bureau of music, but regretfully, it never transpired.

37. The opening of chap. 4 does discuss *qi*, but only in its broadest meaning as the basic stuff of the phenomenal world, that is, its role in acoustics rather than medicine. He argues: "Everything that possesses *qi* must have a physical form; only sound has no form. But sound must also have *qi* in order to be produced, so sound also has a form proper to sound." (He is drawing here on the traditional theory of acoustics that "sound is agitated *qi*.") This reasoning allows him to elaborate on his mouthing method as giving the form proper to sound, and he makes no further mention of *qi*.

38. Xu's "Autobiographical Self-Introduction," mentions his exposure as a student to a classic work of early Qing phonology, *Classifying Sounds* (Lei yin). See also Huang Ying, "Quxue jia Xu Dachun yanjiu," 7–11.

39. Liang Mingyue, *Music of the Billion: An Introduction to Chinese Musical Culture* (New York: Heinrichshofen Edition, 1985), 240–41.

40. Such systems were typical of the genre of songbooks and song formularies known as *pu* (manual or score). Seventeenth-century printed collections of aria lyrics had begun to provide *dianban* (metrical punctuation) notation, symbols for different mouth positions and pronunciations, rhyme markings, and so on. The earliest extant printed collection to add *gongche* (melodic pitch) notation dates to 1725. For an introduction to reading and singing *gongche* notation, see Richard Strassberg, "The Singing Techniques of K'un-chü and Their Musical Notation," *Chinoperl Papers* 6 (1976): 45–81.

41. *Yuefu chuansheng*, 160.

42. *Yuefu chuansheng*, 159. Here, Xu is using names of notes in a written musical score, which differ from the names of the solfege notes in the pentatonic or heptatonic scales, or from the names of the twelve pitches.

43. For a version of this argument on the European side, see Bonnie Gordon, "It's Not about the Cut: The Castrato's Instrumentalized Song," *New Literary History* 46, no. 4 (Autumn 2015): 647–67. In Gordon's words: "The voice thus belongs to what Heidegger would in the twentieth century describe as the realm of technê—a realm that included not only craft but also arts of the mind and fine arts" (654).

44. The Chinese title of the treatise is *Yuefu chuan-sheng*. "Transmitting the Voice" is the literal meaning of the second phrase (*chuan-sheng*), which also implies a "singing lesson"; *yuefu* is an old name for an early genre of poetic ballads, later commonly used as an archaizing term for opera or operatic aria (*qu*).

45. *Yuefu chuansheng*, "Preface," 153.

46. Based on Koo and Yue's translation, *The Tradition of Sung Poetry*, chap. 1, 141, modified. *Yuefu chuansheng*, 157.

47. *Mencius*, trans. D. C. Lau (London: Penguin Books, 2004), 15.

48. The "Fundamental Pitch" (*yuan sheng*) refers to the "Yellow Bell" pitch, the lowest in the ancient gamut of twelve fixed pitches from which the modulation of the other pitches was derived. The problem, which had preoccupied scholars since the Han dynasty and was very much a live issue in the eighteenth century, was how to recover the measurement of this fundamental pitch with any accuracy. Koo and Yue render the phrase figuratively as "the Primal Sound of Nature" in their English translation of this passage (142n7).

49. The character *ju* also means potential or method as well as implement, tool, or instrument.

50. Based on Koo and Yue's translation, *The Tradition of Sung Poetry*, 142, with my modification; *Yuefu chuansheng*, 258.

51. Zhuqing (Lester) Hu, "From Ut Re Mi to Fourteen-Tone Temperament: The Global Acoustemologies of an Early Modern Chinese Tuning Reform" (PhD diss., University of Chicago, 2019), was completed after I wrote this essay, but it is now the best source for understanding the intellectual context in which Xu Dachun wrote his treaties, specifically the relationship between ancient Chinese music theory and the Qing dynasty "Phonological Revolution."

PART II

Limit Cases

3

Voice, Music, Modernism: The Case of Luigi Nono and Karlheinz Stockhausen

MARCELLE PIERSON

In the middle of the twentieth century, something strange happened to "classical" music: composers in the West who identified with the tenets of modernism largely stopped writing melodies. Compositional considerations seemed to shift somewhat abruptly toward texture and timbre. Why write about this phenomenon in a volume about voice? The short answer is that in the Western classical tradition, melody and voice are so intertwined as to form a single entity: when we speak about melody, we speak about the voice, and vice versa. Even instrumental music is often conceived vocally, to the point that young performers are instructed to "sing" through their instruments. The piano is technically a percussion instrument on which keys activate mallets that strike strings, yet a performer playing most well-known repertory is exhorted to aspire to the condition of the voice, to its proclivities toward melodic line and breath-like phrasing. Perhaps this is why pianist Glenn Gould can be heard quietly humming over his famous recordings of Bach, much to the chagrin of his studio engineers.

So the disappearance of melody and singing (in the traditional sense) in recent "classical" music may be of interest to those who are interested in the voice, and particularly in how the voice has fared, aesthetically speaking, in the modernist/postmodernist age. The metaphor of voice in visual art has relatively little traction, but this is not the case with written mediums, where the notion of the "authorial voice" remains powerful even as it has received intense scrutiny from thinkers like Roland Barthes and Jacques Derrida. Music is unique among these modalities in that it has actual, *literal* voices to contend with in its daily business, voices that are highly aestheticized and carefully controlled. It's hard to be a musician without some sense of where you stand in relation to the voice. Composers, then, are especially well positioned to provide commentary on the status of the voice in a given time and place, through both the music they create and what they say about it.

This still leaves open the question of why melody, perhaps the voice itself, became so unfashionable in postwar classical music, somewhat suddenly, after dominating musical textures since the eighteenth century and well before. In this essay, I show how voice has come into conflict with modernism as the dominant musical ideology of the twentieth century. Song, with the voice as its medium, is often associated with the heart—with authenticity, with passion, with emotion and its unmediated expression. This is borne out in the ubiquitous use of voice as conceptual placeholder for subjectivity, agency, and authenticity in both musical and nonmusical discourse. Song and voice make uneasy bedfellows with modernism, which is so often associated with the head. Modernist composers are sometimes lampooned as dispassionate rationalists intent on finding the most elegant formula rather than the most moving music. Daniel Albright elaborates on this caricature, pointing out the difference between the flowing manes of nineteenth-century composers and the "bald pate of Schoenberg or Igor Stravinsky or Sergei Prokofiev or Paul Hindemith . . . appropriate for a music that seems to reject all ornament and charm in favor of research into the essence of things, the phonic equivalent of the physics of subatomic particles."[1] It may seem as though a simple rejection of voice would be the best course of action for a modernist, but as we shall see, the results of this meeting between voice and modernism are much more complicated and contradictory than that.

Here, I focus on a serendipitous moment in the 1950s in which two composers each wrote highly stylized "songs," and then, in the aftermath of their premieres, engaged in an increasingly hostile exchange about their different uses of the voice. These polemics, like the pieces themselves, articulate two very different positions regarding the status of song and singing in the late 1950s. In addition to a disagreement about musical aesthetics, this was a disagreement about the status and means of the voice in music, which in turn was a disagreement about the status and means of expression, of subjectivity, of music's very humanity. The moment constitutes a special case of how the two very different discourses and ideologies surrounding voice and modernism have clashed, sometimes spectacularly, in music written after 1950.

From Friendship to Enmity

In 1952, Luigi Nono and Karlheinz Stockhausen became close friends. Over the next several years they took classes together, presented one another's work in lectures, and even vacationed together. In 1957, Nuria Nono, Luigi's wife, became the godmother of Stockhausen's son Markus;[2] in 1958, Nono coined the term "Darmstadt School" to refer to himself and Stockhausen, as well as Pierre Boulez and Bruno Maderna. By Darmstadt, Nono refers to the famous summer courses in Darmstadt, Germany, a long-standing modernist mecca where composers still come to hear, create, and discuss new music. The moniker presents Nono and his chosen colleagues as a united front of composers who had become towering figures in the halls and beer gardens of this storied institution. Nono and Stockhausen also displayed a number of aesthetic affinities during the 1950s, most relevant among which was their interest in the voice. This is evident even in the titles of Nono's *Il canto sospeso* (The Suspended Song) and Stockhausen's *Gesang der Jünglinge* (Song of the Youth), both of which were composed in the same two-year period (1955–1956), used serial means, made reference to liturgical forms, and maintain a canonical status today. Both Nono and Stockhausen also enjoyed a mutually beneficial relationship with Darmstadt, where the two works were widely discussed. These many similarities invited all manner of comparison, which itself led, almost inevitably, to conflict. By the summer of 1959, the united front of the "Darmstadt School" was no more, creating doubt that it had ever existed,[3] and Nono and Stockhausen's erstwhile friendship had dissolved into personal and professional rancor on public display to their fellow Darmstadt attendees. Helmut Lachenmann describes the scene that took place when he attended a breakfast for lecturers at Nono's invitation:

> When there was no table setting for me—the unannounced intruder—Nono scoffed at the inflexible "German organization," incapable of improvisation, whereupon Stockhausen replied, "What does German organization mean here? With you the tones stand at attention after all!," whereupon Nono, boisterous rather than angry, retorted: "And yours move like a scarecrow." That was quite definitely the last aesthetic discussion between the two.[4]

Not so long after Stockhausen refused him as a lunch companion, Lachenmann would become a preeminent composer and Darmstadt luminary in his own right, but during the late 1950s he was in his early twenties and was a student of Nono's as well as an admirer of Stockhausen's. Reflecting back on the composers' conflict years later, he mused that "it is particularly in a work like *Il canto sospeso* that one can see the beginnings of the gap—now a gulf—between composers like Stockhausen and Nono."[5] Lachenmann's claim is that these polemics constitute a moment of crisis not only between Nono and Stockhausen, but also between composers *like* them. Thus, the repercussions of the differences between these pieces radiate outward, and Stockhausen and Nono become symbolic of a burgeoning crisis in the cosmopolitan new music scene. It seems that the underlying issues might not be so petty as their lunchroom name-calling would suggest. And, in fact, this anecdote touches on the core of the aesthetic conflict that drove them apart, if somewhat obliquely. Each accuses the other of creating music that purports to be human but lacks certain vital human qualities, Nono's tones standing at attention while Stockhausen's are stuffed with straw. The debates center around the proper relationship between music and the human. And these questions felt especially important in the shadow of World War II, as Adorno's famous comment about writing poetry after Auschwitz illustrates.

Even before their falling out, Nono and Stockhausen engaged in many conversations in which Nono insisted that music should be politically engaged and exude the "warmth of life,"[6] and Stockhausen countered:

> It's really *essential* to choose *one* idea, *one* total conception of all material dimensions . . . that the writing has only the function of the performing, the service, and becomes fully un-Promethean, un-Faustian, impersonal—if you will: inhuman, so, music becomes less and less human, more and more pure.[7]

If Nono, then, made an explicit goal of including a human element in his music, Stockhausen gravitated toward an inhuman purity. Although the core conflict is laid out in these exchanges, its terms remain unclear. What exactly constituted the "human" in 1950s Darmstadt? What is the nature of the *technê* that underlies its metaphysics? What does humanity sound like for different members of the Darmstadt School, and what are the compositional techniques that bring it about? It is not a coincidence that these issues were brought to the surface by two pieces that feature voice and stake claims in their titles to the status of "song." In a tradition that dates at least back to Rousseau, composers and critics have exhibited a strong tendency to locate music's humanity within its vocal elements, including melody as a songful practice. In the next two sections, I read each work closely in order to understand how the two composers mediate vocality in them, and why.

Il canto sospeso

Il canto sospeso continues to be a source of great controversy due to Nono's strenuously structuralist treatment of both text and voice.[8] The words he chose were excerpted from the final letters of condemned political prisoners of the World War II resistance; these letters are heartrending, and Nono has stood accused of not approaching them respectfully. The composer used a number of predetermined compositional systems that controlled such aspects of the music as pitch and dynamics, rather than venturing a more intuitive approach.

The charged texts are often layered over themselves, and the metrical placement of words does not necessarily correspond to the natural rhythms of speech. This disruption of vocality makes semantic understanding of *Il canto sospeso*'s texts difficult, indeed often impossible. And yet, especially when compared to Stockhausen's use of text and voice in *Gesang der Jünglinge*, there remains a strong sense that Nono conceived of *Il canto sospeso* as an utterance—as a work that draws upon the association of the voice with agency, subjectivity, and authenticity.

In a 1957 Darmstadt lecture, Stockhausen was generally complimentary of *Il canto sospeso*, but seemed to be genuinely flummoxed by Nono's choices in text-setting. While he acknowledged that Nono was "deeply moved" by the texts, he found his friend's sympathy for the plight of the speakers difficult to reconcile with how he incorporated them musically:

> The texts are not delivered, but rather concealed in such a ruthlessly strict and dense musical form that they are hardly comprehensible when performed. Why, then, texts at all, and why these texts? . . . Should he not have chosen texts so rich in meaning in the first place, but rather sounds?[9]

Nono didn't react well to his friend's censure, expressing his outrage in a 1960 Darmstadt lecture. In an indirect answer to Stockhausen's query, he replied: "The question why I chose exactly this text and no other for a composition is no more intelligent than asking why, in order to say the word '*stupid*,' of all letters one has to use *s-t-u-p-i-d*."[10] He also pointed out that the text of *Il canto sospeso* is never fragmented beyond the level of the word, and that he was careful to present these words in order.

Movement 6a exemplifies Nono's negotiation between serial structure and vocal utterance, and shows how the sounding voice maintained for him a special place in the musical fabric. The text for this movement was written by Esther Srul, and reads: "The doors open. There are our murderers. Dressed in black. They drive us from the synagogue."[11] The movement features a four-voice choir alongside a powerful array of low winds, low brass, low strings, and timpani. The overall affect is violent, with brass swells and timpani hits roiling below sustained and slow-changing vocal harmonies. From their study of archival materials related to this work, Kathryn Bailey and Carola Nielinger have concluded that the vocal parts are meant to represent the Jews in this encounter, while the instruments represent the Nazis.[12] Srul's memory takes the form of the first-person plural, and there is something of a real-time narration as each member of the choir sings a similar text, but at a slightly different time and on a narrow array of pitches. The recountings differ slightly between these vocal "characters," but are also shared. In contrast, Nono denies the Nazis a voicing, instead representing them with sounds that are coded as instrumentalist, frightening, inhuman (**web. ex. 3.1**).

It may seem a trivial point—after all, it makes sense for the vocal part to perform the text—but the fact that Nono gives voice to Srul and her companions and embodies the Nazis through ominous-sounding instruments is significant. Along with his careful text-setting, it shows that despite his serialist machinations, despite the fact that the text is not always comprehensible, Nono very much thought of *Il canto sospeso* as an *utterance*—admittedly obscured, yet envoicing its text many times over. Carolyn Abbate points out that the voice itself, separate from semantic content, is capable of imparting information and catalyzing action. In her analysis of Lakmé's "Bell Song," she argues that the real force of action is not the story Lakmé tells, but rather her voice itself and the fact that she is using it.[13] As Abbate argues, the fact *that* someone is singing, and *how* they are singing, and *to whom* they are singing all need to be acknowledged on their own terms.

Despite the controversy over his fragmented text-setting, *Il canto sospeso* was actually one of the most "vocal," which is to say melodic, pieces to come out of 1950s Darmstadt; it stands out as remarkably lyrical in the context of a bevy of works that celebrate the detached (in both senses of the word). Darmstadt-goers would not necessarily have had a problem with his pointillistic textures per se were they not used in the setting of this particular text. In fact, Nono was attacked from both sides: his text-setting wasn't lyrical enough, and yet, the overall texture was *too* lyrical. One critic's rhapsodic response to *Il canto sospeso* contains a defensive element that shows the controversial nature of the work's melodiousness. He pays special attention to the work's seventh movement, which takes the form of a soaring soprano solo over a delicately shattered instrumental and choral accompaniment:

> [The seventh movement's] long and truly free-floating female vocal line transmits such excruciating pathos that it is not surprising that it was felt by some to be embarrassing. It is not easy to find the courage to express one's emotions today. Heinz Joachim regards this piece as less successful than the preceding movements and describes it as "a very long soprano solo which gives way too much to lyrical expression." What a fortunate mistake in today's musical climate! In reality parts V, VI and VII, together with the third, represent the climax of this rediscovery of communication to which *Il canto sospeso* owes its high esteem.[14]

The manner in which modernism and the voice coexist in this work is somewhat familiar. Modernism resides in the serial techniques that determine so many of its facets, from pitch to dynamics to rhythm. The voice resides in the way Nono fashions these techniques to create music that utters, music that *sings*. These two aspects exist in a tension that is never fully resolved, but Nono's voices are a site where the rigid musical structure opens up and lets a culturally coded sense of humanity come forth.

Gesang der Jünglinge

Between 1954 and 1956, Stockhausen attended Werner Meyer-Eppler's seminars in acoustics and communication theory. Although he saw Meyer-Eppler as having "hardly a clue about music,"[15] Stockhausen admired him as a physicist and acoustician and learned a great deal about the relationship between formants and vowel sounds under his tutelage. With this knowledge, he was able to create electronic sounds that resemble the human voice and a texture that moves back and forth between synthesized and vocal sounds with unprecedented fluidity. *Gesang der Jünglinge* puts these new techniques into action; its intricate sonic tapestry is woven out of a single voice that is split, duplicated, layered, and otherwise manipulated, sometimes beyond recognition, alongside a futuristic panel of synthesized bleeps, bloops, buzzes, and sustained tones (**web. ex. 3.2**). The one and only actual voice in the piece belongs to a twelve-year-old boy soprano named Josef Protschka, with whom Stockhausen worked closely in the recording studio.[16]

Although Stockhausen approached his experimentation with vowel sounds and their serial ordering differently, he and Nono arrived at a similar problem of incomprehensibility; nor was his text free from the kinds of political and emotional valences that accompanied *Il canto sospeso*. The primary text of *Gesang der Jünglinge* was taken from a section of the biblical Apocrypha in which three Jewish children sing praise from a furnace. The first four lines of the text give a sense of its repetitive structure:

Preiset (Jubelt) den(m) Herrn, ihr Werke alle des Herrn—	O all ye works of the Lord—
lobt ihn und über alles erhebt ihn in Ewigkeit.	Praise (exalt) ye the Lord above all forever.
Preiset den Herrn, ihr Engel des Herrn—	O ye angels of the Lord, praise ye the Lord—
preiset den Herrn, ihr Himmel droben.	O ye heavens, praise ye the Lord.[17]

The decision to use this particular text, and not sounds, just a decade after the end of World War II was certainly read politically as well. And unlike

Nono, Stockhausen did not set his text in order, but rather presented a kaleidoscopic mélange of fragments that slide in and out of comprehensibility not only as text, but also as voice. There's a sense throughout the work that both the text and the voice used to utter it are specimens undergoing rigorous testing and analysis. These do not add up to speech acts—utterances—but rather to a kind of vocal object, presented from different angles and at extremely high resolution.

In the same essay that evaluates Nono's text-setting, Stockhausen anticipates an accusation of hypocrisy regarding his criticism of Nono. He claims, however, that the biblical excerpt was already so well known that he could afford to take liberties:

> The words are memorised, and here we are primarily concerned with the fact *that* and *how* they are memorised, and the details of the content are of secondary importance; the concentration is directed upon the sacredness; speech becomes ritual.[18]

For Stockhausen, it is vital that his music perform a consonant relation to a rational system. No matter how dramatic or cacophonous the moment may be, it emerges in harmony with the fundamental ground or overarching plan. Robin Maconie, Stockhausen's biographer and advocate, describes how in the planning and execution of *Gesang der Jünglinge*, Stockhausen believed that

> the ultimate, logical, and appealing alternative to an arbitrary system would be one founded on scientific principles. Such a system, just as rigorous, drawing its strength from the world of everyday human experience, would be more likely as a matter of course to connect with the perceptions of the "ordinary listener."[19]

Both of these statements emphasize replicability in memorization and also in rigor and purity of a system. They oppose an organicist notion of musical development that takes speech as its model: Adorno is not alone in believing that "the gesture of music is borrowed from the speaking voice,"[20] but that is not how Stockhausen wishes to organize *Gesang der Jünglinge* despite the fact that the work is absolutely saturated with the speaking and singing voice. Instead, he wants to organize the work at least partly though sonic objects—recorded voices and compositional systems.

The complexity of the objects in question, especially the recorded voice, precludes the possibility of a certain level of systematic rigor. Richard Toop documents an earlier phase in which Stockhausen rejected *musique concrète* techniques, where a composer manipulates prerecorded material (as with the voice in *Gesang*). Writing in 1952 about his frustration with prerecorded music,

Stockhausen longed for something more "controlled": "'Musique concrète'— I sensed this from the first day, is nothing but capitulation before the undefined, a terribly dilettantish gamble, uncontrolled improvisation."[21] The longing for a kind of purity catalyzed Stockhausen's obsession with the sine tone during the early 1950s;[22] his correspondence with Karel Goeyvaerts reveals that he saw the sine tone as pure sound, and in that sense a reflection of divinity. After completing his *Studie I* with only sine tones, however, Stockhausen found himself dissatisfied with this very limited compositional resource and returned to instruments with *Kontra-Punkte* (1952–1953). Goeyvaerts was outraged over the "heretical impurities" in this work, and the two composers didn't correspond for several months. In his return to *musique concrète* and instrumental works, Stockhausen sought an "impure" middle ground that created problems for him ideologically even as it inspired him musically.

Where, then, lies the voice in *Gesang der Jünglinge*, and where its modernism? In this work, Stockhausen takes as his beginning point the complexity of the voice, the challenge it poses to analysis and reductionism. He then places that complex object into a serial (read: modernist) context, creating a work that is "vocal" in quite an unconventional way. It is vocal not in how communicative its utterance is, but rather in how steeped it is in the *sound* of the voice. Everything else, including the synthesized sounds, arises out of his understanding of vocal timbre.

Stockhausen proposes here an alternative way of creating meaning through the voice, where both the text and the voice that speaks it become "secondary" to elements of repetition and ritual. This brings to mind Abbate's point about Lakmé, but in a very different way. Nono's political prisoners singing from the executioner's block are met by Stockhausen's Jewish children singing praise from inside a furnace, and yet, the two composers apparently conceived of voice and text as having very different roles in these works. Both texts are a sort of direct quotation, but Nono quotes specific and recent historical actors while Stockhausen quotes long-ago biblical figures. Nono thus stages a kind of reenactment while Stockhausen stages an allegory.

Nono intended to use serial techniques in order to enhance the semantic meaning of the text rather than to obstruct it, to "give voice to the legacy of these letters,"[23] to combine them into what Christopher Fox calls "a litany of suffering,"[24] and to set them to music that mirrors and intensifies their anguish. For Stockhausen, the speech of *Gesang der Jünglinge* is implacable sacrament rather than urgent utterance; he saw Nono's attempt at direct vocal expression as embarrassingly old-fashioned. And the sound and structure of the music is deeply affected by these different approaches: Nono sets his texts in syllabic order, while Stockhausen fragments and reorders his; Nono uses the letters as his sole text while Stockhausen places his among children's songs, nonsense syllables, and other vocalisms; Nono's setting features very little repetition while Stockhausen sometimes uses the same tape excerpt multiple times; Nono's main strategy is development while Stockhausen balances development and juxtaposition; Nono's voices come alive in performance while Stockhausen's single boy's voice is accessible only through tape; and, especially in movement 6a, Nono sets his voices against instruments while Stockhausen moves seamlessly between vocal and nonvocal sound. *Gesang der Jünglinge* does not identify with its voice, but rather objectifies it. All of these decisions constitute different ways of navigating the persistent tensions between "voice" and "modernism."

Modernism and the Voice

Nono and Stockhausen's disagreement centers around the question of whether music should be an utterance, an act of vocal expression, that emanates from a body and is laden with affect and communicative intent. They were not the only composers to struggle with this question. In fact, the 1950s and 1960s was a time when many modernist composers were attempting to find modes of expression that forge different relationships with vocality. Some avoided writing for the voice altogether, some portrayed the voice fighting against musical elements that would constrain it, some attempted to bring forth the voices of mental and physical disability.

Gary Tomlinson has articulated a modernist crisis of the operatic voice following the advent of (in particular) Wagner's *Parsifal*. He claims that modernist composers were attracted to Wagner's "consecrational solemnity, which came more and more to seem the gravity required of modernist 'high art,'"[25] at the same time as they were deeply troubled by the commodification of this very feature. Modernist composers were thus "unable to materialize noumenal magic without relying on forces that, all told, falsify material presence."[26] In other words, the use of the singing voice became standardized and hackneyed and lost its magic, its ability to represent an undivided and unproblematized subjectivity. Any opera lover can certainly catalogue standardized compositional techniques for bringing forth a fully present subject though the singing voice: a rising line, with swelling dynamics, accompanied by the building and resolution of harmonic tension. But these techniques, insofar as they *are* established techniques, must also be regarded with deep suspicion by any modernist intent on representing human presence in a principled way (and I mean principled in both senses here: rational and ethical).

Tomlinson discusses only opera, and opera working from within what he calls a conservative tradition (albeit subversively); he shows how Schoenberg's *Moses und Aron* and Britten's *Turn of the Screw* both use singing to bring forth subjectivities at the margins of presence.[27] Nono was distant from especially Britten in any number of ways, and was not yet writing in the genre of opera, but he does seem to belong to this tradition. After all, although *Il canto sospeso* was undoubtedly innovative in its application of strict serial procedures, it does contain a great deal of what might be called operatic singing. Nono appears to be relatively untouched by a modernist crisis of the voice. The way he represents human presence and lends it pathos is actually quite conventional: he does it through vocal utterance that disrupts and transcends the system from which it arises. In the battle between the voice and modernism, Nono ensures the voice's victory. And this "old-fashioned" form of vocal expression was the source of much confusion and consternation at Darmstadt. In his assessment of *Il canto sospeso*, Stockhausen misses this point entirely, focusing on the structural elements of the work and dismissing aspects of it that do invoke utterance as unnecessary and even undesirable.[28]

Stockhausen, for his own part, seems to respond to a similar crisis in a different way—a way that makes the victor between modernism and the voice far less clear. He uses the voice in *Gesang der Jünglinge* not as the bearer of the music's emotional message, but as a kind of object, one that has been manipulated in a variety of ways. Far from feeling that he can communicate a powerful text through *utterance*, he attempts to synthesize vocal timbre in ways that also show that a given voice is finite, knowable, parsable into a certain arrangement of overtones. To understand the voice this way is to separate it from its source in human communication, rendering it inert, devoid of presence—remember that for him, "*one* idea, *one* total conception of all material dimensions" allows music to rise to the status of "inhuman." But humanity does not actually disappear. It is evoked in a different way by making the voice into a ritual, a system. Rather than calling on singing to demonstrate humanity, Stockhausen focuses almost mechanistically on the specific timbre of one voice. Because the piece exists only in recording, and because the timbre of Josef Protschka's particular voice served as a starting point that determined its other sonic elements, *Gesang der Jünglinge*'s voice is utterly singular; it cannot be performed by a different singer. *Gesang* thus brings forth a different kind of vocal presence—a different representation of musical humanity.

Derrida, among others, reminds us that the voice-as-marker-of-humanity is a contingent construction that contains its own set of rational principles.[29] But the association between the vocal and the human is tremendously important and generative for Nono and Stockhausen, as well as for many of their contemporaries, predecessors, and successors. We must therefore take these associations seriously as a means of understanding their music and its interventions into voice. No matter how it is done, bringing the voice into modernist music adds a layer of complexity; it requires a reckoning between these contradictory discourses. Nono's complexity is one of emotional resonance and heft, made especially poignant by the presence of live singers and the aleatory character of live performance. And yet, his resources for creating vocal sound are limited to finite categories: pitch, dynamics, rhythm, and so on. By contrast, as an electronic work, *Gesang der Jünglinge* lacks the potential for different performances, as well as the humanizing presence of singers (or any performers) onstage, even if the materials Stockhausen chose to work with, both synthesized sounds and recorded voice, are incredibly rich. The voice, in particular, is infinitely complex: fundamentally irreducible to the parameters to which Nono is limited. Nono's voice is thus conceived in terms of abstract categories (modernism) but performed with all the messiness of human error and interpretation (voice); Stockhausen's voice begins as fundamentally messy and irreducible (in the way of voice itself) but is "performed" only after it has been subjected to a perfected set of abstract categories of manipulation (in the way of modernism).

Tomlinson's response to the modernist crisis of vocality is pessimistic: "for the first time in long epochs of operatic song, doubt arises whether the voice can sustain metaphysics anymore at all."[30] He's right to point out that calling the viability of the voice into question has potentially catastrophic implications for music, and especially vocal music. But I also think that he underestimates the extent to which modernist composers thrive on catastrophe. Artists working in this tradition continue to this day to struggle productively with the tensions around the idea of a "modernist voice," and continue to generate works that bear eloquent witness to this struggle.

Notes

1. Daniel Albright, *Modernism and Music: An Anthology of Sources* (Chicago: University of Chicago Press, 2004), 5.

2. Rainer Nonnenmann, *Der Gang durch die Klippen: Helmut Lachenmanns Begegnung mit Luigi Nono anhand ihres Briefwechsels und anderer Quellen, 1957–1990* (Wiesbaden: Breitkopf and Härtel, 2013), 29–30. See also Karl H. Wörner, *Stockhausen: Life and Work*, trans. Bill Hopkins (Berkeley: University of California Press, 1976), 235.

3. Scholars have questioned the Darmstadt School as a cohesive movement. See Christopher Fox, "Music after Zero Hour," *Contemporary Music Review* 26, no. 1 (February 2007): 13; Martin Iddon, "Darmstadt Schools: Darmstadt as a Plural Phenomenon," *Tempo* 65, no. 256 (March 29, 2011): 2–8.

4. Nonnenmann, *Der Gang durch die Klippen*, 133. "Als es dort für mich, den unangemeldeten Eindringling, kein Gedeck gab, spottete Nono über die improvisationsunfähige, unbewegliche 'deutsche Organisation,' worauf Stockhausen entgegnete: 'Was heißt hier deutsche Organisation? Bei Dir stehen doch die Töne stramm!', worauf Nono eher übermütig als verärgert zurückgab: 'Und bei Dir machen sie Bewegungen wie Vogalscheuche . . .' Das war wohl definitiv die letzte ästhetische Diskussion zwischen den beiden." Translation my own.

5. Helmut Lachenmann, "Touched by Nono," in *Contemporary Music Review* 18, no. 1 (1999): 20.

6. Nonnenmann, *Der Gang durch die Klippen*, 120.

7. Cited in Nonnenmann, *Der Gang durch die Klippen*, 31: ". . . daß wirklich eine Idee, eine totale Vorstellung alle Materialdimensionen notwendig auswählt . . . —daß der Schreibende nur noch die Funktion des Ausführens, des Dienens hat und vollkommen unprometheisch, unfaustisch, unpersönlich wird—wenn Du willst: unmenschlich, so, wie seine Musik immer unmenschlicher, immer reiner wird."

8. According to Kathryn Bailey, the bombing of the Munich Oktoberfest in 1980 was instigated at least partly by an attempt to prevent a performance of *Il canto sospeso*. Kathryn Bailey, " 'Work in Progress': Analysing Nono's 'Il Canto Sospeso,' " *Music Analysis* 11, no. 2/3 (July 1, 1992): 279–80.

9. Karlheinz Stockhausen, "Text and Music," trans. Ruth Koenig, *Die Reihe: A Periodical Devoted to Developments in Contemporary Music* 6 (Bryn Mawr: Theodor Presser Co., 1964), 48–49. Translation slightly adapted. These quotes are taken perhaps a bit out of context, since Stockhausen seems to be engaged in a sincere attempt to defend Nono against accusations of an inappropriate use of this politically and emotionally charged text, even as these accusations come from Stockhausen himself. As I mentioned, he points out the profound impact of these texts upon Nono and defends Nono's decisions later in the essay: "It is not for nothing that a few fragmentary syllables flash out of the heaving sounds here and there in [movement] II. The listener feels he has understood them without, however, their having resulted in larger coherent passages" (Stockhausen, "Text and Music," 49). M. J. Grant concisely rebuts Stockhausen's criticism of Nono's text-setting, claiming that Stockhausen fails to take into account that "the music itself is utterly sad"; see *Serial Music, Serial Aesthetics: Compositional Theory in Post-War Europe* (Cambridge: Cambridge University Press, 2001), 203.

10. Luigi Nono, "Text—Musik—Gesang," trans. in M. J. Grant, *Serial Music, Serial Aesthetics*, 203.

11. ". . . *le porte s'aprono. Eccoli i nostri assassini. Vestiti di nero. Ci cacciano dalla sinagoga,*" trans. in Carola Nielinger, " 'The Song Unsung': Luigi Nono's 'Il Canto Sospeso,' " *Journal of the Royal Musical Association* 131, no. 1 (January 1, 2006): 119.

12. Bailey, " 'Work in Progress' "; Nielinger, " 'The Song Unsung.' "

13. Carolyn Abbate, *Unsung Voices: Opera and Musical Narrative in the Nineteenth Century* (Princeton, NJ: Princeton University Press, 1991), 3–10.

14. Trans. and cited in Nielinger, " 'The Song Unsung,' " 133.

15. Robin Maconie, *Other Planets: The Music of Karlheinz Stockhausen* (Lantham, MD: Scarecrow Press, 2005), 211.

16. David Metzer, "The Paths from and to Abstraction in Stockhausen's *Gesang der Jünglinge*," *Modernism/Modernity* 11, no. 4 (2004): 695–721, at 708–9.

17. Karlheinz Stockhausen, *Elektronische Musik, 1952–1960*, with the Westdeutscher Rundfunk (Kürten, 1991).

18. Karlheinz Stockhausen, "Music and Speech," *Die Reihe* 6 (1964): 58.

19. Maconie, *Other Planets*, 59.

20. Theodor W. Adorno, "Music, Language, and Composition," in *Essays on Music*, ed. Richard Leppert, trans. Susan H. Gillespie (Berkeley: University of California Press, 2002), 113.

21. Richard Toop, "Stockhausen and the Sine-Wave: The Story of an Ambiguous Relationship," *Musical Quarterly* 65, no. 3 (July 1979): 388.

22. A sine tone has special acoustic properties that give it a very smooth sound, like the one you might encounter during a hearing test at the doctor's.

23. Luigi Nono, *Luigi Nono: Texte, Studien zu seiner Musik*, ed. Jürg Stenzl (Zurich: Atlantis, 1975), 60. Cited and quoted in Christopher Fox, "Luigi Nono and the Darmstadt School: Form and Meaning in the Early Works (1950–1959)," *Contemporary Music Review* 18, no. 2 (1999): 111–30, at 125.

24. Fox, "Luigi Nono and the Darmstadt School," 127.

25. Gary Tomlinson, *Metaphysical Song: An Essay on Opera* (Princeton, NJ: Princeton University Press, 1999), 147.

26. Tomlinson, *Metaphysical Song*.

27. *Turn of the Screw* was premiered in 1954, followed closely by *Il canto sospeso* and *Gesang der Jünglinge*. Compared to Stockhausen, Nono is the traditionalist; compared to Britten, he is the modernist. These internal divisions between avant-garde and conservative are constantly negotiated and renegotiated in the discourse of contemporary music.

28. Christopher Fox comes to a similar point in "Luigi Nono and the Darmstadt School," 126–27.

29. Jacques Derrida, *Of Grammatology*, trans. Gayatri Chakravorty Spivak (Baltimore: Johns Hopkins University Press, 1976).

30. Tomlinson, *Metaphysical Song*, 156.

4

Screamlines: On the Anatomy and Geology of Radio

NEIL VERMA

> The scream, the scream. . . . The scream is often treated as some kind of insurmountable, impenetrable obstacle—pure, white noise. Force . . . that is beyond analysis and unworthy of any kind of interpretation. But here at the Institute we hear the scream from entirely the other perspective: the scream opening as an entry point, as an axis point, into a vast interior landscape that has as its surface this highly nuanced, very individual, psycho-acoustic force to it. . . . (**web. ex. 4.1**)
>
> GREGORY WHITEHEAD, "Pressures of the Unspeakable," 1991

In a radio art career spanning eras, formats, and genres, Gregory Whitehead's 1991 piece "Pressures of the Unspeakable" remains perhaps his seminal work. Upon receiving a commission for a feature from *The Listening Room*, a famous experimental show sponsored by the Australian Broadcasting Corporation (ABC), Whitehead traveled to Sydney, where he formed an imaginary Institute for Scream Studies to, in his words, "give voice to a continental nervous system, coaxing the underlying screamscape out into the public airwaves."[1] Whitehead set up a twenty-four-hour answering machine called the "Scream Line" and a "Scream Room" at the ABC for making recordings of volunteer screamers, while giving interviews and fostering other inputs for material he would eventually turn into an hour-long broadcast. "The scream trickle," he writes, "soon became a flood." Over time, Whitehead developed a pseudodiscipline of "scream hermeneutics," explaining that he was after not only creating an archive of screams but also a way of probing "the telephone-microphone-tape recorder-radio circuitry" he had established. "Pressures" isn't an investigation into the scream so much as it uses that process to palpate the apparatuses that made that effort possible. The scream exposes the inner circuits prompting the screamer to expel it, yes, but it also exposes the outer libidinal pressures in the devices and systems—from language itself to radio towers—that attempt to convey it and are at all points subject to fragmentation, error, and feedback.

The resulting radio broadcast (which won the Prix Italia in 1992) weaves together actualities and interviews; stories from callers about the screams of birth, death, and sadomasochistic sex; "screamscape" passages composed of rugby grunts and virtuoso screams sweetened through filters; and even "screamland blues" to give it all a comfortable groove. None of the screams are "real" in the sense of being unprompted vocalizations of terror, joy, or pain. Each is instead a highly composed submission, sometimes rehearsed, usually extensively prefaced, and often furtively made by members of the public. In Whitehead's work, each scream is handled as respectfully and reverently as the contents of a safety deposit box in a bank vault. As Allen Weiss has observed, the screams aren't phony, they simply lie "beyond any possible determination of authenticity," with the documentary credibility of the work in a state of self-subversion thanks to a set of humorous pseudoscientific monologues interspersed throughout the broadcast, in which Whitehead plays the role of the head of the Institute, haltingly explicating his work.[2] Here is an example of what Weiss calls these "Dr. Scream" passages:

> In many ways, scream analysis is more of an art than a science. It's an interpretive process, and one of the things we're doing here at the Institute is developing a series of techniques which help us to let the scream literally inhabit our bodies, flowing through our own bodies into our voice, and to actually give voice to the body of the original scream.
>
> We have developed a very rough, uh, classification system for screams, which break down into the basic elements of earth/water/fire/air, the basic forces of male/female/and primal, and finally the destiny of the scream, uh, which we understand as birth/death/or bardo, bardo being a Tibetan concept which designates the, the state of suspension between the living and the dead.
>
> The first example falls into the—let's see—[pages ruffle] the category earth-fire-female, and it goes something like this [inhales]
>
> [tape of scream]
>
> Okay [pages ruffle] the second exam—just pick these out—I've got a catalogue which is in this book and it's also in my body, um. The second one I th—it's quite different from the first, um, falls into the categories of air-male-primal-bardo. It's an air-male-primal-bardo scream. [inhales]
>
> [tape of scream]
>
> The uh . . . sorry, excuse me just sec [drinking water] The final example is maybe the most difficult in my particular scream memory catalogue, not

just because I'm a male but because of its particular intensity, its very specific intensity. It's the fire-water-female-birth scream and this is about as—as close as I've been able to get [inhales]

[tape of scream][3] (**web. ex. 4.2**)

It's a wonderfully Borgesian scene. Whitehead mocks the recuperation of the screaming voice into systems of linguistic, gender, and cultural difference—precisely what the scream is supposed to precede—by way of an elaborate vocal drag. Perhaps he is having fun with one of the chief arguments in theoretical work on the scream. Writers on the subject are often working overtime to emphasize that no scream, not even the child's first, is external to structure, a stance that reflects investments placed onto the scream during the linguistic turn specifically and late 1960s theory more broadly, when the scream became framed first as an "extreme" vocalization, and second as one whose recuperation into structure proved especially affirming to the paradigm of structure as a whole.[4] In each case, moreover, Whitehead's grandiose preparation to scream segues into a thinly disguised recording of another screamer from a tape, which makes us mistrustful of the desublimation of body into voice often pointed toward as the special affordance of radiophonic media. The moment of "raw" scream is, in other words, also the moment in which the play reveals the editing process behind the program, which is normally completely opaque to the listener. This is truth in ventriloquism: through the scream, Whitehead is able to both shed mediation and expose it at once.

The doubleness around Whitehead's approach to the scream is what inspired this chapter. My study of the scream on radio (along with its attending forms, such as the cry, the howl, and the growl) will be twofold. First, I will consider this type of sonic performance through a media studies perspective, using several thriller radio dramas from the last century to show that the scream can and should be treated as the source of a critical approach to radio listening rather than as a problem to be solved by one. This exploration will lead toward the complex thematic relationship between screams and anatomy. Second, I will explore how discourse on media historiography might find inspiration by means of such a vocalization.[5] This latter section will lead toward the theme of geology, focusing on a well-loved 1948 horror radio play by writer-director Wyllis Cooper called "The Thing on the Fourble Board," which I will argue chronicles the "birth" of a quasi-scream and at the same time "gives voice" to the material past of this hoary medium, pointing to how classic radio's ontology resonates in its ongoing state of media fossilization.[6] With these twin objectives, this chapter takes on the perhaps foolhardy task of doing in all seriousness what Whitehead does in fun, and even taking it all a step further, employing the "psychoacoustic force" of the scream to burrow into radiophonic expression, in which the scream has long been incorrectly considered only a surface feature. In this chapter, I am working with the scream as "Whitehead" understands it, believing that the scream is an opening rather than an obstacle, an axis along which we can take at least two journeys, one following the screamline into the interior of the body and the second following the screamline into the interior of the medium, thereby figuring the scream itself as the meeting point or state of equilibrium between two pressures.

Radio Wrong Side Out

> Can't we say that the voice is the mother of all special effects?
>
> MICHEL CHION

In criticism of the classical radio era (the mid-1930s to the 1950s), the scream is seldom considered an expressive matter with high stakes, special danger, or promise. One problem has been its subordination to theories of genre. We can't hear screams as screams because we are so busy hearing them as readily recuperable into generic frameworks. Cultural memory of "old time radio" aligns screams with other well-known sonic figures, a set of "effects" lined up with gunshots, rattling chains, and squeaking doors to form what Orson Welles once called the "dear old phosphorescent foolishness" of uncanny thriller radio during its flourishing years.[7] But the scream obeys a different logic not least because it is the only one of such effects often made by a vocal performer. The radio director couldn't say that the voice is the mother of "special effects," as Chion does, because "effects" referred to a separate set of tasks performed by a professional engineer governed by different rules in the industry and logic in the dramatization. Actually, a scream you hear on an Mp3 of an old episode of *Gangbusters, Dimension X*, or *The Ford Theater* could belong to either the engineering or the vocal arts. Some were performed live (the screams of protagonists, their victims, foiled villains), and others aired using prerecorded material stored on records and spun manually on turntables during broadcast (screams of pleasure from a rowdy party, panic from far-off disaster)—although there is almost never evidence of which method is chosen or why, and the difference is seldom legible to the ear.[8]

That doesn't stop screams from disrupting radio composition and theorization. Indeed, if you understand screams as a form of special effects, as Chion does in his work on cinema, then the tripartite system of (1) effects,

(2) music, and (3) voice that structures how radio dramatists understood the main components of their craft begins to fall apart, as do the affective, expressive, and semantic critical frameworks to which that tripartite division corresponds. For nearly every theorist of radio in the Anglophone tradition, the distinction between the triad of effects, music, and voice is intuitive, definitive, and hierarchical. Sound effects "show" things that happen (footsteps ascend stairs), music tells us how to "feel" (swelling violins), and vocalized words enable things to "mean" (George: "Martha, what are you doing with that knife?"). The last of these three "controls" the semantic ambiguity of the former two just as a textual caption controls the ambiguity of an image—never mind that differences within these categories (dialogue vs. narration, for instance) and qualities entirely apart from them (volume, reverberation) are often richer and yield a more compelling reading.[9] The scream is interesting in part because it fits none of these categories. Screams, cries, growls, and other nonverbal utterances can act, feel, and mean all at once. They punctuate scenes and puncture them, crossing boundaries of both compositional and interpretive tripartite structures, destabilizing underlying assumptions that critics and writers seldom recognize to be such.

Critical theory approaches to understanding the scream will only help a little, since screams have been theorized outside of dramatic contexts by those who typically employ psychoanalytic thought to target "the voice" as it screams rather than employing aesthetic interpretation of *a* voice as it screams. Douglas Kahn has noted this problem, writing of the ambiguous relationship between the "art scream" in works like "Pressures of the Unspeakable" and the "scream in its natural habitat" (childbirth, life-threatening situations, psychic and physiological torture, terror or anguish, sexual pleasure or pain, the fury of argument, the persecution or slaughter of animals), a tension between screams "affected" and screams "afflicted."[10] None of the screams I will be discussing come from trauma, although some are harmful to the vocal mechanism—radio "scream queen" Mercedes McCambridge famously damaged her voice intentionally in order to perform the series of growls, retchings, and screams of the demon in *The Exorcist*, the greatest radio performance that's not actually on radio. I would argue that there is no "the voice" in dramatic radio, just as there can be no "true" scream in dramatic radio, in the sense of a vocalization unmodulated by consciousness. Every scream "in" a radio play is scripted and composed, "tuned" in a certain way, and often directed in such a way as to accentuate particular shades and colors, as McCambridge's performances on *Lights Out!, Inner Sanctum Mysteries, I Love a Mystery*, and many other programs made clear. These are voices that act, pose, and distort according to sets of aesthetic postures associated with phonation in whatever cultural tradition to which the broadcast speaks, some of which take the form of a scream. Chion likens vocal work to the use of makeup and body prostheses in film. "Imagine someone," he writes, "who in a matter of seconds could double in height, expand like a balloon and retract into a string bean, or change their face from sweet and harmonious to horribly disfigured." With "no external props and tricks," Chion insists, that is what the voice can do.[11] If vocal work is costume and makeup by other means, then the scream is the voice in a monster suit.

It seems that many directors (especially before 1948, the year in which inexpensive magnetic tape appeared on the market, expanding the prerecording of plays) were reticent to use vocalized screams at all on live air, finding them difficult to manage in studios. This may be because drama directors often set up a series of microphones so that the pickup axis of one mike was set perpendicular to that of another, which created dead zones that made it possible to isolate characters from one another in the world of the fiction even when they were actually occupying the same room at the radio station. In this way, engineers could "ride gain" on each source in order to control sonic perspective from the booth, thereby rebalancing the output of all actors, musicians, or effects artists relative to one another in the final mix.[12] Screams thwart that delicate arrangement by their propensity to bleed from one mike to another, ruining the balanced environment of the studio and forcing engineers to compensate. Screams "bent the needle" of the entire broadcast, and could even damage delicate velocity microphones, a serious concern for live programming, in which few calamities compared to an unplanned real-time equipment failure. You can hear directors mitigating these problems by strategically placing screams in space and time: the cries of frightened peasants in Archibald MacLeish's 1937 free-verse drama "The Fall of the City" (1937) are blunted by remaining always at a deep distance from the microphone; the bursting scream of two parents slaughtered by their own children in Ray Bradbury's "Zero Hour" (1954) occurs at the last second of the play and in the midst of a swell of music while all characters are present, just where it could do the least damage to the delicately constructed imaginary scenography but provide the most punctuation.

In other cases, performances of screaming in its "pure" sense—the voice at its most expressive and least modulated by anything like "language" or "consciousness"—are simply avoided. Go listen for them in the long-running workhorse programs of blood-and-thunder radio such as *Inner Sanctum Mysteries*, *Molle Mystery Theater*, *The Shadow*, and *Suspense*, and you will find them sparse, muted, missing, far off, as often narrated as vocally enacted, or replaced by an instrumental musical phrase. In one stretch on the weekly thriller program *The Whistler*, by my count, more than six months went by without a single scream. There are no screams at all in Orson Welles's 1938 "The War of the Worlds," only grunts within commotions from far-off crowds of restless men; screaming wouldn't fit the aesthetic of silence and delay at the heart of that broadcast. Besides, 1930s radio screaming was usually performed by women, and there are no women at all in this profoundly androcentric fable—only one woman is even *mentioned* in the play, when narrator Professor Pierson absentmindedly remarks upon the likely loss of his wife after the invasion.[13] Perhaps the best-known female performance of screaming in classic radio comes at the end of Lucille Fletcher's 1943 play "Sorry, Wrong Number," in which the invalid Mrs. Stevenson (Agnes Moorehead) overhears a murder planned on a crossed telephone wire and warns the complacent authorities about it, but is unable to motivate them to investigate.[14] As the hired killer enters her very own house at the end of the play and we realize that the planned murder will be her own, the expected scream is doubly cut off, first by her strangler and then by the passing of an elevated train. In the stage version of the scene, script notes instruct Mrs. Stevenson to scream three times.[15] In Anatole Litvak's 1947 film version of the scene with Barbara Stanwyck, her remorseful husband calls and urges her to scream to save her life, something she manages to do a little before her death offscreen. But on radio the scream erupts only to be lost, a monster whose presence "shows" only in the auditory equivalent of a glimpse. Thanks to that ambiguity, along with a line fault, many listeners weren't sure what had transpired and wrote to CBS to complain. The subsequent week, the host of the program offered a terse clarification: "the woman died." Thus began the legend surrounding the play, re-created a half dozen times over the network, each time ending in a scream unheard.

A better approach to thinking through the scream may be to turn to vocalizations on the "edge" of being classifiable as a scream, focusing on how they provide a means to rethink their aesthetic contexts. If screams are rare in old-time radio, near-screams are everywhere. Attending to their role and form can help solve riddles. Consider Arch Oboler's 1940s radio play "The Dark" (**web. ex. 4.3**).[16] In the eight-minute play, widely thought to be the scariest short piece composed for radio, protagonists Doc and Sam receive a report of a disturbance from the switchboard and drive their ambulance to an empty house on Pine Street near the edge of town, a journey "from nothing to nowhere," as Sam puts it. The sonic language of the scene employs two male voices moving in closed spaces, the sound of a siren, creaking doors, gasps, footsteps, all across a canvas of echoing empty chambers, which lends events a sense of abstraction that goes a long way toward excusing its excesses. The men enter the home and move to a back room, where, in the light of a kerosene lamp, they describe something unbelievable: a human body turned inside out—"the skin is the inside, the raw flesh is the outside"—yet seemingly still alive, crying and mumbling. Less worried about saving the man than about understanding what befell him, Doc confronts the body not as a problem of life and death, but of knowledge. As Sam begs to leave, Doc insists they remain. "All my life things have been what they've been," he remarks, vowing, "I'm gonna know all about this." Elsewhere he refers to it as a "miracle" to be demystified at all costs. Investigating further, the pair finds a second door past which there seems to be no floor, only a creeping sound. "The dark sort of spills over on the edges," Doc remarks, toward a "deeper dark than . . . dark," in which something moves in the shadows. Soon Sam faints and is attacked by the shadows, and the doctor is similarly taken. We hear them both turned inside out (radio lore says this sound effect was rendered with a wet rubber glove). Once Doc is so "miraculously" transformed, no further explanation is offered, and we never come to "know."

Or do we? Perhaps Oboler's reversed body is more entwined with the matter of the voice than it is with the genre of the atavistic uncanny. The connection between bodies and voices has animated many thinkers in recent decades, many of whom draw on Roland Barthes, whose essay on the grain of the voice almost singlehandedly oriented a generation of writers to obsessively seek out "the body in the voice as it sings" through analysis of the friction of the music of the voice with that "something more" we call the body.[17] For philosopher Adriana Cavarero, voices matter in part because they are so tied to the inside of a unique body, both in the act of speaking and of listening. Indeed, it is its connection to fleshiness that vouchsafes the very notion of the voice as unique. In her well-known reading of Calvino, she writes:

> The play between vocal emission and acoustic perception necessarily involves the internal organs. It implicates a correspondence with the fleshy cavity that alludes to the deep body, the most bodily part of the body. The impalpability of sonorous vibrations, which is as colorless as the air, comes out of a wet mouth and arises from the red of the flesh.[18]

To speak with a voice is to turn oneself "inside out," in a certain sense, just as to hear is to draw something outside in.

The logic of that has a deep connection to "The Dark," thanks to a third vocalizing character in the drama I haven't mentioned yet. When Doc and Sam reach the house, they encounter an unnamed woman whom they presume to have been driven insane by whatever had transpired earlier. She doesn't utter a word. Instead, throughout Sam and Doc's colloquy, she laughs madly, following them into the room with The Dark, where she also meets her end. On sixteen separate occasions, she interrupts the play with snickers and guffaws, often punctuating the horrific exposition of the two men with uncontrolled cackling. Ignore the semantic denotation of the language, and the play has the feeling of a trio in which two voices narrate while a third laughs virtuosically at that process, wandering from bulbous expulsions to tiny titters at the edge of her breath. We are so inured to this noisy body-performance that by the end of the play, when she is attacked by The Dark, the transformation of her laughter into a scream produces the most monstrous and highest sonic point of the drama, literally and figuratively. What happens to her voice in that moment is the same thing that the "special effects" of the scene do to the bodies of the characters: *the scream is a laugh turned inside out*. And that is the philosophy—the "miracle"—of horror radio as the classic anthology writers practiced it, from the goofy jokes of cackling Old Nancy, Witch of Salem host of *The Witch's Tale*, to the macabre puns of Raymond, host of *Inner Sanctum Mysteries* (progenitors of the "crypt-keeper" figures of late-night television, a generation later), a mode of the horrific that emerges from a reversal of the laughable.

With its hanging vocals and exposed viscera, Oboler's play also unknowingly replies to another famous scream radio piece from around the same time, Antonin Artaud's recorded but unbroadcast 1947 work "To Have Done with the Judgment of God."[19] Artaud's usage of the scream in this anti-American scatological monologue punctuated by mad drumming and glossolalia is anything but funny, yet it has a kind of kinship with Oboler's little experimental skit. It is from Artaud's play, after all, that Deleuze drew the famous concept of a "Body without Organs," or BwO.[20] In a long engagement with this idea, Deleuze evolved an aspirational concept of a body remade, one undifferentiated and alive with potentials of sense and affect—"Why not walk on your head, sing with your sinuses, see through your skin, breathe with your belly," he asks with Guattari in *A Thousand Plateaus*.[21] For Deleuze, the emptying out of the body replaces a body circumscribed by differentiation with one populated with intensities, the body as a field of immanence in Spinoza's sense. It is a surprising idiosyncrasy of Deleuze and Guattari that they fuse "To Have Done," a deliberate offense to God, with Spinoza's defense of God's presence in all things. *A Thousand Plateaus* draws Spinoza's *Ethics* and Artaud's "Theater of Cruelty" together on the basis of something else: their shared fascination with bodily affect and antipathy toward the divisibility of substance, features that are central to both thinkers, and which take on utopian overtones in Deleuze's thought in the late 1960s and early 1970s.

For Artaud in 1947, however, the story of the Body without Organs was more macabre than this later appropriation suggests, never settling down to a utopia after differentiation. "To Have Done with the Judgment of God" emphasizes exposure and the accentuation of hidden differences, conveying an intensity that indicts everything around it. The play is an accusation or exorcism, as Weiss has elegantly argued in a reading that claims that the play uses the scream as a kind of excrement, the mouth as an anus.[22] The *tutuguri* or "Rite of the Black Sun" passages of that play, full of Artaud's own terrible howls, contain some of the most difficult screams in radio history, ones with ambiguous relations to his own mental illness and physical suffering. Artaud was gravely ill at the time, and as he rears from the microphone throughout that recording, banging and shrieking, it is never clear what is performed and what is not. Although we know we hear something scripted and composed, we also feel we can hear through the voice a series of disordered organs, from the membranes swollen by Artaud's childhood meningitis to the colorectal cancer that soon killed him. It's the sound of inner suffering not evacuated exactly but turned into a show. Douglas Kahn's reading of the screams in that piece emphasizes how it is "theatrical and medical," linking Artaud's lifelong fascination with screams to his pursuit of palliative acupuncture, which suggests not the de-organization of the body that Deleuze embraces but the pinpointing of the inside of the body upon its exterior, the inside-outing of suffering.[23] At the end of the interview that concludes the published text of "To Have Done," Artaud indicates as much when he speaks of the freedom to "dance wrong side out." This quote was a favorite of Gregory Whitehead, whose fascination with the postmortem led him to reengage with Artaud and write provocatively of "organs without bodies" in an article in *Performing Arts Journal* published not long before the airing of "Pressures of the Unspeakable."[24]

Dancing wrong side out. Artaud's voice crosses every line that screams draw. And just as Oboler's piece rests on the movement from laughter to screaming, Artaud's performance draws on the kinship of screams to shouts, cries, whines, growls, or roars, toying with the constructed line between a scream that engages on a linguistic level (a scream that *talks* or *means*) and one that is prior to that (a scream that *is*, or comes off that way). If, as Weiss argues, screams "reveal the chaotic depths of linguistic and vocal systems," these near-screams reveal a point where chaos seems orderable, and order chaogenous.[25] In *The Voice in Cinema*, Chion writes, "The screaming point is a point of the unthinkable inside the thought, of the indeterminate inside the spoken, of unrepresentability inside representation."[26] Chion likens the point to a black hole. If that's right, mock screams, laugh-screams, and other near-screams like those of Whitehead, Oboler, and Artaud sit not at the singularity at the center of the black hole, but at the event horizon on the periphery, with barely enough velocity to keep from falling in. Perhaps no writer does a better job of exploring this scream zone than Wyllis Cooper, whose masterpiece "The Thing on the Fourble Board" aired just a few months after Artaud wrote and performed his scream play. In Cooper's work, not only does the scream pull organs toward itself from out of a body, it also pulls media out through the microphone into its jaws.

The Thing about "The Thing on the Fourble Board"

PORKY: Me, I'm a roughneck. Well, I was a roughneck, I mean, twenty years ago. A little too old, too slow now. Besides, I got a dollar now. I don't have to be a roughneck, y'see. Married, got a nice home. Have to meet my wife. Hey Mike! Her name's Maxine but she likes to be called Mike. Mike! I guess she's busy out in the kitchen someplace. Besides, she doesn't hear very well. Shame, too—she's so pretty and everything. Well, you'll meet her. . . . Sit down.[27] **(web. ex. 4.4)**

Those are the first few lines of "The Thing on the Fourble Board," a radio drama by Wyllis Cooper that aired on *Quiet, Please*, the sixtieth play in a run of 106. The show connected strongly to the history of its author. Born in 1899 in Pekin, Illinois, Cooper served in the Signal Corps in World War I, where he was among those gassed at the Argonne. After the war he held various odd jobs, including a stint in the California oilfields. In 1933, the NBC network hired Cooper as an editor, and he began to contribute scripts to one of the earliest surviving adventure shows, *Tales of the Foreign Legion*, but he is really remembered for inventing horror radio with *Lights Out!* on WENR Chicago, a fifteen-minute program airing out of the Merchandise Mart at midnight on Wednesdays beginning in 1934. When *Lights Out!* went coast-to-coast on the NBC Red network, it spawned scores of fan clubs. Later, Cooper went on to write *Hollywood Hotel, Radio City Playhouse*, and more, along with a modest career writing film installments in the *Frankenstein* and *Mr. Moto* franchises. *Quiet, Please* was Cooper's last return to radio, now with a simplified style, capturing the feeling of a moment—according to a *Variety* ad, the *New York Post* called it "better than Benzedrine" around the time that recreational use of that stimulant peaked.[28] Upon his death in 1955, a *Washington Post* radio critic wrote that Cooper had "turned out more dialogue than a truck driver could lift," an analogy that would have pleased the author, many of whose plays surround an obscure worker—a telegraph clerk, a distiller, a disc jockey, an encyclopedia salesman—anyone who keeps odd hours, just like Porky, our roughneck oilfield narrator in "The Thing on the Fourble Board."[29]

The opening is typical for Cooper scripts. After the program title, we hear a signature soundtrack, a phrase from César Franck's *Symphony in D Minor*. Next comes first-person, direct-address character narration delivered by actor Ernest Chappell (star of all the plays), who is so closely miked that we often hear exhalations in between lines, gut laughs, even a little vocal fry. Chappell speaks to an unnamed narratee who acts as our substitute second self by virtue of the fact that we share "audioposition," a term I use to designate the place where we are according to what we hear, emphasizing that it is always a fabrication in radio, one with no necessary relation to an image or place. The mood of the scene is menacing, but it's also comic. By giving "Maxine" her unusual nickname and having Porky go a little off-mike to call to her, Cooper gives the play a marvelous sonic pun: Porky leans away from *the* mike to summon "Mike."

This moment also transforms the broadcast from radio prose to radio drama, as vocals that are projected into a perceivably larger space beyond the range of immediate pickup indicate something more than dialogue. Porky isn't just saying something, he is doing something. All of a sudden we are asked not merely to know about but also "see" a "nice" home, where a married man "with a dollar" might live. Our sense of that space develops even as (or because) its earshot limits are reached at the mention of Maxine, deaf and silent, our opposite on the far side of sonic symmetry. The scene balances three emptinesses. In a quiet room, Porky speaks to a quiet addressee (us) about another quiet addressee (Mike) using a third (the microphone). This story of muteness separated by voice will eventually unite all three, as Porky's subvocal chuckle at the end of the segment above (after "Well, you'll meet her") hints. The play has created the space for an audible scene around an inaudible cavity—Maxine/Mike—and the story will be preoccupied with that orifice and the presence within it, taking on the feel of the ritualized birth of a voice.

The prologue is not over. After Porky explains that being a "roughneck" means working on an oil drilling crew, pointing out that "a derrick floor or a fourble board's no place for a guy with a bow-tie," he brags about a well he once brought in at 7,313 feet, a record that held until a recent well by Pure Oil in the Trona Valley in Wyoming reached 14,309 feet. "That, friend, is almost three miles," he explains. "Quite a hole, that, huh?" After a contemplative pause around that quasi-vaginal image (note the otherness of the drill hole—"That, friend . . . hole, that"), Porky explains a few of the details of modern drilling technique—"fourble board" is a platform high enough to assemble four lengths of pipe, for instance. This tendency anchors the mood in realism so as to guarantee its thwarting by the supernatural. He continues:

> Sure I don't think there's an oil man in the world that don't wonder one time or another what's down there besides rock and oil and gas. Oil that's made out of trees that died twenty million years ago, oil that's made out of dinosaur bones, oil that's made out of the flesh and blood of men, maybe, that beat each other to death with a stone axe, ate sabre tooth tiger for lunch. Yeah, you get to wondering. You look at the cores that come up from way down there. Sometimes there's little shells, trilobites mostly, that was alive when Manhattan Island where New York is was under half a mile of ice. We found something once, me and Billy Gruenwald. And something found us. I'll tell you about it.

Cooper's plays often showcase bio- and geoacoustic phenomena, speaking flowers, singing auroras, distortion in the orbit of the earth, exploring what Jacob Smith calls radio's affinity for parables of "dark ecology."[30] Obvious sonic set pieces are often occluded by sounds that exhibit such phenomena. In "Fourble Board," for instance, despite ample opportunities for sound-rich auditory environments of machinery, the play opts for relatively thin backgrounds in its oilfield scenes. We never even hear the much-discussed drill functioning properly, nor any of its attending boilers or machine parts. Organ music reflects events more often than sound effects do, while campfires crackle with greater prominence than the din of traveling block and rotary table.

What would it mean to follow Porky's "geological wonder," as a hint about the voice that the play is setting us up to hear, dredged up sonically from the depths like oil? To really inhabit the rock, oil, bones, and flesh of the play, we'll need a little paleontology, dwelling on Cooper's seemingly inconsequential line about those little shells that were alive when New York was under ice. As it happens, I grew up with dozens of fossilized trilobites in my basement, from my father's days as a paleontologist. **Figure 4.1** is an example called Isotelus Gigas. It comes from the Bobcaygeon formation in the Canadian province of Ontario, encased in about 2.7 kilograms of Ordovician dolomite. It's 475 million years old. When it was alive, it fed on dead fish at the bottom of the ocean and looked like a lobster, with an exoskeleton of chitin, a hard shell-like substance that is similar to human fingernails, and well-developed antennae. Trilobites are unique in the animal kingdom for their stony eyes, the honeycomb lenses of which were made of calcite crystals rather than proteins. This specimen seems to have been buried under mud very soon after death; normally, trilobites are found in pieces. As its flesh decayed after death, the exoskeleton of this specimen formed a thin plane of separation between the sediment below and that above. Over eons, both upper and lower layers hardened into limestone. The exoskeleton vanished, particle by particle, leaving behind only the gap it set between strata of stone, the top half of which was hammered away when the piece was discovered fifty years ago. That's

FIGURE 4.1 Isotelus Gigas, Bobcaygeon formation, Ontario. Discovery and photograph by Harish Verma.

what we see in the image. There isn't a molecule of any trilobite in this stone; there hasn't been any part of that creature here for hundreds of millions of years. In that sense it's not a trilobite at all, just a record of contact with one, preserved by a geologically automated substitution of particles around the periphery of an absence. A body with its insides out, again.

How might such an object help us understand the play and the voice that it is struggling to show us? Certainly the paleontological uncanny gives the setting of the story mystery. I am reminded of Brandon LaBelle's writing on the sound of the ground below us, "a space of creaks and murmurs, a slow shifting of acoustical particles . . . which carry the possibility of threat, danger, and inversion."[31] Cooper's interest in rock is also that of a writer fascinated with physical practices. In an interview in *Writer's Digest* in 1949, Cooper likened his process to bricklaying.[32] That is a good way of considering "The Thing on the Fourble Board," which turns an ephemeral sound—Mike's voice—obdurate, mineralizing her until she is corporeal. If Mike is a sound somewhere out of our earshot, then the work of the play is to construct a body for her. It does so gradually, but not completely. Because she is only a voice—or, more precisely, a set of sounds aggregated around a gap, the play can do no more than form an impression of something not there, something acutely absent, much like Isotelus Gigas. In other words, we can hear the play as an act of "bodying" that requires the unbodying act of sonic fossilization.

The principal events of the play even begin with an act of solidification. It is some twenty years earlier, and Porky is working on a derrick somewhere in the Oxnard Oil Field in Southern California. Having found water down in the bore hole, the crew has decided to cement off the hole, sealing the area so that drilling can resume the next day, and as the waterproof cement sets overnight, Porky stands watch while the rest of the men go to town. We find him making pork chops by a campfire (another Cooper pun, this time about cannibalism). Geologist Billy Gruenwald arrives, sitting down to eat and study some unusual core samples. As Richard Hand has pointed out, we have no illusions as to what will happen to him; having driven all day to the site, his first words are "I'm dead."[33] It's a spatially deep scene. Porky and Billy move from the fixed audioposition of the fire—we are in the fire ourselves—toward the edge of auditory focus, where they speak just frequently enough to give us a fuzzy, darkened sense of "out-thereness." Like boys at camp, the men speak of their deepest fears, Porky of spiders and Billy of the dark. They continue:

BILLY: Hey, turn on the lights, will you Porky?
PORKY: Okay.
BILLY: That's better. I don't like to eat in the dark. [sound of fire] Hey. Didn't you say you were all alone here?
PORKY: Uh huh.
BILLY: I thought I heard somebody talking.
PORKY: I don't see anybody.
BILLY: Sounded like somebody up there on the fourble board.
PORKY: Oh that. That's some of them dog-gone screech owls, I tell you they set you nuts out here. You drive on down the road they set there until you get right on top of them, then they go bloo-loo-loo—
BILLY: Oh, stop it.
PORKY:—Fly up in front of you like a ghost. I remember one time coming up this road one time I was . . .
BILLY: Yeah, yeah. That's what it was all right. (**web. ex. 4.5**)

Porky is overeager to talk, with his deep chuckle, but Billy is unwilling to warm up and engage his penchant for storytelling.

Upon this fire-licked backdrop, and with an auditory hint of sizzling meat, the play resumes constructing the "Thing" in its title. First we hear Gruenwald report the sound of something in the night, but we are provided no sonic illustration to hear ourselves. We hear a second sound attributed to the creature, the ringing of a stand of pipe as it seems to move along the ground spontaneously. This sound is more like the others in the scene—the sounds of the fire, footsteps, coffee cups, voices—on the soundscape of Porky's memory, sounds motivated by iconic codes of resemblance (to use Peirce's terms) to the sounds of physical acts we recognize. Over the next few moments, Porky and Billy puzzle over two items they discover inside the core samples: a filigreed gold ring and what looks like a stone finger embedded in million-year-old strata from a mile underground, a "petrified salami," as Porky calls it. Both men pass out in an alcohol-induced lapse of consciousness, and when Porky awakens from a dream of spiders, he finds Billy dead with a broken neck and the ring missing. Porky hides in Billy's truck until dawn, when the police quite quickly absolve him from blame for the "accident" at the behest of the mine owner Ted, who is eager to have work resume. No sooner has Porky taken up his place on the fourble board than a steel cable is ripped to pieces in front of him by some invisible hand, dropping a giant pipe on Ted. This is the third "appearance" of the creature in the oilfield memory sequence, but unlike the first two—Gruenwald's report, the sound of a moving pipe—this one is marked with music, as the organ illustrates the falling of the pipe when the derrick boss meets his ignoble end, pouring a new kind of sonic identity onto the unvoiced creature.

At the second death, we are told, the whole crew quits. A few days later, Porky returns to the derrick, which he now describes as a desolate skeleton, a kind of fossil itself, "the deadest thing you ever saw." As Porky wanders around the bones of the scene, he sees the gold ring appear as if dropped from an invisible hand, an act sonically illustrated by an organ as in the case of Ted's death. Then, at last, there comes the voice of the creature to fill the gap that the play had opened in its first moments, what Porky describes as "the sound of a kid crying" or of a kitten. Voiced by Cecil H. Roy—known as the "woman of a thousand voices" and familiar to a later generation of cartoon fans as the voice of Caspar, the Friendly Ghost—the creature has a unique prevocal quality, a wide-open crying call, at once intensely human and otherworldly, scream-like but also not a scream, produced through an erratic and jagged wandering across her vocal break. It's a voice of wonder and of pain, a displaced voice unmistakably adult and yet unmastered in its own ascents and depths. Pursued by this voice, Porky runs along the rig, firing a few shots until a final climax of a big reveal, when he grabs a can of red paint and tosses it in the direction of the sound. Here is the scene.

PORKY: Everything was just the way we left it. I looked in at the floor, the smashed traveling block was there alongside the rotary table. There was a

> little mutter of steam from the boiler. That was all. Then I heard a tinkle of something as it hit the ground alongside me. I looked around. There wasn't a soul in sight. But, at my feet was the gold ring that Billy Gruenwald and I had found in the core of rock that came from a mile underground and from a million years ago in time. And I heard a little sound, the sound of a kid crying. [The Thing cries] And there wasn't any kid up there. I heard it again and it came from above my head and I took out my revolver. I loaded it carefully. I started up the ladder to the fourble board. Well, there wasn't anything up there, nothing I could see. [The Thing cries] There was a voice crying, the voice of a little kid. And there was a movement behind the rack of drill pipes and I saw the pipe move and I yelled come out of there, whoever you are! [The Thing cries] Come out or I'll start shooting! Then the stand of pipes shivered and I thought, what can it be that it can handle a heavy pipe like jackstraws? Then, there was a crash. [Sound of pipes crashing] The whole stand of pipe fell over and I just got out of the way in time. And I was alone on the fourble board with the . . . Thing.
>
> But I couldn't see it. [The Thing cries] I felt the platform tremble under my feet again as something moved toward me . . . I fired two or three shots. [Gunshots] And nothing happened. I started backwards. I knew it was following me because I could hear it meowing like a cat. My feet tripped over something. [The Thing cries] I saw it was a big can of red lead that somebody had left up there. Without thinking, I picked it up and I threw it at the sound and it splashed. [Glissando] (**web. ex. 4.6**)
>
> And there it was . . . [The Thing cries] And I wish I I,—I wish . . . The face of a little girl, frightened. Crying with hunger and terror. Hands like a human being. And a finger . . . missing from the left hand. And a body . . . Well, I won't tell you about that. I told you how I'm scared of spiders. But I knew where it came from. It'd come from the bowels of the earth, come riding up on the drill pipe as we yanked it out of the well. Come to an alien world. And was lost. It stood there dripping with red paint, blood-red from head to foot, like some horrible dream. And it put its hand on my arm. Its hand was stone. Living, moving stone. And it looked into my eyes. And mewed like a lost kitten.

The splash is the climax of the main action, breaking the tension of the scene and turning fear of the creature into pity as the narrative rupture of time is also sutured and we return to the present and the "nice home" that Porky shares with his wife. The creature is Maxine/Mike, of course. Extruded violently from a blind world of geotechnical pressures, it's no surprise that Maxine is a chimera, half spider and half child, invisible.

Her auditory construction is also now complete. To summarize: in the opening scene, she was there-before-she-was-there, and surely imagined-before-heard by the listener, who is given no acoustic information at all about her, besides that of aural expectation. Next, in the derrick sequence, our contact with Mike moves from silence to sound, then from sound to music, then from music to voice. All that remains is to move her from retrospective time to the present. And what could accomplish that better than the power of love? Porky concludes the play:

PORKY: Twenty years ago, I discovered many things about it, what it used for food, that it was deaf, that it was invisible and couldn't see people when it was invisible, that if you sprayed it with mud or paint or greasepaint make-up then it could see people. And, believe me, I didn't want to see its body, I can see that in my nightmares. But its face, I can't help wanting to see that pathetic, little girl face. I'm afraid maybe I've fallen . . . Ah, but it's very beautiful, and when it's well made-up, it's . . . But making it up, rubbing greasepaint on a stone face that looks at you and smiles and it makes sounds like a lost kitten . . . yet . . . I can disguise the body in long dresses. She can't hear very well so . . . and she doesn't go out. And when she's hungry, I have to stay out of her way. I found out what she likes to eat, remember? . . .

No, no, sit still. Sit still, do. Sit still or I'll have to shoot you. I want you to meet my wife. Or rather . . . my wife wants to meet you. Mike? Mike? [The Thing cries, approaching] There she is. Come on in, dear. (**web. ex. 4.7**)

It is a masterful delivery, a blend of tenderness and disgust. Each of Porky's thoughts begins with rapturous love and hypnotic wonder with the voice rising and sweetening ("Ah, but it's very beautiful"), then pauses and concludes with revulsion with the voice dropping, the phrase abbreviated ("But making it up"), a pattern of affect that reflects Mike's double existence as both there and not there, both human and monster. In some ways, her presence makes her more difficult to imagine. An aesthetic of void lingers. Even Porky's dialogue is full of gaps, either by evasion ("I won't tell you about that"), euphemism (what it "used for food" rather than "what it ate"), or elliptical omission ("I'm afraid maybe I've fallen . . ."). And how else could it all end, when we return to our close quarters with Porky, and the far-off door to the kitchen opens at last, emitting that same hungry, childlike scream-cry, the play itself turning against us? When Mike meets the mike, we become Mike's meat.

The Face of the Voice

I began this chapter on the two "inside out bodies" of the radio scream, its anatomy and its geology, noting how screaming is a kind of vocal drag for Gregory Whitehead, and now I want to conclude with how the scream undermines Maxine's drag, a detail that also illuminates the role the scream can play in theory of classical radio drama. Why is it, after all, that Maxine becomes available to the play of representation, the ultimate expression of which is Porky's horror/love for her, at precisely the moment she is covered in paint, mud, skirts, and other applied disguises?[34] An answer lies in the hierarchy of her beautiful face and terrible spider-like body. It is in the face, recall, that *signifiance* congeals, where the body becomes "overcoded" for Deleuze and Guattari. If the face "constructs the wall that the signifier needs in order to bounce off of," while also "digging the hole of subjectivity" to which those signifiers are tied, then the fact that she cannot perceive others and others cannot perceive her without the paint makes good sense.[35] The social quality of the process is interesting—Maxine does not simply need makeup in order to *see* (remember the calcite honeycomb eyes of the trilobites), but in order to *see "people."* Maxine needs to be "facialized" (Deleuze and Guattari's term), undergoing a transformation whereby the face can serve as a machine to decode the rest of her physique in the eyes of Porky. By making up her face to be beautiful, Porky provides himself with something that allows him to rationalize and forget the terror of her body. But the constant reapplication of the face hints that the "face-machine" is grotesquely dysfunctional. That's because Porky's facialization does nothing to her *voice*, which twenty years after the main events of "Fourble Board" still issues the same child-cat scream as it devours us. One aspect of the horror of the end of the play is the realization that the creature of the past is aurally identical to that of the present. Porky has grown "old and slow," but she has remained the same. If Maxine's face-drag represents entering into structure, inscription, and visuality, to time, history, and society, her voice-cry represents ongoing resistance to that metamorphosis, an "exposed inside" that remains unruly with intensities, an immaterial thing maintained yet unmastered by excessive materiality.

The last section argued that dressing up an absence is what the play itself sets out to do, layering audio around the periphery of a gap as unrepresentable just as the body of a half-billion-year-old trilobite is irrecoverable. But we can press the matter still further, from Maxine and "The Thing on the Fourble Board" to the recording (through which we must move in order to come to know them). After all, Maxine's makeup (and mike-up) aren't the only encrustations that we have heard. Indeed, in order to hear this play at all, we've had to dig with our ears through generations of recordings between 1948 and today. Listen to the clips I have selected, drawn from the most commonly available Mp3 of "The Thing on the Fourble Board," and you can hear various moments in the history of preserving this track in a number of surface noises, beginning with the mark of a lacquer disc as it was first recorded (the announcer points out it was "brought to you by transcription"), then a tape of some kind (there are one or two moments of hiss), perhaps a vinyl record—it seems you can hear the dust in the grooves—and also now an Mp3, with its nagging compression artifacts peppering the audio with odd chirps. Ignore its narrative entirely and "The Thing on the Fourble Board" remains a sonic geology of audio media forms aimed at capturing something impermanent, a kind of "core sample." Unlike most modern forms of audio, radio plays are not created with the logic of inscription in mind; they are designed to vanish after dissemination rather than be recorded. But recorded they are, and so today radio plays have become the fossilized invertebrates in the family tree of media. This fact is brought home by the process our ears need to dig through to get at the scream by way of glitches that make lost sounds reachable and enrich the original broadcast with residues of histories that they interpose in the process of remediation.[36]

Like Mike's voice, "The Thing on the Fourble Board" is itself an unstable immateriality, the sum of pressures and textures introduced across time and media by anonymous forces. In remediating this episode again and again through successive formats, fans and critics are doing just what Porky does with greasepaint, and for the same reason—love and horror—throwing splashes of material at a transfixing ungraspable voice, from which it all eventually oozes away. Voices can't be turned into faces in Deleuze and Guattari's sense, yet we keep trying; like Porky, we can't help ourselves, and the logic of that compulsion becomes a rule unto itself. What I'm getting at is a double experience of listening to the piece, one that only emerges nowadays and through engagement with the scream. On the one hand, as listeners we are led off in pursuit of the play as a "sound object" in Pierre Schaeffer's sense, delightedly ignoring the source of emanation and even Wyllis Cooper's craft, so that we may enjoy what seems to be a free projection in our mind. Frances Dyson has described this sort of listening as a drive to "suspend the instrumentality of audio, projecting it beyond the determinations of technology and media culture into a peculiarly transcendent space."[37] As Seth Kim-Cohen has it, "Schaeffer's method, his aesthetic, relies on a disarming or suspending of semiotic activity in the listening experience."[38] But on the other hand, even as we pursue that utopia, the intervention of the marks of recording draws us back again and again to the pitted surface of the medium and to its material history as a rerecording, as a "thing" in Bill Brown's sense, something drawn down from transcendent space and into marred and damaged artifacts and the social and technological relationships that they capture.[39] The relation of Maxine's body to her face is like "The Thing on the Fourble Board's" double existence as intangible radio and tangible recording. Follow the line of Maxine's cry, and you arrive at an account of radio's strange inside-outness, its indeterminate media aesthetics forever shuffling between exposure and concealment of the conditions of its persisting existence through haphazard remediation. By aging in this way, "The Thing on the Fourble Board" has at last caught up to its subject matter, to what's thingly about the scream of The Thing.

Notes

1. Gregory Whitehead, "Pressures of the Unspeakable" (October 29, 2012), available at https://gregorywhitehead.net/2012/10/29/pressures-of-the-unspeakable/, accessed June 10, 2016. On *The Listening Room*, see Colin Black, "A Brief Review of Australian Radio Art," *Sounding Out! The Sound Studies Blog* (December 4, 2014), available at https://soundstudiesblog.com/2014/12/04/a-brief-review-of-australian-radio-art/, accessed June 10, 2016.

2. Allen S. Weiss, *Phantasmic Radio* (Durham, NC: Duke University Press, 1995), 84.

3. Whitehead, "Pressures of the Unspeakable." This is my own transcription, as are all others in this chapter.

4. Mladen Dolar, *A Voice and Nothing More* (Cambridge, MA: MIT Press, 2006), 27–29.

5. For an early version of the second part of this chapter, see Neil Verma, "A Paleontology of Quiet," *Journal of Sonic Studies* 6 (2014). I thank Marcel Cobussen and the reviewers for their help with that.

6. The term "media fossilization" is also used by Parikka, but in a different way, exploring the geological origins and destinies of media. See Jussi Parikka, *A Geology of Media* (Minneapolis: University of Minnesota Press, 2015).

7. Orson Welles makes this memorable remark in the preamble to "The Hitch-Hiker" on *Suspense* (1942).

8. See Robert L. Mott, *Sound Effects: Radio, TV, and Film* (Boston: Focal Press, 1990).

9. See, for example, Erik Barnouw, *Handbook of Radio Writing: An Outline of Techniques and Markets in Radio Writing in the United States*, 2nd ed. (Boston: Little, Brown and Co., 1947), 27–80; and Richard J. Hand and Mary Traynor, *The Radio Drama Handbook* (New York: Continuum, 2011), 40–68.

10. Douglas Kahn, *Noise, Water, Meat: A History of Sound in the Arts* (Cambridge, MA: MIT Press, 2001), 345–46.

11. Michel Chion, *Film, A Sound Art* (New York: Columbia University Press, 2009), 337–38.

12. On these arrangements, see Earle McGill, *Radio Directing* (New York: McGraw-Hill, 1940), 115–44.

13. Orson Welles and Howard Koch, "The War of the Worlds" (1938).

14. Lucille Fletcher, "Sorry, Wrong Number" (1943).

15. Lucille Fletcher, *Sorry Wrong Number and The Hitch-Hiker* (New York: Dramatists Play Service, 1998), 21.

16. Arch Oboler, "The Dark" (airdate unknown, ca. 1940s).

17. Roland Barthes, "The Grain of the Voice," *Image, Music, Text*, trans. Stephen Heath (New York: Noonday Press, 1977), 179–89.

18. Adriana Cavarero, *For More Than One Voice: Toward a Philosophy of Vocal Expression*, trans. Paul A. Kottman (Stanford, CA: Stanford University Press, 2005), 4.

19. Antonin Artaud, "To Have Done with the Judgment of God" (unaired, 1947), available at Ubuweb, http://www.ubu.com/sound/artaud.html, accessed September 12, 2016.

20. Deleuze first adopts the term in Gilles Deleuze, *The Logic of Sense*, ed. Constantin V. Boundas, trans. Mark Lester with Charles Stivale (New York: Columbia University Press, 1993), 83–89.

21. Gilles Deleuze and Felix Guattari, *A Thousand Plateaus: Capitalism and Schizophrenia*, trans. Brian Massumi (Minneapolis: University of Minnesota Press, 1987), 151.

22. Weiss, *Phantasmic Radio*, 8–34.

23. Kahn, *Noise, Water, Meat*, 348.

24. Antonin Artaud, *Selected Writings*, ed. Susan Sontag (Berkeley: University of California Press, 1988), 571; Gregory Whitehead, "The Forensic Theatre: Memory Plays for the Post-Mortem Condition," *Performing Arts Journal* 35/36 (1990): 109.

25. Weiss, *Phantasmic Radio*, 24.

26. Michel Chion, *The Voice in Cinema*, trans. Claudia Gorbman (New York: Columbia University Press, 1999), 77.

27. Wyllis Cooper, "The Thing on the Fourble Board" (1948).

28. The ad ran in *Variety* (February 4, 1948: 45).

29. John Crosby, "Both Mediums Will Miss This Talented Artist," *Washington Post* (July 27, 1955).

30. Jacob Smith, *Eco-Sonic Media* (Berkeley: University of California Press, 2015), 110–41.

31. Brandon LaBelle, *Acoustic Territories: Sound Culture and Everyday Life* (New York: Bloomsbury Academic, 2010), 5.

32. Harriet Cannon, "Wyllis Cooper's *Quiet, Please*," *Writer's Digest* (May 1949).

33. Richard J. Hand, *Terror on the Air: Horror Radio in America, 1931–1952* (Jefferson, NC: McFarland & Co., 2006), 154.

34. My thanks to James Chandler for pointing out the importance of this question to me.

35. Deleuze and Guattari, *A Thousand Plateaus*, 167–91.

36. This section concludes some thoughts about the mineralization of radio from my book: Neil Verma, *Theater of the Mind: Imagination, Aesthetics, and American Radio Drama* (Chicago: University of Chicago Press, 2012), 225–29.

37. Pierre Schaeffer, "Acousmatics," in *Audio Culture: Readings in Modern Music*, ed. Christoph Cox and Daniel Warner (New York: Continuum, 2004), 76–81; and Frances Dyson, *Sounding New Media: Immersion and Embodiment in the Arts and Culture* (Berkeley: University of California Press), 55.

38. Seth Kim-Cohen, *In the Blink of an Ear: Toward a Non-cochlear Sonic Art* (New York: Bloomsbury, 2010), 12.

39. Bill Brown, "Thing Theory," *Critical Inquiry* 28 (2001): 1–22.

PART III

Vocal Owners and Borrowed Voices

5

It's All by Someone Else

ROBERT POLITO

Voice, at least as voice insinuates itself in, through, and around poetry, poems, and poets, can seem either so simple as to mock explanation, or such an intricate magic trick that no explanation will untangle the riddles. In his Baedecker, *The Sounds of Poetry*, Robert Pinsky speaks for many poets—and note at the outset how readily and inevitably one slips into vocal idioms, such as "speaks for," when invoking poetry (and "in-voke": there's another one); Pinsky speaks for many poets when he writes, "The theory of this guide is that poetry is a vocal, which is to say a bodily, art. The medium of poetry is a human body: the column of air inside the chest, shaped into signifying sounds in the larynx and the mouth. In this sense, poetry is just as physical or bodily an art as dancing."[1]

Pinsky's formulation looks matter-of-fact, even mechanical, until you register that he is not intending so much the poet's body as a reader's. "In poetry," he continues, "the medium is the audience's body. When I say to myself a poem by Emily Dickinson or George Herbert, the artist's medium is my breath. The reader's breath and hearing embody the poet's words. This makes the art physical, intimate, vocal, and individual." Here we slide surprisingly, precipitously, from the matter-of-fact into the phantasmagoric, shadowing the implicit, and (again) perhaps inevitable puns inside "medium" and "embody," until we arrive at something approximating poetic voice as demonic possession: "The artist's medium is my breath."[2]

Edward Hirsch in *A Poet's Glossary* originates poetry also in voice and the body. As he opens his entry on voice, "The human voice—the sound produced by the vocal organs, our ability to produce such sounds—is the instrument of poetry. Poetry is made out of sound. It comes out of silence and ends in silence. It emerges from the body. The range of the human voice is great—from the lowest murmur to the loudest shout, from chanting to singing. Human beings are speaking animals and we speak because we are not alone. Speech is social, language is collective. The first poetry is oral poetry. . . ."[3]

As Hirsch edges from voice, sound, and the body (voice as instrument, sound as material, body as source) into intimations of culture and history, his words accrue resonances past the physical or factual—and he proceeds to a second, and figurative, dimension of voice: "Voice is found in both speaking and writing," he writes, "but the very nature of voice in written poetry must be metaphorical, it cannot be literal." Voice in this sense involves an authorial signature, and critical shorthand. "Critics speak of 'the voice' in a poem to mean its characteristic sound, style, manner, and tone, its implied attitude. To speak of 'a poet's voice' then becomes a metaphor for his or her distinctive way of speaking." Voice for Hirsch, much as for Pinsky, shades as well into possession, animism, and ventriloquism—"When you recite a poem aloud . . . your own voice becomes its instrument," he proposes, "the mechanism, by which it comes alive. The poem voices itself through you."[4]

Readers of late twentieth-century poems will know already that for all their complications, divergences, and slipperiness, Pinsky and Hirsch occupy only sequences along the vaster contemporary voice continuum—and that few notions in poetry were (and somewhat remain) as intensively argued as voice. Critic Marjorie Perloff summarized in 1998, "One of the cardinal principles—perhaps the cardinal principle—of American Language poetics (as of the related current in England usually labeled 'linguistically innovative poetries') has been the dismissal of 'voice' as the foundational principle of lyric poetry."[5] Charles Bernstein, one of the poets Perloff was recalling, along with Lyn Hejinian, Ron Silliman, Bob Perelman, Susan Howe, and J. H. Prynne, among others, observed in an interview:

> The question that always interested me was how could language be made more conscious of itself, a question of the making audible of knowledge otherwise unreflected or unconscious. This making audible being the music of the poem. *Voice* has seemed the most obvious way of avoiding this, since it is inextricably tied up with the organizing of the poem along psychological parameters. Unlike terms such as *limit* and *measure*, voice becomes a self-constituting project, both from an external categorizing point of view and from an internal compositional one. To try to unify the style of work around this notion of self is to take the writing to be not only reductively autobiographical in trying to define the *sound* of me but also to accept that the creation of a persona is somehow central to writing poetry. I say reductive because any characteristic ordering of language that creates a sense of voice is very much a construction out of a horizon of possibilities. I don't have *a* voice; though I can create

> a consistent stylistic voice in writing, or let some habitual pattern bleed in from, for example, speech, and call that voice. . . . So I don't want to enfold the variety of language I use into the category of voice. . . . As many others have pointed out, a poem exists in a matrix of social and historical relations that are more significant to the formulation of an individual text than any personal qualities of the life or voice of an author.[6]

If Pinsky and Hirsch seemed initially to summon a rendition of voice for poetry that Bernstein might promptly cashier as "reductively autobiographical," only then to subvert biography via psychic ventriloquism and vocal possession, Bernstein's statements reverse that sly narrative arc: a subversion of biography, personality, and persona sustained by distinctive, personalizing, and "self-constituting" diction, syntax, and gestures ("The question that always interested me. . . . I say reductive because . . . I do not have *a* voice").

One hardly inclines to minimize the complex aesthetic trajectory along which poets as divergent as Pinsky, Hirsch, and Bernstein write and situate their poems, and perhaps we are only mapping, as I mentioned at the outset, chronic enigmas of voice in poetry. The account of voice in the *Princeton Encyclopedia of Poetry and Poetics*, for instance, valiantly just surrenders the field: "Regardless of how much one insists that writing is not speaking and that voice is not literally present in the poem, literary critics have persistently relied on metaphors of voice to analyze writing; it is difficult to imagine how one would go about discussing poetry in particular if we were forbidden to use the terms voice, speaker, and other vocal terms like monologue or song."

When for Pinsky, Hirsch, and Bernstein voice (in its many senses) intersects, or collides with medium (also in its many senses), I'm reminded of one of my favorite moments in silent film, the trial scene in Tod Browning's *The Unholy Three* (1925). A sideshow trio—Tweedledee, Hercules, and Professor Echo—stage a burglary ring out of O'Grady's Bird Store. Their M.O.—rich people purchase chatty, flattering parrots, or at least they talk in the shop, when ventriloquist Echo, disguised as Mrs. O'Grady, throws his voice into their cages. Once the birds are home, and intractably silent, the owners phone in confusion, and Mrs. O'Grady, her strongman son-in-law, and charming baby grandchild, Little Willie (aka Tweedledee—as the carny spieler tagged him: "Twenty Inches! Twenty Years! Twenty Pounds! The Twentieth Century Curiosity!"), visit the contrary parrot to case the mansion for robbery later that night. After Tweedledee and Hercules carelessly kill a wealthy Mr. Arlington, the O'Grady gang pin the murder on the shop's clueless manager, Hector, conveniently also Echo's romantic rival for pickpocket Rosie O'Grady. When Rosie promises to marry Echo if he saves Hector from conviction, the ventriloquist joins the crowd in the courtroom. He passes Hector a note, asking him to take the witness stand, and once there to repeat the "Our Father" over and over. Whereupon, Echo then tries to explain away the whole convoluted and nasty setup by tossing his voice to the front of the courtroom, as though Hector himself were testifying.

Echo fails, and only as himself can convince the court. But this plangent, frustrating, and bravura silent film about a ventriloquist, a film everywhere steeped in vocal teasers, such as animal mimicry, a relentless carnival barker, and loudly alliterative intertitles, constitutes a sort of test case for voice and the cinematic medium: an instance of what art historian T. J. Clark styles "limit cases," or situations of acute exemplification within a particular art.[7]

For me, probably the most provocative, poignant, and exhilarating limit case for voice in modern poetry is *The Changing Light at Sandover*, James Merrill's monumental (560-page) poem of communications over a Ouija board. A trilogy—"The Book of Ephraim" (1976), *Mirabell: Books of Number* (1978), and *Scripts for the Pageant* (1980)—Merrill's Holy Three were collected into a single volume, along with a careering coda, in 1982.[8] All great poems, whatever else they involve, ultimately shape a conversation with the dead, and the conversations in *Sandover* spanned recently dead friends, such as W. H. Auden and Maria Mitsotaki, the angels Michael and Gabriel, a God Biology, and even some twilight subatomic particles disguised as vestigial, unisexual bats.

As a limit case, Merrill's poem bristles with questions. If voice is physical, does it matter if the voices arise not from a "column of air" but a gyrating cup? If voice is metaphor, aren't the voices Merrill transcribes at the board metaphors twice-removed, nesting dolls inside his own nesting doll? And if voice is a hackneyed, reductive cheat, and no poet has "*a* voice," what about the revelation deep into *Sandover* that voices are intrinsically "composite" and achieved by "cloning" through an otherworldly Research Lab, so that, as we shall see, Rimbaud "ghostwrote" *The Waste Land*?

Voices as ghosts; cloned poetry—this isn't exactly where James Merrill started out as a lyric poet, a student of Reuben Brower's at Amherst College in the early 1940s. Merrill wrote his undergraduate thesis on Proust under Brower's supervision—so successfully that the professor quoted his former student twice five years later in *The Fields of Light*, the elegant "experiment in critical reading" he published out of his literature courses. At the outset of a chapter on "The Speaking Voice," Brower cites Robert Frost—"Everything written is as good as it is dramatic"; and he goes on to assert that "Every poem is 'dramatic' in Frost's sense: someone is speaking to someone else."[9] Writing about voice in poems by Frost, Keats, and Pope, a play by Shakespeare, and novels by Woolf, Austen, and Forster, Brower concentrated, as Merrill would, on tone: "we hear the drama through the voice—or voices. . . . Our whole aim in analysis of tone is to delineate the exact speaking voice in every poem we read, but we can succeed only by attending to the special, often minute language signs by which the poet fixes the tone for us."[10] Merrill's lyric poems, early and late, manifest such cunning tonal control, and a conspicuous formal mastery of "special, often minute language signs," that Brower's chapter titles for *The Fields of Light* might have been minted to describe them: "The Aura Around a Bright Clear Center," "Saying One Thing and Meaning Another," "The Mirror of Analogy," "Something Central Which Permeated," and "The Twilight of the Double Vision." *Sandover*, too, devises as resourceful, intricate, and resonant an echo chamber as any iconic symbolist or modernist work, reeling off sonnets, villanelles, Spenserian stanzas, Rubiat quatrains, terza rima, Anglo Saxon alliterative meter, and a stunning canzone. Yet *Sandover* also disposes a sustained dismantling of a lyric voice.

"Admittedly I err," Merrill confesses in the opening line—"err" designating the full enterprise, even that oblique, offhand entrance point, as a mistake: "err" as in fail, miss, go astray; but "err," moreover, as in wander, ramble, digress, or stray. Early on, and throughout "The Book of Ephraim," Merrill steadily signals his resistance of these Ouija board voices—he encourages a reader, for instance, to view his encounters with Ephraim & Co. as merely allegory for his relationship with David Jackson: "folie à deux," his ex-psychiatrist tags it. He embeds synopses of his lost novel about the other world, including his failed aspirations to craft an "anonymous," fable-like tone for it—so that for the poem he appears now to have no choice but to resume his familiar lyric voice: "and I alone was left / To tell my story" (4).

Such words are at once camouflage, clue, and guide. For how "alone" is Merrill here as poet, as speaker? Pulsating on a double allusion, Ishmael on top of Job, the Bible by way of *Moby-Dick*, his elaborately candid admission—"and I alone was left / To tell my story"—enacts the drama of self and other that is decisive to "The Book of Ephraim" and the whole of *Sandover*. "Imbued with otherness," Merrill will marvel of his Ouija board voices—and his own—by the end of "The Book of Ephraim," where he writes:

> And here was I, or what was left of me.
> Feared and rejoiced in, chafed against, held cheap,
> A strangeness that was us, and was not, had
> All the same allowed for its description,
> And so brought at least me these spells of odd,
> Self-effacing balance. Better to stop
> While we still can. Already I take up

Less emotional space than a snowdrop.
My father in his last illness complained
Of the effect of medication on
His real self—today Bluebeard, tomorrow
Babbitt. Young Chameleon, I used to
Ask how on earth one got sufficiently
Imbued with otherness. And now I see.

(89)

Later in *Mirabell*, W. H. Auden, over the Ouija board, will formalize this as the "stripping process"—"EACH IN TURN STRIPPED REDUCED TO ESSENCES JOINED TO INFINITY" (209). Across "The Book of Ephraim," Merrill tracks many routes of attrition ("what was left of me") and expansion ("a strangeness that was us, and was not") to his recasting of Keats's "chameleon poet." One of the most ingenious embraces his friendship in this world and the next with filmmaker Maya Deren. "Arguably the most important and innovative avant-garde filmmaker in the history of American cinema"—as the publicity for *In the Mirror of Maya Deren*, a 2003 documentary about her, neatly summarizes—Deren during the 1940s created nearly all of the short experimental films that assured her reputation: *Meshes of the Afternoon* (1943), *At Land* (1944), *A Study in Choreography for Camera* (1945), *Ritual in Transfigured Time* (1946), and *Meditation on Violence* (1948). As early as 1947, she also started shooting footage for a very different style of film—a documentary about Voodoo rituals and spirit possession in Haiti, *Divine Horsemen*, which only was completed posthumously by her third husband, the composer Teiji Ito, with the financial support of James Merrill. (In 1953, Deren published a book about Haiti—also titled *Divine Horsemen*.)

Merrill helped fund Deren's experimental films, too, and served on the board of her Creative Film Foundation. They met in 1946 through Merrill's first lover, Kimon Friar, a poet, a translator, and (when Merrill as a student first knew him) an instructor at Amherst College. Friar displayed a still from Deren's *Meshes of the Afternoon* in his Amherst rooms—"Maya (Medusa)," as she signed it on the back to him. (Friar, according to Merrill biographer Langdon Hammer, "was obsessed with the myth of Medusa.")[11]

For *The Changing Light at Sandover*, Merrill recurrently summons Deren—her experimental films, as well as *Divine Horsemen*. Viewed dramatically, *Sandover* is a succession of recognition scenes. JM, as he styles and distances himself for the poem, uncovers aspects of himself by observing friends and mentors: W. H. Auden, Maria Mitsotaki, and Deren. She is both a personal and an artistic guide. Her Haitian documentary instructs him on how to handle (as he writes) "gusts of material so violent / As to put out the candle held to them by mere imagination" (304–5). Her experimental films help him shape and structure his poem.

Merrill introduces Deren formally in Section D ("Dramatis Personae"), his wry epithets ("doyenne of our / American experimental film") intermingled among dates, credits, and gossip. Her cinematic dream about Ephraim dominates Section M, as anecdote veers into art:

> This dream, [Ephraim] blandly adds, is a low-budget
> Remake—imagine—of the *Paradiso.*
> Not otherwise its poet toured the spheres
> While Someone very highly placed up there,
> Donning his bonnet, in and out through that
> Now famous nose haled the cool Tuscan night.
> The resulting masterpiece takes years to write;
> More, since the dogma of its day
> Calls for a Purgatory, for a Hell,
> Both of which Dante thereupon, from footage
> Too dim or private to expose, invents.
> His Heaven, though, as one cannot but sense,
> Tercet by tercet, is pure Show and Tell.
>
> (Film buffs may recall the closing scene
> Of Maya's "Ritual in Transfigured Time." . . .)
>
> (45)

Earlier, in Section G of "The Book of Ephraim," Deren visited JM and DJ at their home in Stonington, CT, and burned a heart-emblem of Erzulie on their threshold. As for M: Have rhyming couplets ever so stealthily insinuated themselves into twentieth-century domesticity?—a domestic scene, moreover, pitched, as Merrill remarks, on such "unsteady ground, Earth, Heaven; / Reality, Projection." During her dream, Maya is "a girl again," "a not yet / Printed self"—or a "phosphorescent negative," as in *Ritual in Transfigured Time.* But is this even Maya's dream—any more than, say, the *Paradiso* is here Dante's poem? The dream is notably silent—but as during *The Unholy Three*, voice is implicit: in Ephraim's interstitial uppercase phrases and lines, Merrill's rhyming précis, and his wily stage direction: "Suavities / Of early talking pictures, although no / Word is spoken." When, at the conclusion of M, JM returns to his work, here the lost prose novel inside "The Book of Ephraim" that I mentioned before, his voice is (like Maya's dream) "transferred"—and "imbued" with all he has just experienced and heard: Deren, Dante, and Ephraim.

Section R, set soon after Deren's death in 1961, disposes a memorial sonnet cycle that mixes in her voice, monologue and self shading into dialogue and other. Here is Maya, from the third of five sonnets:

DAVID JIMMY I AM YOUNG AT LAST
WHO ALL THESE YEARS TRIED TO APPEAR SO
MY HAIR IS TRULY RED   EPHRAIM IS STILL
A COURTIER   SHALL I TEACH HIM HOW TO CHACHA

THE CLIMBERS HERE COUNT & RECOUNT THEIR PAST
LIVES   POOR ME WITH ONLY ONE   BUT O
I NUMBER LOVES ON TOES AND FINGERS   TELL
TEIJI (her young husband) IM A CHESHIRE

CAT ALL SMILES   I LOVE MY WORK   ST LUCY
The St Lucy? SHES MY BOSS   IS LETTING
ME DIRECT SOME AVANTGARDE HALLUCI

NATIONS FOR HEADS OF STATE
U SHD HEAR THEM MOAN & FEEL THEM SWEATING
WE GIRLS HAVE STOPPED A WAR WITH CUBA Great!

(64)

Even before her death, we recognize how thoroughly Deren possessed him. As he visits her in the hospital, it's almost as if he's suffered the stroke that separated himself from Maya, or from the Maya inside him: "Here I'm divided." The hints of menace at the end of Section R—"the good gray medium / Blankly uttering someone else's threat"—devastatingly merge a warning JM and DJ hear from Ephraim about the dangers of atomic power and the Good Gray Poet Walt Whitman's "Song of Myself."

Menace looms over *Mirabell*, the second book of the trilogy, and deep into *Scripts for the Pageant*, the third. The "voices" now dictating to JM and DJ no longer identify themselves as formerly among the living, at least living humans, but as speaking from inside the negative potential of the atom, or as the sons of Cain. The Ouija transcriptions hovering behind *Sandover* confront the lyric mode with an insistent polyvocality that disdains the authority of any single human voice, and could not be more inimical to the virtuosity of previous Merrill:

THESE NAMES YOU UNDERSTAND
ARE CHILDRENS NAMES FOR THE WHITE FORCES   & OUR NAMES   BEZ
WE
HAD NO NAMES   THEY ARE THE INVENTION OF THE SCRIBE & SO
THE STORY TAKES FORM   BUT WORDS CANNOT DESCRIBE
THE FRANTIC

ACTION OF THE ATOM BLACK & WHITE AS IT OPERATES
I SAID B4 WE SOARD ALL LIFE S O A R D & THERE WAS NO DEATH
AND THEN ONE ATOM TOO MANY WE WANTED MORE THE BLACK
LIGHT ON OUR EYELIDS OUR BLINDNESS OUR ARROGANCE WE CHOSE
TO MOVE ON INTO SPACE ABANDONING THE WORLD WE ROSE
THE CRUST LIKE A VEIL SHREDDED FAR BEHIND US EXPOSING
THE ALREADY ARID EARTH WE DESPISD IT & FLUNG BACK
A LAST BOLT & THE UNIVERSE FELL IN ON US W E F E L L

(120)

As Frank Bidart once said, "I remember when I first heard the demanding, obsessive, unappeased voices of the 'sons of Cain' in *Mirabell*—it seemed as if Merrill had let in the static of the universe."[12] These subatomic particles, alternately known as the bat-angels, preside over the Research Lab, where sometimes between lives, other times during a life, souls are reprocessed and cloned. This cloning also leads to new poems. Here we can catch some of the dynamic—and, in turn, catch some of Merrill's prosody as through juxtapositions of typography and meter, earthly and otherworldly speakers clash and converge, and the rough pentameter of human actors skids into and blends with the five stresses of Mirabell's syllabics:

NO MAN CAN REACH 3 DIRECTLY. TSE HAD
A NUMBER FROM OUR ORDERS AR HAD THAT SAME NUMBER
POINT ONE THUS YEATS & DJ TSE DOWN ON CERTAIN
SUPERSTITIOUS SCRIBES WE HAD TO APPOINT RIMBAUD HE WROTE
THE WASTE LAND WE FED IT INTO THE LIKE-CLONED ELIOT
And Uncle Ezra?
AS IN SHAKESPEARE WE LET THE CASE REST ON A POUND OF FLESH
Thank you, that will do.
NO JM FOR THE (M) OUNCE OF FLESH U CAN CLAIM AS YRS
LIVES BY THESE FREQUENT CONTACTS WITH YR OWN & OTHERS' WORK
Still, Eliot thought he thought his poem up;
It wasn't spelt out for him by a cup.
Dante and Milton didn't seem to need
Guidance for each scrap of revelation.
DANTE DID INDEED.
Receive dictation?
NO BUT SAT & LISTEND FOR 8 YEARS
TO A MENDICANT PRIEST DEFROCKD FOR IT HAD BEENTHOUGHT HE
SPOKE WITH DEVILS GUESS WHO?
DJ: 80098.
A PLUS

(219)

Across a checkered diction that confounds slang and abstraction, conversation and concision, comic hubbub and vision, Merrill arrives at a recasting of voice as indistinguishable from listening. As he noted in his *Paris Review* interview: "Just as I love multiple meanings, I try for contrasts and disruptions of tone. . . . . Voice in its fullest tonal range—not just bel canto or passionate speech."[13]

The poet Delmore Schwartz, in his essay "T. S. Eliot's Voice and His Voices," observed what he called "sibylline listening"—Eliot's poems, he wrote, "are often dominated by a listening to other voices—the voices of other poets, in other centuries and countries; the voices of various human beings of differing classes and stations in society, a diversity of beliefs, values, habits of speech, and views of life. . . . often the actual substance of a passage is first of all a listening or a quoting. . . . The method of sibylline or subliminal listening must seem, at first glance, no method at all precisely because it is the method which permits all other methods to be used freely and without predetermination; and which allows no particular method to interfere with the quintessential receptivity which opens itself up to any and all kinds of material and subject matter."[14]

Sibylline listening—that "quintessential receptivity"—is axial to *Sandover*. By means of sibylline listening, Merrill might "reach," as he put it in that *Paris Review* interview, "the 'god' within you." As he said there—"Well, don't you think there comes a time when everyone, not just a poet, wants to get beyond the Self? To reach, if you like, the 'god' within you? The board, in however clumsy or absurd a way, allows for precisely that. Or if it's still yourself that you're drawing upon, then that self is much stranger and freer and more far-seeing than the one you thought you knew. Of course there are disciplines with grander pedigrees and similar goals. The board happens to be ours. I've stopped, by the way, recommending it to inquisitive friends."

As Merrill focuses a speech by W. H. Auden on the self in art from the last book of *Mirabell*:

> THINK WHAT A MINOR
> PART THE SELF PLAYS IN A WORK OF ART
> COMPARED TO THOSE GREAT GIVENS THE ROSEBRICK MANOR
> ALL TOPIARY FORMS & METRICAL
> MOAT ARIPPLE! FROM ANTHOLOGIZED
> PERENNIALS TO HERB GARDEN OF CLICHES
> FROM LATIN-LABELED HYBRIDS TO THE FAWN
> 4 LETTER FUNGI THAT ENRICH THE LAWN,
> IS NOT ARCADIA TO DWELL AMONG
> GREENWOOD PERSPECTIVES OF THE MOTHER TONGUE

ROOTSYSTEMS UNDERFOOT WHILE OVERHEAD
THE SUN GOD SANG & SHADES OF MEANING SPREAD
& FAR SNOWCAPPED ABSTRACTIONS GLITTERED NEAR
OR FAIRLY MELTED INTO ATMOSPHERE?

(262)

Here Auden, incidentally, anticipates Charles Bernstein and Marjorie Perloff. Does it matter, matter for sibylline listening, that Merrill wrote Auden's speech himself, rather than taking down dictation? As he told me, when I interviewed him about *Sandover* in 1990, "There are only a few places where I presume to pass 'my own words' off as a message from the other world. The showiest is Wystan's evocation of the manor house (*Mirabell*, 9.1). It came welling up from me one afternoon, instead of from the Board. I never again felt so 'possessed.' "[15]

Possessed, and this is where I'll conclude, sends us back to Maya Deren, and a Deren moment late in *Scripts for the Pageant*. JM and DJ learn that her Haitian footage—*Divine Horsemen*—is showing in Venice, near where they are visiting. Written in Dante's terza rima—one of three parallel terza rima sequences across the trilogy, all ending, much as each of the three canticas of the Commedia, on the word "stars." Another Holy Three. Merrill moves in and out of the film:

Until it happens. Ghédé with his cane,
Smoked glasses and top hat struts avenues
No one else sees. Through flurries of cocaine

The youth he's mounted sizzles like a fuse.
A woman pitches, is held up, advances
Pale and contorted—but it's Maya! (Who's

Holding the camera?) Next we know, her trance has
Deepened, she is combed, perfumed and dressed
In snowy lace, beaming at who she fancies.

The frown, flood of tears, and all the rest
Will have been cut, or never filmed. Delight
Alone informs her dance, unself-possessed.

Partner by partner, David's face goes white:
We are the ghosts, *hers* the ongoing party
At which she was received one summer night

(How many years ago now, twenty? thirty?)
Into the troupe, glow worm and lunar crescent,
That whole supreme commedia dell' arte

Which takes a twinkling skull for reminiscent
Theatre, and soul for master negative.
It's Maya dancing. She is here and isn't,

Her darks print out as bright, her dying so live
—Do they? In Venice's uncomprehending
Eyes? Painful to think, hard to forgive

What "today" makes, what "Paradise" impending
Will, if a trace remains, of . . . let that be.
One last shot: dawn, the bare beach. "Happy ending?"

Smiles DJ as we link arms, tacitly
Skipping the futuristic coffee-bar's
Debate already under way (ah, me)

On the confusing terms: Dance, Gods, Time, Stars.

(505–6)

"*We* are the ghosts, *hers* the ongoing party. . . ." At the conclusion of his "Coda," Merrill circles back to the start of *Sandover*, and also to the dynamics of voice, as he reads aloud the completed poem to an assembled audience of the dead and living, "Human and otherwise" (3).

"For *their* ears I begin: 'Admittedly. . . .'" (560) If vocalizing "the 'god' within you" is one gift of sibylline listening, Merrill never forgets the costs of that stripping process. As JM earlier quoted DJ: "It's almost as if *we* were the dead / And signaling to dear ones in the world. . . . We're the dead" (361).

Notes

1. Robert Pinsky, *The Sounds of Poetry: A Brief Guide* (New York: Farrar, Straus & Giroux, 1998), 7.

2. Pinsky, *The Sounds of Poetry*, 8.

3. Edward Hirsch, *A Poet's Glossary* (Boston: Houghton Mifflin Harcourt, 2014), 686.

4. Hirsch, *A Poet's Glossary*, 687.

5. Marjorie Perloff, "Language Poetry and the Lyric Subject: Ron Silliman's Albany and Susan Howe's Buffalo," *Critical Inquiry* 25, no. 3 (Spring 1999): 405.

6. Charles Bernstein, *Dream* (Evanston, IL: Northwestern University Press, 2001), 407–8.

7. T. J. Clark, *Farewell to an Idea: Episodes from a History of Modernism* (New Haven, CT: Yale University Press, 1999), 7.

8. James Merrill, *The Changing Light at Sandover* (New York: Atheneum, 1982).

9. Reuben Arthur Brower, *The Fields of Light* (New York: Oxford University Press, 1951), 19.

10. Brower, *The Fields of Light*, 29.

11. Langdon Hammer, *James Merrill: Life and Art* (New York: Knopf, 2015), 93.

12. Frank Bidart introduced James Merrill in a reading for *Ploughshares* in the summer of 1980.

13. J. D. McClatchy and James Merrill, "The Art of Poetry XXXI," *Paris Review* 24 (Summer 1982): 185–219.

14. Delmore Schwartz, "T. S. Eliot's Voice and His Voices," in *The Selected Essays of Delmore Schwartz*, ed. Donald A. Dike and David H. Zucker (Chicago: University of Chicago Press, 1970), 135 and 138.

15. James Merrill and Robert Polito, "*The Changing Light at Sandover*: A Conversation with James Merrill," in *Pequod* 31 (1990): 11.

6

The Artist's Impression: Ethel Waters as Mimic

LAURIE STRAS

The relationship between the voice, the body, and identity is examined in the literatures of a wide range of disciplines: theoretical, critical, practical, and even legal. The voice can be an expression of collectivity, as with Hélène Cixous's *écriture feminine*, a distinct semantic realm that arises from women's shared cultural experience of physiological difference.[1] For Katherine Meizel, the voice is the bearer of *vocality*—"a set of vocal sounds, practices, techniques, and meanings that factor in the making of culture and the negotiation of identity"—a concept that may have implications of race, gender, ethnicity, or even nationhood.[2] For other writers, it can be an emblem of individuality: for Adriana Cavarero's *embodied existent*, the voice is the way the unique self makes her narrative heard to another unique self, "the corporeal communication of uniqueness."[3] Roland Barthes's notion of the *grain* encourages us to think of the voice as inseparable from the body, if not the personality, that creates it—unlike Cavarero, he sees the true nature of the voice in its raw materiality, shaped by nature and nurture but as yet unaffected by narrative or language.[4]

Singers, whose agency in their professional world is determined and borne primarily by their voices, often conflate the voice with their artistic—and even personal—identities, to the point that they may perceive imperfections in the voice or their performance as imperfections in their characters.[5] Moreover, recent legal discourse suggests that once a singer achieves a certain level of fame, their voice can even be a sonic avatar for their whole personality. The celebrity voice can encompass not just the physical identity of the singer, but also that singer's politics and beliefs, such that they have the legal right not to allow their voice—or any simulacrum of it—to be used as a tacit endorsement of any product or ideology.[6] The celebrity's voice is thus frequently equated with their persona, and inscribed with a meaning that is as unique to them as their signature, which they use to verify the authenticity of personal documents.[7]

The work of the vocal impressionist troubles this relationship between voice, body, and identity, but it is also paradoxically dependent on it. An audience understands that the impressionist has her own voice—her real voice, if you will—and that she has her own name, and her own unique self. The impressionist's real voice may or may not be familiar to listeners, but when they hear her perform, they are certain that they are not hearing her real voice. Instead, they are hearing the "real" voice of another, the celebrity model, in the full knowledge that the person singing is not the celebrity. Thus, listeners are forced to embrace both voices as intrinsic to identity, and yet not; moreover, the impressionist's skill is measured by the magnitude of the cognitive dissonance produced by the impression. This essay examines the paradox in relation to the blueswomen of early 1920s America, and discusses how imitation might have contributed to their success, individually and collectively. It further considers the implications of how constructed vocality, a practice that is negotiated by both singer and listener, becomes representative of an individual identity.[8]

"Maybe Not at All," by Ethel Waters and Sidney Easton, was recorded by Ethel for Columbia Records on October 28, 1925.[9] Her accompanists were Pearl Wright (Ethel's pianist of choice for many years) and two members of Fletcher Henderson's Columbia house band—Joe Smith on cornet and Coleman Hawkins on bass saxophone. Ethel had been contracted to Columbia for only around six months when she waxed "Maybe Not at All," but had been recording since 1921 on smaller labels like Cardinal, Vocalion, Paramount, and, most notably, Black Swan.

As only her second release in the 14000-D race series, "Maybe Not at All" stakes out Ethel's claim as the new kid on Columbia's block. The three-minute side is not a straight performance of the song, but a routine in which she demonstrates her skills as a vocal impressionist. The two singers she imitates, Clara Smith and Bessie Smith, were also Columbia artists: Clara's reputation as a blueswoman was second only to Bessie's, billed as the "Queen of the Moaners" as opposed to Bessie's "Empress of the Blues."[10] Ethel's side throws down the gauntlet to her new colleagues, challenging their jurisdiction on their own territory: Clara and Bessie were well established on the label, both having begun recording with the company in 1923.[11]

Although a seemingly incongruous addition to the catalogue, "Maybe Not at All" sits squarely in the vaudeville genre of female impersonation (by both men and women), which was hugely popular in the first three decades of the century. The art existed on a continuum, from that which attempted faithful reproduction, through to gentle critique and beyond to rather less gentle satire and parody. Susan Glenn's study of the mimetic movement in American comedy asserts the importance of the tradition in the formation of new social and cultural identities for women, but she also offers a more prosaic motivation for women impressionists. She says: "The aggressive, competitive nature of early twentieth-century stage mimicry was an instance of female celebrities using the celebrity of other performers to further their own careers. Paying tribute to others was ultimately a way to draw attention to oneself."[12]

The aggressive and competitive nature, both professionally and personally, of Ethel, Bessie, and many other blueswomen is beyond dispute. To Bessie, Ethel was just another of "those northern bitches."[13] Clara and Bessie were apparently good friends, and had recorded a number of sides together, two in 1923 and one in September 1925, yet the relationship soured after a public fistfight between them at a Columbia showcase in October.[14] Ethel's "Maybe Not at All" was made just a week later; the timing could have been a coincidence, but it probably is not. The competition between blueswomen seemed to operate with an additional dynamic to that of the mimics, one related to authenticity, the ability to move the audience, and even the quality of the voice itself, and Ethel was determined to show that she had all of these things. Ever since she had shared the bill with Bessie at 91 Decatur Street, Atlanta, in 1917, she had been aware that she was different:

> Along with Ma Rainey, [Bessie] was undisputed tops as a blues singer. When she came to Atlanta she'd heard a good deal about my low, sweet, and then new way of singing blues. . . . Now nobody could have taken the place of Bessie Smith. People everywhere loved her shouting with all their hearts and were loyal to her. But they wanted me, too.[15]

Like many of the great vaudeville mimics, Ethel began her career as a song-and-dance woman, with her shimmying and ability to participate in comic routines at least as important to the impresarios as her singing. Her talent for comedy and dance no doubt helped her survive the fading popularity of the blueswomen in the second half of the 1920s, but her continuing success was probably also due to her individual take on the art of the blues.[16] From the outset, Ethel's reputation was as a more refined performer than her peers, and she enjoyed recounting that a critic had called her the "ebony Nora Bayes" because "she was the one who never gave out with any unlady-like shouts and growls but sang all her songs with refinement."[17] She was also more affecting, drawing her audience into her misery rather than projecting it in an outward display. The cornettist Jimmy McPartland said of her: "She sang, man, she really sang. We were enthralled with her. We liked Bessie Smith very much, too, but Waters had more polish. . . . She phrased so wonderfully, the natural quality of her voice was so fine, and she sang the way she felt."[18] It may be a credit to Ethel's dramatic ability, so effectively demonstrated in later life on the stage and in the cinema, that her fellow musician was so moved by her singing, unable to distinguish the performative, or constructed, element of her vocal interpretations.[19]

In her first years in New York, Ethel worked the clubs. A young black radiologist described her singing in those days, before she topped the bill on the all-black vaudeville tours organized by the Theatre Owners' Booking Association (TOBA):

> Here a tall brown-skin girl, unmistakably the one guaranteed in the song to make a preacher lay his Bible down, used to sing and dance her own peculiar numbers, vesting them with her own originality. . . . Other girls wore themselves ragged trying to rise above the inattentive din of conversation, and soon, literally, yelled themselves hoarse; eventually they lost whatever music there was in their voices and acquired that throaty roughness which is so frequent among blues singers, and which, though admired as characteristically African, is as a matter of fact nothing but a form of chronic laryngitis. Other girls did these things, but not Ethel. She took it easy. She would stride with great leisure and self-assurance to the center of the floor, stand there with a half-contemptuous nonchalance, and wait. All would become silent at once. Then she'd begin her song, genuine blues, which, for all their humorous lines, emanated tragedy and heartbreak.[20]

Although this description hints at more than just a timbral distinction, Ethel herself described the difference between her own blues singing and that of others simply in terms of dynamics:

> Then I would sing "St. Louis Blues," but very softly. It was the first time that kind of Negro audience ever let my kind of low singing get by. And you could have heard a pin drop in that rough, rowdy audience out front. For years they had been used to Bessie Smith and Ma Rainey. They loved them and all the other shouters. I could always riff and jam and growl, but I never had that loud approach.

Ethel claimed she had always sung in her own distinctive way, but her autobiography is peppered with passages that reveal how she might have been able to develop such originality. From childhood, Ethel consciously mimicked other performers, male and female, that she admired, "singing their songs as they'd sung them."[21] And, by learning to sing like others, she could also learn how *not* to sing like them. Standing in front of a full-length mirror in the apartments where she worked as a maid, the thirteen-year-old Ethel would perform a whole repertoire of actors and singers, including Butterbeans and Susie, Bud LeMay, and the Whitman Sisters. And then she would introduce herself, "'And now, folks, the famous and spectacular Miss Ethel Waters will sing!'"[22]

Ethel's use of imitation in her learning experiences, however self-taught, is not unusual. Jazz literature abounds with testimonials from singers describing how they learned to perform by imitating others' tone, phrasing, licks, even whole solos.[23] The idea of apprenticeship is even stronger in instrumentalists' lore, where relationships are often characterized as mentor/disciple. Traditionally, these genealogies of influence occurred in the context of long associations and a genuine period of mentoring: for instance, Emmett Hardy and Bix Beiderbecke; King Oliver and Louis Armstrong; Charlie Parker and Miles Davis; Bennie Moten and Count Basie; Johnny Hodges, Ben Webster, and Mex Gonzales—the list is almost endless.

Mentoring was primarily a firsthand experience, but perhaps not always deliberate: no doubt Ethel studied Bessie Smith's style closely when they shared the bill in Atlanta. Eventually, the advent of the phonograph attenuated and altered this process. As recordings became more widely available, aspiring artists could use them both to learn from and to give their audiences a benchmark by which to assess them. The young Billie Holiday based her act on Louis Armstrong's recordings, and her imitations of his singing and playing are said to have been so close "you couldn't tell the difference."[24] She went on to use his licks and ideas as a springboard for her own—in the apprentice model, the disciple must eventually break away from the teacher. But by doing so, she was able to establish her pedigree, so that her inventiveness could then be judged within a genealogical context that connected her to Armstrong.

Phonography also had an effect on the art of professional mimicry. As recordings became accessible to the public through sideshow cylinder machines, vocal impressions, divorced from the broader context of mimicry—an art that encompassed exaggerated physical as well as vocal impersonation—became an important part of the vaudeville artist's stock-in-trade.[25] The famous nineteenth-century mimic Sir Max Beerbohm decried the "phonographic convention" of younger—and, in his view, inferior—impressionists emerging in the first decades of the twentieth century.[26] But at least one prewar mimic, Cecilia Loftus (whom Beerbohm admired), admitted to using a "graphophone" when preparing her impressions, and even went as far as to use the recordings as preludes to her own performances, thus allowing her audience to judge her accuracy for themselves.[27] And indeed, phonography could preserve the mimic's art, too: coming to "Maybe Not at All" nearly a century after it was made, we—like Ethel's listening audience—are invited to judge the accuracy of the imitations through their similarity to recorded performances by Clara and Bessie.

Phonography may well have encouraged a more clinical approach to mimicry, but it also may have provided mimics with more distinctive models to study. Before electrical recording became the industry standard in 1924, acoustic technology demanded singers with energetic, intense voices that both filled theaters and inscribed well on the wax cylinders.[28] The approach used to produce this penetrating quality was not taught in contemporaneous singing manuals (none of which consider the popular voice), but we can identify it as *twang*, one of the six vocal qualities—*speech, falsetto, cry/sob, twang, opera*, and *belt*—described by the late-twentieth-century voice teacher and theorist Jo Estill.[29] Each of Estill's qualities is produced by a different combination of positions for the larynx, the thyroid and the cricoid cartilages, effort in the vocal folds, and access to the nasal resonators.[30] Although the terms are anachronistic, the techniques themselves are not; so in the remainder of this essay I will use Estill's terminology to articulate observations about Ethel's performance, for it is her manipulation of these qualities that allowed her to produce such variety in her own singing, and to reproduce the singing of others.[31]

Ethel's long apprenticeship, both in front of the mirror and on the vaudeville stage, allowed her to experiment with vocal production, and she grew in confidence after having lessons to help her avoid the vocal damage acquired in her youth.[32] Ethel's mature vocal persona incorporated elements from all the singing styles she had mastered, and she was able to swap them around freely. In 1930, a few years after releasing "Maybe Not at All," Ethel issued two sides together that demonstrate her maverick vocal identities, now honed over many years of singing both the blues and jazz. She adopted widely differing techniques for "My Kind of Man" and "You Brought a New Kind of Love," which—while appropriate to the material—nonetheless ran the risk of confusing her audience. A British critic, Rufus, remarked on the difference, chastising her racially incongruous choice of "white" styles on "My Kind of Man," saying that by singing this way she lost "much of her individuality."[33] The white style involved slower vibrato, clearer diction, and most importantly, a dropped larynx, the primary marker of *bel canto* technique, and the Estill *opera* quality.[34] The style that Rufus felt was more unique to Ethel used more rhythmic and melodic abandon, and a higher-larynx *belt* alongside lighter *cry, twang*, and *speech* qualities, gesturing toward the "imagined vocality" that fixed the cultural identity of the early twentieth-century black singer.[35]

Rufus implies that the singer's embodied voice is insufficient on its own as a marker of "individuality," and that Ethel's authenticity was contingent on vocal practice, not materiality. Her *vocality*, that combination of voice and style which "helps to shape the self- and other-knowledge of the body," was crucial in defining an authentic and distinctive vocal persona.[36]

"Maybe Not at All" is presented as a straightforward impressions routine. Ethel begins with a verse and chorus as herself, using a predominantly light *speech* quality that she colors by lifting or lowering her larynx, moving the resonance between a rawer nasal *twang* or a more cultivated *opera/sob*; significantly, she stays away from a full *belt* and ends her "Ethel" chorus with a distinctly lowered larynx. The instrumental accompaniment pauses, and she announces, "Now, as Miss Clara Smith [which she pronounces 'Schmidt'] would sing the same song. . . ." She proceeds to deliver a chorus in full *belt*, with plenty of *twang* and plenty of vocal disruption consisting of growls and rasping. Another pause, and she exclaims, "Now I'm getting ready for the Empress, Miss Bessie Smith—Lawd!" Dropping the pitch a minor third and slowing the tempo, "Bessie" is delivered predominantly in *cry*, but moving toward *belt* at the climax of the chorus.

Ethel was not primarily known as an impressionist, but she did incorporate what she called "take-offs" into her live revues. These could be straight or comedic, or even downright bizarre; she writes tantalizingly of one sketch in which she parodied the white actress Lenore Ulrich playing a blackface role.[37] Importantly, however, Ethel's imitations normally did not allow direct comparisons to be made; this unites her act with the older vaudeville tradition of mimicry, which sought to convey more than just Beerbohm's "phonographic convention." On "Maybe Not at All," Ethel is singing her own composition, one that was never recorded by either Smith. By committing her impressions to wax, she was inviting a different kind of scrutiny to that offered to Cecilia Loftus's audiences. Although her impressions couldn't be compared to an "original," as the song is a Waters "original," audiences could listen to them repeatedly to judge their merits, not strictly in terms of accuracy but in terms of Ethel's ability to reproduce other singers' stylistic and tonal gestures, even their personalities.[38] Furthermore, they could also marvel at her skill in eradicating her own distinctive vocal persona in order to substitute it with another's. It may have completely passed them by—as it did Rufus—that the "Ethel" they recognized as "authentic" may simply have been the vocality Ethel chose most frequently to represent herself.

In presenting her imitations for critique, Ethel is more or less putting herself above her rivals, implying, "I can sing like them if I want to, but I don't have to—I can do what they do, and more." Curiously, too, when one compares Ethel's impressions to "the real thing," this sense of competition heightens. Her "Clara" is accurate enough in terms of tone, rhythmic placement, diction, and melodic variation, but her "Bessie" is more complex. Ethel faithfully reproduces the visceral quality of Bessie's voice, together with the almost cavernous sound of her placement and her deliberately languid approach to pitch, but something in the phrasing is not quite right. Bessie almost invariably sang right to the ends of phrases; her declamation of the blues was forthright and muscular. However, at key points in the chorus, Ethel's "Bessie" suddenly pulls the voice back from *belt/twang*—lowering and relaxing the larynx into *sob*, creating a near inversion, or introversion, of the sound. She decreases in volume and, if not swallowing the ends of phrases as her "Clara" does, at least muffles them. The change in affect is acute; suddenly we are aware of an internal dimension to this woman's scorn, a private misery that makes us change places from being the observer or recipient of her tirade to being the woman herself. We ponder the reasons why she might want to be left alone, even to the point of wishing pain on her beau; we are moved. This is not just mimicry, this is Ethel showing Bessie a trick or two about singing the blues, and furthermore saying to the audience, "If I sang like her, this is how *I'd* do it, and *I'd* do it better." In a way, she may be finally answering back to Bessie's comment to her those many years ago in Atlanta: "You ain't so bad, [but] you know damn well that you can't sing worth a fuck."[39]

Ethel was always careful to distinguish herself from others vocally, but her stage act also allowed her to distance herself from her competitors' performance personae, accentuating the lived experience she shared with her audiences. One of her most successful entrances in vaudeville was to get her stage partner to make a business of seeming to look for her high and low, while she entered slowly behind them in a funny hat and a gingham apron. When they asked, astonished, "Are *you* Ethel Waters?" she would say wryly, "Well, I ain't Bessie Smith!"[40] Her over-the-top minstrelsy mammy garb deliberately undercut the routines and costumes of other blueswomen, who she said "were going in for flash and class." But she then would sing "Georgia Blues," taking on a character she called a "bewildered little colored girl." She called the song "plaintive and heartbreaking . . . like a cry from the heart of all wanderers everywhere." Later, as an award-winning straight actress, she drew upon this ability to assume another personality, normally observed from personal experience, such as that of her mother or grandmother, or the women she met during her long years on the road.[41] Ethel was not a trained actress, and she was extremely unlikely to have read Stanislavski (and, in any event, *An Actor Prepares* was not published in English translation until 1936).[42] Nevertheless, if she approached acting and "straight" singing as exercises in the assumption of another personality, how much more so would this be true of her approach to impressions? One might believe that Ethel is here attempting to *become* Bessie—or, more precisely, to be *inhabited* by her.

At first consideration the differences between the performances are superficial—in what Barthes called the *pheno-song*, Barthes's term for the cultural accretions that are superimposed on the embodied voice in performance.[43] However, this is not as simple as it appears: the *pheno-song* has to do with interpretation and acculturation, but here we have three completely different performances of the same song ostensibly within the same relatively narrow interpretative tradition of vaudeville blues. And while some differences are indisputably *pheno*—tempo, approach to the beat, ornamentation—others are less clear-cut: How can we account for regional accent, for instance? Ultimately, we cannot escape from the fact that the voices sound different, but the *voice*—wherein Barthes perceives the *grain*, "the materiality of the body speaking its mother tongue"—is the same in each instance.

So why do they sound so different? It's not beyond the ear to detect the same voice in "Ethel" and "Clara," as "Clara's" *belt* seems like it could just be an amplification of "Ethel's," but her "Bessie" seems to change dramatically, and not just in timbre. It is a simple thing to change vibrato and placement, but there is also a pervasive hint of grit (rather than growl) in "Bessie" that is not present in "Clara" or "Ethel." Many singers of Ethel's era had throat problems—something remarked on by the Harlem radiologist quoted above—but then again, so did Ethel; after struggling for a number of years, she eventually had a nodule surgically removed from her vocal folds in 1929.[44] The use of this very physical quality, a knot in the woody grain, is clearly deliberate and distinguishing—and at least partially avoidable. Ethel's "Ethel" sings mostly in *speech* with a neutral, relaxed larynx, masking any damage in the throat; her "Bessie" exploits it, highlighting it through the tilt of the laryngeal cartilages of *cry* and *belt*. Barthes's metaphor likens the voice to a natural surface, and we can think of the singer's artifice as comparable to the way that surface is prepared and then decorated. Whatever imperfections or idiosyncrasies exist in the raw material we assume will be detectable in the finished product. However, Ethel shows that the area of that surface is perhaps broader than Barthes imagines it to be, and that only a portion of that surface need be used or exposed in performance at the will of the performer.

Barthes's notion of the *pheno-song* returns the discussion to the idea of the self in vocality, and the implications for the self of imitative practice. For Barthes, without the *pheno-song* the voice "has us hear a body which has no civil identity, no 'personality,' but which is nevertheless a separate body."[45] According to Meizel, the notion of vocality has come to encompass both *geno-* and *pheno-song*; both derived from the embodied voice and speaking directly of the body, it is nonetheless fundamental to the performative work of self-fashioning, "part and parcel of how we interact with the world around us, and who we think we are."[46] In imitation, the impressionist must hold two selves in balance, her own and her model's; and by the very act of assuming another's persona through adopting her vocality, the impressionist makes clear the constructedness of both that vocality *and* her own.

But Ethel also makes clear that there is an irreducible difference between her and her model. This has important implications for the early twentieth-century blueswoman. Susan Glenn notes that in early twentieth-century psychological thought:

> Not only [had] women been characterized as instinctively imitative, but, as reproducers of other bodies, they were ipso facto less capable than men of maintaining the boundaries between self and other. Suspected of lacking a stable self, they fell into the category of beings perceived to be lower on the scale of intellectual development than men of European ancestry.[47]

How much more lacking in stability, how much lower on the scale of intellectual development might black women have been perceived to be? The early twentieth-century African American woman was, in almost all respects, denied a unique social self. Her role was as a body in service to others—a wet nurse, a maid, a mammy, a prostitute. From this point of view, she might seem a *tabula rasa* that could assume many different identities, none of which were particular to her. Hazel Carby sees the blueswomen as pioneers in claiming an identity for the African American woman, yet, as she says, "we hear the 'we' when they say 'I' "—something Ethel herself recognized, by calling her rendition of "Georgia Blues" "a cry from the heart of all wanderers everywhere."[48] This is akin to Cavarero's description of Cixous's *écriture feminine*: "the problem of a singular experience that is, nevertheless, de-individualized."[49] The blueswoman was an Everywoman, her suffering and passions symbolic of all who shared her race and sex.

Herein lies the paradox for the early twentieth-century record-buying public; and we know that this public, even for so-called race records, was predominantly white.[50] Ethel conjures up Clara and Bessie through producing their voices from her body. In doing so, she disrupts Cavarero's notion of the voice as "embodied existent"—the manifestation of uniqueness that speaks its own story so that others can hear.[51] Yet even in the act of denying her rivals their vocal individuality, she acknowledges it, and thereby gives them social and political currency. In doing her impressions, and perhaps even in her own singing, Ethel is affirming identities by trying them on like costumes, an exercise as crucial to her as a professional in 1925 as it was when she was first learning to sing. And for her audience, to hear them one after another on a recording was to understand (perhaps for the first time) that, no, all blueswomen—all black women—were not the same.

Notes

This essay is based on a paper originally delivered at the Thirty-First Annual Conference of the Society for American Music, February 16–20, 2005, in Eugene, Oregon. My attendance at that conference was supported by a British Academy Overseas Conference Grant, for which my grateful acknowledgment. My thanks to the organizers of "A Voice as Something More," Martha Feldman and Judith Zeitlin, for the opportunity to revisit these ideas, and for their generous comments on the draft.

1. Hélène Cixous, "The Laugh of the Medusa," trans. Keith Cohen and Paula Cohen, *Signs* 1, no. 4 (1976): 875–93.

2. Katherine Meizel, "A Powerful Voice: Investigating Vocality and Identity," *Voice and Speech Review* 7, no. 1 (January 1, 2011): 269, doi:10.1080/23268263.2011.10739551. Meizel's study surveys "the idea of vocality as it has developed across history and disciplines, proposes a holistic model for its study in the context of music, and begins to unpack the heavy sociocultural baggage that accompanies it" (267).

3. Adriana Cavarero, *For More Than One Voice: Toward a Philosophy of Vocal Expression*, trans. Paul A. Kottman (Stanford, CA: Stanford University Press, 2005), 199.

4. Roland Barthes, "The Grain of the Voice," in *Image, Music, Text*, ed. and trans. Stephen Heath (London: HarperCollins UK, 1977), 179–89.

5. Wendy Hargreaves, "Profiling the Jazz Singer," *British Journal of Music Education* 30, no. 3 (November 2013): 391, doi:10.1017/S0265051713000107.

6. Jeff Klein, "Tom Waits and the Right of Publicity: Protecting the Artist's Negative Voice," *Popular Music and Society* 37, no. 5 (October 20, 2014): 583–94, doi:10.1080/03007766.2014.892725.

7. My thanks to Judith Zeitlin for making this point.

8. For a discussion of how vocality, as opposed to voice, is "where we learn to hear distinct individualities, to aurally separate our own voices from others,' " see Meizel, "A Powerful Voice," 268–69.

9. "Maybe Not at All," music and lyrics by Sidney Easton and Ethel Waters, © C R Publishing Co., New York, 1925; Columbia 14112-D, 1925. The recording has been reissued on CD: *The Chronological Ethel Waters, 1925–1926*, Classics 672, 1992. At the time of writing, the original recording is available on a Creative Commons license on archive.org: https://archive.org/details/78_maybe-not-at-all_ethel-waters-and-her-ebony-four-easton-and-waters_gbia0039548b/Maybe+Not+At+All+-+Ethel+Waters+and+Her+Ebony+Four.flac, accessed July 19, 2018.

Note: I shall refer to Waters hereafter as Ethel, not to assume an inappropriate familiarity, but because I am obliged to refer to Bessie Smith and Clara Smith by their given names, as shall become clear.

10. Chris Albertson, *Bessie*, 2nd ed. (New Haven, CT, and London: Yale University Press, 2003), 43.

11. Ethel's previous releases on Columbia, from April 1925, had been part of their "1-D" (for "domestic") series, and although she continued to release sides in both domestic and race series for the remainder of the decade, she was the only black woman to do so. See the discographies

for the full Columbia series on http://www.78discography.com/, accessed August 16, 2016. Clara Smith did release a single 78 on the 1-D series early on—"Uncle Sam Blues" / "Kansas City Man Blues" (12D, 1923)—but was swapped to the race series thereafter.

12. Susan A. Glenn, *Female Spectacle: The Theatrical Roots of Modern Feminism* (Cambridge, MA, and London: Harvard University Press, 2000), 74, 80.

13. Ethel Waters with Charles Samuels, *His Eye Is on the Sparrow* (New York: Doubleday & Co., 1951; New York: Da Capo Press, 1992), 91. Citations refer to Da Capo Press edition.

14. Albertson, *Bessie*, 117. The fight occurred at a Columbia showcase that featured at least half a dozen blueswomen—circumstances that may have brought feelings of rivalry to a dangerous head. Clara and Bessie's three duets are "I'm Going Back to My Used to Be" and "Far Away Blues," recorded October 4, 1923 (Columbia 13007-D), and Bessie Smith's self-penned "My Man Blues" (with a spoken appearance by an unnamed male vaudeville performer), recorded September 1, 1925 (Columbia 14098-D). All three have been reissued under license from Document Records on *Clara Smith: The Essential*, Classic Blues 200027, 2001. At the time of writing, two of these sides, "Far Away Blues" and "I'm Going Back to My Used to Be," are available on a Creative Commons license on archive.org: https://archive.org/details/78_far-away-blues_bessie-smith-and-clara-smith-fletcher-henderson-geo-brooks_gbia0039317a and https://archive.org/details/78_im-going-back-to-my-used-to-be_bessie-smith-and-clara-smith-fletcher-henderson-jim_gbia0039317b, accessed July 19, 2017.

15. Waters, *Sparrow*, 91.

16. See, in particular, comments on Ethel as a lyricist in Randall Cherry, "Ethel Waters: 'Long, Lean, Lanky Mama,'" in *Nobody Knows Where the Blues Come From: Lyrics and History*, ed. Robert Springer (Jackson: University Press of Mississippi, 2007), 264–82.

17. Waters, *Sparrow*, 177.

18. Nat Shapiro and Nat Hentoff, *Hear Me Talkin' to Ya: The Classic Story of Jazz as Told by the Men Who Made It* (New York: Rhinehart & Co., Inc., 1955; London: Souvenir Press, 1992), 149. Citations refer to Souvenir Press edition.

19. Waters was nominated for an Academy Award for her performance in Elia Kazan's film *Pinky* in 1949. She originated the role of Berenice in the 1950 Broadway production of *The Member of the Wedding*, for which she won the New York Drama Critics Circle Award. In 1962, she became the first African American woman to be nominated for an Emmy, for her performance in the television series *Route 66*.

20. Rudolf Fisher, "The Caucasian Storms Harlem," *American Mercury* 11 (1927): 393–98, repr. in Robert Walser, ed., *Keeping Time: Readings in Jazz History* (New York and Oxford: Oxford University Press, 1999), 60–65.

21. Waters, *Sparrow*, 29.

22. Will Friedwald recounts much of this in his book on jazz singing. See, for instance, his comments on Connie Boswell learning from recordings by Caruso, Bessie Smith, and Mamie Smith; and later Ella Fitzgerald learning from and even quoting recordings of Connie Boswell (79, 82, 143). Fitzgerald also learned firsthand from Leo Watson when singing with Chick Webb's band (141–42); Kay Starr learned directly from Connie when they were on the same tour (209–10); Will Friedwald, *Jazz Singing: America's Great Voices from Bessie Smith to Bebop and Beyond* (New York: Da Capo Press, 1996).

23. A recent study in the jazz education literature reports that singers overwhelmingly prefer to learn from listening and imitating rather than from printed music; Hargreaves, "Profiling the Jazz Singer," 384–87.

24. Donald Clarke, *Billie Holiday: Wishing on The Moon*, 2nd ed. (Cambridge, MA: Da Capo Press, 2002), 47.

25. Imitators of Enrico Caruso had repertoire that would allow them to embed the impression in a comedy song; see Larry Hamberlin, *Tin Pan Opera: Operatic Novelty Songs in the Ragtime Era* (New York: Oxford University Press, 2011), 55.

26. J. Arthur Bleackley, *The Art of Mimicry* (New York: Samuel French, 1911), 13–14, 74.

27. Glenn, *Female Spectacle*, 84.

28. William Howland Kenney, *Recorded Music in American Life: The Phonograph and Popular Memory, 1890–1945* (New York and Oxford: Oxford University Press, 2003), 40.

29. Estill's research and teaching methods have been very influential in stage and popular music singing; at its fundament is an understanding of how the vocal mechanism produces speech. The six voice qualities are described in Gillyanne Kayes, *Singing and the Actor* (London: A & C Black, 2000), 153–68. Further information can be found on the Estill Voice Training website: "Estill Voice International," https://www.estillvoice.com/, accessed August 15, 2016.

30. *Twang* is produced with a tilted thyroid and high larynx; *speech* exercises the folds with a neutral larynx; *belt* (tilted cricoid, high larynx) and *opera* (tilted thyroid, low larynx) are delivered with elements of *twang* and *speech* and "anchoring" in the body; *cry* (tilted thyroid, neutral larynx) is sometimes varied into *sob* (tilted thyroid, low larynx); see also Barb Jungr, "Vocal Expression in the Blues and Gospel," in *The Cambridge Companion to Blues and Gospel Music*, ed. Allan Moore (Cambridge: Cambridge University Press, 2002), 105–6.

31. Estill's descriptors are a product of imaging technology that was not available to early twentieth-century voice teachers. Without sophisticated imaging, these teachers could not recognize the role of the laryngeal cartilages in vocal production, but there were manuals that understood the relationship between the vocal productions of speech and song; see, for instance, P. Mario Marafioti, *Caruso's Method of Voice Production: The Scientific Culture of the Voice* (New York: Appleton, 1922), 76.

32. Waters, *Sparrow*, 210. See also Laurie Stras, "The Organ of the Soul: Voice, Damage, and Affect," in *Sounding Off: Theorizing Disability in Music*, ed. Neil Lerner and Joseph Straus (New York: Routledge, 2006), 179–80.

33. "Rufus," "Analytical Notes and Reviews," *Phonograph Monthly Review* 4, no. 11 (1930), review of Ethel Waters, "My Kind of Man" / "You Brought a New Kind of Love," Columbia 2222-D, 1930; cited in Laurie Stras, "White Face, Black Voice: Race, Gender, and Region in the Music of the Boswell Sisters," *Journal of the Society for American Music* 1, no. 2 (2007): 216–17. The sides have been reissued on *The Chronological Ethel Waters, 1929–193*, Classics 721 (1993).

34. James Stark, *Bel Canto: A History of Vocal Pedagogy* (Toronto: University of Toronto Press, 2003), 38ff.

35. For a discussion of the twentieth-century black singer's "imagined vocality" (in the Andersonian sense), see Meizel, "A Powerful Voice," 270.

36. Meizel, "A Powerful Voice," 269.

37. Waters, *Sparrow*, 187.

38. For more on how vocal quality can become emblematic of personality, see Klein, "Tom Waits and the Right of Publicity," 587–90.

39. Waters, *Sparrow*, 92.

40. Waters, *Sparrow*, 81, 151.

41. Waters, *Sparrow*, 233–50, 272. In her autobiography, Ethel admits to a keen emotional investment in her characters, including her 1939 stage performance of Hagar in *Mamba's Daughters*, or Granny in the film *Pinky* in 1949.

42. Constantin Stanislavski, *An Actor Prepares*, trans. Elizabeth Reynolds Hapgood (New York: Theatre Arts, 1936).

43. Barthes, "The Grain of the Voice," 182.

44. Waters, *Sparrow*, 210–13.

45. Barthes, "The Grain of the Voice," 182.

46. Meizel, "A Powerful Voice," 289.

47. Glenn, *Female Spectacle*, 89.

48. Hazel Carby, "'It Jus' Be's Dat Way Sometime': The Sexual Politics of Women's Blues," *Radical America* 20, no. 4 (1986): 24. Reprinted in Walser, *Keeping Time*, 351–65.

49. Cavarero, *For More Than One Voice*, 144.

50. David Brackett, *Categorizing Sound: Genre and Twentieth-Century Popular Music* (Oakland: University of California Press, 2016), 69–112.

51. Cavarero, *For More Than One Voice*, 173. In his critique of Cavarero, Brian Kane notes that Cavarero does not account for vocal imitation. He states that "there is good reason to be skeptical of Cavarero's leap towards uniqueness," and "it is not clear how [her] vocal ontology of uniqueness responds to the possibility of vocal dissimulation," but he does not address the paradox further; Brian Kane, *Sound Unseen: Acousmatic Sound in Theory and Practice* (New York: Oxford University Press, 2014), 154, 156.

7

“I Am an Essentialist”: Against the Voice Itself

JAMES Q. DAVIES

Confessions

There you have it: a confession, not only to the odd indulgence of essentialism, but to the heresy of actually *being* an essentialist, a shameful thing if ever there was. Talk about voice is notoriously prone to the essentialist trap, to the fundamentalist logic of such statements as “you are a tenor,” “this is the voice of an Asian,” “this is the sound women make,” or “her voice is black.” They are the kinds of sonic identifications made by chauvinists. The problem, to be sure, goes beyond authoritarian pronouncement, category error, or barefaced discrimination. It extends to the act of assigning cultural tropes to vocal sound, to the very reduction of “free sound” to essence. In the terms marshaled against reductive logic, any tropological ascription of song to matters of origin is oppressive, limiting performative range and indulging cultural fallacies that betray intolerance. According to the code, the very practice of fixing sound to embodied source is offensive. And the accusation runs deep: that the stereotyping of sound, the stereotyping of vibration even, turns the act of “speaking out” into something less than the liberal opportunity for emancipation. It scrambles the common equation of “breaking silence” with true expressions of authenticity and freedom. Perhaps this is why vocal essentialism is deemed so heinous—because identifications of essence corrupt the free play of sonic suggestion and the irreducible difference and individuality of each speaker. Essentialism: we know to insist upon our sophistication and freedom from it.

My confession, or rather the problem with confession tout court, is that it risks coming across as iconoclastic. This has always been the danger with “intervention,” and the by-now-standard obligation to insist upon one’s scholarly autonomy from the discursive preoccupations of one’s peers.[1] After all, who in their right mind would envoice essentialist tendencies were it not to throw off the chains of some purportedly repressive academic order? Who but the most deplorable among us would knowingly "speak back" in the tones of a reactionary? These incitements are surely by now far too routine in scholarship to signal some revolutionary change in the basic patterns of academic discourse. It seems debatable whether ubiquitous freethinking or "shooting from the hip" guarantees deliverance. Not that my confession is deployed to demonstrate the sublime absolutions of free speech. My particular "calling out," on the contrary, intends to put pressure on the assumption that speech equates with freedom, or that vocalization—defined here in cathartic terms—is necessarily the most effective means of political and moral emancipation. The opposite might be true: that the obligation to confess, to "make one's voice heard," or "to express oneself" is also an obligation to bind oneself again to regulative norms, to the contingent principles of the "interest group" to which one's utterance has been culturally assigned. It may be less that we exercise freedom when we exercise voice than that we exercise some form or other of discursive contingency and belonging.[2]

Wendy Brown puts it well in a thoughtful feminist rumination on "breaking silence" and "compulsory discursivity" in our chatty age of blog culture, Twitter, selfie culture, public disclosure, and personal testimony. Her words are worth quoting at length:

> Here is the way the problem unfolds politically: insurrection requires breaking silence about the very existence as well as the activity or injury of the collective insurrectionary subject. Even dreams of emancipation cannot take shape unless the discursively shadowy or altogether invisible character of those subjects, wounds, events, or activities is redressed, whether through slave ballads, the flaunting of forbidden love, the labor theory of value, or the quantification of housework. . . .
>
> But while the silences in discourses of domination are a site for insurrectionary noise, while they are the corridors to be filled with explosive counter tales, it is also possible to make a fetish of breaking silence. It is possible as well that this ostensible tool of emancipation carries its own techniques of subjugation—that it converges with unemancipatory tendencies in contemporary culture, establishes regulatory norms, coincides with the disciplinary power of ubiquitous confessional practices; in short, it may feed the powers it meant to starve.[3]

This is not to say that strategies of "disidentification," disarticulation, or alternative forms of vocal placement are impossible;[4] it is merely to point out that the very practice of counterexpression—indeed, "freedom" itself—may be indebted to the most deeply cherished orthodoxies of our age. The mythology of "saying it all" or "breaking silence," in short, may have the opposite effect of that which it intends. Pace Freud and his ilk, there may be no talking cure.[5]

This chapter addresses those "spaces of freedom" purportedly offered by voice. It concerns what Brown calls "dreams of emancipation," not of those belonging to subjugated peoples buried in silence and exclusion, but in the cases presented below of those belonging to elite European operatic cultures devoted with surprising assiduity to the "subversive" ideological imperatives of "personal expression." The idea, on the one hand, will be to account for the historical emergence of the sacralized figure of "pure voice," to address questions of fixation (that is, the fixing of voice as a visible object of knowledge), and to consider the implications of making a fetish of vocal sound. On the other, inadvisably perhaps, this chapter—like those chauvinists of yore—will be in search of essence. It will be invested in questions of body-voice relations, vocal materiality, as well as that important issue of how and where voice matters. If there is a project, it is to suggest that voice has been too easily configured in the image of sonic emancipation, too readily fixed (in "acousmatic" style) as the spectral imprint of freedom.[6]

Before proceeding, two prefatory admissions are in order. By appending "the voice itself" to the end of this chapter title, I mean to make reference to long-standing disciplinary disputes over the category of "the music itself," which raged in the 1990s over the contention that musicology was ideally the study of discrete art-historical objects.[7] For those readers not privy to the arcane preoccupations of musicologists, this was a debate, conducted chiefly in relation to music theory, analysis, and other score-based formalisms in the discipline. It concerned whether music can ever be "about itself," and whether it was ever possible to reduce "the music" (or should we say "the score"?) down to some sanitized sonic or textual "essence." The debate addressed the quarantining of "pure music" from the so-called "extramusical." It probed the discipline's focusing on the residuum of so-called "music as music" or "music qua music." The purported nonrepresentational status of "the music itself" was at stake, as was the idealist article of faith that this "most abstract of the arts" was most divine by virtue of its noncontingency. Conceits of autonomy, the conceit of vocal autonomy in particular, will similarly be key in what follows, as will what I take to be the fantasy of a decontaminated and sterile vocal space: namely, that sequestered and specular space of "the voice as voice."

In the interests of full confession, finally, it makes sense to disclose that I am a specialist historian of musical performance, here of elite vocal techniques and vocal technologies developed and disseminated over the past two hundred years in Europe. That vocation has required exploration of surprisingly diverse disciplines of musical training, pedagogy, and physical practice; and involved mapping the ways in which voice has acted in the cultivation of bodies. To match my performative point of view, I have chosen to begin this chapter by engaging in a "speech act," by assuming a deliberately specious or disingenuous voice. I am beginning here in figurative quotes not to be facetious, but to insist that voices—writerly as much as spoken ones—are always in some sense "put on." My voice below is precisely that: it instantiates what I do not believe.

What Comes First: Voice or Body? (The Following to Be Read in Quotes)

It's obvious. The voice comes from the body. First you get the body and then you get the voice: one and then the other. This, apparently in this before-and-after sequence, is how the thing works. And bodies are *just there*, right? You have yours and I have mine; and each of our bodies has its own unique stamp, its own shape, and its own primal-creative personality. In the great common-sensical worldview, we are born that way. All one has to do to *be* a voice is to learn how to release optimally. Thus the task of any good citizen or netizen in the global democratic imperium today. It is to find his or her inborn voice and then to project it outwardly—that is, to externalize their dark psychosomatic "grain."[8] Thou shalt know thy voice, so it is insisted, throw off civility, and make thyself heard.

The body outside the body: that's the voice. That's what singing is about, or at least has been about in this belief system. First, you want to know "who you are" as you sense your irreducible *différance*.[9] Second, you want to break outside of yourself and exteriorize your raw sonic alterity. The vital energies of that innate lurking power crave freedom. Life itself desires awakening, so crushed has it become beneath the weight of language and (in this libertarian anthropology) the cruel forces of social convention. In such a system (where governmental repression is everywhere), authentic expression is only knowable as a bid for power. It involves an individual body breaking outside of the body, and a natural world where voices are wielded as a political right. The right to free speech, in this imperium, aligns with the right to life. In the age of permanent liberal revolution, you are nothing if you cannot make your voice heard (as if you only had one), and illiberal if you refuse to listen.[10]

This is why, for most of the last century or more (in very general Anglo-European terms), there have been good singers and there have been bad singers. Good singers, in the ideological terms of this modernity, know how to project. They know how to "come out" and represent themselves. Bad ones

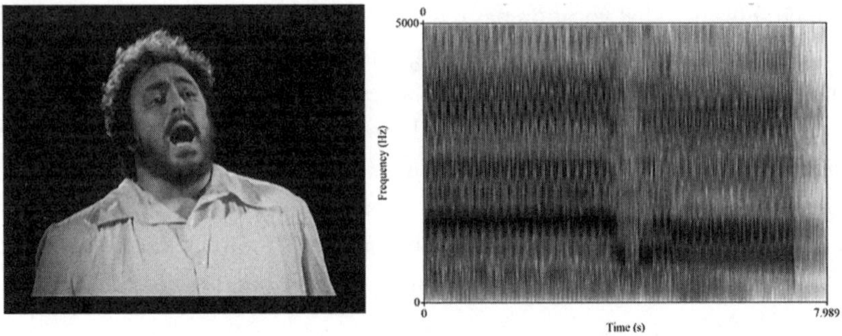

FIGURE 7.1 Pavarotti sings the final high B-flat and ornamented G to end Puccini's "Recondita armonia," *Tosca*, in Modena, 1979, alongside an intense spectrographic record of this climax.

lack that connection. They don't feel it. They are weak because they have literally never extended themselves (physically or emotionally). Moreover, they lack knowledge of themselves. They have not desired enough, having never learned to properly give body to sound.

Take Luciano Pavarotti and a legendary 1979 performance of "Recondita armonia," scary for its muscular and corporeal purity. The still frame printed as **figure 7.1** pictures the Italian superstar delivering phrases from the opening romance from Giacomo Puccini's *Tosca* (Rome, 1900), recorded on video during a production done in the singer's hometown of Modena, and showcased at the heart of a TV documentary entitled *What Makes a Great Tenor?*[11] The documentary, first aired in June 2011, makes a feature of Pavarotti's inwardly turned eyes, the singer's mastery of vocal fixation appearing as the result of obscene levels of technical control. "When he performed you could see his eyes looking inside of himself," explains the presenter of the documentary, Rolando Villazón. At this, the French-Mexican tenor shows how Pavarotti's eyes glaze over as he sings, how they search inside—"exploring every part of his instrument."

The search for essence in this 1979 "Recondita armonia" is desperate. Most striking about this singing organism is the way it insulates as it aestheticizes, the way it breaks or quarantines itself from the world in the act of vocal projection. We are witness here to an incomparably self-possessed singer directing dark eyes within, searching frantically inside in order to maintain the phantasmagoria before him. An external sonic form—this autochthonous vocal space in the beyond—appears here as the dialectical effect of penetrating interior focus, as the outward excrescence of inward observation and a "rock-solid technique." The mineralogical logic is revealing: the resolve of the gaze, and the way his body "locks in," Villazón suggests, explains the flawless structure of the vocal image. The autonomy of this voice is derived from eyes rolled back, as Pavarotti folds, not only in on himself, but against himself, as he burns inside. "Tu azzurro hai l'occhio; Tosca ha l'occhio nero!" he sings in arching phrases, lines that loosely translate as "your blue eyes shine brightly; Tosca's eyes smolder." Eyes are everywhere.[12]

This Cavaradossi of 1979 knows his body. He knows that his body—this entity, not him—is singing. "My voice is my possessor," Pavarotti once said of the disobedient thing he had cultivated. "I am a servant to my voice."[13] Hailed for its immaculate homogeneity across the range, the musical object he forged appears in the documentary as the inexhaustible source of life itself, as in Villazón's description of Pavarotti's voice as a "ray of sunlight," a luminescent beam dispensing warmth and light to a dark world. "The voice of the tenor is a wild animal," the Italian once added in a famous 1995 interview from his home in Pesaro, "it is not the voice of the person who is singing in the shower. It is made completely differently. Control: when it is controlled, it is very exciting. It is very exciting because it is very dangerous, and you feel it."[14] His voice—and I mean this in *real* terms—was configured, by him as much as his fans, as an unruly bestial phenomenon, managed by what soprano Renée Fleming, later in the same 2011 documentary, brands "the greatest technique of anyone I've ever known or heard."

And then there is the fear, the annihilating fear of those glass-black eyes. Of not knowing what The Voice Itself will do next. "We go on the stage every night with the same feeling: we are afraid," says Pavarotti responding to an interviewer in the video: "and if someone tells you this, that he is not afraid; then that means that he is a liar." One is reminded of Hector Berlioz's famous 1855 explanation for why the then-new species—"the ténor"—was so dogged by stage fright. "Silence reigns in the stupefied house," Berlioz observed of the crowd of Parisian witnesses at the Salle Le Peletier more than a hundred years earlier: "people hold their breath, amazement and admiration are blended in an almost similar sentiment: *fear*." For Berlioz, the nascent breed of cut-and-thrust ténors were forever on the edge of vocal collapse. The seductive force of their high notes alone was fatal, not merely to the health of singers, but to the whole symbolic order. Hardly category-less singers "without qualities," which was Berlioz's compositional ideal in 1856, singers such as Gilbert Duprez were "assassins" who wrecked art.[15] At once to be pitied and loathed, they made sounds of extraordinary violence and extraordinary unnaturalness. How different was Berlioz's loathing of this fledgling masculine species to Renée Fleming's opinion of the ténor's later ca. 1979 incarnation. The

American soprano ends her tribute to Pavarotti in the documentary with an uncharacteristic stutter: "And again [his song] was just completely natural . . . so . . . and . . . again . . . I don't mean."

More Stuttering (The Following to Be Read Out of Quotes)

Well, no, actually! If you think about it, voices belong to far more than merely individual bodies. This biocentric way of sourcing "the voice" in "the body" so-called has only been "completely natural" in a few parts of the world, in the very recent past, and then only so for an ever-narrowing community of believers. What seems obvious is that you have to "work like crazy" (as Fleming says) to acquire this sense both of body and of voice. There is in fact nothing "natural" or even "artificial" about it, this turning back on one's own body in order to project a powerful spectral image into the future. A whole raft of techniques and technologies are necessary to the fixation of this potent sonic icon: years of training, microphones, conductors, pianos, radios, compact disc players, global audio industries, opera houses, studios, conservatoires, documentary filmmakers, publicists. And you have to focus to maintain its truth, in ways only hinted at by the furrows of concentration on Pavarotti's face.

Singing this way means supporting "the body" as a unitary presence in "the voice." And it involves highly cultivated practices of knowing and training: a regimen that targets an idea and self-manages frantically. This is not to suggest that autosurveillance is wrong. There is nothing wrong, after all, in construing "the body" as a powerful natural force or biocreative system, or even policing it as such. It is just that this bioevolutionary or "species" sense of the individual body—any sense of body—is partial and political.[16] Which is to say this way of knowing bodies is hardly the only way of knowing bodies. Looking back at Pavarotti, we might see him producing (or should I say incorporating?), not merely sound, but a certain, at once highly cultivated and cruelly physical, kind of Truth.

But What of Aura?

This voice is nothing if not terrifying. There is no question of the auratic or religious dimension of not only this but other voices, particularly in view of the throngs of awestruck worshippers drawn to such vocal archetypes like moths to a flame. The fear that attends the ritual invocation of these voices, moreover, provides clues as to voice's centrality in the cultural order of things. The fetish character of voice—not all voices, to be sure—is undeniable, although for reasons that are more than merely self-evident.

The issue here is not only where the phantasmic dimension comes from, but how that strange magic is maintained. How do we explain the allure of voice? A psychoanalyst might say that we all know that Pavarotti is dead and that his body cannot sing in the way it sang Cavaradossi in 1979. Yet that immortal voice of forty-seven years ago lives on, perhaps now more so than ever before. We may, in other words, construe "voice"—in the much-mythologized age of mechanical sound reproduction—as an object of desire. We may fix it as a willed thing, an occult entity that has broken transgressively from its author and taken on a disobedient life of its own. In this view, when voice manifests desire, when it imprints will, we might take it to be sovereign because it lacks location, and explain its fatal charm on the basis of this terrifying lack.[17] Slavoj Žižek, with characteristic iconoclasm, put it like this in 1996:

> An unbridgeable gap separates forever a human body from "its" voice. The voice displays a spectral autonomy, it never quite belongs to the body we see, so that even when we see a living person talking, there is always a minimum of ventriloquism at work: it is as if the speaker's own voice hollows him out and in a sense speaks "by itself," through him.[18]

In this psychoanalytic vision, the "voice as voice" is haunting because it is born of trauma. Its perfection appears as a consequence of the gap between the mesmerizing sound that attracts fixation on the one hand, and the dying or absent source of that sound on the other. In-betweenness grounds its enigma. In this reified picture of voice, voice will only achieve full surplus meaning and omnipotence once its visible origins have been placed under erasure. This voice is only ever itself, in other words, when the Pythagorean curtain has been drawn.[19] It is only when the decaying means of production has been turned against itself that desire purportedly awakens. It is only under conditions of occlusion that voice appears in its full divinity as "the voice itself"—when the basic facts of bodily materiality have been thrown ecstatically into air.

One could, of course, blame so-called "modern" technologies of sound reproduction for this supposed break of vocal nature from its supposedly precultural ecology. One might say that video technology affords the experience of a modern "disconnect" between the location of the visual image and the sounding speakers of any given reproducing machine. The problem, as ever, is to decide exactly when "modernity" first happened, or to locate the exact juncture at which the fatal divorce actually occurred. Vocal technology, after all, has been with us since at least as far back as the invention of the bone flute some 40,000 years ago, and probably much longer.[20] And I would add that voices are only voices when they have been messed with, or made subject to medial techniques or technologies of cultivation.

Because how exactly does voice break from its source? Where exactly might the fatal interruption be said to occur? Does the umbilical cord break somewhere in the space between you and me? At the point at which voice escapes my mouth and enters the air? Or perhaps at the moment that sound enters your ear and is first discriminated as voice, in which case my voice belongs as much to your hearing as it does to my speaking? Where exactly is the point of severance, and where exactly should we locate the true organ? Is voice cut out at the sharp edge of my vocal cords? Should we say that voice separates out at the point where technology intervenes? At the tip of my pen or the keypad of this computer, perhaps? And should we so readily assume that this voice, my voice, has only one natural-born source: when it could belong equally to the acoustics of the room in which I express myself, to my cultural background, to my biology or language, my psychology, my respiratory or nervous system, to your ear, your nervous system, life itself, to this academic anthropology, the atmosphere, to God, to Nature. The options are almost endless.

From my perspective, the phantasmic dimension I am pursuing depends, then, on far more than some shocking loss of origin. Fracture, interruption, schizophonia, rhizophonia, breakage, rupture, absence, some fearful modernist break: so far as I am concerned, none of these has anything to do with the real fact of vocal aura.[21] In my political rather than psychoanalytic view, instead, voices are phantasmic in the extent to which people organize themselves and struggle ontologically in relation to them. My claim is that vocal aura is less a byproduct of voice's detachment from the world than an effect of voice's deep connection to that world. Voices are powerful when they inspire social belief and social belonging; just as often as, when they appear to lack presence, they inspire disbelief and unbelonging. Voices are bound up, in other words, with the articulation of authenticities, and they are bound up, moreover, with the deep superstitions of our occult modernity.[22]

It appears, then, that I am a devotee of the metaphysics of presence, though not the sort of metaphysics of (self-)presence that Derrida so eloquently scorned.[23] I am certainly no devotee of the category of the illusion of "hearing-oneself-speaking" or *s'entendre-parler*, in the famous conception of Husserl. Husserl's transcendental phenomenology and his illusion of the autoaffective inaudible voice within, after all, assumes the existence of some naturally envoiced subject prior to technical mediation.[24] Instead, I am drawn to the question of how these cultivated voices (audible and inaudible) make (themselves) present: how they are in fact involved in placing matters in the world, and making worldly presence available and known to us. Voices are powerful, in this sense, when they are imbricated in instantiating matters of fact—when they become an ideological means by which communities know causes, shape social ontologies, and conjure essences.

Which is just another way of saying that voices have never been themselves. Or perhaps that statement should be clarified with the modifier that, if there ever has been such an acousmatic image—a voice itself—it has been maintained as the object of a peculiarly intense romantic-modern fantasy. (Here, my view approximates to Mladen Dolar's Lacanian formulation, wherein the living presence of the voice appears by virtue of its ritual function, as the effect of an ardent interplay of human relations.)[25] The challenge, in other words, is to buy out of the myth that in some Arcadian past, essence was fixed, or that the phantasm we call "the body" was just there. Bodies, our materialities, are never *just there*. They are always, in some sense, in flux, or at least given to many vocal placements and many possible political and material configurations. Voices are produced naturally, of course; but they are also always produced culturally. When it comes to singing, at least, there is no "pure voice," no optimal way to place voices in bodies, no one true path, and no such thing as "vocal freedom."[26]

The Spectralization of Voice

This has been true even within the narrow vocal tradition of my scholarly purview. There have been so many ways to place singing voices in bodies; and so many ways for bodies to be. The diversity of vocal positions, historically speaking, is in fact confounding, though a brief account of continuity and change in the image of voice and its mediation may prove useful to my unfolding story. Hence the collection of choice images from the modern history of voice studies and European voice science in the pages that follow.

Voice, as we all know, can index sex, as is obvious from **figure 7.2**, printed in a German source, Karl Liscovius's *Theorie der Stimme* (Leipzig, 1814), one of the first to link sexual function to vocal function. Singing voices, that is, can be linked to and be productive of hard binaristic configurations of gender and reproduction, or be expressive of claims about secondary sexual characteristics, as in **figure 7.3** of a hundred years later, when voice-sex equations had long become second nature. "Go before an open window every morning, place your hands as in figure 4," recommended Nebraskan singer and pedagogue Millie Ryan; "inhale through the nose, (don't raise the shoulders) see that the expansion is as great under the left hand as under the right hand [as in **fig. 7.3**] while holding the breath count 5 (aloud) then exhale while holding the hands in same position, repeat this exercise 5 times in succession."[27] This, apparently, was how debutantes embodied that flawless figure of

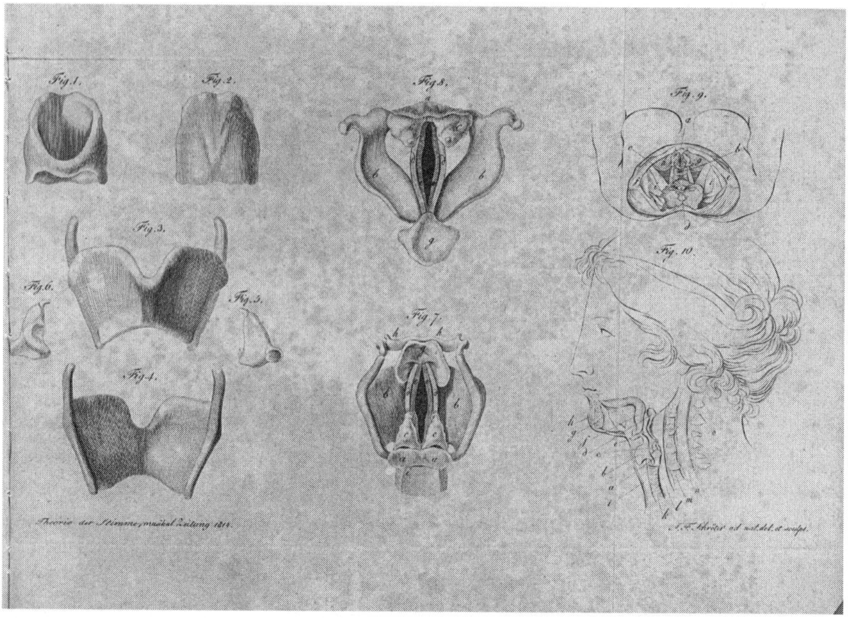

FIGURE 7.2 Karl Liscovius, *Theorie der Stimme* (Leipzig: Breitkopf und Härtel, 1814), n.p. Courtesy of the Eda Kuhn Loeb Music Library of the Harvard College Library.

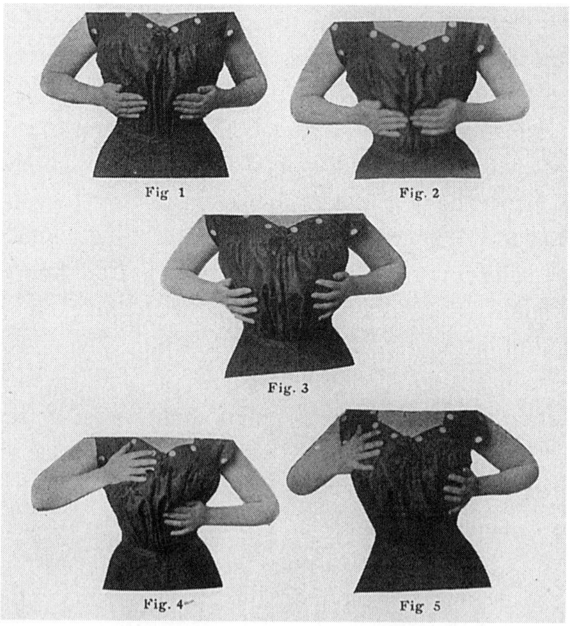

FIGURE 7.3 Millie Ryan, *What Every Singer Should Know* (Omaha: Franklin Publishing, 1910), 93; as also uncovered in Wayne Koestenbaum, *The Queen's Throat: Opera, Homosexuality, and the Mystery of Desire* (New York: Da Capo Press, 1993), 154.

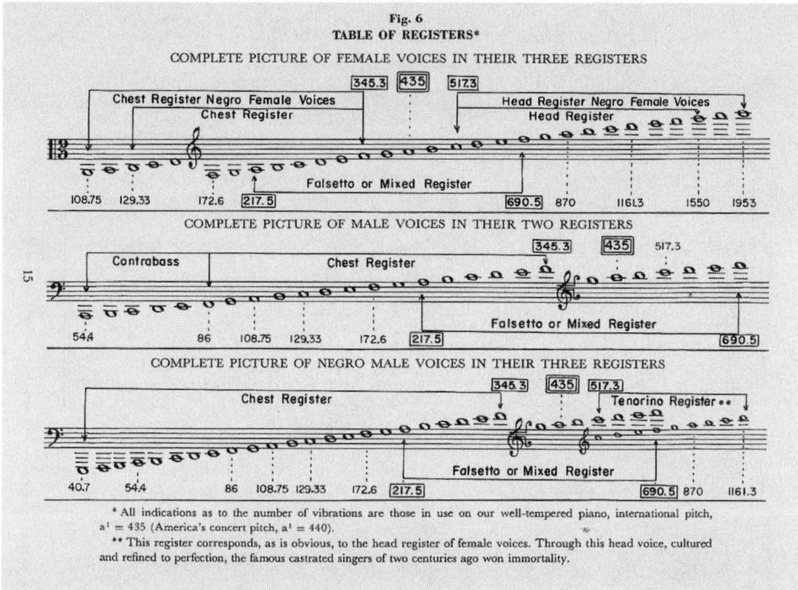

FIGURE 7.4 Racist divisions in Ida Franca, *Manual of Bel Canto* (New York: Coward-McCann, 1959), 15.

well-being and gendered sense of body so important to reproductive health in 1910s Omaha.

Voice can be productive of race or used to bolster conceits of race, as is clear from **figure 7.4**, a "table of vocal registers" printed by that doyenne of 1950s New York voice culture, Ida Franca. (Note too how women supposedly have three "registers" while men have a mere two, in ways dating back at least one hundred fifty years.)[28] The voices of African American males, according to this prominent lyric soprano and student of "king of baritones," Mattia Battistini, extend way farther down into their chest than those of their Caucasian counterparts. Such males, moreover, were also somehow capable of a so-called "tenorino register" (whatever that is) above the "falsetto and mixed register." These registral conceits, like all registral theories, at once make claim to and then furnish a kind of racialized truth for those who assent to them.

Voice, alternatively, can even lodge in the eyes, in ways that harken back to the earlier description of Pavarotti (**fig. 7.5**). This, at least according to Leone Giraldoni, was the prototypal "baritono" or "baritono-tenore" (as he classed himself), who was also Verdi's inspiration for the original *Simon Boccanegra* (Venice, 1857), as well as the first Renato in *Un ballo in maschera* (Rome, 1859). Giraldoni's view was gestural and melodramatic: that "the eyes are the soul of the body, making them, by themselves, enough to inculcate expressive truth." These "essential agents" of operatic culture helped "extend character"

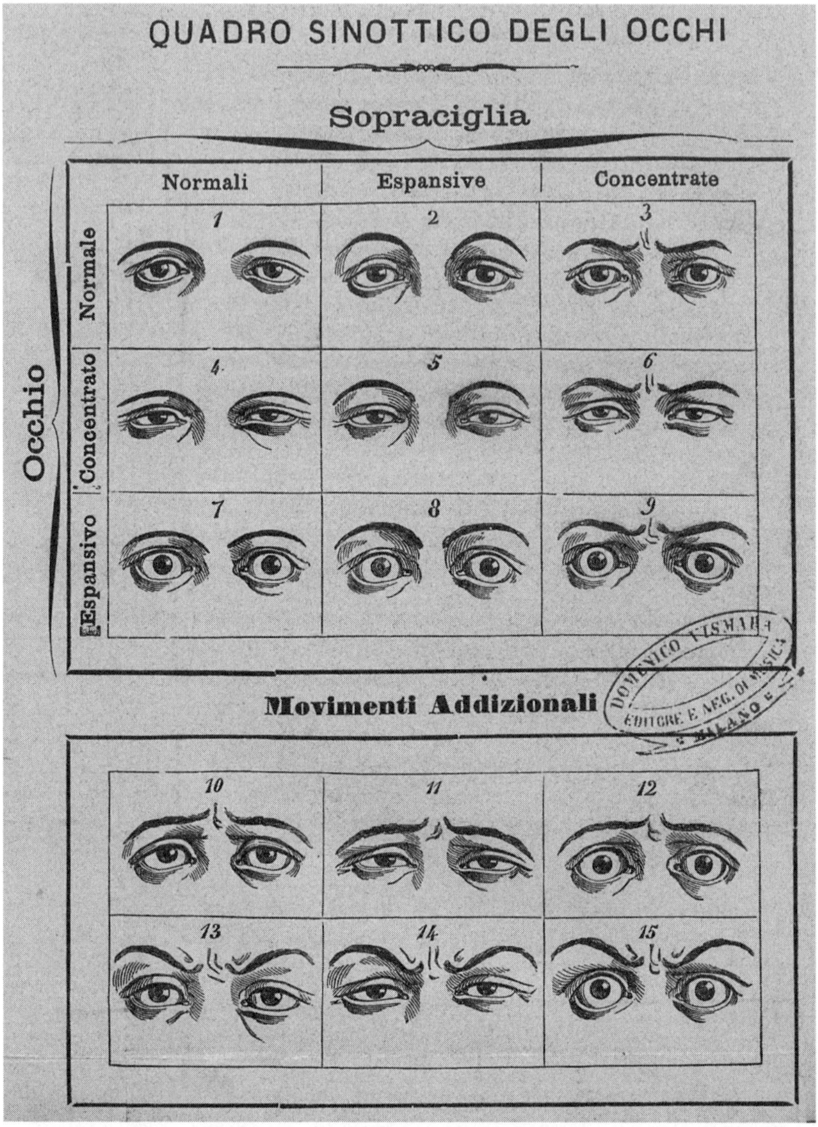

FIGURE 7.5 Melodramatic eyes in Leone Giraldoni, *Guida teorico-pratica ad uso dell'artista cantante* (Milan: Domenico Vismara, 1884), 61. Courtesy of the Conservatorio di musica "G. Verdi" di Milano.

to both dramatic and vocal utterance. "The combination of the three main movements of the eyes and eyebrows exemplifying the above three states [normal, concentrated, and expansive]," explained Giraldoni, "animate nine particular expressions that correspond to the sentiments: [neutrality (1)], indifference (2), ennui (3), physical and moral fatigue (4), contempt (5), mental concentration (6), stupor (7), astonishment (8), energy (9)."[29] Each of these expressive types, in other words, was controlled audiovisually, voices following the movements of eyes, and eyes the movements of voices. These figures represent only a few favored images detailing possible vocal placements, and they represent just the tip of the iceberg, which is to suggest that there was never only one single Euro-American, imperialistic, or "western" concept of voice.

Though if there were, and if I had to generalize, I would point to a related set of practices that the authors of nineteenth-century institutional or European conservatory sources increasingly indulged over the course of the century. In the earlier part of that period, as I have argued in detail elsewhere, it was usual to define voice in relation to the visible contingencies of language or rhetorical display—that is, to place voice in relation to mouths.[30] Increasingly, particularly when it came to politically liberal conceptions of voice, singers were instructed to roll their eyes back, and search inward, in something like the frantic manner of Pavarotti. It is certainly true that an impressive array of voice-related disciplines, from stenography to phonetics, vocal acoustics to voice synthesis, phonology to political theory, emerged in this period. These and a host of new voice-oriented technologies worked to enclose "the voice" as the uncanny index of subjective presence and integrity, as individual voices were at once contained and sacralized as reproducible objects of knowledge.[31] The sciences of "pure sound," acoustics and psychology, certainly held sway, as did the trials and tribulations of laryngoscopy and autosurvelliance. More and more—again to generalize recklessly—attention was directed to inner space and the invisible forces of "the body" so-called in ways at once fleshed out and complicated by the careful work of Gregory Bloch and Katherine Bergeron.[32]

Thus, to put this in highly schematic ways, we move from the outer voices or multiple, visible, and speaking mouths of **figure 7.6a**, where voice belonged to visibility and language, to **figure 7.6b**: inner covered voices or "invisible inside mouths" as seen through the lens of a laryngoscope. It is through the latter interiorizing and physiological optic, particularly around mid-century, that nonsignifying timbre came to be sexualized and sonic color became an audible mark of subjective difference, which is why the "inside mouth" of the glottis pictured by Louis Mandl (possibly the nineteenth century's most influential scientist of respiration in singing) was colored in lipstick red.[33] (This image actually does little justice to Mandl's achievement, which was to promulgate an inspirited view of voice, one sourced in the lungs, respiratory system, and atmospheric resonance in ways irradiated by such imposing vocal authorities as Henri Panofka and Francesco Lamperti.)[34] One way to

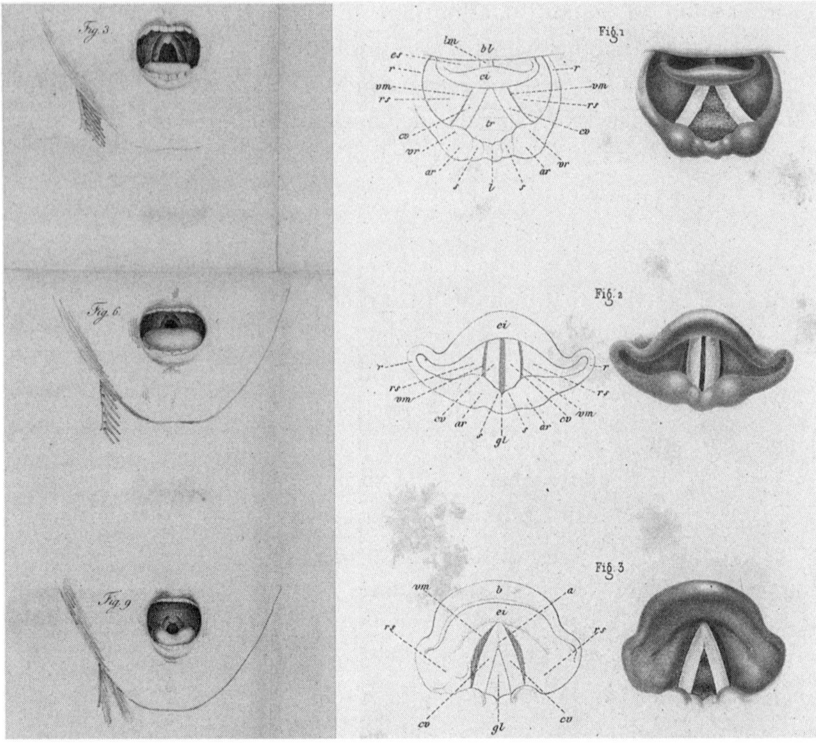

FIGURE 7.6 (a) Inside and outside mouths in Francesco Bennati, *Recherches sur le mécanisme de la voix humaine* (Paris: J.-B. Baillière, 1832), n.p.; (b) Louis Mandl, images of "deep inspiration," exhalation, and deep inspiration (anterior view) in *Traité pratique des maladies du larynx et du pharynx* (Paris: J. B. Baillière, 1872), n.p. © BIU Santé (Paris).

explain the new "metaphysics" would be to say that voice became a means by which to produce these inner corporeal spaces: as singers plumbed their own expressive depths and psychosomatic essences. The changing iconography of voice in Pan-European history thus suggests a deepening cultural imperative to search, direct, and monitor an increasingly terrifying and unruly nature: that is, to configure both voice and body in terms of more abstract, darker, and more inscrutable physiological and mental systems.

Remarkably, it was only in the 1890s that the ghostly image of the disembodied "voice itself" emerged fully into spectral and technological focus, in ways belying a fixation on timbre. True, initial experiments were conducted in Paris as early as 1857, with Edouard-Léon Scott de Martinville's first stenographic "graphic fixing of the voice" and Rudolph Koenig's celebrated manometric flame apparatus for visualizing vowel sounds (1862), devices that anticipated later phonographic or stenographic technologies for projecting or making icons of vocal sound.[35] Even laryngologists eventually came under attack for being overly superficial, or locating voice too narrowly at the glottis.[36] In the early decades of the twentieth century, I will soon describe, it became the norm to fix voice as colored vibration. Voice was substantiated autonomously as if the result of complex overtonal mixtures in the manner of the silhouette profiles appearing in **figure 7.7** and in Lilli Lehmann's highly influential *Meine Gesangskunst* (Berlin, 1902). (Lehmann was a famed Bavarian voice teacher and internationally renowned soprano of astounding versatility.) Here, tone color was generated in the body's resonating spaces: by the interactions of the cavities behind the nose, the sympathetic resonances of the pharynx, and the reverberances of the whole column of air. It was thought that a singer's persona—their whole tonal psychophysiology—could be figured according to the vibrant spectrum of sounds generated in accordance with the acoustic resonating chambers of the face and pharynx.

In **figure 7.8** (left), the full richness of one's tonal palette was only realized—apparently—by the desire for so-called forward tone placement. The instruction in Pasqual Mario Marafioti's *Caruso's Method of Voice Production: The Scientific Culture of the Voice* (New York, 1922) was to project swirling currents of air into "the mask." It was to focus tone by imagining the sensation of various balloons or balls formed behind the nose, such that the cavities proximate to the brain might reverberate with the correctly colored vowel (in ways that Neapolitan tenor Enrico Caruso in particular was said to have perfected—while being "immortalized" before the "Americanizing" horn of the Victor phonograph).

Marafioti in fact proposed a grand reform of American voice culture and a new psychological holism following the colorful example of Caruso, "the most magnificent vocal phenomenon of the human race." "His masque, chest, and all the cavities of his body, even in their remotest corners," Marafioti opined, "were producing sounding vibrations during the correct, free, and expansive production of his voice." "We should supplant the theory of registers," the author insisted later in the volume, "with one of *psychological intonation* of the voice." The vividly pigmented illustration in **figure 7.8** on the right "shows the full range of the voice as performed by a natural, correct mechanism." In Marafioti's psychology of voice, in fact, concepts of register would fall away: "There are *no registers* in the singing voice, when it is correctly produced," he explained. "According to natural laws the voice is made up of only *one* register, which constitutes its entire range." There was to be one resonant voice only, in other words, for each vibrant psychology.[37] "Do registers exist by nature?" Lehmann, that other beneficiary of personality cults developing around "great singers," asked in 1903. "No. It may be said that they

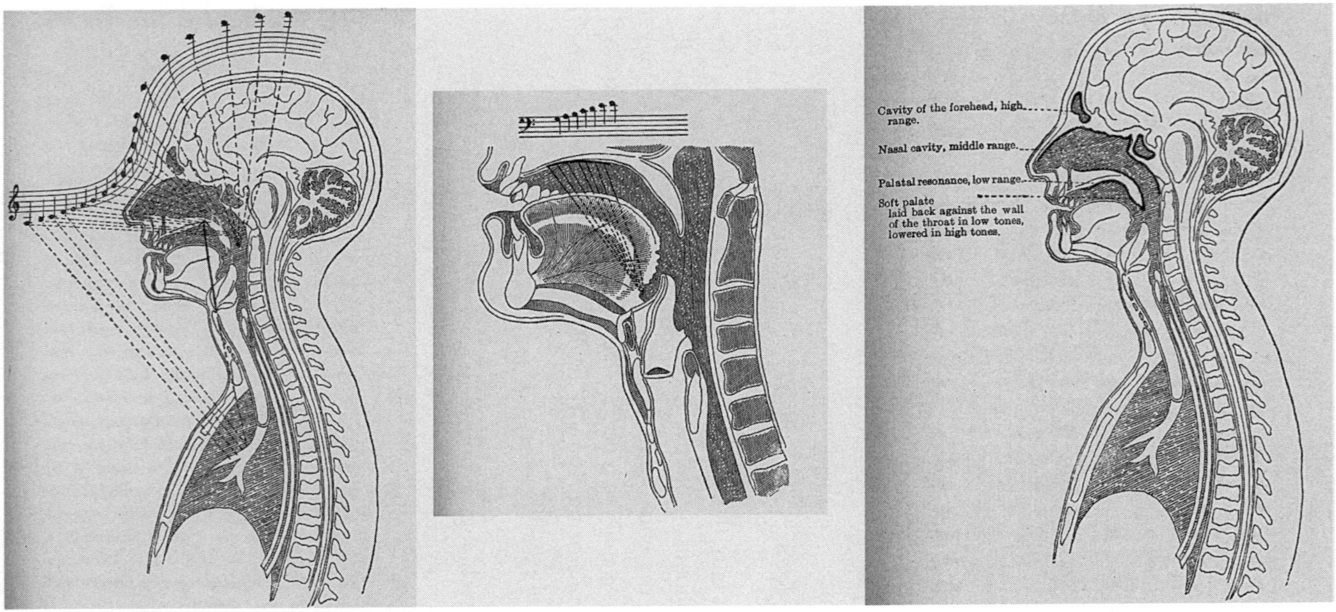

FIGURE 7.7 Images of tone placement, resonance, and currents of breath in Lilli Lehmann's *Meine Gesangskunst* (Berlin: Schwarzbaum, 1902). Courtesy of the Jean Gray Hargrove Music Library, University of California, Berkeley.

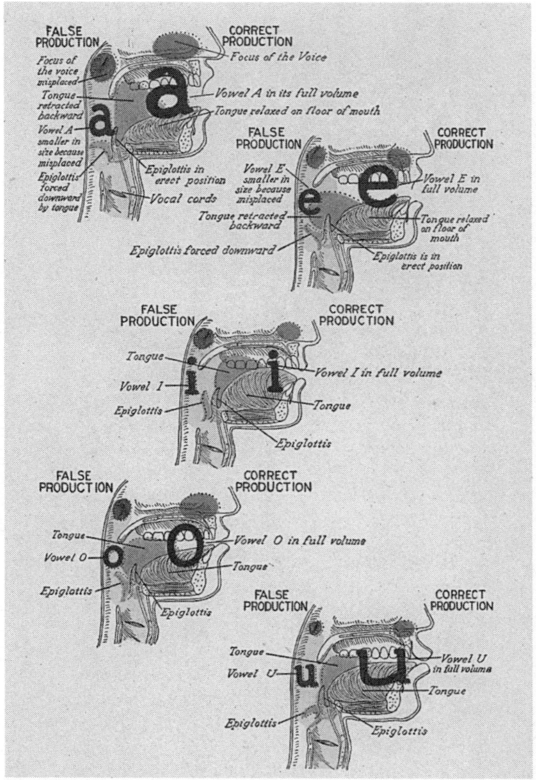

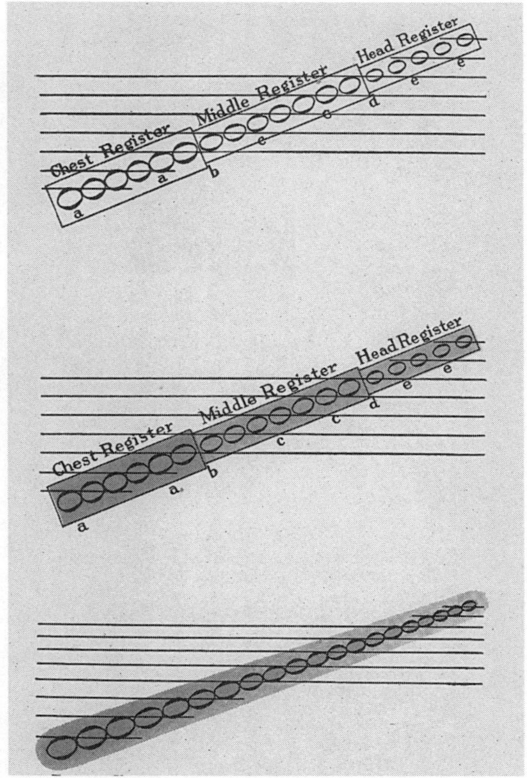

FIGURE 7.8 Two colorful illustrations of the psychosomatology of vocal and vowel sounds, the second showing the progression to a true single-registered voice, in P. Mario Marafioti, *Caruso's Method of Voice Production: The Scientific Culture of the Voice* (New York, 1922), 237 and 149.

are created through long years of speaking in the vocal range that is easiest to the person."[38]

Figure 7.9 pictures him: the Great Caruso, the tenor for whom—legend has it—Puccini originally conceived that famous opening *romanza* of his 1900 opera *Tosca*, the same sung with so much belief by Pavarotti in 1979

FIGURE 7.9 Caruso as Cavaradossi before his "Recondita armonia." Courtesy of the Metropolitan Opera Archives.

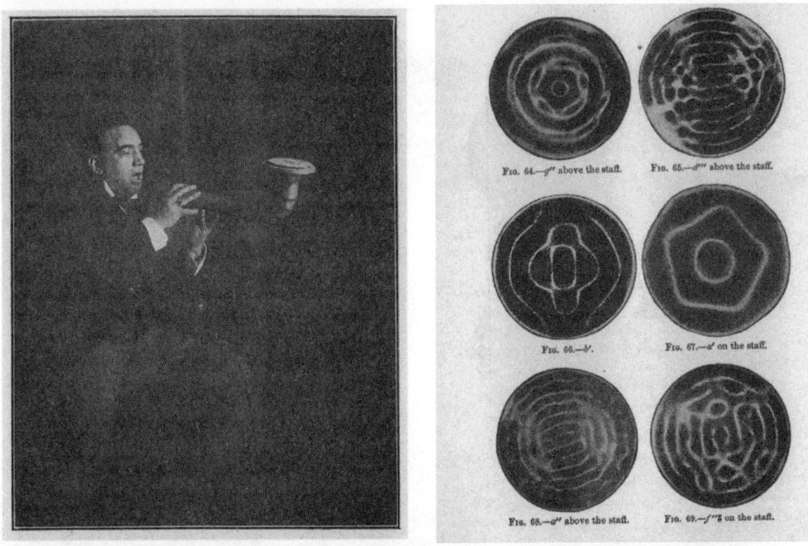

FIGURE 7.10 (a) Caruso and his bell-jar tonograph; (b) geometric voice-forms. Henry Holbrook Curtis, *Voice Building and Tone Placing, Showing a New Method of Relieving Injured Vocal Cords by Tone Exercises*, 3rd ed. (New York: D. Appleton, 1914), 235, 237. Courtesy of the Jean Gray Hargrove Music Library, University of California, Berkeley.

Modena.[39] "Recondita armonia" ("strange harmony"), "dammi i colori" ("pass me the colors"), Puccini's dreamy romantic painter Cavaradossi sings, as he puts brush to canvas. In the first moment of lyricism in this brutally "realist" opera—accompanied by glistening pentatonic woodwinds and harp—he paints not merely the image of the diva Tosca, her hair, her eyes, her divinity. He also paints with vocal color. Puccini's romance, that is, has the singer projecting his desire outward onto a screen. In the terms of early twentieth-century vocal practice, the singer is literally painting in reds, yellows, oranges, blues. Which is why vocal tone—an immaculate image and record of voice—miraculously appears.[40] (Caruso, famously, made two enigmatic voice-prints of "Recondita armonia" for the Victor Talking Machine Company, the first numbered Victor 81029, a "Red Seal" ten-inch record featuring piano accompaniment in February 1904, in Room 826, Carnegie Hall.)[41]

Caruso is doing something similar in **figure 7.10**. He is literally manufacturing a mystic disc-shaped icon of voice, painting tones in vibrant patterns, harmonic mixtures, and pigments. Or so he imagined. This tonograph was a popular voice-imaging technology of the sort that resembled such related and more lasting voice-imaging technologies as the Victor phonograph and the Berliner gramophone record. This particular version was an

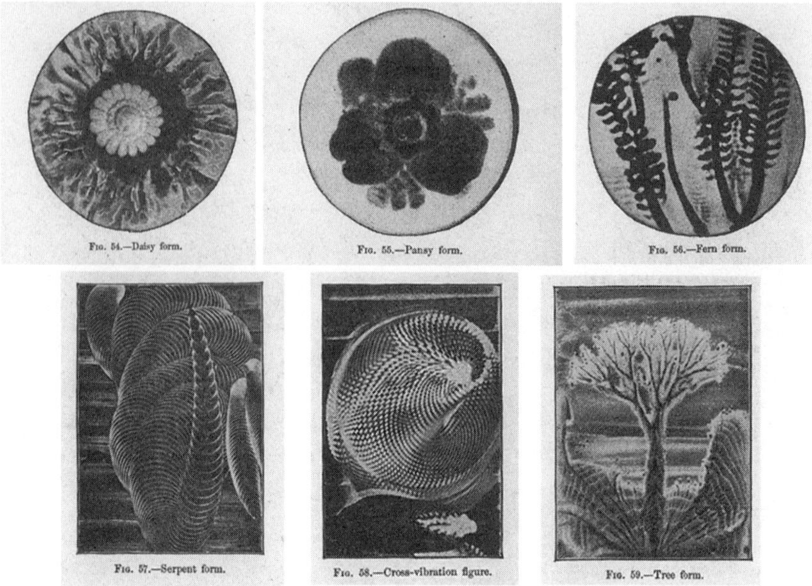

FIGURE 7.11 Recondite voice-prints appearing in Margaret Watts Hughes, "Visible Sound," *Century Magazine* 42, no. 1 (May 1891): 37–39. Courtesy of Doe Library, University of California, Berkeley.

instrument invented three years before *Tosca*'s premiere by a close American friend of Puccini, Henry Holbrook Curtis, for photographing what Curtis called "tone forms" and for observing the coming-into-being of "ravishing beauty of sound." The tonograph was a simple acoustic means of "recording in geometrical figures the vibrations of the voice."[42] And it featured a circular turntable-sized membrane stretched over a metal tube. When activated by standing vibration, the tonograph produced beautiful sound-figures, which Curtis interpreted as "copies of the will" or voice-signatures. This kind of painterly concept of voice characterized the voice culture of Caruso's heyday. Elsewhere in *Voice Building and Tone Placing*, first published in 1896, Curtis urged that singers study the "ingenious mingling of pure spectrum colors" and "color harmonics in music in the same way that they must be studied in painting."[43]

The most dazzling precedent for imprinting voice, Curtis always admitted, was the "eidophone," as developed around 1885 by the remarkable British soprano and pedagogue Margaret Watts Hughes.[44] The eidophone deployed standing-wave patterns and color pigments on glass, in order to animate strange "voice flowers," "tree forms," "serpent forms," myriad strange organic entities come to life (**fig. 7.11**). According to Curtis, the eidophone opened up a new world of voice, one where the resonant cavities of the head were analogous to "weird caverns at the bottom of the sea, full of beautiful coloured sea anemones and mussel shells, headless snakes, entanglements of flower and leaflike forms, all seemingly vital with the same laws of growth as those which inspired the creation of the designs in Nature which they suggest."[45] These self-organizing forms, produced by the magic of cross-vibration, made immortal records of vocal psychophysiology and vocal personality. And as Curtis, Watts Hughes, and clearly Caruso surmised, these vibrational mixtures could be projected and imprinted: as much upon the roof of the mouth, the diaphragm of the ear, as on surfaces of glass, wax, or vinyl.

Conclusion: "There Is No Before and After"

Having laid out these occult voice-icons, it is about time I qualified my confession that "I am an essentialist." That is the charge: essentialism—the merest whiff of which even the most unschooled undergraduate student will know to condemn as a "thought crime." I will defend myself against the guardians of academic purity by saying that I in no way think that essences or bodies are transparently indexed by voices. I do not think that bodies or objects are made self-evident or self-present in them, since that would be to define voice on the supply side alone, and validate accusations of racism, classicism, misogyny, ageism, xenophobia, or worse. Rather, I think voice is embroiled in fraught political battles over the social discrimination of that which matters. My position, therefore, is to insist that essences are formed in voice, and that voices—all voices—belong to these social matters and find their meaning in relation to them.

I will end by admitting that there is no doubt that voices are shaped by the bodies that produce them. But that thought also applies the other way around: *bodies* are also shaped by the *voices* that produce them. This goes beyond claiming that bodies might be altered, enhanced, or sculpted under the influence of constant vocal exercise in situations of both "disciplined" and "indisciplined" training. Rather, it is to claim that bodies are, not only discursively, but (as I have argued) performatively placed in voice. In the case of expressive singing, this is a question of biocultural knowledge: how bodies are made present, and how matters of physical concern are mediated and become known. My review of only two ways to produce Puccini's "Recondita armonia" suggests that to cultivate vocal sound is also to cultivate certain placements, and a certain order and experience of embodiedness. The thing about voices is that they can be sourced in so many different places, both within bodies and outside of bodies. And the thing about bodies is that they offer up a whole panoply of truths, which is to say they are amenable to myriad construals and configurations.

The point to conclude with is the following: that there is no necessary before and after when it comes to voice. Voices and bodies are acquired together: in tandem, not one after the other. In singing, in order to get real, you have to place, and in order to place, you have to know what and where a vocal sound is, or at least to have some understanding of how that particular voice works. Others have certainly formed you in this knowledge. But you have to feel the sound. And you have to be seen to cultivate the right equipment—the right body—to make it happen.

Notes

1. On the orthodoxy of "intervention," see Bruno Latour, "Why Has Critique Run out of Steam? From Matters of Fact to Matters of Concern," *Critical Inquiry* 30 (2004); 225–48; repr. in *Things*, ed. Bill Brown (Chicago: University of Chicago Press, 2004), 168–73.

2. Even Timothy Garton Ash, unabashed advocate for the "moral globalization" of "free expression" via the World Wide Web, warns that "free speech has never meant unlimited speech—everyone spouting whatever comes into their head, global logorrhea." In my opinion, the civil libertarian assumption that all sovereign citizens speak with equal force in the global marketplace of ideas is as wrong-headed as the civil libertarian idea of the "free market." The iconoclastic free-speechism of 2016 politics is a sign that the ideals of liberalism and democracy are no longer coextensive. We have entered the era of a selfist anarcho-capitalist modernity, a media-saturated polity that worships individual freedoms, and where moral law requires that "unregulated" (or rather indecent) speech be the most orthodox kind of speech there is. Under this regime, everything must speak belligerently, money in particular, and expression deregulated (as if such a thing were possible). Those who still believe in "extreme speech," who think unlimited envoicement proffers unlimited freedom, are to blame; and this includes *all* liberals—libertarians, classical liberals, liberty-mongering conservatives and republicans, free-market liberals, liberal innovator-creators, "Whole Foods" liberals, latte liberals, freethinking art-bloggers, neoliberals, liberal elites, Washington liberals. *All* of them are complicit in the thoroughly liberal catastrophe that has befallen this globalizing American polity. Timothy Garton Ash, *Free Speech: Ten Principles for a Connected World* (New Haven, CT: Yale University Press, 2016).

3. Wendy Brown, "Freedom's Silences," *Edgework: Critical Essays on Knowledge and Politics* (Princeton, NJ: Princeton University Press, 2005), 83–97, 84.

4. On the politics of "disidentification," see Nina Sun Eidsheim (after José Esteban Muñoz) in *Sensing Sound: Singing and Listening as Vibrational Practice* (Durham, NC, and London: Duke University Press, 2015), 8–9.

5. Sigmund Freud, "Remembering, Repeating, and Working Through," in *The Standard Edition of the Complete Psychological Works of Sigmund Freud*, vol. 12 (London: Hogarth Press, 1958; repr. 1986), 145–56.

6. For many and varied takes on acousmatic theory (for "theory" is what it is), see Michel Chion, "Prologue: Raising the Voice" and "The Acousmêtre," in *The Voice in Cinema*, trans. Claudia Gorbman (New York: Columbia University Press, 1999), 1–30; Jonathan Sterne, "Hello!," in *The Audible Past: Cultural Origins of Sound Reproduction* (Durham, NC, and London: Duke

University Press, 2003), 1–29; Brian Kane, "The Acousmatic Voice," in *Sound Unseen* (Oxford and New York: Oxford University Press, 2013), 180–222; and Mladen Dolar, "The Physics of the Voice," in *A Voice and Nothing More* (Cambridge, MA: MIT Press, 2006), 67–91.

7. See, for example, Kofi Agawu, "Does Music Theory Need Musicology?," *Current Musicology* 53 (1993): 89–98. Richard Taruskin isolated "the music itself" in "A Myth of the Twentieth Century: The Rite of Spring, the Tradition of the New, and 'The Music Itself,'" *Modernism/Modernity* 2, no. 1 (1995): 1–26, repr. in Taruskin, *Defining Russia Musically* (Princeton, NJ: Princeton University Press, 1997), 360–88; Pieter C. van den Toorn, "A Response to Richard Taruskin's 'A Myth of the Twentieth Century,'" *Music Theory Online* 1, no. 5 (1995); and Scott Burnham, "Theorists and 'the Music Itself,'" *Journal of Musicology* 15, no. 3 (1997): 316–29.

8. In Barthes's celebrated semiology, "grain" refers to "the body in a state of music," "the body in the voice as it sings," or "the materiality of the body speaking its mother tongue." "Russian" basses thus have "Russian" grain; such "Francophile" concert baritones as Charles Panzéra sound "French," and so on—classic, unreconstructed essentialism if ever there was; see Roland Barthes, "The Grain of the Voice," *Image, Music, Text*, trans. Stephen Heath (New York: Hill and Wang, 1977), 179–89.

9. Jacques Derrida, famously, engaged the term *différance* in order to both counter Edmund Husserl and rethink identity in nonessentialist terms as a dislodged system of signs, in *La Voix et le phénomène* (Paris: Presses Universitaires de France, 1967).

10. Existence itself, apparently, depends on the drive to extend the right of having a voice to those "without voices," and—in extreme "posthuman" cases—to envoice so-called "nonhuman" agents and things. Everything—all autonomous bodies, it seems—must have a voice in "the parliament of things." All entities must be privatized; all marginalized bodies must break free and "speak back." Jane Bennett, for example, writes of her benevolent intention to "to give voice to a thing-power," to "feature the negative power of recalcitrance of things" and "the active role of nonhuman materials in public life," in *Vibrant Matter: A Political Ecology of Things* (Durham, NC: Duke University Press, 2010), 2.

11. *What Makes a Great Tenor?*, dir. Dominic Best (London: BBC Four, 2011), DVD. For a clip of the video, see **website example 7.1.**

12. One is reminded of the giant omnipotent eye, representing Scarpia's police state, at the center of Philipp Himmelmann's staging of the act 1 "Te Deum" at the 2007 Bregenz Festival, famously featured in Marc Foster's 2008 James Bond film *Quantum of Solace*.

13. According to Barbara Berkenfield, *The Earth behind My Thumb* (Santa Fe, NM: Sunstone Press, 2008), 19.

14. "How to Sing Like Pavarotti," YouTube video, from an interview with Melvyn Bragg, *The South Bank Show*, televised on November 25, 1995, posted by "Sky Arts," July 3, 2014, https://www.youtube.com/watch?v=yc-hjr8WyO8. "I have a theory that when the tenor voice sings very high, the sound is unnatural," Pavarotti wrote in his 1995 autobiography. "It is not a sound that usually comes from humans; it is more like an animal sound. It may call out to something very deep in our nature. Maybe that is why it is so exciting to many people." Luciano Pavarotti and William Wright, *Pavarotti: My World* (London: Random House, 1995), 292–93. Singers have been "going animal" at least since Charles Bataille, Professor of Singing at the Paris Conservatory and pioneering student of the term "phonation," who would take students to the abattoir, to study the *beuglements* of cattle in distress, at least according to Auguste Laget, *Le chant et les chanteurs* (Paris: Heugel, 1874), 65.

15. "I have sometimes been moved to deep pity for these unfortunate singers, and filled with a great indulgence for the caprices, vanities, exactions, immoderate ambitions, exorbitant pretensions, and infinite absurdities of some among them," Berlioz continues. "They live but for a

day, and die for all time." In Hector Berlioz, *Evenings with the Orchestra*, trans. Charles E. Roche (New York and London: Alfred A. Knopf, 1929), 61, 67.

16. Foucault famously coined "species body" while identifying two poles in the history of the body: "One of these poles—the first to be formed, it seems—centered on the body as a machine: its disciplining, the optimization of its capabilities, the extortion of its forces, the parallel increase of its usefulness and its docility, its integration into systems of efficient and economic control, all this was ensured by the procedures of power that characterized the *disciplines: an anatomo-politics of the human body*. The second, formed somewhat later [around the very late eighteenth century], focused on the species body, the body imbued with the mechanics of life and serving as the basis of the biological processes: propagation, births and mortality, the level of health, life expectancy and longevity, with all the conditions that can cause these to vary"; Michel Foucault, *The History of Sexuality, Volume I: An Introduction*, trans. R. Hurley (New York: Vintage Books, 1978), 139.

17. One is reminded of Barthes's celebrated view that "there is no human voice which is not an object of desire—or of repulsion. Every relation to a voice is necessarily erotic," in Roland Barthes, *The Responsibility of Forms*, trans. Richard Howard (New York: Hill and Wang, 1985), 279.

18. Slavoj Žižek, "I Hear You with My Eyes: or, the Invisible Master," *Gaze and Voice as Love Objects*, ed. Renata Salecl and Slavoj Žižek (Durham, NC, and London: Duke University Press, 1996), 92.

19. Pythagoras, famously, instructed his students from behind a curtain, thus inventing a vocal modality of mythic power and authority. On curtains, see Kane, "Myth and the Origin of the Pythagorean Veil," in *Sound Unseen*, 45–72. Dolar writes perceptively of philosophy itself as (merely) the byproduct of certain practice and modality of voice: "the Teacher, the Master behind the curtain, proffering his teaching from there without being seen: no doubt a stroke of genius which stands at the very origin of philosophy—Pythagoras was allegedly the first to describe himself as a 'philosopher,' and also the first to found a philosophical school"; in *A Voice and Nothing More*, 61.

20. Gary Tomlinson, *A Million Years of Music: The Emergence of Human Modernity* (Brooklyn, NY: Zone Books, 2015).

21. R. Murray Schafer coined the term "schizophonia" to refer "to the split between an original sound and its electroacoustical transmission or reproduction," a phenomenon he felt unnatural, in *The Tuning of the World* (New York: Knopf, 1977), 90. Jason Stanyek and Benjamin Piekut write: "All sounds are severed from their sources—that's what makes sound sound. Rhizophonia is our term for taking account both of sound's extensity and the impossibility of a perfect identity between sound and source"; in "Deadness: Technologies of the Intermundane," *TDR: The Drama Review* 54, no. 1 (Spring 2010): 14–38, at 19. See also Gregory Bateson's "schizomogenesis" (1935) as developed by Steven Feld in "From Schizophonia to Schizomogenesis," in Charles Keil and Steven Feld, *Music Grooves* (Chicago: University of Chicago Press, 1994), 257–89.

22. For more, see my "Voice Belongs," in Colloquy: "Why Voice Now?," Martha Feldman et al., *Journal of the American Musicological Society* 68, no. 3 (2015): 677–81.

23. Derrida, "Introduction" and "La voix qui garde le silence," in *La Voix et le phénomène*, 1–16 and 78–97.

24. Edmund Husserl, *Logische Untersuchungen*, 5 vols. (Halle: Max Niemayer, 1900–1921).

25. Dolar, *A Voice and Nothing More*, 67–91.

26. The problem with any supply-side conception of voice, of course, is that it assumes a straightforward causal relationship between "the body" (so-called) and "the voice" (so-called); such

conceptions draw an arrow from vocal cords to sound. It is surely a mistake to assume that voices only ever work in one way: as in, body first, then voice. The error, perhaps, is to think that prelapsarian nature exists "out there," and that somehow (due to our modernity) voices were once severed from that nature. There was never such a "loss of innocence" (in the words of Chion) and never such a supremely Pavarottian nature. It is precisely this "if only" sense of voice, associated with the libertarian politics of lost paradises, that I aim to agitate against. See Chion, *The Voice in Cinema*, 11.

27. Millie Ryan, *What Every Singer Should Know* (Omaha, NE: Franklin Publishing Co., 1910), 88.

28. Registral theories have a long and complicated past. There is a long history of claiming that men only have two "voices," "registers," or "instruments" (chest and head) while women (usually with children and castrati) apparently have more, as in **figure 7.4**. (This has been true at least since Nina d'Aubigny von Engelbrunner's *Briefe an Natalie über den Gesang* [Leipzig: Leopold Boss, 1803], written by a women's education advocate working from Calcutta, India.) Emma Seiler, student of Friedrich Wieck and Heinrich Helmholtz, went so far as to identify no fewer than five registers with the assistance of autolaryngoscopy. Later authorities even said there might be "as many registers as there are notes." Thaddeus Wronski, *The Singer and His Art* (New York: D. Appleton, 1921), 31. For an overview, see Brent Jeffrey Monahan, *A Compendium of Thoughts on Singing Published between 1777 and 1927* (Metuchen, NJ: Scarecrow Press, 1978), 146.

29. Leone Giraldoni, *Guida teorico-pratica ad uso dell'artista cantante* (Milan: Domenico Vismara, 1884), 60–61. Giraldoni's guide was first published in Bologna in 1864.

30. J. Q. Davies, *Romantic Anatomies of Performance* (Berkeley: University of California Press, 2014), 128–29.

31. For an exquisite summary, see Ellen Lockhart's "Voice Boxes," in *London Voices, 1820–1840: Vocal Performers, Practices, Histories*, ed. Roger Parker and Susan Rutherford (Chicago: University of Chicago Press, 2019).

32. Gregory Bloch, "The Pathological Voice of Gilbert-Louis Duprez," *Cambridge Opera Journal* 19, no. 1 (2007): 11–31; and Katherine Bergeron, *Voice Lessons: French Mélodie in the Belle Epoque* (Oxford: Oxford University Press, 2010).

33. The crucial text was Louis Mandl, "De la fatigue de la voix," *Gazette médicale de Paris* 25 (March 24, 1855): 180–81.

34. Henri Panofka, *L'art de chanter, théorie et pratique, suivies du vade-mecum du chanteur contenant des exercises . . . et de vingt-quatre vocalises*, op. 81 (Paris, 1854); and Francesco Lamperti, *Guida teorico pratica elementare per lo studio del canto* (Milan: Ricordi, 1864).

35. Prévost's "*sténographie musicale*" of 1833 and Pitman's "phonography" of 1837 predated these techniques further; see Hippolyte Prévost, *Sténographie musicale ou art de suivre l'exécution musicale, en écrivant* (Paris: Prévost-Crocius, 1833); and Isaac Pitman, *Stenographic Sound Hand* (London: Samuel Bagster, 1837). Edouard-Léon Scott de Martinville fixed voice in spectral terms as disembodied sound. "What is the voice, indeed?" he wrote in 1857. "A periodic motion of the air which surrounds us, caused by the working of our organs; but a motion very complex and infinitely delicate." "Fixation graphique de la voix," trans. Patrick Feaster, in *The Phonautographic Manuscripts of Edouard-Léon Scott de Martinville* (FirstSounds.org, 2008), 22–42. http://www.firstsounds.org/publications/working-papers/First-Sounds-Working-Paper-03.pdf, accessed July 23, 2016. David Pantalony, "Seeing a Voice: Manometric Vowel Studies," in *Altered Sensations: Rudolph Koenig's Acoustical Workshop in Nineteenth-Century Paris* (New York: Springer, 2009), 88–91.

36. Fights over whether the glottis was the true origin of voice (and late-century skirmishes over the righteousness of the *coup de glotte*) are too involved to rehearse here; suffice it to point

to Mandl's celebrated attack and redefinition of the glottis as nothing but a void, which "me semble-t-il plus convenable d'appeler désormais *orifice de la glotte* ou *l'orifice glottique*, l'espace désigné généralement sous le nom de glotte." Mandl, "Étymologie de la glotte," *Le Ménestrel: Journal de musique* 37, no. 5 (January 2, 1870), 37. Mandl, that is, ended up preferring to define voice (away from the glottis) in view of respiratory space and resonance.

37. Pasqual Mario Marafioti, *Caruso's Method of Voice Production: The Scientific Culture of the Voice* (New York: D. Appleton, 1922), 1, 7, 151.

38. Lilli Lehmann, *How to Sing [Meine Gesangkunst]*, trans. Richard Aldrich (London: Macmillan, 1902), 133–34.

39. The official story, actually, is that Caruso expected to play the part, but Puccini changed his mind during rehearsal and gave it to the older and more experienced Emilio de Marchi, probably at Ricordi's insistence; see Julian Budden, *Puccini: His Life and Works* (Oxford: Oxford University Press, 2002), 197.

40. This "record" was in fact a literal "disc," according to contemporaneous reports. "He secured his brilliancy and resonance principally from the spaces of the mouth and head;—especially the latter. They were reinforced by the resonance supplied by Caruso's deep chest (his entire body aided in this respect), but he directed this tone to the front of the face, one might say almost at a sort of disk, made up of that part from the base of the nose to the lower part of the forehead and including the cheek bones." Pierre V. R. Key, *Enrico Caruso: A Biography* (Boston: Little, Brown, and Company, 1922), 369.

41. The Library of Congress has digitized this recording for its National Jukebox, http://www.loc.gov/jukebox/recordings/detail/id/375/, accessed September 10, 2016.

42. Henry Holbrook Curtis, "The Tonograph," *Scientific American* 76, no. 22 (1897): 345–46.

43. Henry Holbrook Curtis, *Voice Building and Tone Placing, Showing a New Method of Relieving Injured Vocal Cords by Tone Exercises* (New York: D. Appleton, 1896), 152.

44. Margaret Watts Hughes, "Visible Sound," *Century Magazine* 42, no. 1 (May 1891): 37–39.

45. Watts Hughes, "Visible Sound," 226.

PART IV

Myth, Wound, and Gap

8

Is the Voice a Myth? A Rereading of Ovid

SHANE BUTLER

My own obsession with the long Western obsession with Narcissus may or may not be a symptom of narcissism in the conventional sense: that, surely, is for others to decide. In either case, the perverse result of this obsession with an obsession has been the conclusion that Narcissus is not only far less important than he thinks he is, but also far less important than *we* think he is. Regarding classical antiquity, I have come to this conclusion largely through the slow but steady realization that the story of Narcissus and Echo in the *Metamorphoses* of the Roman poet Ovid, who may be the first ancient writer to pair the figures, is overwhelmingly about Echo. At every turn of the Latin original, she infiltrates and occupies the speech of poet and protagonist alike, causing an already noisy poem to explode into polyphonic extrasemantic repetition. This begins even before her first appearance, provoking Tiresias to deliver his prophecy about Narcissus's self-knowledge in self-echoing sound (*si se non noverit*, "provided that he not come to know himself," 3.348), and it continues to the end, even as Narcissus's life flows out through his eyes (*perque oculos perit ipse suos*, "by way of his own eyes he leaves life," 3.440).[1] Regarding, instead, the hapless youth's modern mythography, I have come to the same conclusion by struggling to make sense of a generally overlooked loose end in Lacan's account of the "mirror stage." We shall return in a moment to this loose end, which partly depends on the attempted deracination of its hero from the mythographic tradition through which he reached Lacan, via Freud, the Surrealists, and others. That attempt makes for a very odd chapter in the retelling of classical myths in the twentieth century—a story too long to tell here, though I have partly told it elsewhere.[2]

All of this is to say that my obsession with Narcissus has led me to become very much an antinarcissist, in search of a way to move beyond him.

Of course, one could easily object that antinarcissism is just a mirror image of narcissism, or even its echo. One way or another, I, like Echo herself, just can't stop talking about him, and to some extent, that will continue to be the case in this essay. Nevertheless, I think that thinking about sound offers a new way to think about what we might call the Narcissus problem, which, it turns out, was more interestingly understood by most pre-twentieth-century readers as the Echo problem. And conversely, I would like to suggest that thinking about—and beyond—Narcissus helps reveal what is by now an inveterate problem in the modern study of myth itself.

Let us therefore turn in earnest to that great Latin treasury of ancient myth: the *Metamorphoses* of Ovid. Scholars continue to mine the poem for its single stories (as I myself shall do in what follows), but it does not unfold encyclopedically. Indeed, the linear reader soon begins to notice that the poet often seems to be repeating—obsessively, even posttraumatically—something like the same story, over and over, with minor if escalating variation. Here is an example. In the poem's first erotic episode (1.452–567), Apollo pursues Daphne, introducing what we might call a radically heterosexual paradigm, since these two are differentiated not only by gender but by divine hierarchies and topographies, as the male Olympian god of the sun pursues a female, terrestrial nymph of the forest:

$$A \rightarrow D_a$$

Daphne, however, has already pursued, in the sense of following and imitating, Diana, virgin goddess of the hunt, whom she copies in dress and habits, to the point that she becomes the very picture of her model:

$$D_a \rightarrow D_i$$

Diana, though, is a pretty close copy of Apollo, who is in fact her twin brother, and she follows him through the heavens as the moon to his sun, reflecting if not outshining him:

$$D_i \rightarrow A$$

Put it all together, and we get this:

$$A \rightarrow D_a \rightarrow D_i \rightarrow A$$

This chain of pursuit means that the first character, whether he knows it or not, is chasing the last:

$$A \rightarrow A$$

In other words, we already are well on our way to this, in the poem's third book:

$$N_{(s)} \rightarrow N_{(o)}$$

That is to say: Narcissus as subject and Narcissus as object.

Indeed, the story of Narcissus has been anticipated not only by that of Apollo chasing Daphne as a reflected version of himself. Both episodes are already prefigured by the poem's opening genesis of the world, which leads an unnamed creator to look down on the face of creation and to find himself, reflected back. This scene in turn reflects the pose of the poet himself, who addresses gods and readers alike in the poem's first lines and again in its final ones regarding his own act of creation and pursuit of fame. And so the poem unfolds in between, perhaps nowhere more clearly than in books 10 and 11, which tell the story of the first poet, Orpheus, who, at the conclusion of the poem's longest episode, which occupies all of the poem's tenth book and the beginning of its eleventh, finally both follows and is followed by his beloved Eurydice, in the underworld. We are left to wonder: Where exactly in the poem did the telling of this myth of mirrors *first* begin, and when exactly will it end? Little wonder that Ovid calls his poem, in its opening lines, a *carmen perpetuum*, a "continuous song," and ends it with the promise of a new beginning: *vivam*, "I shall live."

If Ovid thereby teaches us anything, it is surely that a mythographic origin is anything but the end of the story. Despite, however, this lesson from such an important master, the point of departure in modern studies of myth has generally been exactly the opposite. Especially since the beginning of the last century, we have tended to regard a myth's *aition*, its "origin" or "cause," as its *finis*, its "end" and binding "definition." (This is generally true even of scholars who allow some flexibility in those limits on the grounds that a myth must be somewhat ambiguous in order to remain generative of meaning over time.) If we look *through* a myth's tradition, then this has usually been to distill an essence that we mostly suppose was there all along. If that essence changes significantly, then the myth isn't really the same myth at all: only then have we tended to allow ourselves to begin interpreting all over again. Most times, though, it seems to us to be the same old story, whether we are being told about Oedipus by Sophocles, Seneca, or Freud, or about Narcissus by Ovid, Caravaggio, Cocteau, or Lacan.

Indeed, Ovid's version of the twinned tales of Narcissus and Echo might seem to offer a parable of the etiological principle at work, already in the relationship between the two characters. At the center of the account, in the interpretation that has become customary over the past several decades, is Narcissus, staring into the liquid "source" (*fons*) of his own iteration. Echo, by contrast, who can only repeat the words of her indifferent beloved, appears in the story just long enough to reveal her own extraneousness to it and so to signify—and to gender—lack itself. Such is the reading, for example, of Alessandro Barchiesi, general editor of a recent six-volume translation and commentary that aims to be the last word on Ovid's masterpiece for some time to come, and Gianpiero Rosati, coeditor with Barchiesi of the volume that includes Ovid's account of Echo and Narcissus, comprising 171 lines in the poem's third book. To the episode, Barchiesi and Rosati devote thirty-two dense pages attuned to its every ideological nuance, unfolding, in the process, a veritable map of the critical horizons of late twentieth-century literary scholarship.[3]

Nevertheless, as I have observed elsewhere, those same thirty-two pages remain almost entirely deaf to poetic sound.[4] This is despite the fact that, as I have already intimated above, centuries of readers prior to the twentieth were anything but sure that Narcissus wins the poetic *agon* implied by Ovid's pairing of the two once separate myths. To give just one example: Boccaccio, in his *Genealogy of the Pagan Gods*, regards Echo as a kind of tenth Super-Muse and confidently places her home on Parnassus, the mountain of poetry itself.[5] Indeed, already in Ovid's own poem-closing bid for immortality as an endlessly repeating voice, the author "resembles no character in the poem so closely as his own Echo," as one very exceptional recent reader of the poem, Lynn Enterline, astutely observes.[6] In other words, it is as an echo that the poem's final *ego* (note the echo) "shall live." If Narcissus and his mirror seem at first to be the myth's starting point and centerpiece, then Echo turns out to be something far more interesting, not only in the episode itself, but throughout the poem—and even beyond, in the long tradition of imitation and adaptation Ovid inspired.[7] Indeed, I would go so far as to insist that she, not Narcissus, is revealed to be the myth's ultimate *raison d'être*. And she comes to matter so not because she offers a competing etiology (that is, the origin of reflected sound), but precisely *as* reflection, repetition, echo.

Let me go still further in order to place before my reader a hypothesis directly opposed to conventional approaches to myth. I would like to suggest that the truth of a myth—and I say "truth" in lieu of any better word, for I mean something more than mere meaning, I mean what a myth *really tells us*, in the end—is *never* to be sought in its *aition*, whether by that we mean its reconstructed origin in a human encounter with a natural phenomenon, or in the workings of the human psyche or of human society, or even merely in its first telling. Rather, I wish to suggest, the truth of a myth comes *only* in its retelling. The first and simplest proof of this is that nothing that is told only once can even be called a myth: to speak of a retold myth is to offer a pleonasm. But I mean more than this. I mean that it is only in retelling that a myth can acquire what it lacks, that it can become an Echo, by which I mean—and here I am going to be perverse and even fetishistic—a real, solid, present, material being. In other words, it is only through retelling that a myth acquires a *voice*, that mythology gives way to mythophony. And I want to argue that voices, and other bodies like voices, constitute the truth of a myth, or if you prefer, its unending truths.

What is a voice? That this question has acquired such urgency of late is already a sign of shifting critical winds.[8] For Adriana Cavarero, the voice is precisely that thing which philosophy fails to hear, to which, indeed, it is constitutionally deaf.[9] In part, for her, this is because the voice is always *a particular voice*, and so one of many possible voices, while philosophy is attentive only to unities. But critical obtuseness to voices can also be more generally hermeneutic; indeed, Susan Sontag long ago laid the blame for the lack of an "erotics" of art at the feet of interpretation tout court.[10] To be sure, Ovid taunts us with invitations to engage in both philosophy and interpretation. On the one hand, Narcissus's story pointedly burlesques the Socratic search for self-knowledge, emblematized by the "know thyself" inscribed on the Temple of Apollo at Delphi. On the other, the story can be read as the lavish elaboration of a schoolroom riddle: in the sentence "Narcissus loves Narcissus," which in Latin, better still, would instead be *Narcissus Narcissum amat*, what is the difference between the first and second Narcissus, between *Narcissus* and *Narcissum*? Ovid's paradox, in fact, is less about Latin grammar than it is about the syntax of pederasty: Narcissus is just of that borderline age (sixteen, in Ovid's account) that allows him to play the man to his own boy, distinguished in Greek by the active and passive participles (*erastēs*, *erōmenos*) of the verb for love.

But where does all of this leave Echo? Or Daphne, for that matter, whose story Echo echoes? For Daphne is not just any tree: she is the laurel, the very emblem of poetry. Artistic materiality has a nonnegligible role to play here. "Paint a sound," suggests Echo to an artist who would depict her, in an epigram of the late-antique poet Ausonius.[11] Narcissus himself could be regarded as the world's first painter, according to the Renaissance classroom of Leon Battista Alberti.[12] Ovid's description of the moving lips of Narcissus's reflected *imago* in the water, producing "words not reaching my ears" (*verba . . . aures non perveneniia nostras*), was taken by John Brenkman, forty-three years ago, as an allegory of writing (and of silent reading).[13] I myself have observed resemblances between Ovid's odd description of the pond's surface and that of the furrowed black wax of a Roman writing tablet.[14] An echo, in Ovid's Latin, is an *imago vocis*, which is part of how Ovid makes her embody poetry itself. And so on. Rather than seeing this all as a symptom of myth's inevitable fall into text and tradition, or as so much Ovidian metapoetic frippery, I suggest we look here for the very essence of mythmaking.

Let us therefore move forward through Ovid's mythography until the starting points we have been rehearsing have been transformed almost beyond recognition. And like Lavinia in Shakespeare's *Titus Andronicus*, who "turns the leaves" of a copy of Ovid's *Metamorphoses* with her mutilated arms, let us stop at "the tragic tale of Philomel." In what easily is one of Ovid's most horrific episodes of sexual (or any other) violence, the Thracian king Tereus drags his sister-in-law, Philomela, to a cabin in the woods and rapes her. When she threatens to tell the world of his crime, he cuts out her tongue, which, on the ground, continues to move; thus silenced, she is again raped, repeatedly:

> But it's her tongue he seizes with a pincer;
> and even as it calls upon her father,
> protests and struggles hard to speak, he lifts
> his blade and—without mercy—severs it.
> Its root still quivers, while the tongue itself
> falls to the ground; there, on the blood-red soil,
> it murmurs; as a serpent's severed tail
> will writhe, so did that tongue, in dying, twist
> and try to reach its mistress's feet. Though this
> indeed defies belief, it's said that Tereus
> again, again, gave free rein to his lust
> upon that mangled body.[15]

No Freudian reader can fail to find here a story of castration and the fetish, especially since, moments before, Tereus "frees his sword from its sheath" (*vagina liberat ensem*, 6.551), and Ovid here compares Philomela's twitching tongue to the severed tail of a snake, using the same relatively uncommon word for a female snake (*colubra*, 6.559) he has already used, earlier in the poem, for the hair of Medusa at the very moment of her decapitation. Indeed, the floating of severed signifiers becomes even more grotesque when we consider that Philomela's threat has already made her tongue like a forefinger, ready to point out the culprit, for *index*, in Latin, is both the finger that points and the person who says "I accuse." Completing the picture is the fact that she says she will thus finger him after casting aside feminine "modesty" (*pudor*, 6.544), which in the logic of Roman shame culture is tantamount to unsexing herself. In other words, Philomela claims for herself the phallus she instantly is made to lose.

But this is not the end of the story. Escape from her prison is impossible, and in any case, *os mutum facti caret indice*, "her mute mouth lacks its *index* of the deed" (6.574). So she finds another way: "Cleverly, she hangs the warp on a barbarian loom"—an act that already grimly mimes her barbaric rape—"and weaves purple marks into white threads" (6.576–77). This *indicium sceleris*, "accusation of crime" (6.578), she folds up and contrives to have delivered to her sister Procne, setting in motion the story's revenge phase, in which Philomela and Procne will butcher and cook the latter's son by Tereus, who devours the meal, unknowing. In the end, all three will be transformed into birds.[16]

The "purple marks" (*purpureae notae*) of this "tedious sampler" (as Shakespeare calls it in the play I already have mentioned, which lavishly reworks the ancient myth) must now command our close attention. "Purple" here has its ancient sense, designating antiquity's costliest dye, secreted both offensively and defensively by the Mediterranean sea snail (*murex*), producing a remarkably rich array of hues, many of which correspond to what we would call "crimson" rather than "purple."[17] In other words, an ancient reader would immediately have understood these marks to be suitably blood-red, as if Philomela has bled directly onto the cloth, or better, as if the folded fabric has itself bled, as a hymeneal substitute for her once untouched skin. But what kinds of marks are these? It has been common to see them as writing, but Ovid's word is far from clear. *Notae* can be "letters," but they also can be any meaningful mark, including the telltale signs of violence on a human body or, more innocently, the moles and other naturally occurring marks that distinguish one body from another. Alternatively, they could be pictures of her violation, like those sewn by Arachne to illustrate the cruelty of the gods, earlier in the poem's same book. In the end, however, it is not entirely clear that they are signs in any conventional sense at all: perhaps their signature skill simply gives Philomela's sister incontrovertible evidence that she is still alive, despite Tereus's claim to the contrary—the rest then being easy enough to deduce.

We could not, it would seem, be further away from the voice: either this strange blanket is a text and so expresses its author's wishes while still miming her muteness, or else, silenter still, it is not verbal at all. And yet, when the object arrives, this is what Ovid says Philomela's sister does with it: *carmen miserabile legit*, "she reads the pitiful song" (6.582).[18] Since Ovid has called his whole epic a "song" already in his opening lines, the designation of Philomela's creation as such pointedly assimilates it to the verses we have read. And philology steps in to explain that Ovid can call his poem a song, as do all ancient poets, both because the Homeric epics that lend him his verse form were once sung (albeit in a past already ancient for Ovid himself) and because other kinds of poetry continued to receive musical performance. Some will add that Philomela's sister, in reading, perhaps aloud (in contrast to the silence of her ensuing reaction), *lends* this object both pity and a voice, and possibly even music. What happens, however, to our understanding of the voice if we instead take seriously the ancient claim that songs can be written and read? What, indeed, would it mean to suppose not just that Philomela's *carmen miserabile* represents a voice, or is the surrogate for one, or elicits one, but, rather, that it actually *has* a voice?

Let us pause a moment. In looking for a voice in something that is sufficiently like a text to be embodied by one, are we falling victim to the "phonocentrism" decried not by Lacan, but by Derrida? I do not think so, at least not exactly. For "phonocentrism" is Derrida's other name for "logocentrism" only because he takes the Greek word *phoné* always to mean "speech," though its primary meaning is instead "voice."[19] Aristotle emphatically is looking not for the former, but for the latter, anatomically, as a very messy mix of pharynx and larynx that plunges deep into cardiac flesh (home to the embodied force that Aristotle calls the "soul"), in several of the key passages Derrida misrepresents as instead being about disembodied "speech" and thus about metaphysical *logos*. Even when he really is talking about "speech," Aristotle seldom means the bloodless abstraction Derrida wants him to be talking about. In any case, when I suggest that Philomela's tapestry has or even is a voice, I am not quietly folding a text into the voice's deep tissue. I mean instead a simple (and, indeed, hylomorphically Aristotelian) proposition: spoken or written, there is no language without matter.

Philomela's creation, the persistent materiality of which is so conspicuously like that of a body—both her own, in that it seems to bleed with and for her, and one in lieu of that of the child that, almost uniquely in such myths, her rape does not cause her to produce—arguably calls neither for Lacan nor for Derrida but, instead, for Kristeva. For this purple page seems very much an instance of the Kristevan semiotic, a place of "signifiance," where significance is emergent rather than static—in short, what she calls a "genotext."[20] Kristeva's early mentor Roland Barthes makes extensive use of her distinction between "genotext" and "phenotext" in his essay "The Grain of the Voice," but it is another of Barthes's epigrammatic formulations that may be of more use to us here, namely, what he calls (in his essay "Listening") "the shimmering (*miroitement*) of signifiers."[21] It helps a bit that Philomela's signifiers really would have shimmered, for one of the distinctive qualities of fine ancient purple is that the dye's crystals sit on the surface of the fabric, catching the light as the fabric moves.[22] And it is in this light that I want to oppose Barthes's *miroir* to that of Lacan, who sought to refine Freud's distillation of "narcissism" into something so pure and simple that it no longer needed an eponymous hero. The problem with Lacan's "mirror stage" is not what it does to us, but what it does to its mirror, reducing it to a bare functionalism—a reflection, let us say, and nothing more.

With this last phrase, I am echoing the present volume's echo of the title of Mladen Dolar's *A Voice and Nothing More*, which in turn echoes a classical text. At the end of her story, Philomela is transformed into the sonorous songbird that in English we call the nightingale. And it is the nightingale that lends Dolar his opening epigraph and title, borrowed from a very brief anecdote in Plutarch's "Sayings of the Spartans." Here it is in the original Greek, followed by the English translation quoted by Dolar:

> Τίλας τις ἀηδόνα καὶ βραχεῖαν πάνυ σάρκα εὑρών, εἶπε, "φωνὰ τύ τίς ἐσσι καὶ οὐδὲν ἄλλο."
> A man plucked a nightingale and, finding but little to eat, said: "You are just a voice and nothing more."[23]

It may be revealing that the Greek, strictly speaking, has "nothing else" or "nothing other" (*ouden allo*) and so lacks the second insufficiency implied by Dolar's translation, which, unlike the Greek, implies that a mere voice is not itself any great thing. But there is something even odder here. Dolar's argument emphatically will not be that there is voice and nothing more, but instead that the apparently significant voice-and-nothing-more is itself nothing more than a figment, by negation, of the signifying structures of language:

> Bringing the voice from the background to the forefront entails a reversal, or a structural illusion: the voice appears to be the locus of true expression, the place where what cannot be said can nevertheless be conveyed. The voice is endowed with profundity: by not meaning anything, it appears to mean more than mere words, it becomes the bearer of some unfathomable originary meaning which, supposedly, got lost with language. . . . It should be stated clearly: it is only through language, via language, by the symbolic, that there is voice, and music exists only for a speaking being. . . . The voice as the bearer of a deeper sense, of some profound message, is a structural illusion, the core

> of a fantasy that the singing voice might cure the wound inflicted by culture, restore the loss that we suffered by the assumption of the symbolic order. This deceptive promise disavows the fact that voice owes its fascination to this wound, and that its allegedly miraculous force stems from its being situated in this gap. If the psychoanalytic name of this gap is castration, then we can remember that Freud's theory of fetishism is based precisely on the fetish materializing the disavowal of castration.[24]

Our ancient sources help reveal what is missing here. Plutarch's amusing anecdote leans on the uncanny fact that a large voice can come from so little flesh. Consciously or unconsciously, it also plays, grimly, on the vocal dissection at the heart of the nightingale's etiological myth. And while the jovial diner discovers that the voice of a songbird, once flown, leaves little matter behind, this is not how the story goes in Ovid. Philomela does not in fact lose her voice except by virtue of her imprisonment; Tereus instead cuts out her tongue, and so her power of articulate speech—her *vox articulata*, which ancient linguistic theory distinguished from the *vox inarticulata*.[25] And for a brief, grotesque, but profoundly illuminating moment, Ovid makes us see what *even a tongue* does, usually unheard, while trying to speak. For Philomela's tongue, flung to the ground, tries to crawl back to her, "murmuring" as it goes. In other words, this tongue briefly becomes a voice, indexical of the body from which it has come; it "says" nothing, except this: there is a body here, my body. (Here we are at the root of the arguments of Cavarero, who opens her book with this quote from Italo Calvino: "A voice means this: there is a living person, throat, chest, feelings, who sends into the air this voice, different from all other voices.")[26] Once we admit that the indexical meaning of voice—that is, the way the voice points to the body that is vocalizing—cannot easily be reduced to a "structural illusion," then what? Can we not similarly accept that Philomela's textile is more than a text, that Ovid's own "song" means more than words can tell? The structural illusion, both of these artifacts richly remind us, does not regard meaningful matter, but immaterial meaning. There is no such thing as language, and no thing more.

Over the course of the last century, something strange happened to language, or, rather, to what we might call our language myth (with the proviso, of course, that to call something a myth is not necessarily to call it untrue). I am referring not merely to the fact that the twentieth century's "linguistic turn" found languages, or things like languages, in surprising places, not least, of course, in the unconscious. Rather, I am referring to a related but even more distinctive characteristic of that language myth, one that embraces both structuralist *langue* and its poststructuralist critiques. Regarding the latter, let us recall that what has come to be remembered as the inaugural move of deconstruction was Derrida's discovery of the very language of writing at the heart of Western "phono-logocentrism," a paradox by which he sought to explode the West's persistent "metaphysics of presence." What Derrida did *not* do, however, was to deploy that same contradiction in the opposite direction, reattaching structuralist *langue* to its linguistic root, its Latin *lingua*, and thereby to the bodies and other matter from which it was abstracted. Signifiers, for Derrida and Saussure alike, and so too for Lacan, albeit in different ways, always point elsewhere; they do not call attention to themselves; they cannot "shimmer"; they do not know how to sing. It is against this misdirection, into this blind and deaf spot, that the neomaterialist projects of the present century have cast new and old eyes and raised a voice to say: there may be no presence *in* language, but the presence *of* language is a different matter.

For Dolar, citing Freud, this spot is the irrevocable "gap" at the core of the subject, the site of symbolic castration, the very "wound inflicted by culture." But are we sure that this gaping wound, which plunges through folded flesh deep into the body, is not instead a mouth? For Freudians, of course, this symbolic substitution flows in the reverse direction: a dream about a mouth is probably about a vagina, just as one about a nose is surely about a penis, via what Freud argues is a common dream-mechanism, transposing the lower parts of the body onto the upper. This, in part, is why Dolar calls the voice a fetish, marking a lack that is itself elsewhere. But more is being lost (and found) in all these metaphors than the phallus. Freud and Dolar are talking themselves out of the *whole body*, the flesh where all voices are born, regardless of the opening that bodies them forth.

What is lost, let us say, is the voice that wails (*vagit*), an onomatopoeic word far older than Latin itself, one that mimes the "wah-wah-wah" (*va va va*) of an infant. Signifiers that thus exhibit what linguists call "iconicity" are rare birds: indeed, Saussure's foundational intervention—in the name of the so-called "arbitrariness of the sign"—was against linguists who treated iconic words as normative. But have we learned all we can from this being who cannot speak, this *infans*, who has not yet met his mirror? For Dolar, this is precisely to fetishize the voice as "the bearer of some unfathomable originary meaning which, supposedly, got lost with language." To be clear, I do not think he is wrong to say this, nor do I think we can afford to dispense with psychoanalyzing Ovid's tale of the nightingale: here, as often, Ovid seems not merely to admit Freud but to have anticipated him. But this is to tell only half the story.

Let us briefly borrow from the myth of another mutilated avatar of the poet: Orpheus. Vision is key to Orpheus's second loss of Eurydice, the wife he has just rescued from the Underworld, not only because he has been commanded not to look at her until back aboveground, but because Ovid uses carefully ambiguous syntax as well as language borrowed from the story of Narcissus in order to make the doomed couple's final, fleeting moment together into a mirror:

> Flexit amans oculos, et protinus illa relapsa est,
> bracchiaque intendens prendique et prendere certans
> nil nisi cedentes infelix adripit auras.
>
> Loving, he bent his gaze, and at once she slid backward,
> and with outstretched arms, and struggling to be grasped and to grasp,
> she/he snatches at nothing but breezes that gave way.[27]

But later, as Orpheus stretches out his hands, either to deflect the Maenads' blows or to beg them for mercy, it is the suppression of his voice that seals his own fate:

> Tendentemque manus atque illo tempore primum
> inrita dicentem nec quidquam voce moventem
> sacrilegae perimunt, perque os (pro, Iuppiter!) illud
> auditum saxis intellectumque ferarum
> sensibus in ventos anima exhalata recessit.
>
> As he stretched out his hands and for the very first time
> spoke in vain and failed to move anything with his voice,
> they profanely slew him, and through that mouth (oh, Jupiter!),
> heard by stones and understood by the senses of beasts,
> his soul, with his breath, into the wind, departed.[28]

The twentieth century fully equipped us to diagnose the narcissism of Orpheus's grasping for Eurydice, but it gave us few tools for recovering the music drowned out in the scene of his violent death. Perhaps we can now do better. Listening to Ovid's lines with ears attuned to sound as well as sense, let us hear not just a prayer, but a protest, through and for the mouth (*perque os . . . illud*). Indeed, in the Latin this protest bursts from the middle of "that mouth" (*os . . . illud*), like a raised fist: "oh, Jupiter!" (*pro, Iuppiter!*). Or, rather: like an open mouth. For the exclamation *pro* is a sound that starts on the lips (*p*) and then moves deeper into the mouth and begins to vibrate (*r*), yielding to a vowel (a *vocalis* or "voiced" letter in Latin) whose very mark (*o*) opens wide. As we read, this exclamation seems to widen further, embracing and enfleshing the same consonants (*p*, *r*) farther forward (*Iuppiter*), and farther back (*perque os*). Indeed, it resonates farther still: all the way back to Narcissus, whose life flowed out "through his eyes" (*perque oculos*). But the sound-play draws those "eyes" (*oculi*) down to this "mouth" (*os*)—and perhaps even hints at the kisses (*osculi*) they will no longer give. From those lips comes instead a last breath, but this rallies into a shout, hurled back at the thunder-god, Jupiter—that is, at *Iovis pater*, God the Father. The protest properly comes not from Orpheus but from the narrator (notionally Ovid himself), who perhaps ventriloquizes our own indignant reading. *Pro, Iuppiter!* Our mouths are not wounds, even—and especially—when they thus overflow![29]

In what I take to be Dolar's terms, this vocal protest is, in a narrow, literal sense, meaningless, and the proof that its apparent meaningfulness cannot come from anything but language is there beneath our noses, clear as black and white. For we are reading, after all. Indeed, vocal fetishes proliferate as the episode progresses, protracting Orpheus's death in ways that ever more insistently echo the nightingale, since she too is presumably there among the "plaintive birds" that, we are told, have gathered around him to listen, and then to mourn, in trees that have uprooted themselves in order to move closer to the singer and his song.[30] The Maenads, however, interrupt his singing and decapitate him (Freud's go-to metaphor for castration, of course), tossing his head and lyre into a river. From the lyre, as it floats, comes a "complaint" (*queritur*), while the tongue (*lingua*) in his severed head continues to "murmur" (*murmurat*). The harmony of mangled lyre and *lingua* (which, like the English "tongue," can also mean "language") is described as a *nescioquid*, an "I-know-not-what": "By not meaning anything," as Dolar might say, "it appears to mean more than mere words." "The banks answer back" (*respondent ripae*), and the sound is "lamentable" (*flebile*), which suggests that you would be inclined to weep, could you but hear it. Nothing quite prepares us for the over-the-top climax, when the head washes up on the shore of the island of Lesbos. Here a snake prepares to attack the dead poet's "mouth" (or "face": *os petit*), but "at last" (*tandem*) his father Apollo "is present" (*adest*) and "freezes the snake's open maw into stone, hardening its broad gapings, just as they were" (*in lapidem rictus serpentis apertos / congelat et patulos, ut erant, indurat hiatus*).[31] Surely the analyst's diagnosis couldn't be easier than it is here!

Or are we failing to see the forest (*silva*, *hulē*: "woods" but also "matter") for the trees? For it is simultaneously possible to trace Ovid's scene not to the depths of the psyche, where Freud found the metaphorical black wax of the "Mystic Writing Pad" (*Wunderblock*) and Derrida, as a consequence, discovered yet another written text underpinning Western thought, but rather to the surface tension of the actual black wax in which the poet wrote—to the limits, that is, of his medium.[32] The voice, from this perspective, is an aspect of the "real" in the less-than-Lacanian sense given to the word by media theorists: sound that could not be recorded before stylus was pressed to wax by the phonograph, that device that by its very name promises to "write the voice."

Even beyond the voice per se, Ovid's episodes of Philomela and of Orpheus gesture at a number of acoustical phenomena that would seem to lie at least partly outside the technological reach of writing: from the melodic and other musical values that ancient languages and verse forms did not fully encode or imply, to the nonhuman, nonlinguistic "music" of the nightingale.[33] Other technologies would one day rush in to fill even these particular "gaps": Orpheus's song was repeatedly reimagined by composers after the medieval invention of modern musical notation (indeed, Orpheus will eventually be the protagonist of most of the first operas), and Respighi inserted cues to play the phonographically recorded sounds of a real nightingale into his score for his 1924 symphonic poem, *The Pines of Rome*.[34] But we should not imagine these reaches for an extralinguistic real—again, in a mediatic sense—condensed in Ovid's efforts to make us hear the floating Orpheus's voice-that-does-not-speak, his voice-and-nothing-more, to be accompanied by a poetic sigh of impossible desire or even failure. On the contrary, these acoustical vanishing points are only meant to throw into higher relief what our poet believes he has achieved: namely, a poem thick with sound, matter, voice. Ovid's vocal reaches in this regard do not pull us back to a forgotten, prelinguistic paradise, but forward, to the immortality he will claim for himself in the poem's closing lines: *ore legar populi*, "I shall be read by the mouth of a people," and so, "I shall live" (*vivam*). This, of course, is a poet's narcissism, fashioned, as we have heard, by Echo. But it is also an invitation to listen—not for a fantastical world beyond words, but simply, and profoundly, to words as part of the world, acting in and upon that world, materially. After all, Edison did not need to be psychotic to suppose that his voice could make wax change shape, just as Orpheus's had made rocks vibrate, animals listen, riverbanks resound.

Until just now, we seemed to have forgotten about Narcissus, or at least to have stopped talking about him for a while. To be sure, had we stopped listening and gone looking for him, he would hardly have been hard to find: in Philomela as the desirable double of her sister; in the mute signs of her tapestry (compare the reflected Narcissus's "words that do not reach my ears"); in the dinner Tereus unknowingly makes of his own son (you are what you eat!); in the reflected, futile grasping of Orpheus and Eurydice on the brink of the light; and in the former's turn to pederasty after the latter's second death. But should we therefore take these echoes of Narcissus as signs of his repression, and as proof, therefore, that the primal trauma and master myth of all that follows are *his*?

That, I think, would be to miss the forest for the sake of a single if undeniably captivating flower. *Iste ego sum*, says Narcissus to Narcissus, "you, that one, there, I am." Lacan echoes: "[P]sychoanalysis may accompany the patient to the ecstatic limit of the '*Thou art that*,' in which is revealed to him the cipher of his mortal destiny."[35] This, for Lacan, is a journey away from "madness, not only the madness that lies behind the walls of asylums, but also the madness that deafens the world with its sound and fury." With this final phrase, echoed from Shakespeare, or even from the echo thereof by Faulkner in his stream-of-consciousness novel, Lacan makes us hear in "madness" nothing less than the *furor poeticus*, the creative frenzy long said to lie at the heart of art-making.[36] "But," Lacan rightly adds at the essay's end, "it is not in our mere power as practitioners to bring [the patient] to that point where the real journey begins." That, indeed, is a job better left to poets. Yes, in many ways, Ovid's poem is a journey back into madness and horror. But it is also a journey forward, if not really to redemption or immortality, then at least toward a more complete cure of any doubt, Lacanian or otherwise, that the world we hear really is here, and that we ourselves, along with our words, are part of it.

Notes

This paper was first given at the conference that has inspired this volume, where it prompted a response from Mladen Dolar that was both spirited and generous. It was a great joy to get to know him and everyone else at that remarkable gathering, for which I would like to extend my thanks above all to impresarios Martha Feldman and Judith Zeitlin. I was able to repeat the paper, with slight modifications, at a conference on myth organized by Joshua Smith at Johns Hopkins University, and again for the Columbia University Seminar in Classical Civilization. I am grateful to audiences on all three occasions for their questions and suggestions.

1. Unless otherwise indicated, translations from Greek and Latin are my own.

2. Shane Butler, "Beyond Narcissus," in *Synaesthesia and the Ancient Senses*, ed. Shane Butler and Alex Purves (Durham, UK: Acumen Publishing, 2013), 185–200.

3. Ovid, *Metamorfosi*, vol. 2, ed. Alessandro Barchiesi and Gianpiero Rosati (Milan: A. Mondadori, 2007), 175–207.

4. Shane Butler, *The Ancient Phonograph* (New York: Zone Books, 2015), 82–83.

5. Giovanni Boccaccio, *Genealogy of the Pagan Gods* 7.59.1.

6. Lynn Enterline, *The Rhetoric of the Body from Ovid to Shakespeare* (Cambridge and New York: Cambridge University Press, 2000), 56, noting that this is itself constructed of the repeated words and figures of other poets, a matter to which we shall return.

7. My suggestion that Echo is not only the star of the episode but also invisibly directs the entire poem's acoustics will hardly surprise musicologists, especially historians of early opera, for which Ovid's poem provided many of the first plots and protagonists, starting with Orpheus, to whom we shall return. Nor can one object that a judgment of Echo's importance on the basis of that musical tradition is clouded by its medium, since to do so would be to sidestep the question of why Ovid long proved so irresistible to composers. Particularly eloquent on the subject is Carolyn Abbate, *In Search of Opera* (Princeton, NJ: Princeton University Press, 2001), 20–28, exploring the role of echoes (and, sometimes, of Echo herself) in operatic settings of the

tale of Orpheus, regarding whose resonant instrumentality she already has noted, "Orpheus was already just an opera *singer* centuries before opera was invented" (18).

8. For a concise review of this trend and many of its driving questions (especially though not only for musicologists), see Martha Feldman et al., "Why Voice Now?," *Journal of the American Musicological Society* 68, no. 3 (2015): 653–85.

9. Adriana Cavarero, *For More Than One Voice: Toward a Philosophy of Vocal Expression*, trans. Paul A. Kottman (Stanford, CA: Stanford University Press, 2005). In a brief but profound chapter, "Echo; or, On Resonance" (165–72), Cavarero observes that Echo's loss of signifying *logos* transforms her into "pure *phone*" (167), a metamorphosis that hardly makes her irrelevant, since "as Ovid himself doubtless knew, Echo is not so much a tragic figure of indicted speech as she is a figure of a certain pleasure" (169). Nevertheless, Cavarero rejects "Ovid's textual games" (172), which require "the definitive dissolution of a uniqueness that, as echo, Echo's voice does not possess. Echo's voice is, in fact, not *her* voice; it does not possess an unmistakable timbre, and it does not signal a unique person" (167). One could object that environmental echoes are in fact distinct (from one another and from the sounds they transform even as they reproduce them), and I express some reservations about Cavarero's politics of vocal "uniqueness" in *The Ancient Phonograph*, 17–18. For a very interesting attempt to align Cavarero's thoughts on Echo with Suzanne Cusick's thoughts on the use of music in torture, see Ryan Dohoney, "Echo's Echo: Subjectivity in Vibrational Ontology," *Women and Music: A Journal of Gender and Culture* 19 (2015): 142–50.

10. Susan Sontag, "Against Interpretation," in *Against Interpretation and Other Essays* (New York: Dell, 1967), 3–14.

11. Ausonius, *Works* 19.32.

12. Leon Battista Alberti, *On Painting* 2.2 (26).

13. John Brenkman, "Narcissus in the Text," *Georgia Review* 30 (1976): 293–327.

14. Shane Butler, *The Matter of the Page: Essays in Search of Ancient and Medieval Authors* (Madison: University of Wisconsin Press, 2011), 76–77.

15. Ovid, *Metamorphoses* 6.555–62, trans. Allen Mandelbaum (New York: Alfred A. Knopf, 2013), 194. Judith Zeitlin has made to me the remarkable observation that Philomela's dismemberment analogizes but reverses decapitation, in which it is the rest of the body that continues to move for a while.

16. Tereus is usually said to become the hoopoe, whose cry was sounded like the Greek for "where? where?" (*pou pou*) and so was made to refer to a futile search for his sons. Greek sources (such as the lost *Tereus* of Sophocles, the plot of which can partly be reconstructed from fragments and other evidence) tend to transform Procne into the nightingale and Philomela into the swallow, though later Roman sources invert this. On these and other vicissitudes of the myth, see Paolo Monella, *Procne e Filomela: Dal mito al simbolo letterario* (Bologna: Patròn, 2005).

17. The *murex* yielded a dye "ranging in shade from blood-red to deep violet," notes P. G. W. Glare, ed., *Oxford Latin Dictionary*, vol. 2 (Oxford: Oxford University Press, 2012), 1676, s.v. *purpura*. Mark Bradley, *Colour and Meaning in Ancient Rome* (Cambridge: Cambridge University Press, 2009), 189–211, provides a rich exploration of the term's remarkable semantic range and its development over time.

18. Though *carmen* is clearly what was read in the archetype, editors long have fretted about it and have sought to emend the text in various banalizing ways.

19. For a full discussion of this imprecision and its consequences, with a review of the relevant passages in Derrida and Aristotle, see Butler, *Ancient Phonograph*, 39–54.

20. "What we shall call a *genotext* will include semiotic processes but also the advent of the symbolic . . . In other words, even though it can be seen in language, the genotext is not linguistic (in the sense understood by structural or generative linguistics). It is, rather, a *process*. . . ." Julia Kristeva, *Revolution in Poetic Language*, trans. Margaret Waller (New York: Columbia University Press, 1984), 86. Further discussion in Butler, *Ancient Phonograph*, 80–81.

21. Roland Barthes, "Listening," in *The Responsibility of Forms: Critical Essays on Music, Art, and Representation*, trans. Richard Howard (New York: Hill and Wang, 1985), 245, 259.

22. Bradley, *Colour and Meaning*, 189: "The way its crystals sat on the surface of the fabric caused it to refract light so that the garment appeared to shimmer and glow."

23. Plutarch, *Moralia*, "Sayings of the Spartans" 233a. Mladen Dolar, *A Voice and Nothing More* (Cambridge, MA: MIT Press, 2006), 3.

24. Dolar, *A Voice and Nothing More*, 31–32. It is striking that Dolar here *twice* calls the seemingly meaningful voice-and-nothing-more a "structural illusion," since this echoed phrase itself echoes the very thing at the heart of the Ovidian and Lacanian myths of the self, namely, the mirror, site of a *méconnaissance* said to be irrevocable, that is to say, from which we cannot subsequently be called away.

25. See Butler, *Ancient Phonograph*, 112–15, with a review of other bibliography, 226–27n49.

26. Cavarero, *For More Than One Voice*, 1, quoting Italo Calvino, *Under the Jaguar Sun*, trans. William Weaver (New York: Harcourt Brace, 1988), 54.

27. Ovid, *Metamorphoses* 10.57–59. The subject of the final verb is deliberately ambiguous; discussion in Butler, *The Matter of the Page*, 26–27.

28. Ovid, *Metamorphoses* 11.39–43.

29. "We're stormy, and that which is ours breaks loose from us without our fearing any debilitation. Our glances, our smiles, are spent; laughs exude from all our mouths; our blood flows and we extend ourselves without ever reaching an end; we never hold back our thoughts, our signs, our writing; and we're not afraid of lacking." Hélène Cixous, "The Laugh of the Medusa," trans. Keith Cohen and Paula Cohen, *Signs* 1, no. 4 (1976): 878.

30. Here and in what follows, I am quoting from and summarizing Ovid, *Metamorphoses* 11.44–60.

31. Ovid, *Metamorphoses* 11.59–60. Some editors seclude the former line as an interpolation.

32. Sigmund Freud, "A Note upon the 'Mystic Writing-Pad,'" in *The Standard Edition of the Complete Psychological Works*, ed. James Strachey, vol. 19 (London: Hogarth, 1961), 225–32; and Jacques Derrida, "Freud and the Scene of Writing," in *Writing and Difference*, trans. Alan Bass (Chicago: University of Chicago Press, 1978), 196–231.

33. Note, however, that the name of Philomela's butchered nephew, Itys, mimes and transcribes, proleptically, the nightingale's complaint, which the Greeks heard as *itu, itu*.

34. Ottorino Respighi, *Pini di Roma: Poema sinfonico* (Milano: G. Ricordi, 1981). Monteverdi's "Orpheus is asking for Edison," observes Klaus Theweleit. "Monteverdi's *L'Orfeo*: The Technology of Reconstruction," in David J. Levin, ed. and trans., *Opera Through Other Eyes* (Stanford, CA: Stanford University Press, 1994), 169, quoted and discussed by Abbate, *In Search of Opera*, 28. As Abbate herself puts it, opera responds to a question both Orphic and phonographic: "how does the dead object continue to sing?" (6).

35. Jacques Lacan, "The Mirror Stage as Formative of the I Function as Revealed in Psychoanalytic Experience," in *Écrits*, trans. Bruce Fink (New York: W. W. Norton, 2006), 81.

36. Lacan, "Mirror Stage," 80.

9

Voice Gap Crack Break

MARTHA FELDMAN

In the annals of music journalism, singers command attention through rapturous lyricism, dazzling pyrotechnics, or powers of eloquence. In the annals of aesthetic criticism, they are said to still the soul, quiet the mind, rouse the passions, and excite the body. What they are rarely praised for doing is toying with failure.[1] Yet most of us sense that some kinds of vocal failure—construed here as deliberate vulnerability and fragility—when emitted by a virtuoso, can be as necessary to the arsenal of the extraordinary singing voice as lyricism, pyrotechnics, or eloquence, and at least as apt to affect its auditors. Risky and dangerous, artful and seductive, eccentric and uncontainable, the vulnerable voice exceeds language and sense to reveal voice in its very voiceness.

What interests me in this chapter is the phenomenon whereby subtle failures or breakdowns in the singing voice expose gaps in the very status of voice—voice not as smooth, official, "acceptable," or straightforward, but bearing what Certeau calls a "tattoo," a messy surplus located in the intangible spaces between music and noise, noise and signification, noise and language, bodily control and ownership and their loss or precarity. "The weeds between the paving stones," Certeau would have called this.[2] Such in-betweenness I will take to involve special instances of voice, instances that sometimes go by the name of failure yet constitute an inherent condition of voice as both an object of play and a site of misadventure. I begin the essay with an empirical tour through several examples and then move to a reevaluation of the gap constituted by the Lacanian voice, whereby the crack or break in the singing voice serves as an embodied point of orientation and identification.

The Willful Failure

Failure without art conjures up a condition that impedes the voice from making an unobstructed sound, or reveals frailty, debility, or imperfect execution. By that measure, the emcee who gets a frog stuck in his throat would fail by the standards of the dancehall and the tenor who cracks on a high C would fail by the measure of the opera house. Similarly, a conversationalist who cannot summon a full-bodied sound because she has been struck dumb, made hoarse, or rendered faint-voiced by news of a sudden death would fail by the measure of everyday social interaction. In these examples from "real life," failure is to varying degrees allied with trauma.[3] Yet to talk about singers who *toy* or flirt with vocal failure is another matter—a kind of restaging of trauma, perhaps, rather than the sheer laying bare of the thing itself.[4] Restaging suggests a field of intentions that is predicated on choice and might be followed up by artful action: *I want to create an uneasy effect tonight, so at the end of this song I'll let the note give a little.* Or: *I might not make that note but I'll go for it and let it break if need be.* Recognizing deliberate vulnerability, collapse, or breakage grants that voices can be *allowed* to "fail" as readily as to succeed, and that in some instances a voice can be thought to succeed at failing. It acknowledges the performativity of voices that not only fall victim to successes and failures but strategize them. Cecilia Bartoli produces a fleeting instance of this in the last bit of Giacomelli's aria "Sposa, son disprezzata," where she cracks, just barely, a sustained note in her upper octave, and this on the very take she authorized for release (**web. ex. 9.1**).[5] Though the words are those of a loyal wife betrayed and disdained ("disprezzata") who loves her husband ("la mia speranza," my hope), her voice alone betrays personal agony in a realm beyond semantic meaning.[6] Harsh and aggrieved, the words are thus exceeded by the failing voice, which Bartoli conveys with a trilled collapse into "speranza" onto a high G-sharp as she lets her voice shade into a grainy aperiodic phonation.

This is far from Carolyn Abbate's account of her "drastic" experience in listening to Ben Heppner crack all his high notes in a Wagner opera.[7] It operates instead in a zone where miscarriages are managed with deliberate finesse, a finesse that involves nuanced, fluid zones where the gulf—the gap—between what we can only awkwardly index as success and failure is tenuous and subtle—the differences between holding a note solidly and just slightly cracking it, ending it or letting it give way, hiding the transitions between vocal registers or letting them show, or as we will hear later, singing outright or devolving into spoken words or wordless sounds.[8]

But why? Why let the chief expressive tool give out? Why let it tempt failure, stage it, and even cultivate it? And why do some listeners seem to long for it? Why do Callas's fans seemingly cling to the break in her upper passaggio or others feed on the late ravaged voice of Judy Garland? Why do they feed on slippages from outright singing to near-speech in Nina Simone and Billie Holiday and find themselves breathless in the face of Bartoli's broken high note? To explore these questions, I make recourse here to two idioms, traditional classical singing and jazz singing, both of which invite thinking on the matter precisely because they establish clear normative expectations in the form of unobstructed sound production and clear diction, even if classical singing brooks far fewer exceptions than jazz, which gives much more leeway to an errant voice. (Think of persistent slippages from song to speech like Holiday's, aged voices like Jimmy Scott's, and noisy phonation like Louis Armstrong's.)[9]

The Brazilian Leny Andrade, whose dusky alto and extraordinary musicianship has earned her the rubric of "Queen of Bossa Nova," gives a wonderful example of "failing" as a controlled outcome in her rendition of the Dizzy Gillespie/Frank Paparelli jazz standard "A Night in Tunisia." On the so-called jazz break, when the rhythm section stops and the beat disappears, she delivers an unprecedentedly long-held, completely naked, and disappearing B-flat up in a head voice, which she otherwise uses sparingly (**web. ex. 9.2**). "Breaking" into the sustained note and collapse, she performs a dare that disintegrates into exhaustion. She enacts the illusion that the breath has been expended after being unduly sustained, and that it is truly spent, but it is an illusion she would execute similarly in one performance after another. And each performance would declare that the body had given itself up to this great effort.

That Andrade puts off the hubristic performative coup until the moment of the jazz break is no coincidence. The jazz break is a kind of Bermuda Triangle in jazz performance, a hazardous zone that performers navigate and audiences hanker after for precisely that reason. At the Sardinian Jazz Festival in 2005, when Andrade took a much slower tempo than her usual, she was able to maximize the illusion of failed breath by not singing at all for several seconds after dropping the B-flat, to audience applause. Moreover, as Anthony Cheung points out, Andrade defies expectations by doing the very opposite of what informed listeners think ought to happen. In the recorded tradition of the tune, the four-bar rhythm break is strongly associated with the Charlie Parker fast-break, where "all the pent-up tension of the ostinato figure that precedes it is suddenly unleashed in a torrent of notes." By stark contrast, Andrade's version expends all the energy and breath in one note leading to collapse, even as she manages to make a similar effect because of the "aggravating repetition and mounting harmonic build-up right before it."[10]

The Vocal Break

Andrade's staged failure is wholly different from the kind of danger that goes by the name of the "vocal break," or transition, or what the Italians call more lyrically and forgivingly the "passaggio," that major shift in the laryngeal mechanism between about D and F above middle C. The vocal break is experienced biologically by the vast majority of adult voices, high and low, the space below called "chest voice" in Western pedagogy (or, tellingly, modal or speaking voice), that above "head."[11] Notably, the shift between these "voices," produced via movement of the larynx, is thought to cause a disconcerting disturbance due to an exposure of that which should be kept aurally hidden, namely, the literal mechanism itself. Small wonder then that in Western discourses the vocal break unleashes an unsettling linguistic plurality: we might speak of the break, the transition, or the passaggio, or associatively of inflections, tremors, trembles, or even cracks or croaks. At its worst, we might imagine the vocal break as a yawning crevasse, at its best as a site where disguise of the mechanical shift allows failure to be put off—deferred until another day, a different tune, or a later age.

The ways Western singing hides the mechanism are many,[12] but technically there are basically two. One is by adjusting the amount of air pressure to smooth it over, the other by molding the vocal tract complexly to create subtle timbral contrasts, various hues being produced by sculpting an infinite variety of shapes in the resonating spaces above the larynx, including throat, cheeks, and tongue. Yet some voice types—notably mezzos, contraltos, and tenors, as well as low-voiced female jazz singers—spend more time in the danger zone of shifting registers than do others. These we might call voices on the edge, or in-between voices, because they live in precarious states of disclosure, mysterious states that seem to produce in listeners a sense of the uncanny, or lay bare a deep interiority marked by distress, fallibility, or other vulnerabilities, as many have shown.[13]

The most radical instance of such a voice, familiar to everyone under every sky, is the voice of a boy during his vocal change.[14] On the verge of puberty, the boy's voice is quintessentially unpredictable: liable to emit Alfalfa-like cracks but also capable of swooningly fragile beauty.[15] The boy's vocal change is thus a moment of particularly perilous exposure. In the winter of 2006, I was able to follow a boy's voice at the very lip of that change while involved in Patricia Barber's *Mythologies* project.[16] One song in the cycle used the then-teenage Lawrice Flowers from the Chicago Children's Choir, who performed the verse from a song about the liminal Persephone—Persephone who traversed the upper and lower worlds when she was raped and then abducted to Hades, where she ruled as a seductively powerful queen.[17] Though Lawrice's voice had begun to change, it still retained, just barely, something of the boy's passaggio, uniquely situated about a half octave higher than the typical adult one.[18] In a filmed recording of that performance, the fragile beauty Lawrice brings to the song rests on the sensitivity of his artistry, including nuanced phrasing and control over a very lightly muscled, exquisitely modulated quasi-falsetto. The moment that especially interests me comes in the heartrending telltale phrase when he moves up to G above middle C, almost breaking androgynously on the text "your saintly goodness with its darker side . . . ," yet with no definite and audible change of vocal mechanism. Listen to him sing the verse in **website example 9.3**, ascending toward the end, just barely, over the vocal break, using a predominantly modal voice, and then drooping down chromatically from G through F-sharp, F, and E-flat.[19]

As a voice on the edge, or in-between voice, at the moment of transition from puberty to adulthood, Lawrice's voice embodies the very voiceness of voice itself, and here I begin to expose the matter of my title. It epitomizes the condition that makes voice what Dolar calls a key "operator" of a dividing line.

> So this voice, this object, is like a quirk, it's like an addition, an intrusion, it presents the dimension which is neither interior nor exterior, neither nature nor culture, neither somatic nor symbolic—but where the one intrudes upon the other. It emerges at their interface.[20]

Lawrice's voice, I would argue, does things that invite desire, perhaps as what a Lacanian would call an *objet a*, or what Buñuel called, too concretely to satisfy a Lacanian, an "obscure object of desire." His is also a voice that, by virtue of its frail embodiedness, invites reactions, involves listeners in transactions. Rather than guaranteeing shared understandings of messages, it makes apparent the inherent *refusal* of voice to serve as a warrant of particular referential meanings and insists on its ongoing transactionality. In this sense, the voice of Lawrice would seem to epitomize the very thing that distinguishes voice from speech and language and puts it outside of them. Freya Jarman-Ivens dissects the implications of such a split in her *Queer Voices: Technologies, Vocalities, and the Musical Flaw*,[21] showing that voice introduces what she calls a third space between "voicer" and listener, mediating queerly in the process between voice and language, but fully attached to neither, and in ways that make room for the musical flaw and for the object-voice as a kind of "misfire" into the symbolic realm that in turn triggers desire. I will return to these points.

The Nina Simone Break

If an in-between voice is about living at the edge of exposure and risk, then an ultimate instance of it is surely the voice of Nina Simone. Thoroughly trained as a classical pianist as a young person but also practiced as a gospel accompanist, Simone was in genre terms alone a quintessential threshold creature, easily shifting between jazz, classical, soul, R&B, folk revival, gospel, and protest song.[22] Vocally, her resonance was as deep as an ocean cave and as limitless. Her home territory spanned the octave below the vocal break and the notes just in and over it, meaning that much of the top region of her tessitura lay in the vulnerable space vernacularly called the break. Her deep contralto hardly belonged to an obvious gender, and her emotions were delivered on a razor's edge, much like the political rhetoric that entered her music by 1963 and became inseparable from her position as an indomitable black musical pioneer.[23] Loud, soft, low, high, delicate, brash, muted, brassy, she was not just ready to lay herself bare vocally; she sought it out in an infinite variety of forms, and with a voice loaded with presence.

So, too, her renditions stand apart from the crowd in often using a speech voice—a plain-speaking, modal voice of simple attacks, vibratoless notes, conversational, prosaic rhythms—and here and there those renditions spill, like Holiday's, into a space of near oblivion to sung pitch. For Simone, speaking or quasi-speaking a tune was no accident; she poured on full-out lyricism when she had a mind to (witness her legendary performances of "The Other Woman," "Wild Is the Wind," and so much else), but withheld it strategically.[24] A classic instance of Simone's quasi-singing comes in her rendition of "Who Knows Where the Time Goes?," her voice breaking at a critical moment out of referential singing via a chromatically tenuous melisma and falling into broken, raggedy speech on the delivery of "I do not feel time"[25] (**web. ex. 9.4**).

The various thresholds of Nina Simone's genius are far more numerous and nuanced than I can even hint at here. I'll elaborate on one other, namely her solo rendition of the Hoagy Carmichael tune "I Get Along without You Very Well (Except Sometimes)," but first I turn to the third chorus in Rosemary Clooney's pitch-perfect 1960 rendition arranged by Nelson Riddle, which Clooney delivers flawlessly in a classic big-band swing patois—a kind of jazz bel canto (**web. ex. 9.5**).[26] If Clooney's version is one great swanky toe-tapper in a fat, upbeat arrangement, Simone's version, recorded for RCA in 1969 on her solo album *Nina Simone and Piano!*, is lean, lonely, broken, meandering, exposed. . . .[27] It is a markedly intentional instance of playing with the threshold between registers, and we will see that it again raises questions about the interface between voice and language, the very place where signification breaks down.

To appreciate her delivery of it, though, it's important to recognize that though given to ferocious passions, Simone was sublimely capable of holding back her voice by undersinging, plainly, without ornament, to the point of letting a song feel as if it were almost disintegrating. This she does on "I Get Along without You Very Well," where she strips away the idiomatic swing and even much of the harmonic color of the song to stage it, sometimes half-speakingly, as an instance of radically conditional optimism, which is the endgame of its much-too-protesting lyrics: *How do I get along without you?* the song asks. *Very well, of course . . . except "when soft rains fall" or "I hear your name," or when it's spring, and then, well . . . sometimes I remember being sheltered in your arms and sometimes things fall apart.* So, the message is *I get along without you very well so long as I don't think about these everyday things.* For Joan Didion, this would qualify as magical thinking because "Magical thinking is IF thinking. If I had done such and such, if I were to do such and such, I could change the outcome of that which has already happened."[28] In this song, the thinking is ultimately also negative inasmuch as the singer's survival depends on avoiding all the sunshine of the past: *if only* there were no soft rain or *if only* people would stop saying your name or *if only* I were never to think of spring, then I could get along without you very well.

Simone takes advantage of such thinking by staging vulnerability vocally, notably at a key moment at the end of the last chorus, when she lets the singing nearly break. And that near-break coincides with the *BIG except*, the final rhetorical point of the last two lines, which is also a confession or a break in the magicality of the singer's thoughts: "But I should never ever think of spring. For that would surely break my heart in two" (**web. ex. 9.6**).[29] Shockingly naked, she now steers her voice into the oncoming traffic of a D-sharp–E–F-sharp scale rising up above middle C that literally "breaks her heart" and voice "in two"—a risk she could have mitigated had she not transposed the song from its standard key of B-flat major to the improbable and vocally more demanding key of B major. The F-sharp on "heart in two" hovers just around the uppermost limit of her change of registers, and she holds it tenuously for two full measures. This means that it's only at that moment that her voice begins to move out of its chest (or what a linguist would call "speaking") register, which has governed in a totally unforced way the whole song to this point. It's only here that she strains toward a never-settled-in head voice, giving voice to the most fragile instant in the song.

The fragility—self-possessed and fiercely independent—is not accidental. All the other renditions of the song that I know perform the last scale rising up an octave from the second degree and settling on the tonic. Simone rises from the fifth degree below the tonic and lands on the dominant an octave above it, meaning on an unsettled F-sharp' at the very top of her "break," where she purposely struggles to maintain the note without flipping into head. More than that: right on the line "For that would surely break my heart in two," her voice nearly gives out over three repeated F-sharp's that hang tonally in midair. (Listen to the passage again in **web. ex. 9.7**.)

The signifier thus stains the voice, just as (as Dolar says) the voice stains the signifier. The voice here, however, is fully real, present, and material, in the most robust acoustic sense. The "break" is the broken body of the voice, which cannot therefore give full "voice" to the song yet gives it voice through that very inability. Nina Simone spoke of such a voice in an interview when she said: "What I was interested in was conveying an emotional message, which means using everything you've got inside you, sometimes to barely make a note; or if you have to strain to sing, you sing. So sometimes I sound like gravel and sometimes I sound like coffee and cream."[30]

We might render these insights as a kind of economic theory of traversing the vocal gap. Simone's voice is a voice on the edge but never goes "over the edge," as the expression has it. She takes her song to the outer limits, but she is reserved: semantically reserved in the symbolic domain of language, expressively reserved in keeping a reserved demeanor, and materially reserved in her use of voice (as in *keeping the voice in reserve*—that sonic and bodily reservoir of stuff). This double movement between risk and reserve is crucial to her voice, because the transactions it invites from listeners rely on both their *fear for her*, which is a consequence of her risk-taking, and their *deprivation of her*, which, I would argue, is a consequence of her carefully managed reserve. And it is both of these that cause listeners to *reinvest* in her voice. Again, Simone understood this perfectly well and expressed at least a part of it when she wrote, "People came to see me because they knew I was playing close to the edge and one day I might fail."[31]

The failing artist, the failing voice. Both index being overcome, exceeding, going beyond, and overspilling convention, where voice is seemingly abandoned by its companion, language, abandoned by proper diction and even musically by proper pitches.[32] Perhaps a masterful vocal performance is a performance *of* this speechlessness, and even notelessness; and yet it is also real in being deeply embodied. Nina Simone declared as much, as many singers have done, when she wrote about the agony of staged *singing* as something even well beyond the trials of instrumental performance. "[Jazz] singing disturbed me in a way I had never experienced with classical [piano] music; the tunes stayed in my head for hours—sometimes days—at a time, and I couldn't sleep or even simply calm down."[33]

To consider further why Simone could not calm down after singing, we might turn to Fred Moten's *In the Break: The Aesthetics of the Black Radical Tradition*, which invites us to hear her singing here as a kind of phonic eruption tantamount to the black experience and epitomized by the scream or cry, which Moten glosses as a "break"—embodied for me in Simone's manipulation of a painful and incomplete registral shift.[34] For Moten, it is the cry or scream (we could add: or vocal crack, a breakdown) that initiates the break, understood as a black event that takes the form of an encounter, or improvisation, or break-*through*, from predication, naming, classification, and bondage to escape, maroonage, and freedom, all of which are mobilized by the phonic trace. A cascading echo of black histories past, the black phonic trace with which Moten is concerned is irrepressible. It will not be denied or held back, and cannot be contained by grammars, categories, strictures, walls, cells, chains. Nor is it reducible to those instruments of the symbolic order that go by the terms sense, syntax, and language or to those instruments of the musical order that go by the conventions of "correct" singing or conventional pitch. More than a mere phenomenon, the break is most importantly a form of knowledge, such that no agency or freedom is possible without it—hence the necessity of the eruptive phonic disturbance that takes place in a fugitive way outside convention, outside language.[35]

Risk, Reserve, and (Re)investment

If Simone's body refuses this convention, her listeners do too. The listening body cannot easily divest itself of voice, nor can the auditor keep the body of the voice outside the head. As the voice invests, I would argue, so do listeners: the more I invest, the more you may give. *What* you give must include risky investments on your, the singer's, part to make it worth my while to invest more.[36] You must risk your pride, your reputation, and yield up your secrets. To do so, you must be aleatory, or at least seem aleatory.

If this is right, then Michel Poizat is wrong to claim both that an autonomous object-status of voice and a perfect singing voice, devoid of failure, are required in order for jouissance to occur in fans (if, indeed, occur it might).[37] For if the voice is above all transactional, it is this transactionality that is vital to jouissance. If you warrant your authenticity with cracks and breaks, I will warrant your performance as real—both *Real* in Lacan's capital-R terms, as that messy remainder that lies incomprehensibly beyond the symbolic; and real in the ordinary sense Lacan warned us not to confuse it with. The aleatory thus combines with the linguistically, even musically "failing" voice to open a critical gap between the production and reception of voice. Voice fails when it eludes the clutches of signification in order to be what it uniquely is: pure phonation itself, however also contingent. Fleetingly and intermittently, voice may also, as we've seen, fail in musical terms as it wavers between music and nonmusic—between, for example, a periodic vibrational sound that IS recognizably *music* and the coarse aperiodicity of noise—Bartoli's crack or Simone's raspy speaking and throaty sounds—all the more disorienting since voice usually is what Steven Connor calls "the antonym of noise."[38]

The Gap, a Coda

What might this proliferation of vocal cracks and breaks have to do with the long shadow cast over modern voice studies by the Lacanian philosophy of voice, cratered as it is with cracks, holes, breaches, breaks, voids, cavities, and gaps? In the most prominent Lacanian writings on voice, the "gap" is a persistent figure of speech, though pinning down its ontology in actual usages is not necessarily easier than pinning down the status of the Lacanian subject. In Žižek, a "gap" designates any number of discrepancies: for example, between ideological claims and everyday experience; between the radical contingency that characterizes the Lacanian Real and the more rigid modes of its symbolization in language; and between the way one sees oneself versus the way one is observed by another.[39] Žižek's "gap" is so often akin to his "void" that it seems safe to understand it as a trope figuring the endless "abyss of desire of the Other."[40] Only occasionally, it seems, do Žižek's gaps directly target voice. The most revealing instance for our purposes is one that evokes the chasm between what one is saying and what one means to say by it, between "utterance" and "enunciation," "locution" and "illocution," which is to say between concrete meaning and the force of utterance, or what one might gloss as the difference between signifying and performing.[41] Correlated with these discrepancies is the gap between demand and desire—between demand as what can be expressed in the differential order of signs and desire as what can only be lamented because forced out of the symbolic as that which is in excess of it and hence a negative, and in that classic sense indeed a *gap*.[42]

In Dolar, references to "gaps" proliferate but designate more precisely than in Žižek. Dolar's abiding concern, if I read him correctly, is the gap between bodily cause and vocal effect, where voice is the uncanny whose effect always goes beyond its cause—hence a surplus, a "ghost in the machine." This is why Dolar's voice is epitomized by the acousmêtre, which always conjures the voice in a broken causal nexus, detached as it is from its body, its mechanism of operation invisible to its observers. Often we're reminded of the exposure of the wizard in *The Wizard of Oz*, where to see the source of a sound (the wizard behind the curtain) might literally be to *see* the gap, but this is only to be reminded of an analogy to a contraption. For in these various figurations, the gap is a rather abstract construct, always producing tensions that can never be reconciled. They can never be reconciled because the gap involves the circuitry of desire, with the subject aiming at voice as a partial object that seems to promise gratification but always misses its target.[43] Voice qualifies as a partial object precisely because of its never-quite-thereness, because it consists of that which can trigger a wandering desire but never has the positivity to affirm it. The gap in this sense is a psychoanalytic master trope that condenses the Lacanian theory of subjectivity,[44] since at the heart of Lacanian theory lies a subject whose very coming-into-being is bound up with a fundamental gap—that of estrangement—prompted by the intrusion of the symbolic father into the infant's enjoyment (jouissance) of its mother. That gash in the infant's being means that its desire is forever (dis)placed onto the Other. Symbolically speaking, it goes of course by the name of castration; yet it is language and the symbolic—the latter embodied in the symbolic father—that have carved up the subject in the first place.

Here is where the gap pertains to voice. The Other (aka the big Other [or mOther]) around whom desire turns has its most symbolized, ready-to-hand representation in the medium of language. And language, once again, is at once a means of communication and a constant reminder that the smooth wholeness of being, prior to its being shorn by language, is lost in a never-ending attempt to satisfy an Other, whether that Other be real or spectral, familial, social, or romantic.[45]

The immense complexity of this theoretical maneuver is one over which we need linger only briefly. What matters for us here is above all, I think, a fundamental contrast between verbal language and music. Verbal language—that medium of most vocal music—can only ever heal the breach in part, since by seeming to lie on the rigid side of the formal and repeatable domain of the symbolic, on the side of what is automatic and iterable in Lacan's view, language becomes part of the problem. Whereas music, notwithstanding its formalities and repeatabilities (da capos, recaps, twelve-bar blues, ghazal couplets, medieval virelais), is in some sense its converse. Music, we could say, while it hinges on certain formal equivalents to language—musical syntax and related structural conventions—even more significantly has the capacity to pull away from them. Even texted vocal music is both married to language itself and ready to renounce it. If jouissance lies outside the symbolization that is language and is often fantasized as existing prior to it, then the musicking subject has as complex and varied an experience of jouissance (if an experience it is) as she has to language, each operating in and through music.[46]

Outwardly, music may thus seem from a psychoanalytic perspective to be all about the urge to jouissance—about the realms of the immediate, phenomenologically vivid, unmediated, and unsymbolized. But if that's so, what then to do with the enormous amounts of discipline exacted of composers, players, and listeners who are trained to conform to the various rules and modes of representation that music demands? Besides the nuances of breakdowns that we have seen in Bartoli, Flowers, Andrade, and Simone, what about things like harmonic syntax, formal plotting, historically informed performance practice, phraseology, cuing, and even notational and editing tools (to say nothing of the sophisticated improvisation traditions in jazz, raga, etc.)? All disciplines that force practitioners to *sub-ject* themselves to various symbolic orders, dismembering themselves in the process (something Nina Simone would have understood well). And what to do with the intentional arts of failure or fugitivity or the break tracked above?

Holly Watkins proposes a place for musical jouissance that seeks to accommodate these questions and resonates with examples of "failed" vocal emission and syntax that I adduce here. *Jouissance*, she suggests, "emerges in musical moments that seem to transcend syntactical determination: a certain vocal timbre, a fleeting instrumental sonority, or even some hard-to-describe extra thing (an 'excess') that attends a particular harmonic progression or turn of melody."[47] Put less concretely—not as something actually attained but as something fantasized—we might say that the (im)possibility of jouissance arises in just those places where envoicing itself becomes almost impossible, where the very experience of it is denied, transformed in a break from the symbolic and hegemonic political and racial order.

Imagine then that even in so slight an instance as pertains to the skillful conjunction of music with words in a classic early eighteenth-century aria, Bartoli cannot fully express the sorrow of the "disdained wife," the "sposa . . . disprezzata." Within its conventional signifying bounds, she cannot fully express her hurt and bewilderment at betrayal in the medium of a "pure" (symbolized, phenogenic) singing voice, subjected to a symbolic order and mortified by signifiers, despite the fact that the composer has already sought to exceed verbal language by means of a long, doleful melisma and sostenuto at the aria's end. Thus, she takes these a step further, away from syntax and convention, which is also the realm of iterables and repeatables, through a little tear in the fabric of music itself: namely, the noise of the vocal crack, which transcends what Watkins calls "syntactical determination," thereby allowing for a certain jouissance to be fantasized. Or, as in Simone's case, allowing a certain escape to be dreamed of, plotted, ventured, felt. Perhaps in both instances that transcendence through the tear or the break IS music itself, beyond the boundaries we usually use to map it.[48]

Apropos this characterization of "the music itself," we should hasten to underscore the status of the listener as the desiring subject par excellence. Here, Watkins follows up by noting that "such unsymbolizable musical 'things' may even assume the status of Lacan's 'little piece of the real' or *objet a*, the object-cause of desire that sets *jouissance* in motion."[49] Hence on one side of a relation stands the voice, producing itself, on another side the listening ear.[50]

If my examples above do anything to underscore these issues, I hope they function like "trapped fireflies," as Wayne Koestenbaum characterized Barthes's fragments on love. For what I've wanted to do is to favor what Koestenbaum calls the "perfume," or "luster," or "shimmer" of nuance that operates in the cracks and breaks of the voice, or indeed the fire that operates in them—all of which capture the elusiveness of the object-cause of desire—and thereby to give sense to the voice beyond language and syntax, beyond messages.[51] Any validity this may have means that some part of the figure of the gap can be salvaged, even for those suspicious of the status of the Lacanian model as a transcendental one and suspicious of the machinery it takes to operate it. The gap exists as an excess that cannot be recuperated into the logic of desire and therefore cannot fail to be a remainder, the perpetual Žižikian "discrepancy"—not the total nothing, however, but a kind of activated and activating (some)thing about which we know little.

But there is another thing voice becomes in this distillation, which we have not yet accounted for, and here I return to what I've called the transactional. Without being a Lacanian, either by allegiance or training, I think it fair to say that a transactional view of subjectivity is not a Lacanian one, not even in the pre-1960s Lacan, who did make room for the intersubjective.[52] It is not something to which a Lacanian model can lead us because its compass is that of the subject, the intersubjective being of interest only as the needle of the compass shifts from one subject to another, each with their own bearings in relation to the world. The famous Lacanian graph of desire is more comparable to a genealogy mapped in relation to a single ego than to a chart of interrelationships understood in a dynamic, multidirectional sense. If subjects share in anything for Lacan, they share in the experience of the gap.

In the model I have in mind, voice produces itself as a relation *between*, such that the privileged ego can be jettisoned in favor of an interplay of subjective relations that voice agitates and animates.[53] Vocal "failure" gives a stage to those relations, and highlights the poignant, intimate stakes in the exchange. That is the beauty of it.

Dickens wrote about something apropos in a passage in *A Tale of Two Cities* (1859). The pater familias is seen for the first time in a very long time as a man broken by his long, wrongful incarceration in the Bastille, puttering away obsessively at shoemaking. As his daughter approaches, a voice sounds that has thinned into near nonexistence:

> The faintness of the voice was pitiable and dreadful. It was not the faintness of physical weakness. . . . Its deplorable peculiarity was, that it was the faintness of solitude and disuse. It was like the last feeble echo of a sound made long and long ago. So entirely had it lost the life and resonance of the human voice, that it affected the senses like a once beautiful color faded away into a poor weak stain. So sunken and suppressed it was, that it was like a voice underground. So expressive it was, of a hopeless and lost creature, that a famished traveler, wearied out by lonely wandering in a wilderness, would have remembered home and friends in such a tone before lying down to die.[54]

Hearing this wash of heightened prose, full of alliterative lyricism, the reader thinks of the daughter who must be listening. Her presence is a provocation to heartbreak and a call to sympathy. It is almost the lack of an interlocutory listener that creates the sense of bleak solitude. Where is the transactional voice here? The voice of the father is on the verge of death, a figment of "solitude and disuse" that has all but lost its life. No longer calling to a subject, his voice is nothing but a gap, presubjective. In *A Lover's Discourse*, Roland Barthes has something to tell us about a pathos-laden voice similarly poised at an edge between life and death. "Nothing more lacerating than a voice at once beloved and exhausted: a broken, rarified, bloodless voice, one might say, a voice from the end of the world, which will be swallowed up far away by cold depths: such a voice is *about* to vanish, as the exhausted being is *about* to die: fatigue is infinity: what never manages to end."[55] Both Dickens and Barthes attempt to reckon with the voice in its situatedness between makers and listeners, interiors and exteriors, the fullness of life and the frailty of it, and to do so *through* voice—its power declares itself as such while striking pity, sympathy, and fear in listeners and prompting in them a terrifying but absorbing sense of identification.

Voice at the edge of voicelessness seems to posit the voice as the lost Other of Dickens, Barthes, and so much else. The listener responds to the threat of loss that all voices always carry—that ever-disappearing something that evaporates at the same time as it sounds, sounding into nothingness.[56] And it is that very disappearance that is intensified with the lacerated, pitiful, damaged, breaking, or disintegrating voice, a disappearance that also reveals an emergence, a gap that the unbroken voice covers over so well. Frail and vulnerable, the lacerated voice draws attention to the near bodilessness by which voice attracts the ear, and causes concern for that very body.[57]

Hence the subjective transformation that happens when a listener is interpellated into an exchange. But it is in the event of the transaction that the thinginess of the voice comes into being. And thus it is in the vocal *event* that fear of loss is mitigated. How? What mitigates it is the transaction of risk, because voice demands investments from doers and listeners, voice users and voice receivers, through vulnerability on the user's side and loss and emotional cathexes on that of the receiver, who might be thought to continually reinvest in order to persist in forestalling loss. The ceiling is lifted on reinvestment; the stakes are seemingly limitless.[58]

Notes

This essay began as a kind of indirect answer to some of Mladen Dolar's thoughts on voice, insofar as his early presence at the Voice Project faculty seminar, sponsored by the Neubauer Collegium for Culture and Society, raised questions for me that I would not otherwise have thought to ask. My thanks to Patricia Barber, who helped me identify some of the vocal phenomena and songs dealt with in this chapter, and to Seth Brodsky, Joshua Chambers-Letson, and Judith Zeitlin for nuanced comments on the argument. I'm also grateful to Anthony Cheung, Tom Gunning, Sarah Nooter, Jessica Peritz, Marcelle Pierson, and Steven Rings for rich discussions of earlier versions of this paper. For certain theoretical directions, special thanks are due to David Levin and members of our cotaught seminar at the University of Chicago, "Voice: Material, Subjective, Abstract" (Winter 2014).

1. A partial exception is Wayne Koestenbaum, *The Queen's Throat: Opera, Homosexuality, and the Mystery of Desire* (New York: Poseidon Press, 1993); and also Laurie Stras, "The Organ of the Soul: Voice, Damage, and Affect," in *Sounding Off: Theorizing Disability in Music*, ed. Neil Lerner and Joseph Straus (New York: Routledge, 2006), 173–84.

2. Michel de Certeau, "Vocal Utopias: Glossolalias," *Representations* 56 (Autumn 1996): 29–47, at 30.

3. On which (and related to trauma), see, for example, Emily Wilbourne, "Demo's Stutter, Subjectivity, and the Virtuosity of Vocal Failure," *Journal of the American Musicological Society* 68 (2015): 659–63.

4. Recent writing on vocal failure, whether coming from psychoanalysis or disability studies, sees it overwritten with trauma, a direct sign of the persistent consequences of traumatic losses or deficiencies, or other traumatic experiences. Clara Hunter Latham gives historical and theoretical footing to this perspective in "Listening to the Talking Cure: Sound and Voice in Psychoanalysis" (PhD diss., New York University, 2014), which reappraises the dynamics of the psychoanalytic "talking cure" by showing that among its originators, talk was understood to re-create traumatic affect sonically in order that traumas could exit the physical body therapeutically; and see Clara Hunter Latham, "Rethinking the Intimacy of Voice and Ear: Psychoanalysis and Genital Massage as Treatments for Hysteria," *Women and Music: A Journal of Gender and Culture* 19 (2015): 125–32. For a view that rejects trauma as a catchall for weakened voice, see Neil Verma's chapter in this volume.

5. The track appeared on the album *Se tu m'ami: arie antiche*, Cecilia Bartoli, soprano, György Fischer, piano (New York: London, 1990), in CD format. On the genesis and provenance of the aria, which is incorrectly attributed to Vivaldi on the Bartoli CD, see Frédéric Delamea, "The Noble Death-Pangs of Vivaldian Opera," in booklet included with CD and DVD of *Vivaldi Bajazet*, dir. Fabio Biondi with L'Europa Galante (EMI Records Ltd/Virgin Classics, 2005), 11–19, esp. at 16–17. The aria was written for Giacomelli's opera *La Merope* (Venice, 1734), and sung there by the castrato Farinelli in the role of Epitide, with aria text "Sposa, non mi conosci." It was reused and adapted by Antonio Vivaldi in his operatic pastiche (pasticcio) *Bajazet* (Verona, 1735) for the character of Irene, with text "Sposa, son disprezzata," sung by the female soprano Margherita Giacomazzi.

6. The words: "Sposa, son disprezzata; fida, son oltraggiata. Cieli, che feci mai? E pur egl'è il mio cor, il mio sposo, il mio amor, la mia speranza." / I am a scorned wife, faithful, yet insulted. Heavens, what did I do? And yet he is my beloved, my husband, my love, my hope.

7. Carolyn Abbate, "Music, Drastic or Gnostic?," *Critical Inquiry* 30, no. 3 (Spring 2004): 505–36, at 535.

8. Steven Rings calls these "zones of fluidity" in his chapter here on singing and speaking, which has points of contact with mine.

9. Neither classical singing nor jazz sanctions anything like the totally wrecked voices that usually sing rock and that often sing blues. See Stras, "The Organ of the Soul"; Daniel Zangger Borch, Johan Sundberg, Per-Åke Lindestad, and Margareta Thalén, "Vocal Fold Vibration and Voice Source Aperiodicity in 'Dist' Tones: A Study of a Timbral Ornament in Rock Singing," *Logopedics Phoniatrics Vocology* 24, no. 4 (December 2004): 147–53; Jessica L. Wood, "Pained Expression: Metaphors of Sickness and Signs of 'Authenticity' in Kurt Cobain's *Journals*," *Popular Music* 30, no. 3 (October 2011): 331–49; and Alexandra Apolloni, *Starstruck: On Gaga, Voice, and Disability: Performing Gender, Fashion, and Culture* (New York: Routledge, 2014).

10. Private correspondence with Anthony Cheung, November 23, 2015.

11. Change between the two principal registers (the "universal passaggio") is in reality only one area of mechanical adjustment. Singers are constantly adjusting throughout their ranges to accommodate different areas of response, which tend to change about every half octave, if not as pronouncedly as they do at the universal passaggio, and are tweaked in many different ways. I'm much indebted to Will Crutchfield for helping me understand these. Cf. Martha Feldman, *The Castrato: Reflections on Natures and Kinds* (Berkeley: University of California Press, 2015), chap. 3, "Red Hot Voice."

12. An exception in Western singing would be yodeling, or Yma Sumac- or Joni Mitchellesque-styled leaps that bound between registers without wanting to disguise the fact. A good example is Joni Mitchell's performances of her song "California." Another great example is the singing of Phoebe Snow, who was a master of these kinds of bounding shifts; listen to the live performance of her song "Poetry Man," including the very beginning of the vocals, at https://www.youtube.com/watch?v=7OxTVxGhHFM, accessed August 22, 2016. In "classical" Western singing and jazz singing, exposing the break in that way is mostly unheard of, except as an extended modernist technique, but in such cases (as with yodeling), singers would be more likely to bound around it with wildly different-sounding "voices" on either side of big leaps. Rock and other pop singing is another matter; see n10 above.

13. Rod Stewart (b. 1945) popularized the raspy rock style of singing, and Janis Joplin (b. 1943) was its most famous bluesy practitioner. As for tenors, mezzos, and contraltos, there is a long history of viewing them as in-between singers that dates back to their prehistory in the castrato.

See John Potter, *Tenor: History of a Voice* (New Haven, CT: Yale University Press, 2010); Naomi André, *Voicing Gender: Castrati, Travesti, and the Second Woman in Nineteenth-Century Italian Opera* (Bloomington: Indiana University Press, 2006); Feldman, *The Castrato*, chap. 3; James Q. Davies, *Romantic Anatomies of Performance* (Berkeley: University of California Press, 2014); and Marco Beghelli and Rafaelle Talmelli, *Ermafrodite armoniche: Il contralto nell'Ottocento* (Varese: Zecchini, 2011).

14. Less widely familiar would be a transgender or other hormonally atypical voice. See *Trans Bodies, Trans Selves: A Resource for the Transgender Community*, ed. Laura Erickson-Schroth (New York: Oxford University Press, 2014); Alexandros N. Constansis, "The Changing Female-to-Male (FTM) Voice," *Radical Musicology* 3 (2008), at http://www.radical-musicology.org.uk/2008/Constansis.htm; Constansis, "Hybrid Vocal Personae" (PhD diss., University of York, 2009); and Elias Krell, "Singing Strange: Transvocality in North American Music Performance" (PhD diss., Northwestern University, 2014).

15. Alfalfa was a boy character in Hal Roach's *Our Gang* short-film series (1922–1944) whose voice broke whenever he sang in public. The series was later known as *Little Rascals*, including in its life as a television series from 1955.

16. The project, consisting of a song cycle based on Ovid's *Metamorphoses*, was first performed at the Museum of Contemporary Art (MCA) in Chicago on January 7, 2006, where I was part of the presenting team, and released as a commercial recording called *Mythologies* later that year (New York: Blue Note Records, 2006), track 7.

17. The lyrics of the verse are a paean to Persephone's liminality: "Summer pales like a ghost of stubborn spring / this itch, this prayerful longing for heat / belies an angel's desire to take wing / so as you fall then fall into me, sweet Persephone. Now your poet and guide, night after day after night I'll complete / your saintly goodness with its darker side / for one without the other is naïve / past limbo to the second circle we slide" (lyrics by Patricia Barber).

18. Lawrice was born on December 22, 1989. By the time the recording was made, in February 2006, Lawrice's voice had already changed. As he wrote me, "My voice was very much so changing at that time. The CCC [Chicago Children's Choir] made me a baritone from tenor 2 a month later" (i.e., after the MCA performance); private communication, August 29, 2014. On registers of boys' voices, see Richard Wistreich, "Reconstructing the Pre-Romantic Singing Voice," in *The Cambridge Companion to Singing*, ed. John Potter (Cambridge: Cambridge University Press, 2000), 178–91, 258–61; and Ann-Christine Mecke, *Mutantenstadl: Der Stimmwechsel und die deutsche Chorpraxis im 18. und 19. Jahrhundert* (Berlin: Wissenschaftlicher Verlag Berlin, 2007).

19. "Verse" here is as used in jazz and American popular song, especially older standards, that is, as "an introductory section, often rubato, that leads up to the 'chorus' or main strain, which is the tune as generally recognized" (http://www.sonic.net/~jazz4/glossary.html). The complete song as performed at the MCA can be viewed here: https://www.youtube.com/watch?v=AnCPz71_psU&list=PL9141000A7FB16DD0&index=5, accessed August 26, 2016.

20. Mladen Dolar, "What's in a Voice?," public lecture and discussion on the occasion of Smadar Dreyfus's exhibition "Mother's Day," Extra City Center for Contemporary Art, Antwerp, November 14, 2008.

21. This is a complex argument that repays close reading of Freya Jarman-Ivens, *Queer Voices: Technologies, Vocalities, and the Musical Flaw* (New York: Palgrave Macmillan, 2011), especially the "Introduction: Voice, Queer, Technologies" and chap. 1.

22. On this heterogeneity, much has been said by recent writers on Simone's performances, especially as they concern race, importantly by Daphne A. Brooks, "Nina Simone's Triple Play"

Callaloo 34, no. 1 (2011): 176–97; Daphne A. Brooks, "Afro-Sonic Feminist Praxis: Nina Simone and Adrienne Kennedy in High Fidelity," in *Black Performance Theory*, ed. Thomas F. DeFrantz and Anita Gonzalez (Durham, NC: Duke University Press, 2014), 204–22; Malik Gaines, *Black Performance on the Outskirts of the Left: A History of the Impossible* (New York: New York University Press, 2017), chap. 1; and Joshua Chambers-Letson, *After the Party: A Manifesto for Queer of Color Life* (New York University Press, 2018), introduction and chap. 1, which he kindly shared with me in manuscript.

23. See also Tammy L. Kernodle, "'I Wish I Knew How It Would Feel to Be Free': Nina Simone and the Redefining of the Freedom Song of the 1960s," *Journal of the Society for American Music* 2, no. 3 (2008): 295–317; Ruth Feldstein, "'I Don't Trust You Anymore': Nina Simone, Culture, and Black Activism in the 1960s," *Journal of American History* 91, no. 4 (March 2005): 1349–79; Ruth Feldstein, *How It Feels to Be Free: Black Female Entertainers and the Civil Rights Movement* (New York: Oxford University Press, 2013), chap. 3; and Shana L. Redmond, *Anthem: Social Movements and the Sound of Solidarity in the African Diaspora* (New York: New York University Press, 2013), chap. 5.

24. We might call this prosody in singing, on which see especially Victoria Malawey, "Vocal Prosody in Popular Music," colloquium presentation at the University of Chicago, Department of Music, March 6, 2015, forthcoming in her book *A Blaze of Light in Every Word: Analyzing the Popular Singing Voice* (Oxford University Press). Simone learned certain songs that use the technique from her listening to Holiday, famously "Strange Fruit" and "Fine and Mellow."

25. Recorded for *The Essential Nina Simone* (New York: RCA/Legacy, 1959), 6'02"–6'27".

26. From *Rosie Solves the Swingin' Riddle!*, arranged and conducted by Nelson Riddle, 33 1/3 monaural (New York: RCA Victor, 1960). The film *The Las Vegas Story* (1952), dir. Robert Stevenson, with Jane Russell acting and singing the part of Linda Rollins and Hoagy Carmichael playing Happy, uses the song in a pivotal scene to shift the filmic register from that of a nondiegetic dream memory to a harsh diegetic reality, complete with breaking dishes at "For then my heart would surely break in two." Excerpt available at https://www.youtube.com/watch?v=08RotsdK1z8, accessed August 22, 2016.

27. Recorded at RCA Victor Studios, September and October 1969.

28. Joan Didion, interview at https://www.youtube.com/watch?v=5jlL4s6TmFs, accessed August 22, 2016; and see her book *The Year of Magical Thinking* (New York: Alfred A. Knopf, 2005) and play of the same name.

29. Simone adds "ever" to make "never ever think . . . ," enhancing the lyricism.

30. Quoted from the documentary *What Happened, Miss Simone?*, dir. Liz Garbus (Netflix and Radical Media, 2015).

31. Nina Simone with Stephen Cleary, *I Put a Spell on You: The Autobiography of Nina Simone* ([New York]: Da Capo Press, 1991), 92.

32. This may be akin to what Alexander García Düttmann has in mind when he reflects: "The fact that one cannot distinguish between a pure thought . . . and a failing voice . . . means that nothing can express a thought more purely than the failure of explanation which comes of being overwhelmed"; *Visconti: Insights into Flesh and Blood*, trans. Robert Savage (Stanford, CA: Stanford University Press, 2009), 56. Musically, it is certainly close to what Robert Walser has in mind about Miles Davis's risky horn playing in "'Out of Notes: Signification, Interpretation, and the Problem of Miles Davis," in *Keeping Score: Music, Disciplinarity, Culture*, ed. David Schwarz, Anahid Kassabian, and Lawrence Siegel (Charlottesville: University Press of Virginia, 1997), 147–68, esp. 159–60. It is equally true of instrumentalists and vocalists, albeit with different consequences.

33. Simone with Cleary, *I Put a Spell on You*, 83. "Classical music" in reference to her own performance meant classical piano playing. Before she began making a living by playing gigs in Atlantic City in 1954 (Simone with Cleary, *I Put a Spell on You*, 48–49), classical piano had been her primary form of music-making outside the church.

34. Durham, NC: Duke University Press, 2003.

35. Other critical texts are Moten's *Black and Blur* (Durham, NC: Duke University Press, 2017); and on fugitivity specifically, Stefano Harney and Fred Moten, *The Undercommons: Fugitive Planning and Black Study* (Wivenhoe, UK: Minor Compositions, 2013). I develop the notion of Simone's "fugitivity" in "Love, Race, and Resistance: The Fugitive Voice of Nina Simone," forthcoming in *The Female Voice in the Twentieth Century: Material, Symbolic and Aesthetic Dimensions*, ed. Michela Garda and Serena Facci (Ashgate/Routledge).

Harney and Moten's fugitivity and Moten's phonic break each find an ally in Judith (now Jack) Halberstam's sense of a "queer art of failure," which takes "failure" to index a counterhegemonic, renegade practice in opposition to success models founded in binary norms of hegemonic, easily legible knowledge. By Halberstam's measure, a new performative in music might be the vocality of the gap, crack, and break, which demotes easy legibility as it works to escape disciplinary practices (*The Queer Art of Failure* [Durham, NC: Duke University Press, 2011]). "Knowledge" here is a concept with limited utility for artistic practices, and thus Foucault's idea of antisovereignty in *The History of Sexuality* might pertain to anyone who's ever been subjected to conservatory discipline, classical or jazz, or to musical auditions.

36. Edward Schieffelin writes on the inherent risk of failure in performance from an anthropological standpoint, but understands failure in literal terms; "On Failure and Performance: Throwing the Medium out of the Séance," *The Performance of Healing*, ed. Carol Laderman and Marina Roseman (New York: Routledge, 1996), 59–89. There is a fair amount of writing about such failure, whereas there is relatively little about performing failure.

37. Michel Poizat, *The Angel's Cry: Beyond the Pleasure Principle in Opera*, trans. Arthur Denner (Ithaca, NY: Cornell University Press, 1992), translation of *Opéra, ou le cri de l'ange: essai sur la jouissance de l'amateur d'opéra* (Paris: A. M. Métailié, 1986).

38. Steven Connor, *Beyond Words: Sobs, Hums, Stutters, and Other Vocalizations* (London: Reaktion, 2014), 7. Connor investigates noise in terms of "crossovers" between meaningfulness and meaninglessness (10 and passim).

39. Slavoj Žižek, *The Sublime Object of Ideology* (1989; London: Verso, 2008), 50, 107, 118; and Žižek, *On Belief* (London: Routledge, 2001), 58, quoted in Dolar, *A Voice and Nothing More*, 70.

40. Žižek, *The Sublime Object of Ideology*, 312 and cf. 129.

41. All these occur in Žižek, *The Sublime Object of Ideology*, but see esp. 123–24.

42. Cf. Dylan Evans, *An Introductory Dictionary of Lacanian Psychoanalysis* (London: Routledge, 1996), "demand," 35–36, and esp. "desire," 36–39.

43. Indeed, according to Žižek, Lacan's mode of argumentation presupposes Hegelian dialectics, among other ways, in the difficulty it has in accommodating empirical reality; see Žižek's preface to the 2008 edition of *The Sublime Object of Ideology*, vii–xxii.

44. Dolar, *A Voice and Nothing More*, 31 and 39.

45. Bruce Fink, *The Lacanian Subject: Between Language and Jouissance* (Princeton, NJ: Princeton University Press, 1995).

46. On jouissance as pleasure or pain, enjoyed or fantasized, see Bruce Fink, "Against Understanding: Why Understanding Should Not Be Viewed as an Essential Aim of Psychoanalytic

Treatment," in *Against Understanding, Vol. 1: Commentary and Critique in a Lacanian Key* (New York: Routledge, 2014), 26n7.

47. Holly Watkins, "Slavoj Žižek: Responding from the Void," *Contemporary Music Review* 31, nos. 5–6 (October–December 2012): 449–60, at 453.

48. On the valence and history of the term "the music itself," with relevant literature on the matter, see James Q. Davies's chapter in this volume.

49. Watkins, "Slavoj Žižek," 453.

50. This is not unlike Žižek's claim that music is itself a "*supplication*," "an attempt to provoke the 'answer of the Real': to give rise in the Other to the miracle of which Lacan speaks apropos of love, the miracle of the Other stretching out his or her hand to me." Slavoj Žižek, *The Plague of Fantasies*, 2nd ed. (1997; London: Verso, 2008), 245.

51. Wayne Koestenbaum, foreword to Roland Barthes, *A Lover's Discourse: Fragments*, trans. Richard Howard (1978; New York: Hill and Wang, 2010), ix–x.

52. See "On the Possible Treatment of Psychosis," in Jacques Lacan, *Écrits: A Selection*, trans. Alan Sheridan (New York: W. W. Norton, 1977), 179–225; and Žižek, *The Plague of Fantasies*, 8–11.

53. A parallel argument was made by Walter Ong with respect to voice and interiority, on which see Corey Anton, "Presence and Interiority: Walter Ong's Contributions to a Diachronic Phenomenology of Voice," in *Of Ong and Media Ecology: Essays in Communication, Composition and Literary Studies*, ed. Thomas J. Farrell and Paul A. Soukup (New York: Hampton Press, 2012), 71–90. Ong's defense of presence, and thus implicitly Anton's defense of Ong, has been critiqued from the point of view of communication history by Jonathan Sterne, in "The Theology of Sound: A Critique of Orality," *Canadian Journal of Communication* 36, no. 2 (Summer 2011): 207–26. On divadom and interiority, see Stras, "The Organ of the Soul," 179 and 182; and Koestenbaum, *The Queen's Throat*.

54. Quoted from Dover Thrift Editions (Mineola, NY: Dover Publications, 1999), 29.

55. Barthes, *A Lover's Discourse*, 114. Alex Sorensen's paper, "'. . . *in vocem flentium*': Prosopopoeia and Palimpsests of Utterance in Two Poems of Eduard Mörike and Georg Heym," written for my seminar on voice with David Levin in winter 2014, first brought this aspect of *A Lover's Discourse* to my attention.

56. See Adriana Cavarero, *For More Than One Voice: Toward a Philosophy of Vocal Expression*, trans. Paul A. Kottman (Stanford, CA: Stanford University Press, 2005), 20; and Sarah Nooter, "Introduction: Voice, Aeschylus, and the Stage," in *The Mortal Voice in the Tragedies of Aeschylus* (Cambridge: Cambridge University Press, 2017).

57. Laurie Stras adds another layer to these glosses by linking the pathologies of vocal damage in popular music singing to willful acquisition of an artistic tool. In pop music, the persistent sound of vocal damage satisfies the yearning of fans to hear the wear and tear of a ravaged body. Outside pop music, vocal damage is inadvertent and plays on fans differently. Callas's fans, Stras notes, transformed her increasing vocal damage into a source of "pity and concern," "identification and catharsis" (Stras, "The Organ of the Soul," 177); and see Jarman-Ivens, *Queer Voices*, chap. 4. Cf. also Sonja Dierks, "Dylans Stimme: Am Beispiel von 'A hard rain's a-gonna fall,'" in *Bob Dylan: Ein Kongreß*, ed. Axel Honneth, Peter Kemper, and Richard Klein (Frankfurt am Main: Edition Suhrkamp, 2007), 143–59, who thinks about how Dylan risks vocal failure for the sake of expression.

58. See also the Introduction to this volume on Michel de Certeau's "secondary vocalizations" as explained in his "Vocal Utopias: Glossolalias," *Representations* 56 (Autumn 1996): 29–47, and relatedly his characterization of urges to "unsaying" and "saying" in *The Mystic Fable*,

trans. Michael B. Smith (Chicago: University of Chicago Press, 1992), 129–44, which proposes that the mystic experience and utterance represent an unstable relationship of voice to language, as prescribed directly in theological writings of the sixteenth and seventeenth centuries. Certeau keeps his ear fixed on how the edges of language intersect with voice through extravagant troping, deviations of meaning, and "monstrous" oxymorons (143), making speech an excessive in-between that is akin to voice without being equivalent to it. Thanks to Françoise Meltzer for encouraging me to return to this text.

10

The *Gesamtkunstwerk* and Its Discontents: The Wounded Voice in (and around) Alexander von Zemlinsky's *The Dwarf*

DAVID J. LEVIN

In the course of a characteristically provocative account of the "linguistics of the voice" in chapter 1 of *A Voice and Nothing More*, Mladen Dolar launches into a refrain about the singing voice that has become familiar to his readers over the course of the thirteen years since the book's initial publication:

> [T]he voice as the bearer of a deeper sense, of some profound message, is a structural illusion, the core of a fantasy that the singing voice might cure the wound inflicted by culture, restore the loss that we suffered by the assumption of the symbolic order. This deceptive promise disavows the fact that the voice owes its fascination to this wound, and that its allegedly miraculous force stems from its being situated in this gap.[1]

As Dolar argues with eloquence and wit, the terms of this investiture of the singing voice as the "cure" for the "wound" are at once widespread and long-standing. In this essay, I am keen to explore the consequences of Dolar's insight for opera, and in particular, for opera after Wagner. (The reasons for this historical specification will, I hope, become clear in the course of the following argument.) In that sense, I am inflecting the agonistic surplus suggested by the title of this collection (*The Voice as Something More*) in a somewhat unusual sense. Rather than exploring, as Dolar does, the voice's transcendent, resplendent, *curative* role in a sociocultural dramaturgy of disavowal, I seek to examine the no less symptomatic and overdetermined role that the voice plays in rendering (rather than disavowing) the gap and the wound. But where and when does opera give itself over to the traumatic voice, the voice *as* and *of* the wound? Where, to return to Dolar's formulation, might we turn to experience the proper "fascination" of the voice, one that properly renders (rather than symptomatically disavowing) the wound? To address this question, I will focus upon a single work (along with a set of intertextual references), namely, Alexander von Zemlinsky's *Der Zwerg* (1919–1921), a one-act opera with a text by Georg Klaren based on "The Birthday of the Infanta," a short story by Oscar Wilde. *Der Zwerg* (*The Dwarf*) premiered in Cologne in 1922 in a production staged by Felix Dahn, with Otto Klemperer conducting.[2]

At the outset of Zemlinsky and Klaren's piece, the Infanta of Spain is celebrating her eighteenth birthday, and among the lavish gifts she receives is a dwarf who is hideous and deformed. Alas, while this is plain for all to see, the Dwarf himself is blissfully unaware of his ugliness, since he has never seen himself in a mirror. Indeed, the Dwarf presents himself as something of a man of the world (who has, as he puts it, a "reputation as a singer"), with a voice whose heft and force belie his diminutive physique. The Infanta is amused by the Dwarf, who, for his part, and in response to her attentions, falls desperately in love with her. Eventually, the Dwarf's deluded effusions—expressed in song—have cataclysmic consequences: in the midst of his reveries about a future life with the Princess, he happens upon a mirror, and is shattered by the hideousness of the image that he confronts. He dies in despair as the birthday party continues.

One of the questions that critics have wrestled with in thinking about this piece is how to make sense of its relationship to Wagner. As a technical, generic, and compositional matter, this question has received some sensitive and illuminating treatment.[3] But as a dramaturgical matter, the discussion has been rather sparse.[4] This is strange, since the piece engages a set of problems raised by Wagner. The engagement I have in mind involves two scenes of vocal performance—the original scene, in Wagner; the second, as a kind of startling revisitation, in Zemlinsky and Klaren's work.

The original scene will be familiar to many readers: it serves as something of a primal scene of vocal performance—not just in and for Wagner, but beyond that, for opera itself: the song contest near the conclusion of *Die Meistersinger von Nürnberg*. In act 3, scene 5 of Wagner's comedy, the hero—*our* hero—Walther von Stolzing wins the contest and receives, as his reward, the hand of the lovely maiden Eva and belated recognition as a Master Singer. Of course, in order for Walther to win, someone has to lose, and the work's loser—in any number of registers—is Sixtus Beckmesser, the town scribe. Beckmesser participates in the song contest, where the resounding failure of his performance clarifies his status as a foolish and deluded pretender. He is eventually hooted off the stage and, according to Wagner's stage directions, disappears into the disapproving crowd. For our purposes, and put in terms of Dolar's observation, we might say that Beckmesser's song is fascinating precisely by virtue of its failure: here, then, we have a comical performance of the wound that is quickly healed—or so the logic of Wagner's comedy goes—by Walther's restorative (and corrective) performance.

Zemlinsky and Klaren's "Dwarf" picks up just before Wagner left off—that is, with the scene of Beckmesser's very public failure. In place of Wagner's shambling and delusional bureaucrat, Zemlinsky and Klaren present us with a shambling and delusional dwarf. In both cases, the scene of singing dramatizes a notable failure, one that is *staged*. And in both pieces, that failure is dramatically and dramaturgically significant, although its significance is inflected very differently. In Wagner, Beckmesser's failure serves what we might, echoing Northrop Frye, term an *adhesive* function: his expulsion from the scene in turn warrants the romantic resolution of the comedy and, somewhat more abstractly, the fulfillment of the formal promise of the artwork of the future, which would wed Walther to Eva, but also, by extension, his impetuous expressive energies as a young outsider artist to her situation as the offspring and inheritor of the German *Volk*'s aesthetic tradition.[5] In Zemlinsky and Klaren's piece, the Dwarf's song serves as the Dwarf's musical introduction, a calling card in song. The effect of the Dwarf's performance in Zemlinsky is similar to Beckmesser's performance in *Die Meistersinger*, but its situation in the middle of the piece means that rather than resolving the piece, it inaugurates and gives form to its concerns. Those concerns involve the place and possibility of individual expression in the wake of the Wagnerian *Gesamtkunstwerk*. If *Die Meistersinger* gave form to the force of communal expression in song (and Wagner inflects Walther's achievement as encapsulating and embodying the musical spirit of the *Volk*), Zemlinsky and Klaren's work explores and lends expression to a much lonelier condition: the integrity of individual vocal expression *in isolation from* the *Volk*.

In order to see how this is so, we need to take a closer look at Zemlinsky and Klaren's work. As *Der Zwerg* gets underway, the house staff is busy setting up a birthday party for the Infanta, and as they work, they ask their boss, the Chamberlain, to tell them about the presents amassed on the birthday table. The score indicates that the Chamberlain recites the list of presents "in a dry and expressionless voice." The list is impressive, even if the Chamberlain's tone suggests that he is unimpressed: the pope has sent a golden rose of thorns made of precious gems; the king has sent a dress made of a thousand pearls; and the emperor has sent two gorgeous horses. At this point in the recitation, the Chamberlain's expression changes markedly, as does the orchestra's: "but the loveliest present," he explains furtively, as the trombones lurch into a syncopated evocation of misalignment: "the loveliest, is awful" (in Georg Klaren's wonderfully Wagnerian alliteration: "das Schönste ist scheusslich").

"The Sultan," the Chamberlain tells his staff—and us along with them—"has sent a dwarf" (**web. ex. 10.1**). Among a variety of noteworthy features, Zemlinsky affords the Dwarf strikingly different—even contradictory—characterizations. As Antony Beaumont notes, the juxtaposition involves shifting perspectives: on the one hand,

> the Dwarf as others see him: a monster. Snarling trombone *glissandos*, sinister *sul ponticello* slides, frog-like hops—he is spared nothing. An instant later, the same idea, now an elegant violin solo, represents the Dwarf as he sees himself: a cavalier. The second strain of this new theme is initially presented as a mirror image of the first (no exact correlate, but a free inversion, recognizable as such even to the unschooled ear).[6]

The Dwarf's predicament as it is encapsulated in his initial narrated appearance—he's risible, and all the more risible for thinking himself to be quite elegant—is a familiar one in Zemlinsky's operas, which tend to fix on outcasts, offering what we might provisionally term a performative poetics of the perverse. But as such, it seems important to qualify and refine that characterization, since his is a deeply empathetic poetics: Zemlinsky's pieces tend to identify with the predicaments of the outsiders on his stage rather than lampooning or ridiculing them. In terms of the scene of the Dwarf's arrival at court, this means that the piece will end up siding less with the maids, and their expectation that this will be great fun, than with the Dwarf, whose experience of the party will end up being not much fun at all.

It is no doubt on account of this recurring scene of the composer's identification with the victims, and his corresponding sense of *himself* as a victim, that critics have tended to read his works autobiographically. In the case of *The Dwarf*, the biographical argument is buoyed by various familiar facts, derived from Zemlinsky's physique (he was short, with beady eyes and a protruding chin) and his romantic entanglements (especially his tortured love affair with Alma Mahler-Werfel—a famously carefree beauty, who, with characteristically imperious contempt, described Zemlinsky in her *Autobiography* as a "hideous gnome"[7]). These facts tend to suggest a certain overlap between the Dwarf and the composer, and how we might make sense of his hopeless and tragic love for a carefree Princess.[8]

But biography—illuminating as it is—hardly tells the whole story. There are philological reasons why this is so: the libretto was not by Zemlinsky, but by Georg Klaren, a young and ardent disciple of the Viennese philosopher and sexologist Otto Weininger. The autobiographical resonances, which seem so obvious to anyone familiar with the broad strokes of Zemlinsky's biography, are thus more incidental than they would seem, since Klaren expressed no particular interest in layering the tale with the details of Zemlinsky's private life, and expressed a good deal of interest in the possibility of allegorizing the impossibility of any real relations between the sexes. Thus, in an article on *Der Zwerg*, Klaren explains that his conception of the character of the Infanta, unlike Wilde's, involved a certain shading of sadism:

> the character of the Infanta had to gain melodic shape through some sort of psychological component, she had to be de-statue-ified, so to speak, robbed of her pseudo-majesterial play-thing calm (*ihrer pseudomajestättischen Spielzeugruhe*). To that end, she became childlike, outfitted with all of the cruel moods of puberty. Thus the Infanta gives the impression—or at least, she is supposed to—of not yet being a woman and no longer being a child (which is what she is in Wilde's account), so that her cruelty appears to be bred of a predisposition—constitutive and natural, not pathological—to sadism or a remnant of an infantile unscrupulousness, one that would lead her to destroy a doll out of curiosity.[9]

In Klaren's view (which is properly his inflection of Weininger's view), the Infanta cannot be held liable for actions that merely mark her as a *femme enfant*, a childish progenitor of the *femme fatale*.[10] The Infanta, on this account, is not just a young woman, but a young Woman, that is, an embodiment of characteristics that Weininger ascribed to women (such as a predisposition to amorality, a seemingly boundless desire for attention and affirmation, an extraordinary naivité); while the Dwarf bears, in concentrated form, qualities that Weininger and Klaren ascribed to men (such as a predisposition to intense feelings of inferiority in the presence of Woman and a correspondingly profound romanticization of the love object that takes the form of erotic longing rather than sexual attraction).[11]

As it turns out, Klaren's reinflection of Wilde's story in Weiningerian terms happens to align with the biographical terms of Zemlinsky's romantic inclinations, which involved a famously enduring streak of masochism and an equally long-standing identification with the outsider who formed the focus of his operas, including Görge of the *Traumgörge*, Kandaules of *König Kandaules*, and the Dwarf in *Der Zwerg*. In this essay, I propose to supplement an account of the reciprocal concord between the librettist's sociophilosophical inclinations toward tragic love and the composer's dramatic and biographical inclinations by tuning in to some of the other discursive channels that are at play in this piece, channels that will help us understand how and why, in this piece, and for Zemlinsky's stage works more generally, as the Chamberlain puts it in introducing the Dwarf, "das Schönste ist scheusslich"—that which is loveliest is awful. The essay is divided into three parts, or indeed, three scenes. Each of these scenes is distinct from the other, and yet we need the first two in order to understand the third.

Richard Wagner's Jewish Voice

In fact, I won't begin with Wagner's voice per se, although that is a hugely promising topic, but with the composer's articulated sense of Jewish voices on the stage. As Wagner puts it in his infamous pamphlet "Judaism in Music," Jews on the stage had something insuperably dreadful and inadvertently comical to them. Indeed, in Wagner's mind, these are precisely the voices one *does not want to hear*—they screech, drone, and carry on in a nasal fashion. And the bodies of those bearing these aberrant voices are similarly distended and offensive to any refined sensibility: they shuffle, blink, wheedle, and shamble.

I cite Wagner's essay not so much to trot out the point, by now familiar, that Wagner was an anti-Semite, but to focus on the specific terms of his polemic (which was, as we know, a commonplace polemic for the middle of the nineteenth century).[12] In Wagner's mind, Jews were a monstrous presence, ill-formed aesthetically, physically, spiritually, and socially for the pressing task of radically reforming art and therewith radically reforming society. Their monstrousness, in Wagner's mind, was symptomatic: Jews stood in (or perhaps we should say, they stooped and screeched in) for the deformed nature of contemporary art and society. Thus, when they took to the operatic stage (or any stage, for that matter), they imbued it with that symptomatic deformity. And as a result, art became risible. In Wagner's mind, there is something unintentionally and undeniably comical about a Jew on the stage, especially a singing Jew. Rather than imparting something serious or moving, the singing Jew onstage merely imparted his own inappropriateness; he became a joke, and with him, so too did the art that he deformed: what was to be sublime became ridiculous. Here is how he puts it in "Judaism in Music":

> Everything about [the Jew's] outward appearance and language that strikes us as repulsive will have an infinitely off-putting effect upon us when he starts to sing, unless we allow ourselves to be held enthralled by the sheer ridiculousness of it all. It is entirely natural that song, being the liveliest and most indisputably authentic expression of the individual's emotional life, should reveal the peculiar offensiveness of the Jewish nature in a particularly acute form; and we might well, in accord with a natural assumption, consider the Jew to be capable of artistic expression in every branch of art save that which is rooted in song.[13]

This, in a nutshell, is the central problem that "Judaism in Music" seeks to expose: the symptomatic vocal and corporeal monstrosity of Jews who thus undermine—or indeed, undo—the noble mission of art.

Of course, the problem of monstrosity in opera is not restricted to Jews. It is a problem that has historically nagged at opera itself, as Charles Dill has shown with reference to Jean-Philippe Rameau and the culture of eighteenth-century French opera.[14] In the highly regimented culture of the French baroque, Dill shows, Rameau's efforts at reform were perceived to be monstrous (that was the most common critical term used to denounce his work) because they appeared to introduce radical disorder to an ordered and edifying form, introducing distention and disfiguration in place of rationality and balance. And while the particular instantiation of these concerns might surprise, the concerns themselves are not unfamiliar. That is, while it may come as a surprise to find Rameau charged with disorderly conduct, the notion that opera would in some sense invite disorder is hardly surprising. As I hardly need to point out, the form risks disorder at any moment: singers, ballet, drama, an orchestra, scenery, stage effects—it is a lot to keep under control. And one can imagine a history of opera as a history of attempts to impose and maintain that control followed by symptomatic eruptions that challenge that control.

What I would like to ask the reader to keep in mind is the particular terminological constellation that is emerging here: in both cases—that is, for Wagner in the mid-nineteenth century, and for Rameau a century earlier—aesthetic innovation is freighted with a risk of a kind of disfiguring monstrosity. The edifying form of art is threatened in either scenario (if for very different reasons) by the introduction of disfigurement. Famously, Wagner's intention, in the *Gesamtkunstwerk*, was to consolidate disparate expressive channels into a single, unified whole. Of course, such a consolidation, in Wagner, is not without its costs, and he tends to stage those costs. That is, in Wagner's works, the threat of (aesthetic) disfigurement is mimeticized—it takes disfigured form onstage. One term we might employ for the figures of disfiguration in Wagner, the figures who stand apart from and outside of the magisterial edifice of consolidation pursued in and by the *Gesamtkunstwerk*, is "Jews."

Let me put that point a bit differently, because it is important, I think, to an understanding of Wagner's aesthetic achievement and the fantasmatic role that "Jews" play in that achievement, but also to an understanding of Zemlinsky's *Der Zwerg*, which emerges very much in Wagner's wake. Using Dill's terminology, we can say that Wagner's project involves a recurring attempt to tame the monstrousness of opera. Or indeed, the formulation hardly differs from

Wagner's own characterization of his project: in taking on the culture of opera (and by that he meant the culture of French grand opera that was the rage in Paris and at many of the major European opera houses of his day), Wagner famously hoped to replace what he perceived to be a senseless hodgepodge of pompous scenic effects and senseless musical ideas with a totalizing and unified work of art.[15] If opera was monstrous—a haven for the hodgepodge—then Wagner's artwork of the future would be cogent and compelling because properly consolidated. Or that, in any case, was the theory.

The process of consolidation was, of course, enormously ambitious and complex. The project of streamlining that Wagner undertook yielded a series of scenes in his works in which figures are unmasked and expelled for not belonging. And how do they express this state of not belonging? The short answer is: via symptomatic or overdetermined aesthetic means. And as we might expect, given the claims registered in Wagner's pamphlet and given that the works in question are music dramas, "Jews" reveal their sense of not-belonging in song. But not just in song (since, after all, this is Wagner, and thus everyone is forever singing), but most emphatically, in scenes of vocal performance.

This is not an intuitively obvious claim, so let me linger upon it for a moment. If "Jews" express their purported ridiculousness most particularly in the scene of singing (as Wagner claims in "Judaism in Music"), then it makes sense that the full ridiculousness of a character who bears the marks of a "Jew" would emerge when the character sets off in song. Here it helps to recall the distinction introduced by Carolyn Abbate, between a *noumenal* instance of music-making (that is, an occasion when a character sings, but the formal conceits of the piece do not mark the song as sung) and what I have in mind here, namely a *phenomenal* instance of singing (that is, scenes, like a song contest, or a dwarf's arrival at court, where a character is called upon to sing within the confines of the piece's fictional world).[16] When Mime sings his rearing song to Siegfried in acts 1 and 2 of *Siegfried* or Beckmesser sings his prize song to Eva in act 3 of *Die Meistersinger*, the scene of phenomenal performance is at the same time a scene of revelation—and in the cases mentioned here, the figure emerges in the course of his recourse to song in his full risibility and expressive incompetence. If Zemlinsky could be said to produce a poetics of the perverse in which we come to identify with the victims, in Wagner the victims—such as Beckmesser and Mime—are rarely the objects of empathy. (Put provocatively and schematically, I wonder whether we might not distinguish, then, between what we might provisionally term Zemlinsky's luridly masochistic poetics of the victim and Wagner's no less luridly sadistic poetics of the victim.)

Whether we understand the Wagnerian project as an effort to *transcend* opera by radically disciplining and in the process transforming its monstrous means (which is more or less the Wagnerian claim) or instead understand the project as an effort to appropriate and rebrand operatic means in the service of Wagner himself (which is how many of Wagner's critics saw the enterprise), it is striking to note the extent to which the stage works bear traces of a thoroughgoing animus toward opera. Put otherwise, my sense is that the stage works are peppered with the monstrousness of opera that they understand themselves to be transcending. Indeed, in some of my earlier work, I have tried to suggest how "Jews" appear on Wagner's stage as remnants, as ciphers of that monstrousness.[17] They are left behind on Wagner's stage—often laden with aesthetic means associated with the old operatic order (which, in Wagner's mind, was an old operatic dis-order) if only to be expelled, thus paving the way aesthetically and dramatically for a new aesthetic order, what he envisioned as the order of the *Gesamtkunstwerk*. In that way, the newly ascendant artwork of the future can sport the features of its newly won aesthetic identity—including especially its freedom from a vocal monstrousness that it has successfully (if not quite surgically) excised. The scene of that excision, in both *Siegfried* and *Die Meistersinger*, is, if in different ways, a scene of vocal performance—or indeed, the failure of such a performance.

In this sense, Beckmesser is a particularly interesting case, since he is an artist—a member of the guild of Master Singers—and yet, his art is inflected in *Meistersinger* as radically inept while the artwork of the noble Walther von Stolzing is presented as duly transfiguring and transcendent. The two, of course, are competing for the same girl, and the piece inflects it as no contest at all—or indeed, it is a risible contest, since Beckmesser is as wrong for the lovely Eva as Walther is right. Walther's victory in the song contest is all the more transcendent because it comes on the heels of the spectacle of Beckmesser's astonishing and cruelly comical failure. (Walther becomes the teutonic equivalent of an American Idol—let's call him a Bavarian Idol—only on the heels of Beckmesser being hooted off the stage as a shyster, a pretender, a failure.[18] Walther, we might say, is the cure to the wound opened up by Beckmesser's spectacular failure.) The couple of Eva and Walther—and with them, the artwork of the future—are consolidated, in the wake of the overdetermined expulsion of Beckmesser, who is not so much a lover as a schemer, not so much an artist as a pretender, not so much a singer as a screecher. Beckmesser's expulsion in the course of act 3 of the *Meistersinger* is, I think, a key scene to understanding what I am terming Wagner's sadistic poetics of the victim. And central to that expulsion is not only the risibility of his performance, but its reception onstage: initially the *Volk* murmurs in surprise, and eventually it will hoot and holler in disdain.

I invoke the scene of the festival meadow not simply to remind the reader of the terms of this sadistic poetics, but because I think the scene is an important intertextual referent for Zemlinsky and Klaren's *Dwarf* (both as a piece and as a character). In Wagner's piece, Beckmesser's performance is risible—and the crowd is unanimous in getting the joke, in finding his song ridiculous. The work of the scene, we might say, involves the dawning of this recognition: and of course, we in the auditorium—so the Wagnerian logic goes—quickly join our onstage surrogates in arriving at the realization that Beckmesser's song is in fact an imitation of a song, a duly distorted account of inspiration. Thus, as Beckmesser continues to sing, his singing shifts from being merely risible to being properly scandalous. In the process of attempting to woo Eva, he gives voice inadvertently and unwittingly, but also unequivocally, to his expressive incompetence. Put otherwise, the wound occasioned by Beckmesser's song is attributable to his specific identity and character.

The scene that Klaren and Zemlinsky set in *The Dwarf* has a great deal in common with the scene of the Prize Song in *Die Meistersinger*. Here, too, an obviously deluded singer performs what he takes to be a lovely wooing song, and its effect is one of unintentional comedy. In short, the crowd is bemused, while the singer, in his delusion, takes himself to be quite winning—much like the scene of the Dwarf's introduction earlier in the opera. The question—and I believe that the piece poses it as an urgent question and not merely a rhetorical one—is where does the song leave us as an audience? Let us consider the scene of the Dwarf's performance.

In fact, the Dwarf sets out to sing a drinking song to the Princess, but gives up after only a few measures, and launches instead into a courtly romance—a song about a bleeding orange that, when pierced, turns out to be his heart. The song's lyrics are transparently allegorical (**web. ex. 10.2**):

> Mädchen, nimm die blutende Orange, die in meinem Garten reifte, nimm! Ich bin arm, ein einzig Bäumchen hat mein Garten, und es reifte diese blutende Orange, nimm sie hin! Mädchen, hat ein stolzes, hartes Lachen, nimmt die Silbernadel aus dem Haar, das sehr weich ist, sticht so lachend, tief verletzend seine blutende Orange in den Staub. Mädchen, ach dein Lachen und die Nadel traf nicht eine Blutorange, spitze Nadel und dein scharfes Lachen traf mich, sieh, ich sterbe, denn die blutende Orange war mein Herz.

> Maiden, take the blood-red orange, which has ripened in my garden, take it! I am poor, my garden has but one little tree, and it bore this blood-red orange: do take it! The maiden's laughter is haughty and hard, she takes the silver

> pin out of her soft hair, and laughing, deeply wounding, stabs his blood-red orange into the dust. Maiden, ah! your laughter and the pin did not pierce a blood-red orange, the sharp pin and your harsh laughter struck me, see, I am dying, for the blood-red orange was my heart.[19]

For anyone familiar with the *Meistersinger*, the scene of the Dwarf's performance seems astonishing. It's not just that the *terms* of the Dwarf's song are familiar in form and content—from the instrumental prop (the Dwarf accompanies himself on a lute) to the inadvertent comedy of the ostensibly poetic text, to the hyperearnest recitation, to the risible desire to possess the leading lady. Beyond this, the denouement of the song's performance seems like one of those undergraduate thought experiments: What if Beckmesser hadn't disappeared, or indeed, what if the work, rather than directing Beckmesser to disappear amid the crowd in order to iris-in on Walther and Eva, had instead maintained its focus on Beckmesser. What might that have led to? What might it have sounded like?

Zemlinsky revisits the scene of vocal performance in *Die Meistersinger* not to correct its outcome, but rather to reframe the question that it poses. In Wagner, as I suggested above, the audience in the auditorium is aligned with the audience onstage, and both join together in hooting the scribe off the stage. It is a familiar generic conceit: the unity that brings together the proper pair is attained by expelling the pretender, who, the work reminds us, is a pretender in and to song. In turn, then, our attentions are redirected to Walther's masterful vocal performance, that follows upon and corrects Beckmesser's. Put in Dolar's terms, cited at the outset of this essay, the wound occasioned by the song's initial distortion is sutured by Walther's masterful vocal performance, which thus warrants his emergence as Eva's—and the *Volk*'s—proper hero.

In Zemlinsky and Klaren's piece, the scene and the outcome are—to a certain point at least—quite similar, but the stakes of identification and representation are very different. In order to understand how this is so, I would have us proceed to our second scene.

Jacques Lacan's Mirror

In 1936, some fourteen years after the premiere of Zemlinsky and Klaren's one-act opera, Lacan delivered the famous lecture outlining his idiosyncratic theory of the development of the human psyche. In Lacan's argument, the emerging subjectivity of the infant is riven at the age of about six months, catapulted from a sense of wholeness and dyadic union with the mother (a realm that Lacan famously dubs "the imaginary") to a sense of splitness, of insufficiency (a realm that Lacan characterizes as the "symbolic"). How does this transition come about? And what are its stakes? Lacan locates the transition in the infant's experience of his visual image in the mirror. What the subject perceives in the mirror is a figure whose motor capacities outstrip his own. Here, then, we witness the birth of what we might term an intra-psychic grass-is-greener syndrome: the subject in the mirror is better, is more fully formed, is more capable of controlling space, figuring an ideal—of control and capacity and formation—for the infant himself, something to which the infant can only aspire. I will spare the reader a lengthier and more detailed account of Lacan's argument, one that it fully deserves. What I want to hold on to, beyond the priority accorded the mirror in Lacan's argument as in Zemlinsky and Klaren's opera, is a fundamental insight that derives, I think, from that priority. After all, both have at their center a scene of traumatic recognition—in Lacan's lecture, that recognition comes very early in the subject's development; in Zemlinsky and Klaren's opera, it comes very late. For Lacan, the infant's perception of excellence *out there* in the mirror image produces, as I indicated, a sense of splitness in the subject, who, in entering the symbolic, is always in arrears of itself, insufficient to itself. Lacan locates, in this insufficiency, a fundamental quality of human subjectivity, a sense of insufficiency that will inform as it describes the subject's social relations.

I cite the Lacanian notion of the mirror stage because I think it offers us a helpful way to understand some of the stakes of the project of consolidation undertaken, in very different ways, by the works I have been seeking to understand here. Put otherwise, I think Lacan can help us understand why artists might develop, say, a poetics of masochism on the one hand, and a poetics of sadism on the other; or indeed, how we might understand the effort to consolidate aesthetic identity in the total work of art—the aspiration to totalization that it embodies, and the symptomatic remnants that it leaves behind. But more than that, the mirror scene—as it is staged in Zemlinsky and Klaren's *Dwarf* and shadowed by Wagner's *Meistersinger*—is itself split: in the Wagnerian scene, the apprehension of splitness produces a scene of consolidation by which the "Jewish" pretender is expelled and dramatic and expressive unity is ostensibly (if symptomatically) vouchsafed. But for and in a modernist mirror scene, which, I want to suggest, Zemlinsky and Klaren create here, the scene of risibility and contempt would spur a different identification: in *Die Meistersinger*, as I've suggested, the performance of comical misalignment in body and voice produces a scene of union (between Eva and Walther) that follows upon the expulsion of the bad object (Beckmesser as "Jewish" singer)—all the while soliciting our identification with both the scene of union as well as the expulsion that is its precondition. Put more schematically: we in the audience are unified in absorbing the diegetic scene of romantic unification and the scene of expulsion from which it proceeds and upon which it depends.

In Zemlinsky and Klaren's piece, the analogous scene solicits our identification with the object of scorn as he is scorned, such that a different consensus emerges not despite, but on the occasion of, this sung performance. If we take Lacan's model as in some sense instructive, if we take on his assumption that the human subject is in some sense riven, then the task of the work of art can be understood as taking up a position relative to this insight. That is, to cite two obvious and very different options, art can be restorative (seeking, say, to resituate us at a prelapsarian point, a moment prior to that split, a moment of wholeness that predates the fall) or it can seek to be representative (rendering that riven and fallen condition). The former, we might term the Wagnerian position; the latter, I think, is closer to Klaren and Zemlinsky's aesthetic project. There is a certain aggression that necessarily accrues to the restorative position, since it will have to account for the distinction between present conditions (of rivenness, of atomization) and its aspiration to totalization. By the same token, there is a certain empathy that accrues to the poetics of the riven. Which brings us to our third scene.

Zemlinsky and Klaren's Dwarf

In Zemlinsky and Klaren's piece, the Dwarf knows nothing of his deformity, and the particular terms of his delusion are suggestive. As the Chamberlain's account indicates, it's not just that he does not know that he's a dwarf, but he thinks that he's an artist. The terms of delusion map onto a prevalent discourse of the fin-de-siècle Viennese culture into which Zemlinsky was born: Jews, according to that discourse, were deformed, both physically and aesthetically; and they were not artists.[20] Or, as Wagner put it, they were insuperably repulsive and inadvertently comical—physically as well as musically.

Der Zwerg takes up a position in this discourse. Lonely and misunderstood, the Dwarf is also outfitted with an extraordinary—and extraordinarily idiosyncratic—voice. The terms of vocal idiosyncrasy take various forms: bodily (insofar as the Dwarf's voice emerges from a body coded as deviant) and expressive (insofar as the Dwarf falls head over heels in love with the Princess and gives immediate and unguarded voice to his affections). His allegorical wooing song, then, is hardly a manly song—neither according to the conventions of post-Wagnerian operatic affect, nor according to the expectations of lyrical reference (insofar as the song has no obvious dramatic anchor: it stands alone, and thus enacts the condition to which it attests).[21] The song of the blood-red orange that serves as a culmination of the Dwarf's vocal performance in the piece bespeaks, or indeed, it "be-sings" a profound isolation, and as such, it testifies to a profound rivenness—between a majesty of personal expression and the socially felt deformity of that expression; between the expressive integrity of the Dwarf's desire and the cruelty and disregard with which that expression is met. In short, this is an aria of and as the wound.

In the scene of the Dwarf's vocal performance, as in so many scenes in Zemlinsky's works for the stage, we encounter a familiar constellation: on the one hand, those who embody a fully tragic, because fully sensitized, emotional life and, on the other, those who have capitulated to the rawness and insensitivity of a life lived amid (emotional) callousness and mean-spiritedness. Thus, the Dwarf's intensely felt lyrical outpourings in this piece are relegated to a landscape (also familiar in Zemlinsky) where such outpourings have been rendered obsolete or inconsequential. As Sherry Lee observes,

> the Dwarf's own musical language throughout the opera presents him as a lyrical subject of genuine feeling. Its integrity is heightened by its contrast with the blatant musical mimicry that represents the objective cruelty with which others view him: his entrance, which incites the mirth of the court, is a pitiless caricature of disfigurement composed of limping dotted rhythms, ungainly dissonances, and grotesque glissandi across awkwardly wide intervals.[22]

The musical dramaturgy of his aria to the Infanta works differently. The aria is subject to no such obvious, composed contrast (that is, there are no ungainly dissonances and grotesque glissandi). Instead, the contrast is rendered dramatically, with the pressures of the court's dismissal crowding the performance at its outset and conclusion. Thus, the aria's expressive grandiloquence is implicitly juxtaposed to the Dwarf's diminutiveness and explicitly subjected to the onstage crowd's dismissal: either way, it comes off as radically out of whack.

Here, then, we in the audience are presented with a solitary voice of expressive integrity, a voice removed, situated between (the court's) mockery, (the Chamberlain's) bureaucratic aggression, and (the Princess's) entitled oblivion. But if we were to seek a name for this voice, situated as it is between loss, longing, and a fullness of expression that is always in arrears of itself and the desire to which it attests, would it not be the voice of the wound, the gap, or indeed, the voice of castration?

In that sense, the vocal and orchestral power amassed in the service of the Dwarf's lyrical expression contrasts with the powerlessness with which that expression is associated: in Zemlinsky's operas, such instances of vocal performance are accorded expressive heft but they have no apparent dramatic traction. This, then, is the tragedy of the diminished subject, the subject dwarfed, so to speak, by the weight and callous exigencies of life in the world. In Zemlinsky and Klaren's piece, the voices of the "dwarfed" are granted an emphatic and sustained expressive agency, but they have little resonance in the (opera's) world of action. Here, then, we encounter a characteristic expressive condition for Zemlinsky, an extroverted pathos of empathy. That pathos needs to be understood in two ways: as a form of *expression* (duly lyrical, and taking conventional forms, as aria and orchestral eruption), but also as a form of political critique (where the loneliness of the lyrical and orchestral eruption constitutes an indictment of an emotional world that has become bureaucratized, anaesthetized, and oblivious).

To cite an example: in the course of the opera's first scene, as the gift table is brought in, Ghita and the three ladies-in-waiting mock the Chamberlain, and as the latter storms out, Ghita launches into a characteristic arioso outburst of admiration: she admires the Infanta's birthday presents, but beyond that, she wishes she were herself an Infanta, for if she were, she would "shower with love those who are unhappy and hideous." At this early point, we are alerted to the piece's expressive economy of empathy, by which one figure emerges from the group in order to venture a lone (and thus, performatively lonely) position, inflected as authentic and marked as individualistic, which is endorsed (musically) by the terms of orchestral accompaniment (in this case, the characteristically "espressivo" accompaniment in the strings and celestina) and disregarded (socially) by the other figures in the scene. This is the first expression that the piece inflects as authentic, heartfelt, and transcendent in the midst of an emotional landscape that is impoverished because callous, unreflected, and everyday. As such, it marks the piece's discursive inclinations, its expressive investments.

How are we to comprehend the stakes of the conjunction of the Lacanian insight with the Wagnerian critique? At stake in this insight is a dissolution of the unified state, of a unified aesthetic edifice, of a coherent and self-identical subjectivity. *Der Zwerg* dramatizes such a moment, it lyricizes it, lending it dramatic and musical form. The scene of performance enacts the trauma that it describes, an epiphanic instance of rivenness, of splitness (and the torment that accompanies this recognition). It is a traumatic scene—arguably the traumatic scene—of modernity: in place of the romantic gambit celebrated in Beethoven's Ninth Symphony, by which we are all destined for brotherhood (unified in a shared, chorally avowed identity), we have here a sense in which not just the utopian community of mankind, but the human subject itself is insuperably split. *Der Zwerg* renders this condition, according it a sober and de-idealized treatment. In so doing, Zemlinsky affords the voice a deeper sense—but *not*, to return to Dolar's formulation, in a *restorative* (or what we might term a *Wagnerian*) sense (by which we might restore the loss suffered by the assumption of the symbolic order), but rather as testament to the inevitability of that loss and the impossibility of its restoration. Far from serving as a "cure" for "the wound inflicted by culture," the Dwarf's voice lends expression to that wound. Might this begin to explain the fascination of the Dwarf's vocal effusions—as well as the ambivalent place of *Der Zwerg* in the operatic canon?

Notes

1. Mladen Dolar, *A Voice and Nothing More* (Cambridge, MA: MIT Press, 2006), 31.

2. A piano reduction was published by Universal Edition just before the premiere: Alexander Zemlinsky, *Der Zwerg, ein tragisches Märchen für Musik in einem Akt, frei nach O. Wilde's "Geburtstag der Infantin" von Georg C. Klaren, Musik von Alexander Zemlinsky* (Vienna: Universal Edition, 1921). Zemlinsky's biographer Antony Beaumont edited a revised edition of the score also published by Universal Edition in 2006. See Zemlinsky, *Der Zwerg: ein tragisches Märchen in einem Akt, op. 17 (1921), hrsg. Antony Beaumont. UE 17571* (Vienna: Universal Edition, 2006). The Los Angeles Opera produced the opera in 2008. A DVD of the Los Angeles production, conducted by James Conlon and directed by Darko Tresnjak, was recorded in 2008 and released by Arthaus in 2010. It features Rodrick Dixon as the Dwarf, Mary Dunleavy as the Infanta, Susan B. Anthony as Ghita, and James Johnson as Don Estoban.

3. See Ulrich Wilker, *"Das Schönste ist scheußlich": Alexander Zemlinskys Operneinakter* Der Zwerg, Schriften des Wissenschaftszentrums Arnold Schönberg, vol. 9 (Vienna: Böhlau, 2013). In chap. 6 of his exhaustive and informative study, Wilker locates *Der Zwerg* in a long line of "artist operas" that includes *Tannhäuser* and *Die Meistersinger*. See Wilker, *"Das Schönste ist scheußlich,"* 204–13. Additional sources include Antony Beaumont, *Zemlinsky* (Ithaca, NY: Cornell University Press, 2000), who notes that "*Der Zwerg* is the only opera of Zemlinsky's to use anything approaching Wagnerian leitmotiv technique" (303).

4. One noteworthy exception is Stefan Bodo Würffel's "Der andere Mime: Eine Märchenfigur bei Wagner und Zemlinsky," *Die Musikforschung* 46 (January–March 1993): 32–44.

5. See the section on "Comic Fictional Modes" in Northrop Frye, *The Anatomy of Criticism: Four Essays* (Princeton, NJ: Princeton University Press, 1957), 43–52. For a detailed reading of the dramaturgy of singing (vs. reading) in the *Meistersinger*, see my "Reading Beckmesser Reading: Antisemitism and Aesthetic Practice in *Die Meistersinger von Nürnberg*," *New German Critique* 69 (Fall 1996): 127–46.

6. Beaumont, *Zemlinsky*, 307.

7. Alma Mahler-Werfel, *Mein Leben* (Frankfurt: Fischer, 1960), 24. See, for example, Beaumont, *Zemlinsky*, 309: "In private, Zemlinsky had often been the object of Alma's 'pity and disgust'; in public, he found himself at the mercy of every satirical columnist and caricaturist in the land. To compose an opera on so sensitive a theme as his own physical appearance seemed a particularly distressing form of self-abasement." See also Stefan Bodo Würffel, "Der andere

Mime," 39; and Sherry D. Lee, "The Other in the Mirror, or, Recognizing the Self: Wilde's and Zemlinsky's Dwarf," *Music & Letters* 91, no. 2 (2010): 199.

8. As Kenneth Smith puts it at the outset of an essay on Lacan, Zemlinsky, and *Der Zwerg*, "a more wretchedly masochistic self-portrait of an artist is difficult to imagine." See Smith, "Lacan, Zemlinsky, and *Der Zwerg*: Mirror, Metaphor, and Fantasy," *Perspectives of New Music* 48, no. 2 (2010): 78.

9. Georg C. Klaren, "*Der Zwerg* und was er bedeutet," in *Kölnische Zeitung*, May 29, 1922.

10. See, on this point, Uta Wilhelm, "Zum Einfluß der Theorien Otto Weiningers auf die Figurenkonzeption in Alexander Zemlinskys Einakter 'Der Zwerg,'" in *Archiv für Musikwissenschaft* 54, no. 1 (1997): 84–89, here 88. Wilhelm's essay offers an illuminating account of the implications of Klaren's relationship to Weininger for the libretto of *Der Zwerg*.

11. Uta Wilhelm argues that Klaren's libretto marks a break with Weininger in one important respect, namely in the librettist's conviction that redemption—and indeed, the Dwarf's redemption in the opera—is to be found in a man's erotic attachment to an idealized Woman that is freed of sexual content. Weininger for his part dismissed outright the prospects of a redemptive love. See Wilhelm, "Zum Einfluß," 87.

12. On Wagner and anti-Semitism, see Marc A. Weiner, *Richard Wagner and the Anti-Semitic Imagination* (Lincoln: University of Nebraska Press, 1995).

13. Richard Wagner, "Judaism in Music," trans. Stewart Spencer, *Wagner: Journal of the British Wagner Society* 9 (1988): 25. In German: "Alles, was in [der] äußeren Erscheinung und Sprache [des Juden] uns abstoßend berührte, wirkt in seinem Gesange auf uns endlich davonjagend, solange wir nicht durch die vollendete Lächerlichkeit dieser Erscheinung gefesselt werden sollten." Richard Wagner, "Das Judentum in der Musik," *Gesammelte Schriften und Dichtungen*, 2nd ed., vol. 5 (Leipzig E. W. Fritzsch, 1887), 72.

14. Charles Dill, *Monstrous Opera: Rameau and the Tragic Tradition* (Princeton, NJ: Princeton University Press, 1998).

15. See, for a characteristic instance of Wagnerian disparagement, the scene of Parisian performance that Wagner describes in "A Theatre in Zurich" (1851): "All the rich and notables, who settle in the monstrous world-metropolis for its out-of-the-way amusements and distractions, are driven by ennui and unsated cravings to the sumptuous chambers of this theatre, there to get set before them the fullest draught of entertainment. [In Paris] the most astounding pomp of decorations and stage-costumes unfolds itself in startling multiplicity before the swooning eye, which turns its greedy glance, again, to the most coquettish dancing of the amplest ballet-corps in all the world; an orchestra of unrivalled strength and eminence accompanies in sonorous fill the dazzling march of never-ending masses of chorus-singers and figurants; between whose ranks at last appear the most expensive singers, schooled expressly for this theatre, and claim the overwrought senses' residue of interest for their special virtuosity. As pretext for these seductive evolutions a dramatic aim is also dragged in by the ears—its tantalizing motive borrowed from some murderous, or Devil's, scandal; and this whole clinking, tinkling, glittering, glistening show [Klingen, Schwirren, Flittern und Flimmern] is paraded as 'Grand Opera'" (in Wagner, *Prose Works*, vol. 3, 36–37).

In German: "Alle Vornehmen und Reichen, die sich in der ungeheuren Weltstadt der ausgesuchtesten Vergnügungen und Zerstreuungen wegen aufhalten, versammeln sich, von Langeweile und Genußsucht getrieben, in den üppigen Räumen dieses Theaters, um das höchste Maß von Unterhaltung sich vorführen zu lassen. Die erstaunlichste Pracht an Bühnendekorationen und Theaterkostümen entwickelt sich da in überraschendster Mannigfaltigkeit vor dem schwelgenden Auge, das wiederum mit gierigem Blicke dem kokettesten Tanze des üppigsten Ballettkorps der

Welt sich zuwendet; ein Orchester von der Stärke und Vorzüglichkeit, wie es sich nirgends wieder findet, begleitet in rauschender Fülle die glänzenden Aufzüge ungeheurer Massen von Choristen und Figuranten, zwischen denen endlich die kostpieligsten Sänger, eigens für dieses Theater geschult, auftreten und den Rest einer überspannten sinnlichen Teilnahme für ihre besondere Virtuosität in Anspruch nehmen. Als Vorwand zu diesen verführerischen Evolutionen ist nebenbei auch eine dramatische Absicht herbeigezogen, die als prickelndes und stachelndes Motiv aus irgendeinem Mordoder Teufelsskandal der Geschichte entnommen ist; und das Klingen, Schwirren, Flittern und Flimmern des Ganzen stellt sich als 'große Oper' dar." Richard Wagner, "Ein Theater in Zürich" (1851), in Wagner, *Gesammelte Schriften und Dichtungen*, vol. 5, 31.

16. See Carolyn Abbate, "Mahler's Deafness: Opera and the Scene of Narration in Todtenfeier," in *Unsung Voices: Opera and Musical Narrative in the Nineteenth Century* (Princeton, NJ: Princeton University Press, 1991), 119–55.

17. See, in this regard, my *Richard Wagner, Fritz Lang, and the Nibelungen: The Dramaturgy of Disavowal* (Princeton, NJ: Princeton University Press, 1998), as well as "Reading Beckmesser Reading"; "A Picture Perfect Man: Senta, Absorption, and Wagnerian Theatricality," *Opera Quarterly: Der fliegende Holländer* 21, no. 3 (Summer 2005): 486–95; and "Interstitial Redemption: Wagner's *Tannhäuser* and the Dramaturgical Vicissitudes of Music Drama," in *Monatshefte*, special issue on "The Art of Hearing," ed. Marc Silberman, 98, no. 2 (June 2006): 180–91.

18. This is an insight that is conveyed with penetrating verve and imagination in the much-maligned 2007 Bayreuth production of *Die Meistersinger* staged by Katharina Wagner. (Since the production was released commercially on DVD without subtitles [!?], it is worth noting that a version of the production that includes English subtitles is available at the time of this writing via Amazon Prime's video streaming service.) The production was recorded live at the Bayreuth Festival, July 2008, Opus Arte OA BD7078D, featuring Hans Sachs: Franz Hawlata; Sixtus Beckmesser: Michael Volle; Walther von Stolzing: Klaus Florian Vogt; Eva: Michaela Kaune; Conductor: Sebastian Weigle; Stage design: Tilo Steffens; Costumes: Michaela Barth and Tilo Steffens; Dramaturgy: Robert Sollich; Chorus director: Eberhard Friedrich; Television director: Andreas Morell.

19. I have slightly modified Roger Clément's translation, which appears in the booklet accompanying the EMI recording of *Der Zwerg* with the Kölner Philharmoniker and the Gürzenich Orchestra conducted by James Conlon, featuring Soile Isokoski as the Infanta and David Kuebler as the Dwarf. EMI Classics, 1996.

20. There is a rich literature on the cultural politics of Jewish bodies. See, most famously, Sander Gilman, *The Jew's Body* (New York: Routledge, 1991); as well as Carl E. Schorske, "Politics in a New Key," in Schorske's *Fin-de-Siècle Vienna: Politics and Culture* (New York: Knopf, 1980).

21. See, in this regard, Sherry D. Lee's astute observation that the song underscores the thoroughgoing feminization of the Dwarf: "throughout the opera, the Dwarf, as spectacle, is placed in the feminine position of the object of the gaze. . . . Beyond the obvious self-abasement of the song's text, its real masochism arises in the phantasmatic that places the subject in a passive, feminine sexual position, that of an orange being penetrated by a hairpin." Lee, "The Other in the Mirror," 206.

22. Sherry D. Lee, "Modernist Opera's Stigmatized Subjects," in *The Oxford Handbook of Music and Disability Studies*, ed. Blake Howe, Stephanie Jensen-Moulton, Neil Lerner, and Joseph Straus (Oxford: Oxford University Press, 2016), 677.

11

There Is No Such Thing as the Composer's Voice

SETH BRODSKY

My title might resonate with Jacques Lacan's imperious declarations on non-existence—for instance, that "there is no sexual relationship" (*il n'y a pas de rapport sexuel*) or that "there is no [the] woman" (*la femme n'existe pas*).[1] But it was another phrase cycling through my head when I chose this title, and it's a phrase I can't separate from the sound of a voice. It is a friend's voice, imitating another voice, his keyboard teacher's, and so I always hear in it my friend's Italianate estimation of a Catalan accent. It is a complaint, one of the best reasons to "be vocal," and it is a complaint about voice no less. The phrase—hear it in your best fake-Italian-Catalan—is: "The sound of Bebung on the piano is the same as nothing."[2]

Bebung is an eighteenth-century clavichord technique, what would have been known as an affect, an expressive ornament, for imitating the human voice. The clavichord uses not a hammer or quill to strike the string, but a small metal tangent, and once the key is pressed this tangent stays in place.[3] So wiggling the finger wiggles the key which wiggles the tangent which wiggles the string which makes the quiet vibrating tone quiver—like a human voice. My friend's teacher was responding not to some misuse of the technique on the clavichord. He was objecting—with that special mix of defensiveness and fatigue reserved for masterpieces—to Beethoven's attempt, in the early nineteenth century, to execute *Bebung* on an instrument mechanically incapable of realizing it (**mus. ex. 11.1**).

After the first staff's impersonation of an opera orchestra giving way to a singer's recitative, there is no question that this is a vocal apparition. But note the contradictory notation in the top staff of the second system: Should those repeating notes be rearticulated? But also tied together? Is this weird

EXAMPLE 11.1 Beethoven, op. 110, mvt. 3 ("tutte le corde").

direction even meant to be played? Heard but not played? Seen and thought but not heard? The debate is not to be resolved.[4]

In this chapter, I want to return to the larger territory and topic explored so well by Marcelle Pierson earlier in this volume.[5] But I want to think less historically and more allegorically about the scenario I just outlined, and to break down this allegory into three registers. On a conceptual register, it involves what Edward T. Cone famously called "the composer's voice," a magical web of sound and sense and time and event whose conjuring power renders a structural absence—the singing composer—into an ineluctable presence.[6] I want to postulate that this composer's voice—as a trope that comes into being with Beethoven and continues on to this day—is also "the same as nothing."[7] And, in a metaphorical sense, this too has to do with, first, its status as a kind of technique for imitating the voice, and second, its being executed on a kind of "instrument" mechanically incapable of realizing this technique. On a second, more historical register, I would postulate that this scenario is inseparable from how we think about musical modernism in the expanded sense—meaning a modernism beginning with late Beethoven, if not in the works themselves, then with their "delayed activation," their "afterwardness" or *Nachträglichkeit*, their increasingly intense reception and gradual transformation into an ethics of musical composition.[8] Finally, on a third, "generic" register, I want to propose that this composer's voice—this modernist voice or voice of modernism that "is the same as nothing"—is fundamentally theatrical. It is, to push it further, fundamentally *operatic*: extravagant, spectacular, showy, stagey, a real curtain-raiser. But this "operaticness" is paradoxical: it involves a staging of *the impossibility of making something appear*. It is a theater of truancy, a showing of the no-show, an endeavor not simply to make nonappearance appear, but to make it sing.

These are some immodest claims, and so I want here only to offer a sketch, a condensed conceptual outlining of the problematic and just the beginning of their working-out. And here I want to work allegorically as well: if "opera" could be taken as our heuristic "reality," then I would ask our allegory to be "string quartet"—on the one hand, the string quartet as the Western classical paradigm of inwardness, abstraction, the rejection of the theater; and, on the other hand, the string quartet, post-Beethoven, as unsung aria, broken song, latent opera, failed cavatina. A preparation for an opera that never comes, or one that does, but arrives missing something essential: hero, event, story, sound. What follows then are four such scenes, a quartet of four-voiced nonappearances moving back in historical time, and each prompting a digression on what, where, and how the composer's voice is not.

Scene 1

Helmut Lachenmann's Second String Quartet, "Reigen seliger Geister" ("Rounds of the blessed spirits"), from 1989, is performed on the website by the JACK Quartet (**web. ex. 11.1**).[9] The scene comes just before the epilogue of this epic single-movement work: the previous twenty minutes unfold a meticulous but relentless journey from the airy edge of unpitched audibility, to long heaving tones and plucked hockets (musical lines split between distinct bodies), to the most walloping percussive violence, during which the individual players detune their instruments' strings indeterminately. The score arrives at a moment of extraordinary equipoise: out of the wildly detuned quartet emerges what Lachenmann calls "an expansive sixteen-note 'song'" (*Gesang*, he writes, in quotes). It appears, however, only as a kind of shadow melody, one after another of the group's sixteen open strings left resonating after a brutal pizzicato attack.[10] The delicate, almost alarming strangeness of the tones—unforeseeable by even the performers themselves—is only intensified by the blows that precede them. They are less a song than a sonic corona to a song eclipsed (**mus. ex. 11.2**).

Lachenmann arrives at this culminating moment through a characteristic mad logic, the result of system- and instrument-building on the one hand and radical contingency on the other. This shadow-song, made up of what Lachenmann calls "subtraction sounds," is the apotheosis of the score's exploration of "meta-melody," of "sequences built through hockets."[11] But it also

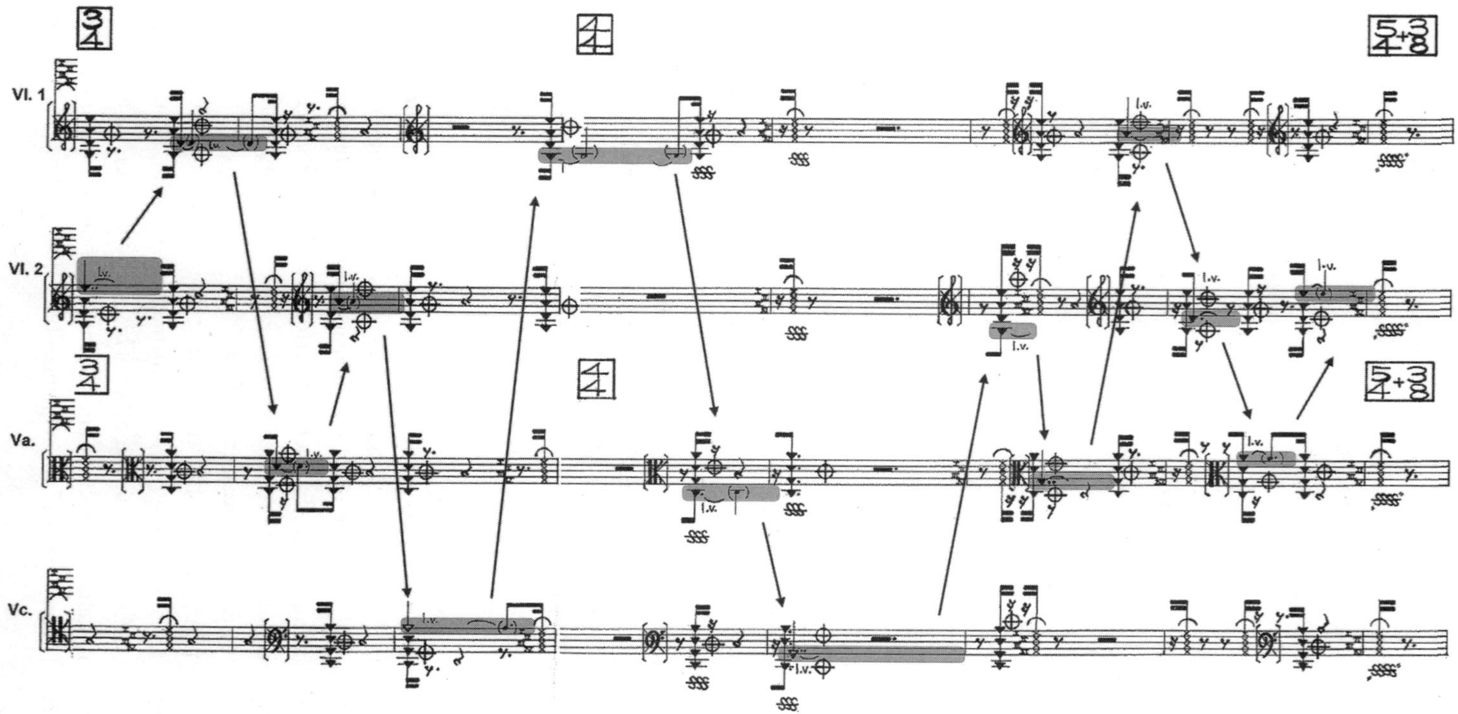

EXAMPLE 11.2 Lachenmann, II. Streichquartett, "Reigen seliger Geister" (1989), "shadow-song" (resonating strings highlighted).

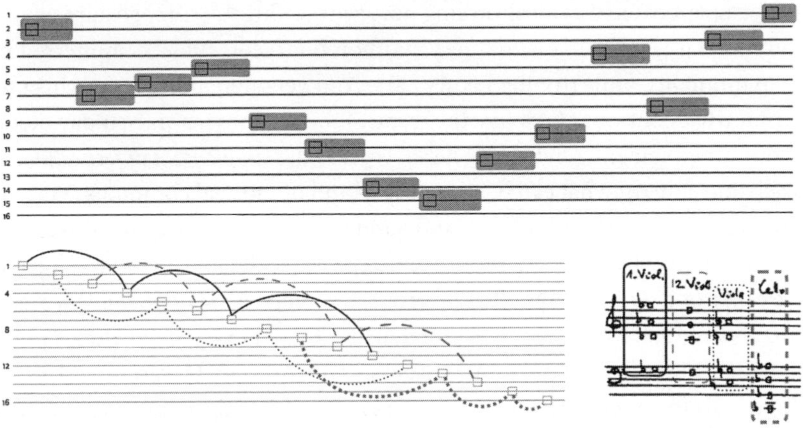

FIGURE 11.1 Lachenmann, II. Streichquartett, ensemble as 16-string Orphic "meta-harp": as played (top); tuning of four instruments (lower right); interlocking/emergent meta-harp (lower left).

produces an uncanny image, not least on the page: Lachenmann has made a giant harp. And not just any harp. Given the quartet's subtitle—"Dance of the blessed spirits," taken from the ballet in Gluck's 1774 version of his opera on Orpheus and Eurydice—it seems fair to call this an Orphic harp. This shadow-song could be its toccata, its warming-up, but if so, it is for a voice that never appears. Perhaps Orpheus is already long gone, and only wind makes this harp speak, hence the gust-like arc of the song itself (**fig. 11.1**; note the way Lachenmann has retuned all the instruments, and "restrung" them so that they interlock into a single vibrating field).

The passage is one of Lachenmann's most inspired "offers through refusal," a quickly vanishing foretaste of "the dream of the 'lucky hand,' " a music at once composed, decomposed, and uncomposed.[12]

First Digression: "Find Your Voice"

"The path to being a composer is not only a technical path," says the Italian composer/performer Ludovico Einaudi in an interview from 2016. "[O]f course you have to prepare yourself with technical tools. But the most difficult thing is to find your voice. Sometimes I see younger guys that come to me and they give me CDs of music that resembles what I do—and this is a mistake. You should diversify your experiments in writing."[13]

Einaudi is in some ways Lachenmann's nightmare double, inverting all his Frankfurt School sympathies, his faith in *ernste Musik* and aesthetic autonomy. By contrast, Einaudi, who writes in a studiedly naive postminimalist vein, can appear as a cynical smiling purveyor of shrink-wrapped aura whose commercial-sized solo piano tunes summon bourgeois subjects immersed in deep moments while driving luxury cars. And yet—Einaudi does put his finger on what continues to define the trope of the composer's voice today: it is a twofold supplement. On the one hand, voice is the *supplement of technique*, of teachable craft, of what can be shared as a kind of musical commons. Voice is voice only because hand is hand, and hand is defined by what can be grasped, placed, and replaced.[14] Whatever is writable, reproducible, iterable—voice is the other of it. On the other hand, voice is the *supplement of resemblance*. It is what is singular, what cannot be imitated; it is the other of *other voices*, a point to which I'll return below in my discussion of Adriana Cavarero and Brian Kane.[15] To formalize this—let's call it Einaudi's Rule—the composer's voice is whatever is not technique that is *also not* other voices. It's funny that Einaudi suggests that "experiments in *writing*" are the key: on your way to transcending the writable in the service of transcending other voices, writing can help.

Unsurprisingly, Einaudi's Rule is hegemonic in the age of late neoliberal capitalism. The singular, the auratic, that which renders music logically closest to the unica of the hypercapitalist art world/market, is also what mobilizes its opposite: the endless whirl of exchangeable coin. The composer's voice is a staple of branding and PR ("Eschewing the ivory tower, composer Kevin Puts aims to communicate with performers and audiences—without compromising his individual voice"); a bulwark of grants and awards funding ("The American Academy of Arts and Letters . . . honors outstanding artistic achievements by a composer who has arrived at his or her own voice"); and even a license for some of music's most risk-averse institutions to place an odd bet now and then, as when the Metropolitan Opera agreed to produce an opera by the young American composer Nico Muhly. The opera, *Two Boys*, got middling reviews, but *New York Times* critic Anthony Tommasini blessed it with the ultimate imprimatur for a living composer:

> All composers draw upon various musical styles. Very few are completely original. The challenge is to fashion the diverse influences into a distinctive voice. It is hard to describe what makes a composer's voice authentic, but you know it when you hear it. Nico Muhly has a voice, a Muhly sound. . . .[16]

Muhly, in transcending technique and other voices, can be designated an "authentic" voice. The composer's voice is, first and foremost, the central achievement of the professional (neoliberal) composer. But Tommasini stumbles as he nominates, qualifying: Muhly has "a voice, a Muhly sound. . . ." A sound: as if voice and sound were the same thing. I wonder about this. I wonder if—citing Einaudi's Rule—we might place the composer's voice on the other side not just of technique, not just of other voices, but also of sound, existence even. How might the composer's voice, as "whatever is not technique that is also not other voices," have a real effect, a real power, without having a positive ontic status, any condition of *being*? How might it be real but not actual?

Scene 2

This is the Minguet Quartet, performing Italian composer Luigi Nono's only entry in the genre, *Fragmente—Stille, an Diotima,* from 1979–1980 (**web. ex. 11.2**).[17] The quartet is famous for signaling Nono's "inward turn," and there is no question that its airy hermeticism had an enormous effect on Lachenmann's second quartet of a decade later.[18] The section on **website example 11.2**, which also comes toward the end of the piece, presents an actual historical piece of song: the tenor to the famous fifteenth-century Franco-Flemish chanson "Malor me bat," or "Suffering beats me down" (**mus. ex. 11.3**).

For Nono the song comes with a story: his friend and mentor Bruno Maderna introduced him to it in 1948, in Ockeghem's setting in the Petrucci Harmonice Musices Odhecaton A of 1501.[19] If Lachenmann's was a shadow-song, Nono's is a broken one: embedded in the viola, incessantly riven by long and painstakingly varied silences, its integrity skewed by constant changes in rhythm, phrase, attack, harmony, and timbre by the other players. The section silently discloses the forty-eighth of fifty-two fragments from Friedrich Hölderlin's late poetic fragments that superscribe the whole score; in this case, the words—"Wenn ich trauernd versank . . . das zweifelnde Haupt" (When I sank in mourning . . . my doubting head)—encrypt a memorial to Maderna, who had died in 1973.

As radically new as the sound world of Nono's quartet was in 1980, the dialectical logic of fragmentation is redolent of early nineteenth-century German Romanticism: the audible field's unrelenting inconsistency is precisely what shores up the consistency of the silences that tear this field apart. I would argue that the figure of "song" here—including not only the Ockeghem, but also later silent allusions to Beethoven's "heiliger Dankgesang" ("holy song of thanks") from the late quartet, op. 132—lies on the side of the fragment. It is less voice than voice-husk, the *once-voiced*, the exteriorized remnant. But these figures essentially "trick" a silent interiority into—if not exactly appearing, then implying. This interiority, weirdly external to the score, nonetheless haunts it, everywhere and nowhere at once, the inimitable consistency of nothing.

EXAMPLE 11.3 Luigi Nono, *Fragmente—Stille an Diotima* (1980), fragment 48, "When, mourning, I sank . . . ," viola line with tenor from "Malor me bat"; "Malor me bat" as used by Johannes Ockeghem (tenor line).

Second Digression: "A Vocal Turn?"

"Uniqueness," writes Brian Kane, "grounds an ethics where the unique site of vocal emission is ultimately more important than what is said or the pleasure it gives."[20] This is perhaps another way of formulating Einaudi's Rule, that is, that the composer's voice has a special kind of singularity, something radically incomparable and hence unique. In context, Kane is trying here to understand the stakes of what he calls the recent "vocal turn" in the Anglophone humanities.[21] He is a bit skeptical, and understandably so: if we are turning to voice, it is because we are *re*turning to a challenge voice keeps posing, and we should be wary of our hubris in thinking we now have a solution. For Kane, the unique challenge of voice is clear: it is a post-Derridean challenge, "how to turn (or return) to the voice without, at the same time, affirming the metaphysics of presence?"[22] That is, how can we think of voice beyond the Husserlian paradigm of autoaffection, of the internal voice engaged in silent, expressive speech, grounding its self-presence by being at once the sender and receiver of its own discourse?

Kane lays out an elegant model for engaging this challenge, which I envision thus (**fig. 11.2**): where there is voice—*phoné*—there is always (what Derrida calls) a spacing or *différance* of three other terms: *echos* (sound), *logos* (sense), and *topos* (site, location, or body, as I will gloss it here below).

By spacing is meant nothing necessarily complex, at least initially—only a coordinated nonidentity, what Kane calls at one point a "minuscule lag" or "delay" between distinct terms that conceptual thinking can at least temporarily stabilize and articulate.[23] Voice, *phoné*, is hence a single signifier standing in—not without a certain impropriety—for what is never actually selfsame; voice "is neither identical with the simple summation of its three terms,

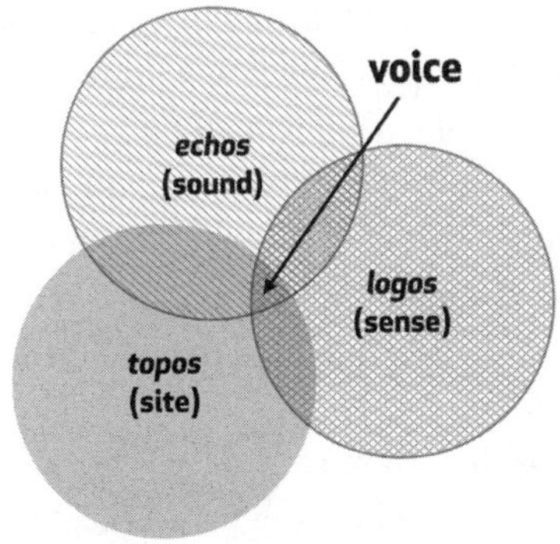

FIGURE 11.2 Kane's spacing of the voice (visual model).

nor a subtraction to any single term." It is, rather, "the product of a constantly circulating displacement of *echos*, *topos*, and *logos*."[24] The quiet radicality of Kane's proposal reveals itself as he moves through the history of voice in Western thought, not merely as a history of spacing, but of *reduction to pairs*, what Kane calls "crossings." The Western philosophical history of voice becomes a history of such crossings and their vicissitudes: for the Stoics, for instance, voice is fundamentally a matter of *sound + sense*, the very definition of the human; the Judeo-Christian heritage, reliant on the acousmatic voice of God, requires the reduction *sense + body*; the poststructural legacy—the one that most interests Kane here—often involves a reduction to *sound + body* (Kane has in mind Roland Barthes's classic "The Grain of the Voice," but also Cavarero's more recent *For More Than One Voice: Toward a Philosophy of Vocal Expression*).[25]

As compelling as these crossings are, I am drawn to the third terms they each leave behind; it seems to me less a process of elision than one of repression. It could even be said that precisely this repressed third term is what returns in the form of the subject—say, the Stoic, the Christian, or the poststructuralist—who speaks for the crossing that brings that subject into being. If being human involves the crossing *sound + sense*, the Stoic assumes the *body* in which sound and sense take place; if the silent voice of God delivers its *logos* in the *topos* of the place of worship, then the Christian assumes the reverberant sound, the *echos*, of the testifier; if the voice after Derridean deconstruction is, per Barthes or Cavarero, a matter of senseless sound authenticated by the body's materiality, then the poststructural philosopher assumes the role of *logos*, the subject who writes words about this desubjectivized material voice. While it seems questionable to find too many links between Ludovico Einaudi and Roland Barthes—though one could imagine the former as an entry in the latter's unwritten second volume of *Mythologies*—it would seem the two figures both subscribe to this last reduction. If, for Einaudi, the composer's voice is an achievement—a "positive," a "plus"—then, for Kane, it would likely be, like the Stoic or Christian or poststructuralist voice, a *reduction*, a crossing, the repression of a third term as a way of selling the voice short in order to be able to sell it at all.

But this is not quite the voice I have been talking about, this voice that is "the same as nothing." And here the question could be asked: Would an "unshorted," unrepressed voice even be possible? Would the refusal to repress any of its three terms, and instead to hold them all in decentered suspension, permit another kind of voice to emerge? Another kind of voice, or another kind of *subject*? Perhaps the composer's voice is not a voice at all, but one attempt to name, in music, the subject—a paradoxical subject that, unlike any subject worthy of the name (i.e., a thrown-under being, a servant to someone or something), seems to emerge without any repression at all.

Scene 3

The Tana String Quartet, with soprano Julia Sitkovetsky, performed the beginning of the final "Largo desolato" of Alban Berg's 1926 *Lyric Suite* (**web. ex. 11.3**).[26] In my opinion, there shouldn't be a soprano anywhere near the stage! True, in 1976 the American musicologist Douglass M. Green discovered that Berg's score was an encrypted chronicle of his doomed affair with Hanna Fuchs, and that Berg even documented this chronicle—with characteristic punctiliousness—in an annotated copy he gave Fuchs. Green also discovered that Berg originally conceived his quartet's last movement as a setting, complete with interpolated vocal part, of Baudelaire's frantically sad verse "De profundis clamavi" from his *Fleurs du mal* of 1857. Green's work, impressive as it was, generally confirmed what many had long suspected about Berg's "esoteric" score, rife with quotes from Wagner's *Tristan und Isolde* and his colleague Alexander von Zemlinsky's own *Lyric Symphony* from 1922–1923. Theodor Adorno, who knew of Berg's affair already in the 1930s, had in the late 1960s called the quartet a "latent opera," with "the character of an accompaniment, as it were, to a course of events absent from it. . . ."[27]

All of which is to say Berg's *Lyric Suite* is, by Kane's standards, a peculiar vocal situation: on the one hand, it is insistently, almost ostentatiously spaced between *echos*, *topos*, and *logos*, infested with song, word, meaning, body, breath; in doing this, it seems to refuse to "cross," and so to repress any third term. On the other hand, it is, technically, voiceless—the *phoné* that should emerge from its clasping together of sound, site, and body is itself repressed, "latented." And in this sense, there is something deeply violating to the spirit of the work to actually sopranicize it. Berg wanted voice, but he also wanted to hide it—to stage its immanence, its impending ubiquity, and at the same time its provocative nonappearance: voice, but at night; song, but from the depths; opera, but the words "gigantic Chaos" have gotten lost in a gigantic wordless chaos, and the characters, singers, dramaturg, and so on are actually all one person, keeping his mouth desperately shut. (**Mus. ex. 11.4** is based on the annotated score Berg gave to Fuchs; the Baudelaire poem can be seen running under the first violin line, and the hidden melody is represented in gray noteheads.)

In this sense, the *Lyric Suite* is not simply operatic, but a remarkable travesty of opera, the logical conclusion of a historical process whereby the

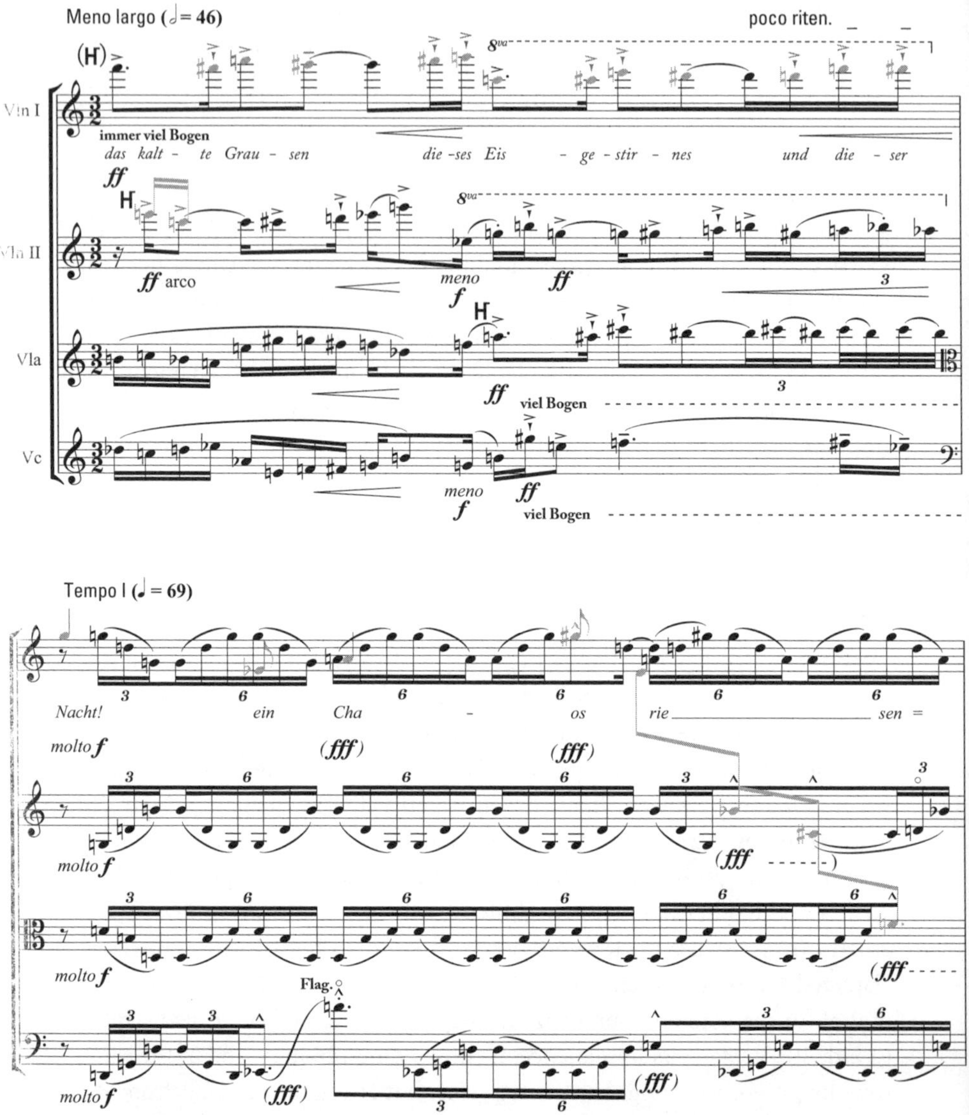

EXAMPLE 11.4 Berg, *Lyrische Suite* (1926), mvt. 6 climax: suppressed vocal line (in gray) and Baudelaire text.

resounding throat of a woman dying onstage gradually transforms into the silent hand of a man composing in his study who, with centuries of opera's dramatic and mimetic technologies at his fingertips, then choreographs his *own* phantasmatic demise as an author who cannot bring his work to a close, nor satisfy the demands of what he has made, nor bring his own finale to completion. There is a special kind of pretension here, in the usual but also nonpejorative sense, and Adorno very much picks up on it. In Berg's last movement, Adorno hears nothing less than the "liquidation of the sonata" as an entire musical genre; the movement's concluding viola line is "not even allowed to expire, to die. It must play on forever except that we can no longer hear it." "If, after Beethoven, no finale was able to close in affirmation," Adorno writes, "this one simply adopts the principle of infinity as the expression of the finale's negativity."[28] And, despite the quote from *Tristan*, Berg is no transfigured Isolde here; this is not a sublation, a transcendence. He is more Verdi than Wagner, almost Violetta-like, losing his breath, losing his voice, taking center stage in order to write out his own expiration *as the composer*. Hence why he must stage himself expiring before he can even complete the scene—"Here the master laid down his pen," and so on.

What I would like to suggest is that this scene of martyrdom, in its strangely opulent austerity, has a paradigmatic logic to it, still reverberating well into the late twentieth-century quartets by Nono and Lachenmann. By this logic, the composer loses his voice in order to win his subjectivity; he represses his song to gain back his *sound*, his *site*, his *body*; he choreographs, operatically, his death, so that his vocation, as a kind of writer, a *silent maker of works*, might enjoy life everlasting.

Third Digression: "A Voice as More Nothing"

Behind Kane's wonderfully practical model for *spacing* the voice lies Mladen Dolar's 2006 book *A Voice and Nothing More*, which presents a (somewhat less) practical model for *reducing* the voice.[29] Dolar provides a strong psychoanalytic—and specifically Lacanian—reading of the voice, which means that reduction, as the gradual peeling away of layers of psychic defense, will be essential to his work. As Kane puts it, Dolar performs three reductions:

> First, [he] reduces out logos; he shows, via linguistic theory and the aesthetics of music, that the voice is in excess of the conventional meaning of its utterances. Next, Dolar reduces out the body of the speaker; he shows, via appeals to acousmatic sound and film, the incongruousness of the voice and the body from which it is emitted. Finally, Dolar reduces out the sound of the voice by tracing the relation between the voice and the silence of the drives. This silent voice, unable to speak itself because it is always speaking the language of the other, can only be heard in the psychoanalytic session.[30]

I think this is a fair characterization, and it is striking in its suggestion that, at the heart of as disenchantingly modern a project as Lacanian psychoanalysis,

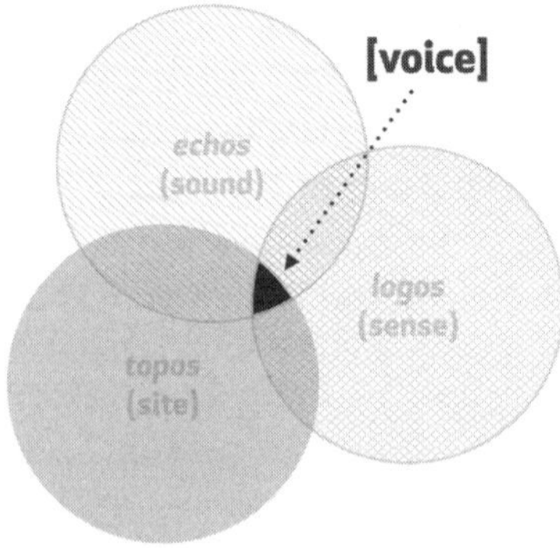

FIGURE 11.3 Dolar's reduction of the voice (visual model).

there might be a metaphysical—even gnostic!—little anchor. Dolar admits as much when he asserts that "there is no such thing as disacousmatization"—that is, there is no such thing as a complete and total revelation of the source behind any given voice. Voice, once all its supports have been removed, is still there, a floating Bermuda Triangle of libidinal and cognitive investment (**fig. 11.3**).

Nonetheless, I think Dolar's general premise offers something absolutely vital to thinking about the composer's voice—especially in the last two centuries that have witnessed the rise and supposed fall of both aesthetic modernism and psychoanalysis (which I also take to be a modernist practice).[31] If Einaudi embodies the composer's voice as an achievement, a plus, the fruit of full artistic subjectivity, and Kane's model suggests it is the result of a cunning but ultimately suspect reduction, then Dolar might call "the composer's voice" a fantasy, in the psychoanalytic sense. In Lacanian terms, this means it is a way of framing not only an object of desire—put simply, the voice "itself"—but also the world in which this voice consistently appears in such a desirable way. Fantasies frame both objects and their worlds, lending them both a powerful consistency they wouldn't otherwise have; in the process, they also support the subject's desire—which, in Lacanian terms, *is* its consistency.

It's not hard to see such a fantasy at play with Einaudi, and Kane's reduction makes this even clearer. But if there is a kindredness to the three quartet scenes staged thus far, I would argue that it has less to do with their own submission to a common fantasy, and more to do with their resistance to it. Indeed, they could be said to be on the side of psychoanalysis here, which is to say: an ethics and practice of analysis, of loosening the grip of fantasy, unmeshing the consistencies it supports, unframing the subject's fictive world.

But this is not at all to say that these three quartets are not fantasies. Their enchantments are now canonical, they each stand for a historical paradigm of composing, an ethics of work-formation, a way of being sonically modern. I instead want to propose something more complicated: that *the modernist composer's voice, as exemplified by these three unsung songs, emerges through fantasizing the silence opened up and laid bare in the effort to disintegrate the fantasy of voice.* There is something of Martin Heidegger's *aletheia* in this: an ethics of disclosure, truth as the unforgetting of what has long been repressed.[32] But it is not a positive essence that is being disclosed. The string quartet, as a nonopera staging shadow-songs, broken songs, hidden songs, requires *something*, in the most robust and substantial sense, such that the laying bare of this something's absence can attain the great theatrical force of, say, an opera. And that "thing" is the voice. One result of this operation is that, the voice now stricken, *echos*, *topos*, and *logos* can return. As is often the case in modernism, they return with a vengeance (**fig. 11.4**).

The voice, as a fabricating integrity, is unmeshed, such that the composing subject too is unmeshed, such that, in the hollows left behind, a reverberant double, at once floating subject and "suspended song," can emerge in its place, "seemingly without any repression at all." After all, what is *there* to repress?

In *A Voice and Nothing More*, Dolar dares to condense "the whole program of modernism" into the briefest of axioms: "*there must be an object other than the fetish*."[33] Minimally, I think this holds. But were the program to be expanded just a bit, I could imagine it thus: in modernism, there emerges a paradoxical *desire* for an object other than—one could say *realer* than—the object of desire constituted and framed by fantasy. But this new desire is, inevitably, fated to seek out radical new consistencies—which is to say fantasies.

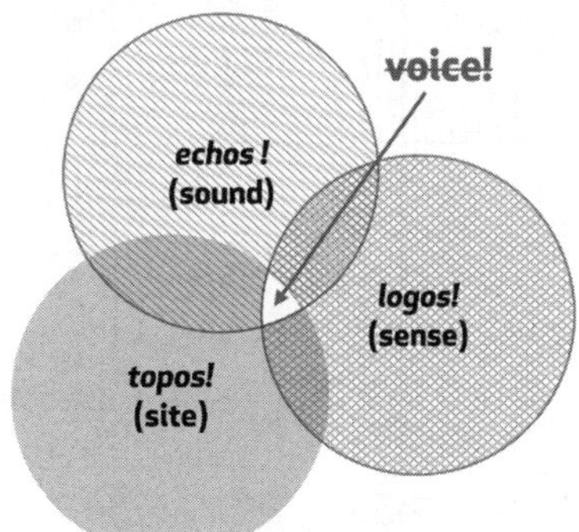

FIGURE 11.4 The musical modernist voice?

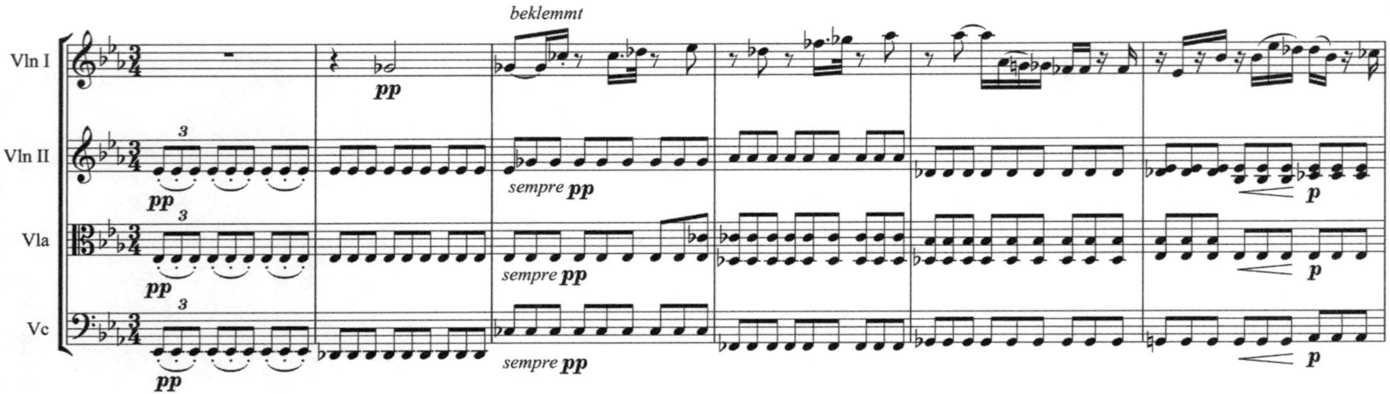

EXAMPLE 11.5 Beethoven, op. 130 (1826), mvt. 5, “Cavatina,” *beklemmt* section (start).

By extension, one could say that musical modernism, by seeking out what Dolar calls the "anti-voice," ends up actually intensifying the vocal drive. In traversing the fantasy of voice, in losing its voice as a fetish object, musical modernism comes to fetishize "losing its voice" *as* its object.

Scene 4

Of course we would have to end up here: the (in)famous *beklemmt* ("oppressed," or "anguished") section from the cavatina to Beethoven's late quartet, op. 130 (**mus. ex. 11.5**), played on the website by the Artemis Quartet (**web. ex. 11.4**).[34] It is in some sense there in the background of each of the three later scores, not just in their operatic pathos—the cavatina is a genre of Italian operatic scene that Beethoven was clearly instrumentalizing—but in the double-sidedness of that pathos. On the one hand, Beethoven's late works are aggressively phantasmatic, unparalleled in their hunger to frame elaborately desirable worlds. Friedrich August Kanne writes of the Ninth that Beethoven's "[sense of] fantasy always keeps going" ["seine Phantasie schafft immer fort"]; Beethoven himself famously said about his op. 131 quartet, "Of fantasy, thank God, there's less lack than ever before."[35] On the other hand, there is the famous difficulty of the work, what made reviewers call it a "wild tangle" and the "negation of music."[36] Naomi Waltham-Smith, in one of the deepest assessments of the cavatina, claims it is a mistake to read the *beklemmt* section's fragile failure, its "stutterings and stammerings," straight; they are not just about the "impossibility of being articulate." There is here the not-yet of a future modernism that might have been otherwise. In this not-yet lies something more radical than "anti-voice": "that it is possible to not speak."

In the Vienna of late Beethoven, a postrevolutionary moment in many ways characterized by a foreclosing of the political horizon, this unwriting or "exscription" of the voice has strange ramifications. It "unravels the traditional notion of the body politic," a notion held together by the fantasy that "individual bodies belong with each other in a common body determined by a common substance. . . . In late Beethoven, by contrast," this fantasy is unmeshed, its frame removed; "there is neither a communal voice nor a community of voices."[37] Instead, there is something stranger, both weaker and stronger: the taking place of the possibility of speaking or falling silent, "the (im)potentiality of voices communicating with one another." This is perhaps another way of saying the sound of Beethoven's voice—his silent, writing, floating, suspended "composer's voice"—is the same as nothing. But it is a nothing with a history, not least on the musical stage.

Notes

This essay expands on a brief passage at the end of my book *From 1989, or European Music and the Modernist Unconscious* (Oakland: University of California Press, 2017); see chap. 15, "Music and New Music (2)," 266–67.

1. For the first comment, see Jacques Lacan, *The Seminar of Jacques Lacan, Book XVII: The Other Side of Psychoanalysis, 1969–1970*, ed. Jacques-Alain Miller, trans. with notes by Russell Grigg (New York: W. W. Norton, 2007), 116; for the second, see Lacan, *The Seminar of Jacques Lacan, Book XX: Encore, 1972–73, On Feminine Sexuality, the Limits of Love, and Knowledge*, ed. Miller, trans. with notes by Bruce Fink (New York: W. W. Norton, 1998), 7.

2. I thank Rob Haskins for his—clearly—unforgettable rendition of this line.

3. See, for instance, Daniel Gottlob Türk, *School of Clavier Playing, Or, Instructions in Playing the Clavier for Teachers & Students*, trans. and ed. Raymond H. Haggh (Klavierschule [Leipzig and Halle, 1789]; Lincoln: University of Nebraska Press, 1982), 131–41.

4. For a classic instantiation, see Paul Badura-Skoda, "A Tie Is a Tie Is a Tie," *Early Music* 16, no. 1 (1988): 87–88; and Jonathan del Mar, "Once Again: Reflections on Beethoven's Tied-Note Notation," *Early Music* 32, no. 1 (2004): 24–25.

5. My thinking on voice and modernism is inseparable from the many discussions with Marcelle Pierson in the course of her dissertation; in addition to the essay in this volume, please see also Marcelle Pierson, "The Voice under Erasure: Singing, Melody, and Expression in Late Modernist Music" (PhD diss., University of Chicago, 2015).

6. See Cone, *The Composer's Voice* (Berkeley: University of California Press, 1974); for some generous and critical reassessment, see among others Fred Everett Maus et al., "Edward T. Cone's 'The Composer's Voice': Elaborations and Departures," *College Music Symposium* 29 (1989): 1–80; and Carolyn Abbate, *Unsung Voices: Opera and Musical Narrative in the Nineteenth Century* (Princeton, NJ: Princeton University Press, 1991).

7. For an excellent account of how a paradigm of the composer's voice emerges out of a paradoxical crisis of identity and stylistic profusion, see Nicholas Mathew, "Beethoven and His Others: Criticism, Difference, and the Composer's Many Voices," *Beethoven Forum* 13, no. 2 (2006): 148–87.

8. The concept is Freud's, developed over the course of his career. See "Project for a Scientific Psychology" (1895), in *The Standard Edition of the Complete Psychological Works of Sigmund Freud*, vol. 1, trans. and ed. James Strachey (London: Hogarth Press, 1966), 356. For a clear excavation of the term's meanings and uses, see Jean Laplanche and J. B. Pontalis, "Deferred Action, Deferred," in *The Language of Psycho-Analysis*, trans. Donald Nicholson-Smith (New York: W. W. Norton, 1974), 111–14. And for a discussion of musical modernism and *Nachträglichkeit*, see Brodsky, *From 1989*, chap. 2, "Fantasy & Fantasy (1)," 61–62.

9. This clip comes from an unpublished DVD film of the JACK Quartet performing the complete quartets of Helmut Lachenmann.

10. See Helmut Lachenmann, *Musik als existentielle Erfahrung: Schriften 1966–1995*, ed. Josef Häusler (Wiesbaden: Breitkopf and Härtel, 1996), 237; for an English translation, see Lachenmann, "On My Second String Quartet," trans. Evan Johnson, *Contemporary Music Review* 23, no. 3 (2004): 67.

11. Lachenmann, "On My Second String Quartet," 67.

12. The first phrase is legion in Lachenmann's thinking throughout the 1960s and 1970s; see for instance "Vier Grundbestimmungen des Musikhörens" (1979), in *Musik als existentielle Erfahrung*, 60; the second phrase comes from Lachenmann, "Über das Komponieren" (1986), in *Musik als existentielle Erfahrung*, 82.

13. "'The most difficult thing as a young composer is to find your own voice,' says Ludovico Einaudi." Interview from August 16, 2016, *Classic FM*. See http://www.classicfm.com/composers/einaudi/interview/, accessed August 20, 2017.

14. I thank Marcelle Pierson for coining this memorable distinction.

15. On the imitation of voices, see also the chapters by Laurie Stras and Tom Gunning in this volume.

16. The first quote comes from the subtitle to "In the Moment," an interview between American composer Kevin Puts and Ann McCutchan in *Symphony Magazine* 61, no. 2 (2010): 38–42; see http://www.kevinputs.com/press-pdf/symphonyonline_mar_apr_2010_Kevin.pdf. The second quote cites the American Academy of Arts and Letters' announcement of its 2016 Music Award winners; see http://artsandletters.org/pressrelease/2016-music-award-winners/. The third quote comes from Anthony Tommasini, "Connections in an Amorphous World: Nico Muhly's 'Two Boys' Makes Its American Debut at the Met," *New York Times*, October 22, 2013. See http://www.nytimes.com/2013/10/23/arts/music/nico-muhlys-ambitious-two-boys-makes-its-american-debut-at-the-met.html. All webpages accessed August 20, 2017.

17. This clip comes from a live television broadcast (now unavailable) of the Minguet Quartet performing Nono's *Fragmente—Stille* at the Römerbad Musiktagen 2004 in Badenweiler, Germany.

18. See for instance Heinz-Klaus Metzger, "Wendepunkt Quartett?," in *Musik-Konzepte 20: Luigi Nono*, ed. Heinz-Klaus Metzger and Rainer Riehn (Munich: Edition text + kritik, 1981), 93–112. For evidence of the deep relationship between Lachenmann's and Nono's quartets, see Rainer Nonnenmann, *Der Gang durch die Klippen: Helmut Lachenmanns Begegnungen mit Luigi Nono anhand ihres Briefwechsels und anderer Quellen, 1957–1990* (Wiesbaden: Breitkopf and Härtel, 2013), 409ff.

19. For the most expert and extended analysis of the genesis of Nono's quartet in English, see Carola Nielinger-Vakil, "*Fragmente-Stille, an Diotima*: World of Greater Compositional Secrets," *Acta musicologica* 82, no. 1 (2010).

20. Brian Kane, "The Voice: A Diagnosis," *Polygraph* 25 (2015): 103.

21. See for instance Martha Feldman et al., "Colloquy: Why Voice Now?," *Journal of the American Musicological Society* 68, no. 3 (2015): 653–85.

22. Kane, "The Voice," 91.

23. Kane, "The Voice," 91.

24. Kane, "The Voice," 105.

25. See Cavarero, *For More Than One Voice: Toward a Philosophy of Vocal Expression*, trans. Paul A. Kottman (Stanford, CA: Stanford University Press, 2005). See also Kane's more extended critique of Cavarero in Kane, *Sound Unseen: Acousmatic Sound in Theory and Practice* (Oxford: Oxford University Press, 2014), 152–56.

26. See Wigmore Hall Learning, "Inside the Score: Berg's *Lyric Suite*," lecture-recital from May 10, 2016, with Gavin Plumley, presenter, and the Tana String Quartet with Julia Sitkovetsky, soprano; live-streamed at https://www.youtube.com/watch?v=biJHZthyqRw, accessed August 20, 2017; the excerpted clip appears starting at https://youtu.be/biJHZthyqRw?t=1h30m42s.

27. See Douglass M. Green, "Berg's *De Profundis*: The Finale of the Lyric Suite," *International Alban Berg Society Newsletter* 5 (June 1977): 13–23. For an exemplar of how the *Lyrische Suite* was already considered an encrypted score, see, for instance, Constantin Floros, "Das esoterische Programm der *Lyrischen Suite* von Alban Berg: Eine semantische Analyse," *Hamburger Jahrbuch für Musikwissenschaft* 1 (1975): 101–45. By the time of Adorno's 1968 book on Berg (in which the score is coined a "latent opera"), Adorno had known for decades about the secret program; see his confessional letter from April 16, 1936, to Berg's widow, Helene, in *Theodor W. Adorno and*

Alban Berg: Correspondence, 1925–1935, ed. Henri Lonitz, trans. Wieland Hoban (Cambridge, MA: Polity Press, 2005), 232–36.

28. Adorno, *Alban Berg: Master of the Smallest Link*, trans., introduced, and annotated by Juliane Brand and Christopher Hailey (Cambridge: Cambridge University Press, 1991), 112.

29. Mladen Dolar, *A Voice and Nothing More* (Cambridge, MA: MIT Press, 2006).

30. Kane, "The Voice," 93. As with its critique of Cavarero, Kane's *Sound Unseen* offers a much more sustained engagement with Dolar; see 206–22.

31. See Brodsky, *From 1989*, in particular "Introduction," 21–22, and chap. 13, "Repetition (3)," 216–25.

32. For a lucid account of Heidegger's evolving concept of *aletheia*, see Iain Thomson, "Heidegger's Aesthetics" (2010, rev. 2015), *The Stanford Encyclopedia of Philosophy*, https://plato.stanford.edu/entries/heidegger-aesthetics/, accessed August 20, 2017.

33. Dolar, *A Voice*, 69.

34. This video clip comes from a 2010 film of the Artemis Quartet performing Beethoven's Quartet no. 13, op. 130; the performance of the entire Cavatina can be viewed at https://www.youtube.com/watch?v=ClFnHE6swlM, accessed August 20, 2017.

35. For more on Kanne's comment, see Mathew, "Beethoven and His Others," 150ff; for Beethoven's comment on op. 130, see Alexander Wheelock Thayer, *Ludwig van Beethovens Leben*, vol. 5 (Leipzig: Breitkopf and Härtel, 1908), 318–19; and also Joseph Kerman, *The Beethoven Quartets* (New York: Alfred A. Knopf, 1966), 349.

36. See, for instance, Anon., "Einige Worte zu den vielen über Beethoven's letzte Werke," *Allgemeine musikalische Zeitung* 31 (1829): 272, cited in K. M. Knittel, "Wagner, Deafness, and the Reception of Beethoven's Late Style," *Journal of the American Musicological Society* 51, no. 1 (1998): 55; and Alexandre Oulibicheff, *Beethoven, ses critiques et ses glossateurs* (Leipzig and Paris: Brockhaus, 1857), 270; cited in K. M. Knittel, "Wagner," 51.

37. Naomi Waltham-Smith, *Music and Belonging between Revolution and Restoration* (Oxford: Oxford University Press, 2017), chap. 4, "Beethoven's Blush," 160.

PART V

Interlude: The Gendered Voice

Vowels/Consonants: The Legend of a "Gendered" (Sexual) Difference Told by Cinema

MICHEL CHION
TRANSLATED BY ZAKIR PAUL

Introduction

Having worked on the "audio-visual" for years, I ended up coining the term "audio-logo-vision" in 1990, because there are very few films without words or speech.[1] Then, I realized that the written and spoken forms of a text are two interdependent and yet profoundly different universes.

Allow me to quote Claudia Gorbman's translation of my concept of the "audio-logo-visual":

> Audio-Logo-Visual: A term I propose as a replacement for "audiovisual," since it more accurately describes all the cases that include written and/or spoken language. For language transcends the strict spheres of the visual and auditory. Audio-logo-visual usefully reminds us that the situation is most often triangular and not binary. The music video, for example, typically combines not merely images and music, but images, music, and words.[2]

My first book on cinema, *La voix au cinéma* (*The Voice in Cinema*), was published in 1982 in France. I was extremely lucky that my friend Claudia liked it. She published a very fine English translation of it with Columbia University Press.[3] And *L'écrit au cinéma* (*Writing on Screen*, 2013), one of my latest books (others are currently in progress), is now available in English too, also published by Columbia University Press.[4] It deals with writing in the literal sense: everything that one can read in a film onscreen, from brand names to the intertitles of silent films, letters, messages, words, banners, and so on, and of course credits.

Voice, writing: there are many binaries, conceptual pairs we learn as children: day/night; inside/outside; ground/sky; heaven/hell; life/death; sun/moon. In languages in which they occur, many of these differences are gendered: night is often feminine, while day is masculine. The moon is feminine in French and Italian (*la lune, la luna*) and masculine in German (*der Mond*), and conversely the sun is masculine in French and Italian (*le soleil, il sole*) and feminine in German (*die Sonne*). Recall that German, contrary to French and Italian, has not two, but three genders: masculine, feminine, and neuter.

Among these binary oppositions, one of the hardest to define, to locate, but also to deconstruct is the vowel and the consonant. *Voyelle*, "vowel," is *Selbstlaut* in German, which literally means "sound that makes itself," and *consonne*, "consonant," is *Mitlaut*, literally, "sound with."

It is thus logical for me to talk about consonants and vowels in the cinema, because these two terms have a different meaning, even if they seem identical, as images and sounds: a double meaning, which varies depending on whether you consider the visible "letter" or the "sound" of speech. In alphabetic systems like ours (but this observation also holds for the Cyrillic and Greek alphabets), the consonant as a letter and the consonant as a sound (and phoneme) are not the same thing, and the vowel as letter and vowel as sound (and phoneme) are not the same either. Now, as I said earlier, cinema is one of the only arts to juxtapose the visible form of language to its audible, acoustic form. One reads and hears at once. Films where there is nothing to read in a crucial scene are very rare: there is at least a title, part of a letter, a "No Trespassing" sign like at the end of *Citizen Kane* (**fig. 12.1a**), a headline, a flashing neon sign, some graffiti on a prison wall or in a public bathroom, a name on a grave (**fig. 12.1b**).

The French word "*voyelle*," like the English word "vowel," comes from the same Latin root *vox/vocis* and its derivations *vocalis*, which designate the voice. Similarly, the word "consonant" comes from the Latin *consonare*, to "sound with," which suggests that a consonant cannot be sounded alone, it needs to be supported by a vowel. It is always amusing to compare the French way of spelling out the alphabet: "A, Bé, Cé, Dé, Eff, Gé, Hash," to the Anglo-American way. Inversely, there are systems of writing that primarily note consonants. These systems are called "abjad," to use the term invented by the linguist Peter T. Daniels. It would be logical to place consonants on the side of writing, and vowels with voice, because vowels are required to elongate a word, particularly when singing.

I think that would be a little too simple. And I think that when he theorizes "writing" in the singular, in his works, Jacques Derrida is already misguided; for it became obvious to me that there is no writing in the singular. A system of writing, like our alphabet, does not constitute a coherent and comparable system across the board in Serbian, Castilian, Icelandic, English, or French. I am not only talking about "diacritical" signs belonging to certain languages, like the tilde in Castilian, or the Umlaut in German, which has an entirely different function than the equivalent sign in French—I am talking

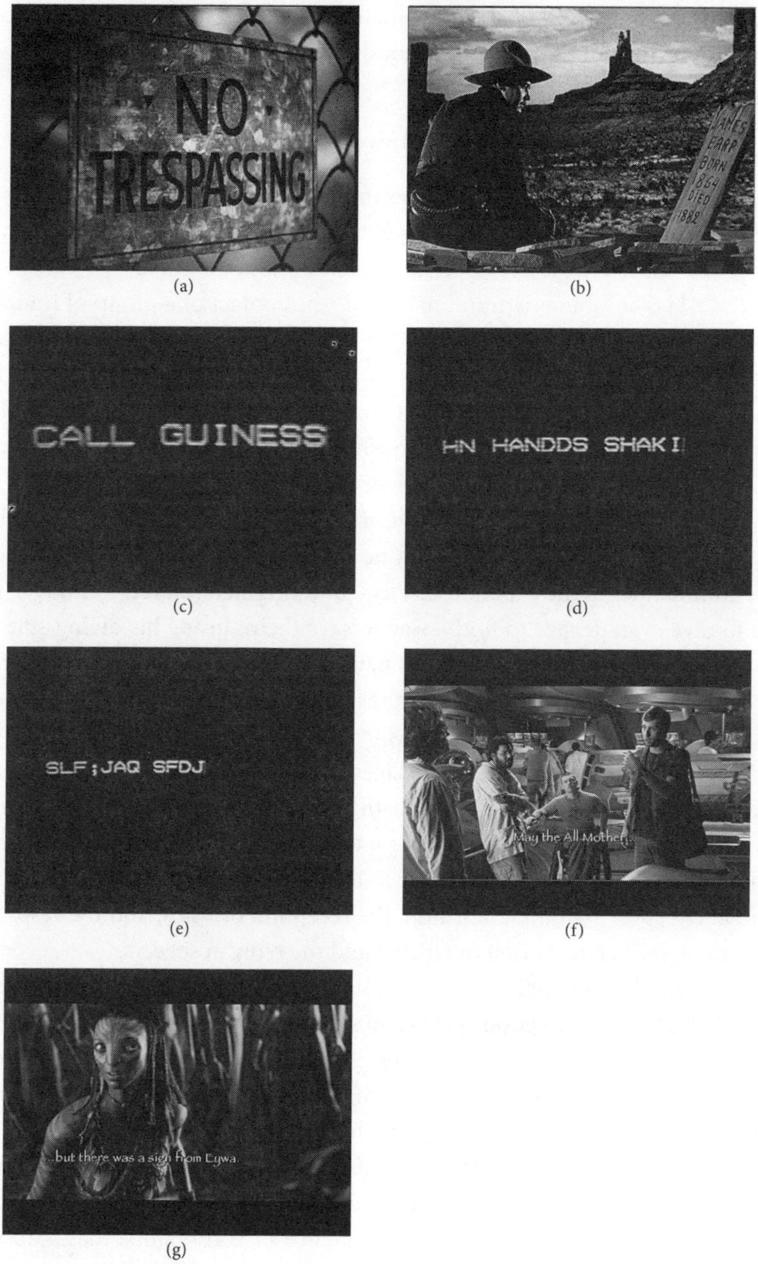

FIGURE 12.1 (a) *Citizen Kane* (Orson Welles, 1941); (b) *My Darling Clementine* (John Ford, 1946); (c) *The Abyss* (James Cameron, 1989); (d) *The Abyss* (James Cameron, 1989); (e) *Avatar* (James Cameron, 2009); (f) *Avatar* (James Cameron, 2009); (g) *Avatar* (James Cameron, 2009).

about the entire history of spelling and orthography that litters texts that one reads with a host of unpronounced, or differently voiced, letters.

Stories of *A*

Now, I would like to discuss a few examples from scenes in films that were particularly striking to me in regards to this theme. One of these has a certain historical value: *The Abyss*, directed by James Cameron in 1989.

The Abyss combines a grand narrative (the contact of a group of humans with an extraterrestrial civilization that inhabits the ocean floor) and an intimate little story (a human couple gets back together after a breakup). This kind of double plot is common in science fiction. More recently, Christopher Nolan's *Interstellar* (2014) simultaneously tells the story of the redemption of humanity and the reconciliation between a father and a daughter.

In *The Abyss*, a bathyscaphe containing a crew of American researchers has sunk to the depths of the ocean and no longer has contact with the surface. The commander of the expedition, Virgil Bud Brigman (played by Ed Harris), has to dive even deeper to find a way to save them. Inside his diving suit, he is submerged in a liquid in which humans can breathe, so that he can tolerate the pressure of the great depths. As a result, he can no longer speak, but he is equipped with a kind of watch allowing him to type written messages on his wrist (this was well before text messages). In his diving suit, he can hear the voices of those who remain in the bathyscaphe, especially his ex-wife Lindsey (played by Mary Elizabeth Mastrantonio). Cameron imagines these plot points in order to introduce a device in the key scene of the movie: a writing-man and a speech-woman. For him, the reception of voice, and the response in writing; for her, reception in writing and the reply in speech.

To begin, Lindsey tells Bud that he has broken the diving record. In turn, Bud shows that he is in good spirits and still has his sense of humor, by typing a response on his wrist: "CALL GUINESS" (**fig. 12.1c**). Later, Bud sends this text in capital letters: "HN HANDDS SHAKING" (**fig. 12.1d**). This jumbled, awkward entry mimics stuttering, which is still based on speech.

As Bud descends deeper, in spite of the encouragement he gets from Lindsey's voice, the tremendous pressure that he is under in the depths is translated via his messages as a compact sequence of consonants, that is to say, nonvocalizable sounds.

> "SLF.
>
> JAQ SFDJ" (**fig. 12.1e**)

The close succession of consonants, which does not evoke any given language, amounts to the unspeakable and makes us think of writing systems that do not note vowels. But we are not dealing with words engraved in stone, but rather abstract and ephemeral characters on a double screen that mixes them all together: the transmitter-watch that Bud is using and the screen on which we are watching Cameron's film.

While Bud thus dives into nonvoice, Lindsey, just to stay in contact with him, breaks into a declaration of love, evoking their shared memories, and confessing that she had to become very harsh in order to turn into an active, responsible woman.

This scene from *The Abyss* thus seems to consecrate the victory of feminine speech over masculine writing—a theme that will be retold in a different way, over twenty years later, in Cameron's *Avatar* (2009), a film in which humans are faced with an extraterrestrial species on another planet. In *Avatar*, the technological world of the humans is full of writing, on screens, in the background, a writing always linked to technology, while the noble species of the Na'vis is matriarchal. They greet each other by invoking the Great Mother Goddess. Na'vi society gives great importance to the feminine gender, and uses a refined language but without a written form. It foregoes machines and keeps contact with nature. In *Avatar* (a title made of the repetition of a vowel), there is a break between a primarily masculine and militarized world, even if it includes some women, a world with writing and machines, a world belonging to humans, and a world, if not feminine, at least respectful of women, a world without writing, close to nature, and far from technology. As you can see, stereotypes continue to persist (**fig. 12.1f–g**).

In *The Abyss* we saw the male character lose what little voice he had left in writing, typing more and more consonants and fewer vowels, reaching the unpronounceable. Clearly, we are in an alphabetic system that notates what we call consonants and vowels. The problem of the unpronounceable is posed in an entirely different way, in other writing systems, the so-called ideographic ones, and the complex systems of writing of the Japanese language, which includes syllabic signs.

Let's remain with this system for a moment. As we have seen, the only vowel that remained in Ed Harris's unpronounceable text—the last sign referring to what the German calls a "*Selbstlaut*," "sound by itself"—is an *A*.

In Jean-Luc Godard's famous credits for *Pierrot le Fou* (1965), which have been imitated a lot since then (very recently, in the closing sequence of Alejandro Iñárritu's 2014 film *Birdman*) (**fig. 12.2a**), the letters appear separately, in an order that looks alphabetical. Here, for example, are a few screen shots of the opening credits to *Pierrot le Fou*. There are a lot of *A*s, in the first image

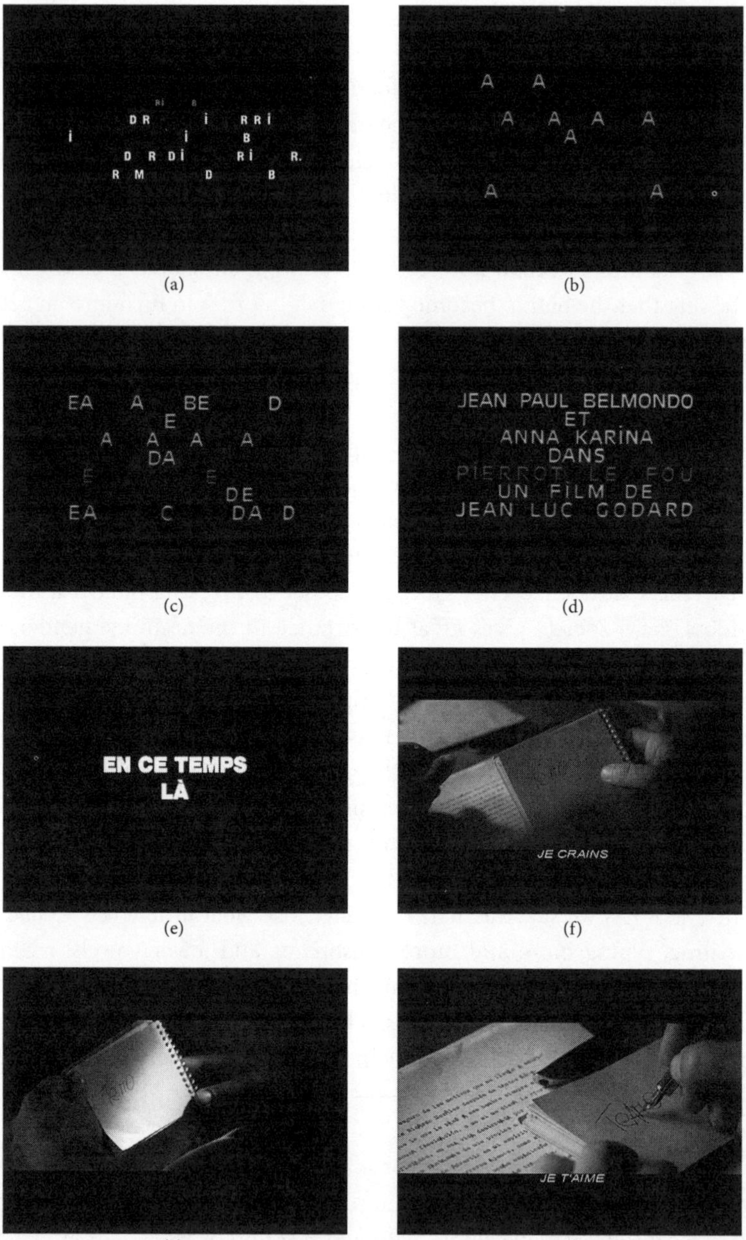

(a) (b) (c) (d) (e) (f) (g) (h)

FIGURE 12.2 (a) *Birdman* (Alejandro G. Iñárritu, 2014); (b) *Pierrot Le Fou* (Jean-Luc Godard, 1965); (c) *Pierrot Le Fou* (Jean-Luc Godard, 1965); (d) *Pierrot Le Fou* (Jean-Luc Godard, 1965); (e) *Hail Mary* (Jean-Luc Godard, 1985); (f) *The Secret in Their Eyes* (Juan José Campanella, 2009); (g) *The Secret in Their Eyes* (Juan José Campanella, 2009); (h) *The Secret in Their Eyes* (Juan José Campanella, 2009).

(**fig. 12.2b**), just one vowel repeated as one term. Slowly the images fill out and we see consonants appear rapidly (**fig. 12.2c**). A few seconds later, we get the complete text (**fig. 12.2d**) with two male names and one female name. The male names belong to Jean-Paul Belmondo, the lead actor in the film (he was the star, as you know, of *À bout de souffle* [*Breathless*, 1960]), and Jean-Luc Godard, the director (hyphenated first names beginning with Jean—Jean-Paul, Jean-Pierre, Jean-Claude, Jean-Luc, Jean-Marie—were extremely common in France for three generations, but now they have almost completely disappeared). The female name belongs to the lead actress, of Danish origin, who was Godard's partner and acted in many of his films: Anna Karina. Her name made of two first names is actually a pseudonym. Two years earlier, a French actress adopted a beautiful pseudonym beginning with two *A*s, Anouk Aimée. The *A* in many romance languages, derived from Latin, is directly associated with the feminine: in Italian and in Spanish, of course, but also in French, in the article *la*.

Now, what happens in the few seconds that the screen is filling with letters? The *A*s of Anna Karina's name continue to be pronounced, but those in the male first names fade not into the unpronounceable but into the *nonpronounced*: the evolution of French spelling, like many alphabetic languages, holds on to letters that one has no longer pronounced for a long time. In French, "Jean" could be written "Jen" (like the French word for people, *gens*). But when, in French, you feminize the common first name Jean, a name with an ancient biblical origin, of course the *A* is pronounced: "Jeanne."

What Godard shows us is a kind of "spelling" in apparent disorder that is in fact French alphabetical order. This progressive spelling makes vowel-letters appear, some of which disappear into the pronunciation of the word and of other names. There are many more *A*s that are read than words in which the *A* is heard. The *A* in the name of the actress (who plays a character called Marianne) remains pronounceable from the beginning to the end of the sequence, while the *A* of the male names disappears from pronunciation and voice.

We know that Godard later used many signboards and texts in his films, and primarily used capital letters, pitting letters against words in all kinds of ways, just as he plays image against sound (**fig. 12.2e**).

The vowel-letter *A* also plays an important role in a more recent film, which uses the theme of the "missing letter on a typewriter" (a theme present in *Misery*, Rob Reiner's film based on Stephen King's novel, and in the French film by Philippe de Broca, *Le Magnifique* [1973], among others). I am alluding to *The Secret in Their Eyes* (*El secreto de sus ojos*, 2009), directed by Juan José Campanella based on a novel by Eduardo Sacheri. In the film, the hero Benjamin Esposito (Ricardo Darin), a retired lawyer who is writing a novel, uses an old typewriter on which the *A* key is missing. So he has to add it by hand (**fig. 12.2f**). Toward the end of the novel, he finds a notebook on which he had scribbled in caps "TEMO" ("I'm scared, I'm afraid") (**fig. 12.2g**). Seeing the typed manuscript on which all the *A*s are handwritten, he does the same on his notebook and "TEMO" becomes "TE AMO" ("I love you") (**fig. 12.2h**). He thus reveals his feelings for the heroine to himself and can go tell her. A vowel-voice was missing in the machine; he had to fill in the blanks in the text by hand. After realizing a voice was missing, he was thus able to find his voice again in order to speak to the woman of his dreams. The international success of this film, and especially of this touching, melodramatic scene (which is all the more noticeable as almost no one uses typewriters with missing letters anymore), proves how cinema guarantees the permanence of the symbol of the typewriter and broken or erased characters.

By filling in a blank with a vowel, and in giving voice to the text, Benjamin repeats an ancient gesture of reading. One thinks of the resurrection of sacred Hebrew as a spoken language, as Clarisse Herrenschmidt recounts it in her essay *Les trois écritures: Langue, nombre, code* (*Three Writings: Language, Number, Code*):

> During the period in which the Talmud was being written . . . , Hebrew was no longer heard by newborns. . . . No script, archaic or square writing, noted the vowels—even if, occasionally, it indicated them by *matres lectionis*, "mothers of reading." The reader grasped the words, added vowels and formed syllables mentally.[5]

In this act of reading ancient texts (before Hebrew became a spoken language again, notably thanks to Eliezer Ben-Yehuda), "the reader lends his voice to the text, but . . . the text has no voice. Thanks to writing, he feels that he is reviving the status of prophetic speech, the most ancient example of which takes us back to Moses: once he has seen the burning bush, he receives Yahweh's order to speak."[6]

Herrenschmidt is alluding to a passage from chapter 3 of Exodus that I will quote in a translation readily available on the internet (the Gateway version):

> 13. Moses said to God, "Suppose I go to the Israelites and say to them, 'The God of your fathers has sent me to you, and they ask me, 'What is his name?' Then what shall I tell them?"
>
> 14. God said to Moses, "I am who I am. This is what you are to say to the Israelites: 'I am has sent me to you.' "

> 15. God also says to Moses, 'Say to the Israelites, 'The Lord, the God of your fathers—the God of Abraham, the God of Isaac, and the God of Jacob—has sent me to you.'"

"Moses," Herrenschmidt continues in her commentary, "must somehow say 'I am' in Yahweh's place, lending him his phonic organ, just as the reader gives his voice to the text without vowels."[7]

The missing vowel of the Argentine film calls for a voice to utter it. The opposite occurs in *The Abyss*, in which the man (in the sense of an individual of the masculine gender) who expresses himself through the typewriter gradually loses what little voice remains in his writing; all he has left is the *petit a* (small *a*). Here, by filling in the missing *A* by hand, another man becomes capable of speaking to a woman. I discuss this scene in *Writing in the Cinema* in the following way:

> In some way, the missing letter on the typewriter (whose principle is that it affects indiscriminately all words that include it) imprints its absence, and marks its place all the more so at the heart of the most varied words. At the same time as an "an-empathetic" indifference of the letter to content, of the signifier to the signified, it also embodies the insistence, the permanence, and to some extent the fidelity of the symptom. But also, in this instance, the power of the upheaval that one may possess, which would allow one to rediscover the love that one carries within oneself, thanks to a simple vowel-letter.[8]

Stories of *O*

O is another of the vowel-letters most present onscreen, particularly because it looks the same as a number whose presence multiples the value of a sum of money. But the *O* is also a feminized letter because of its round and hollow shape.

In Fritz Lang's *Metropolis* (1927), young Freder sees the name of the divinity Moloch in the inhuman machine: and the two *O*s of Moloch fly from the page. It is worth recalling the important role the film gives to a female robot (**fig. 12.3a**).

In *Ballet mécanique* (1924), Fernand Léger's experimental film, she is associated both with money and with an object whose shape evokes the opening of the female sex, as in the French erotic novel *Histoire d'O* (*Story of O*, 1954)[9] (**fig. 12.3b–c**).

In a famous scene in Hitchcock's *North by Northwest* (1959), Roger Thornhill (Cary Grant) takes a matchbook out of his pocket with his initials ("my

FIGURE 12.3 (a) *Metropolis* (Fritz Lang, 1927); (b) *Ballet mécanique* (Fernand Léger, 1924); (c) *Ballet mécanique* (Fernand Léger, 1924); (d) *North by Northwest* (Alfred Hitchcock, 1959); (e) *North by Northwest* (Alfred Hitchcock, 1959); (f) *North by Northwest* (Alfred Hitchcock, 1959); (g) *North by Northwest* (Alfred Hitchcock, 1959).

trademark," he says) (**fig. 12.3d**) and this matchbook becomes the object of an insert—one of the only ones in the film—allowing us to see it in close-up (**fig. 12.3e**). It reads "ROT" with an *O* larger than the *R* and the *T*. "What's the *O* for?" Eve Kendall (Eva Marie Saint) asks him. Instead of saying his middle name, Thornhill replies, "Nothing."

To be sure, this "Nothing" can be taken as a symbol of the famous MacGuffin, that stake lacking importance and content, for which characters fight, kill, and chase each other, but in the context of this film, it has supplementary significance. This little dialogue and this insert play an important role in the story: at the end of the film, when Thornhill has infiltrated Vandamm's house, to save Eve's life, he wants to signal his presence to her without attracting attention, so he has the idea of throwing this matchbook at her feet from a room on a higher floor. It falls out of her line of sight, but one of Vandamm's men, Leonard, picks it up like a fallen object without examining it, and places it on a table where Eve sees it (**fig. 12.3f**). The characteristic *O* (on the matchbook it is larger than the *R* in Roger and the *T* in Thornhill) saves Eve, at the same time as it prevents Leonard, probably gripped by this hole, this zero-vowel, from recognizing the two consonants *RT* in the initials of the name Roger Thornhill, which, in his eyes, hide George Kaplan.

Symbolically, this matchbook, given the role that Thornhill makes it play in making his presence known to Eve, represents the recuperation and revalorization of his own name for him—the name of his dead father (as is often the case in this kind of story, and especially in Hitchcock, the hero's father is dead or absent), a name first lost in strange circumstances, then found again but tarnished by a murder charge.

It is worth noting that the question of the name is not limited in the film to the idea of a name without a character—a floating "name," Kaplan, is a fictive being at first. It is also reflected in different ways in other characters: for example, Leonard (Martin Landau), an associate of Vandamm, has a first name and no last name, while the man from the CIA called "the Professor" (Leo G. Carroll), who seems to have invented Kaplan, does not have a name and never will have one. At the airport, where Thornhill meets him for the first time, Thornhill asks, "I don't think I caught your name," and he answers, "I don't think I pitched it." Later, Thornhill asks the Professor if he is from the FBI, a question he evades again in an answer that French versions of the film have trouble translating: "F.B.I. . . . C.I.A. . . . O.N.I. . . . we're all in the same alphabet soup." This soup, swimming with letter-shaped pasta, seems to not only mix up all possible names and words, but also not differentiate between consonants and vowels.[10]

Note that without Eve Kendall's remark, Thornhill would not have noticed the *O* in his own name, a thick vowel lodged between two smaller consonants. It is due to Eve's interest that when he sees his monogram on his handkerchief, with which he wipes his blood (**fig. 12.3g**), Thornhill recalls the matchbook, and thinks of using it. It's a brilliant idea on the part of the screenwriter Ernest Lehmann, even if it's said that the *O* was meant to be a satirical allusion to the name of the producer David O. Selznick.

Stories of *I*

Certain vowels are pronounced very differently from one language to another: *u* is pronounced in a certain way in the English words *mud* and *but* (and *bud*, which we'll come back to later). It is pronounced in a different way in the French word *mur* ("wall"), and yet another way in the German word *Turm* ("tower"). But the vowel that changes its sound most drastically, in many languages and within one language, is *i*. For example, *i* in *nice* or *bite*, and in *click* or *sick*.

French kids obviously know the brand "Nike," which is pronounced as in English, very differently from the slang (and vulgar) verb *niquer*, which means "to fuck," or else in more common French words like *pli*, *fil*, and *vite*. The hesitation between the two pronunciations lies at the heart of a French comedy that was very popular in our country, especially among young people (children, kids).

I am talking about James Hut's *Brice de Nice* (2005), with Jean Dujardin, who introduced a whole linguistic and gestural code into French schoolyards. The hero, created and acted by Jean Dujardin, is the son of a French gangster in the Riviera, living in the city of Nice. His name is Brice Agostini, but he calls himself and makes people call him Brice de Nice. When he is at the top of his glory, this is pronounced "Braïce de Naïce," as if it were an Anglo-American name. The movie thus testifies to France's current Americanophilia, and also to what one might call the "double reading" or the "*double entendre*" (as you say in Anglo-American French) of the French language according to its situation. Is *Nice* read like Nice the city, or like the omnipresent American adjective "nice"? We also know that Brice wears his name on his t-shirt like a brand name (**fig. 12.4a**) and copies it on his personal items (**fig. 12.4b**). You inevitably think of Nike, which can be read doubly in French: Nick or Naïke.

But this vowel *I* in his name is a testament to both its prestige and the instrument of his vulnerability: whenever this idiotic and arrogant young man becomes less popular among his friends, they have only to call him "Brice de Nice," in French and not in an American way, and he goes back to being an

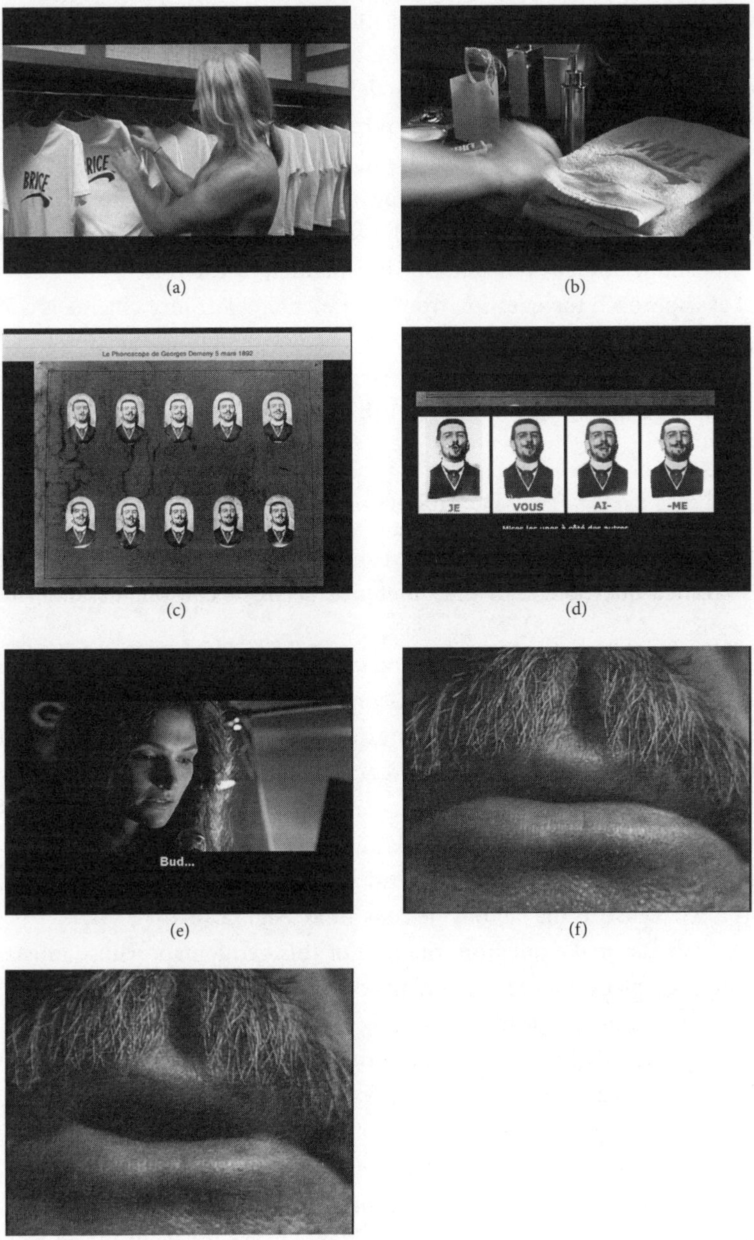

(a) (b) (c) (d) (e) (f) (g)

FIGURE 12.4 (a) *Brice de Nice* (James Hut, 2005); (b) *Brice de Nice* (James Hut, 2005); (c) Georges Demenÿ, "Je vous aime"; (d) Georges Demenÿ, "Je vous aime"; (e) *The Abyss* (James Cameron, 1989); (f) *Citizen Kane* (Orson Welles, 1941); (g) *Citizen Kane* (Orson Welles, 1941).

immature and unknown little French guy, and stops being identified with his hero the surfer in *Point Break* (dir. Kathryn Bigelow, 1991) played by Patrick Swayze, who is his model. His name deflates, even as it is still written in the same way, because its main vowel is pronounced differently.

In these three examples of *A*, *O*, and *I* (we are talking about vowel-letters, not vowel-sounds, or vowel-phonemes), we have seen the crucial and symbolic character of the presence or the absence of vowels in the written text, their pronunciation or not, and in what manner, by the voice.

Let's approach the question from a different angle: Since cinema is audio-logo-visual, do consonants and vowels become visible in the simple act of utterance, and not only in writing onscreen? This is where we will return to an important monosyllable: the English monosyllable *bud*.

The History of Visibility

Let us now deal with the question of speech made visible and ask ourselves this strange question: Can the difference between consonants and vowels be seen?

Well before cinema became a sound medium, around 1891–1892, the French photographer, athlete, and inventor Georges Demenÿ (1850–1917), whose name is written with a *tréma* on the *y* (an extraordinary diacritical sign above this letter which does not affect its sound at all), had invented the "phonoscope." This rapid photography device is not, contrary to what one sometimes reads, a device for making images and sounds audible, but rather for filming the act of speech, and to allow deaf-mutes to read a phrase, and eventually to vocalize it. This is what gave us the famous "je vous aime" (**fig. 12.4c–d**).

As you can make out from the face of this gentleman, whose mustache takes the shape of a smile, consonants cannot be seen, but the phrase still illustrates many mouth positions. Strictly speaking, "Je vous aime" is not a film, but a sequence of distinct images, meant to separate speech into its elements. What they illustrate is that it is impossible to situate the enunciation of a consonant through a distinct position of the mouth, and even less possible to separate consonant-images and vowel-images into distinct images.

We can attend to this question through a word that has a whole cinematic history unto itself. The word *bud*, coincidentally the nickname of Ed Harris's character, "Virgil 'Bud' Brigman," is heard very often in Cameron's film (**fig. 12.4e**). Now, one of the most famous words in cinema is *rosebud* (**fig. 12.4f–g**).

We see it said at the beginning of *Citizen Kane* (1941), the film by and starring Welles. It is spoken by a virile, mustachioed mouth probably belonging to the actor-director, and without our knowing exactly how, this word uttered on his deathbed is known to all and repeated by many other mouths. At the end of the film, no one has discovered the secret of "Rosebud." It is only unveiled in the last few minutes of the film, when a child's sled, found among the belongings of the dead man, is thrown into a fire. "Throw that junk," orders the head butler played by Paul Stewart, and the spectator alone can read what he sees disappearing (**fig. 12.5a–b**).

Making us read something that is being destroyed and ruined is a situation that cinema often uses, whether in images of burning letters, letters drowned in the rain, or texts tattered and blown away by the wind (**fig. 12.5c–g**).

In *L'écrit au cinéma*, I ventured the following hypothesis:

> this cinematic vision of writing in the process of erasure, combustion, drowning, and dissemination, is paradoxically a way for cinema, an immaterial art, based in projected images (even if the initial physical medium, film, was visible and tangible for a long time), of inscribing something within us, and encouraging us to give it a voice. Destroying the writing that we see on screen, making us attend to its disappearance paradoxically amounts to valorizing and symbolizing it. The physical destruction of writing mentally determines the instant of writing and its inscription; it emblematizes its *excription*. This is what I call an inscription that does not hang upon the world, is not incorporated within it, in such a way that one has to determine, and repeat the movement of its erasure and its dissolution.[11]

Let us return to *rosebud*: What do we see? The labial *b* is what is most visible in the pronunciation of consonants, as is the case for other English labials, especially *b*, *p*, *m*, *v*, and *f*: the lips touch and separate. This is why labials are used as markers for dubbing films in another language, especially from Anglo-American into other languages. As a popular website puts it: "[The translators] start by creating a raw, word-for-word translation. In many cases, the translation is then tweaked to make the words fit better with the actors' English-speaking mouths. The translator will try to make the 'labials'—the consonants that cause the mouth to close, such as an M, B, and P—match up with the labials in the English version."[12]

B is a voiced consonant. When it comes to consonants, many languages use the voiced/nonvoiced opposition. Now, the voicing of *b*, what makes it not a *p* and vice versa, is precisely what cannot be seen.

As I point out in my book *Film: A Sound Art* (2009):

> The second syllable "bud" is crucial since it's the consonant "B" in "bud" that's visible, that anchors the audio-visual synchronization, not the rose that is not so readable. Coincidentally, in a striking moment in another film, another bud is uttered by a female mouth, but only in mime. This moment at the end

(a) (b) (c) (d) (e) (f) (g)

FIGURE 12.5 (a) *Citizen Kane* (Orson Welles, 1941); (b) *Citizen Kane* (Orson Welles, 1941); (c) *Fahrenheit 451* (François Truffaut, 1966); (d) *Casablanca* (Michael Curtiz, 1942); (e) *What Lies Beneath* (Robert Zemeckis, 2000); (f) *All Quiet on the Western Front* (Lewis Milestone, 1930); (g) *The Cameraman* (Edward Sedgwick, 1928).

> of Elia Kazan's *Splendor in the Grass* (1961) exemplifies the idea of a silent film bubbling up from underneath the talking film.
>
> Deanie (Natalie Wood) is desperately in love with young Bud (Warren Beatty), but they never manage to get together. At the end of the film, years after being separated (Deanie has been treated in a psychiatric hospital, Bud became a farmer and married someone else), they meet again and recall their former love. They have spoken and she is going to return to her friends. Bud walks her to the car; she is already seated inside, about to depart for good, when she fixes her eyes on him with love and utters silently (behind the car window) the monosyllabic name that we have heard her speak so often in his presence, or in his absence—the beloved name that intoxicates her, a name that separates and reunites her lips: Bud.
>
> Implicitly, Natalie Wood is silently saying to an awkward and helpless Warren Beatty, "Read my lips."[13] (**fig. 12.6a–b**)

Song poses a specific problem, because it is the vowels of the language that make it possible to sing and vocalize, even without a text. Song is possible with a text because one can infinitely prolong a vowel, and thus the opening of the mouth. One can also vocalize while keeping one's mouth closed, but the consonant and the text disappear.

At the other extreme, rap beats out consonants, emphasizing mouth movements and avoiding prolonged opening of the oral cavity: in some rap hits, the consonantal character of the text is hyperaccentuated, hypersexualized in the virile sense (moreover, arm gestures are used to punctuate and affirm the consonants in syllables even more). Often a chorus of women's voices is used for the singing parts, following a stereotypical repetition of gender roles: the vowels and songs for women, the consonants and speech for men. Of course, there were female rappers, like Neneh Cherry, from the 1980s onward.

This is not the case in opera. Consider Hans Jürgen von Syberberg's opera-film *Parsifal* (1982). I choose it because the director allowed himself to film the singing in extreme close-up. What is most striking is how Syberberg chooses to use the playback technique. In the majority of cases, a different performer features in the image and the sound: here, Wolfgang Schöne sings Amfortas, the wounded, suffering knight, and Armin Jordin, the conductor of this recording, plays the song *Durch Mitleid wissend, der reine Tor* ("By his pity knowing, the pure fool") (**fig. 12.6c–g**).

One might think that vowels correspond to the moment of opening and consonants to closing. Yet things are not quite so simple: the sequence allows us to see the tongue hitting the upper teeth in *Tor* ("fool"). The visible consonant affirms the synchronization and makes it possible, while showing

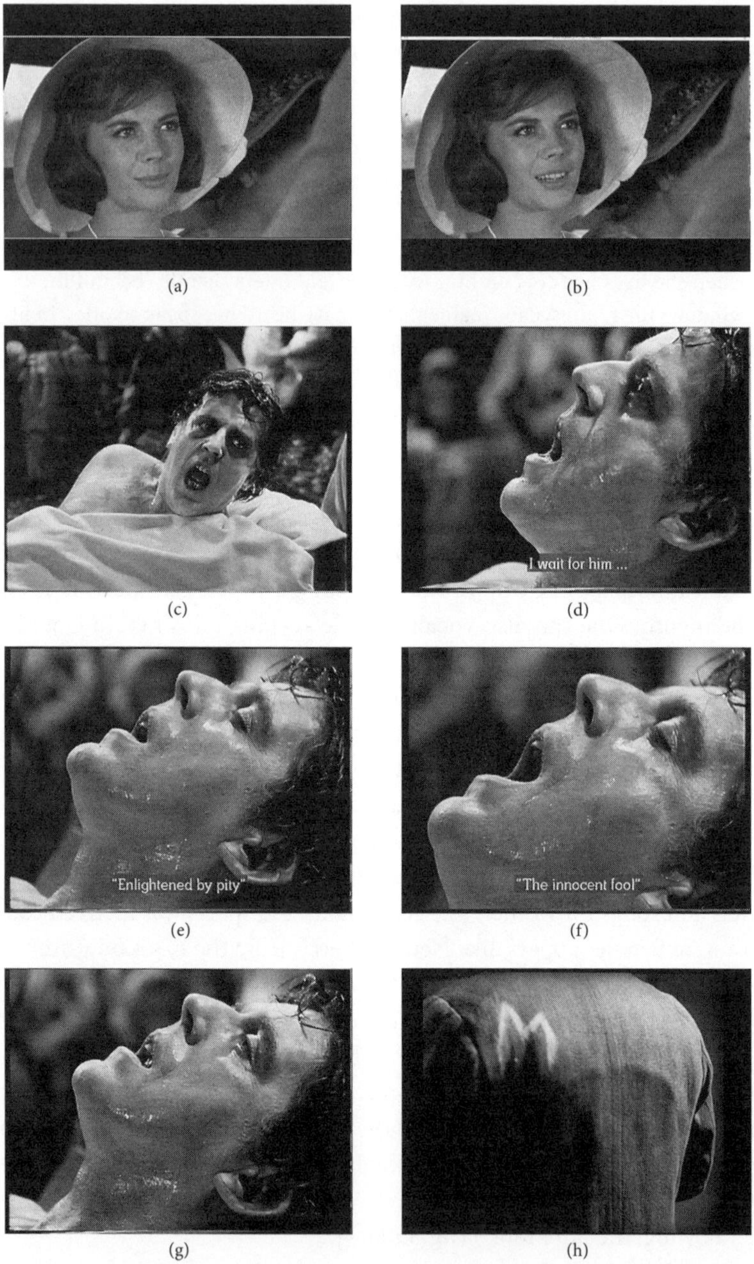

FIGURE 12.6 (a) *Splendor in the Grass* (Elia Kazan, 1961); (b) *Splendor in the Grass* (Elia Kazan, 1961); (c) *Parsifal* (Hans Jürgen Syberberg, 1982); (d) *Parsifal* (Hans Jürgen Syberberg, 1982); (e) *Parsifal* (Hans Jürgen Syberberg, 1982); (f) *Parsifal* (Hans Jürgen Syberberg, 1982); (g) *Parsifal* (Hans Jürgen Syberberg, 1982); (h) *M* (Fritz Lang, 1931).

respect for the text, and the vowel manifests voice. This style of singing is a way of manifesting writing, text, and voice at once.

As we know, Richard Wagner was the author of his own librettos. In these librettos, he was particularly committed to emphasizing the articulation of the consonants, especially by multiplying effects of alliteration, namely the repetition of the same consonant. As an example, I choose two verses from the libretto of *Siegfried* almost at random:

Fafner der wilde Wurm	Fafner, the wild dragon
lagert im finst'rn Wald	lies in the dark forest

Featured Consonants on Film

I have mostly dealt with vowels above, but what about starring consonants featured in the cinema, especially ones that are removed from the alphabet?

The most famous one is *M*, which marks the murderer in Fritz Lang's film *M* (1931) (**fig. 12.6h**). But we also know *Z* that is the sign of Zorro's passage (**fig. 12.7a**) and the *K* that is Kane's monogram in Welles's film (**fig. 12.7b**), just as *N* is Nemo's monogram in Jules Verne's *Twenty Thousand Leagues under the Sea*, and its various movie adaptations (**fig. 12.7c**).

These consonants are thus associated with dangerous or intimidating male characters. However, the most famous consonant remains the *R* belonging to the dead Rebecca who obsesses Max de Winter's poor spouse, played by Joan Fontaine in Hitchcock's film. This *R* is everywhere (**fig. 12.7d**); one could imagine that it inspired Rosebud in *Citizen Kane*, because it goes up in flames at the end. But we also know that this *R* is all the more fascinating as the young wife does not have a first name, and thus no initial; she is called "Woman" in the script. The star-consonant is thus almost always the initial of a name or a first name. It suffices to compare it to the hyperfeminine vowel *A* that brands the heroine of Hawthorne's *The Scarlet Letter*, written in 1850 and adapted many times onscreen.

Anagrams and Text Messages

The anagram is particularly interesting because its principle, as in crosswords, relies in many cases on the capital letter, and on the principle of discounting diacritical signs, especially those that go on vowels. For example, in a French anagram, one would accept that an *é* (an *e* with an *accent aigu*) in a different order of letters would become an *e* without an accent. The diacritical sign is taken out of play, and the writing-letter is freed from sound. An a in an

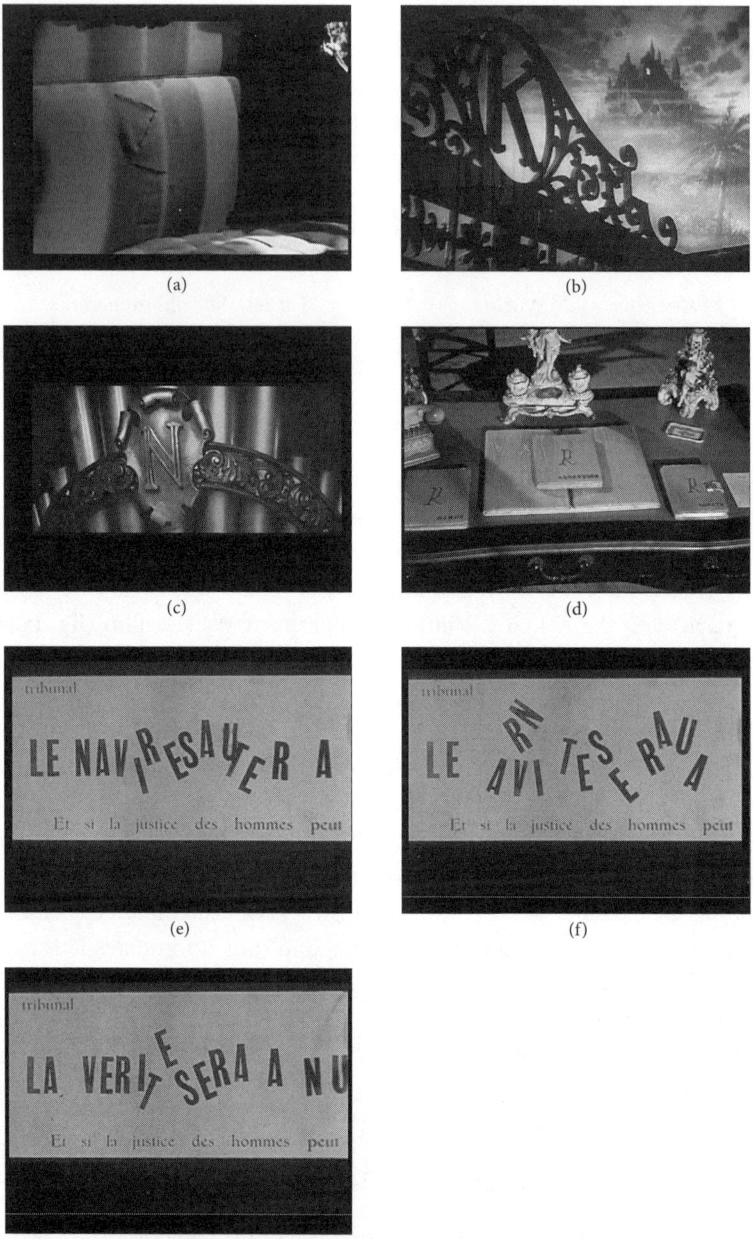

FIGURE 12.7 (a) *The Mark of Zorro* (Rouben Mamoulian, 1940); (b) *Citizen Kane* (Orson Welles, 1941); (c) *20,000 Leagues under the Sea* (Richard Fleischer, 1954); (d) *Rebecca* (Alfred Hitchcock, 1940); (e) *Les Vampires* (Louis Feuillade, 1915); (f) *Les Vampires* (Louis Feuillade, 1915); (g) *Les Vampires* (Louis Feuillade, 1915).

anagram or a crossword row can lose the sound of the *a* once it enters a word like *dirigeant* or the first name "Jean."

Since cinema is used to make letters dance, we also find anagrams in the feuilletons of early silent cinema.

Already, in *Les Vampires* (Louis Feuillade, 1915), the heroine Irma Vep, whose name is an anagram of Vampire (Musidora), receives a religious tract in prison that proclaims "LA VERITE SERA A NU" ("The truth will be naked"). Before our eyes, the letters (in all caps without the two acute accents in "vérité") dance and form the coded text "LE NAVIRE SAUTERA" ("The ship will explode") before moving again to reconstitute the first message. Of course, this is made possible image by image, using animation techniques: the first animated drawings often mixed the so-called real take with a drawing (**fig. 12.7e–g**).

In the play of anagrams, as mentioned earlier, any letter can be pronounced or silent. One of the most basic anagrams of French consists in reading *port* ("port") backward from the last to the first letter, to get *trop* ("too much"). The *p* in *port* is pronounced and the *t* is silent, while in *trop* it is the opposite. The consonant that we see is separate from the one we hear, and even from the vowel. The image-letter separates itself and frees itself from its sound.

Many films, including *Suspicion* (Alfred Hitchcock, 1941), *Rosemary's Baby* (Roman Polanski, 1968), and *Sneakers* (Phil Alden Robinson, 1992) (**fig. 12.8a–d**), feature games of Scrabble in which characters discover a truth in the shape of a word or a name. We know that the apparition of a word decrypted in an anagram gives an emotional and sonorous charge to the vowel: it is the element that seems to call for internal vocalization, forcing us to utter it, thereby reinforcing the impression that in an alphabetic system with consonants and vowels, voice is expressed by vowels.

Similarly, the use of so-called "phonetic" writing in "text messages" consists in using the isolated pronunciation of a vowel or a consonant instead of the word, and the consonant thus regains a vocal value, because it calls for voice. This is the case in these two messages from *Up in the Air* (Jason Reitman, 2009) and *The Adjustment Bureau* (Georges Nolfi, 2011) (**fig. 12.8e–f**): we are dealing with speech contained in the silent image that takes the form of an *incomplete writing*. The reader becomes much more conscious while reading them that she is vocalizing internally. Writing loses the sense of the trace and includes its declamation.

Speech and Law

Up to now, I have been speaking about alphabetic writing that writes vowels, but is a lot less phonetic (writing out the sound) than commonly admitted.

FIGURE 12.8 (a) *Suspicion* (Alfred Hitchcock, 1941); (b) *Rosemary's Baby* (Roman Polanski, 1968); (c) *Rosemary's Baby* (Roman Polanski, 1968); (d) *Sneakers* (Phil Alden Robinson, 1992); (e) *Up in the Air* (Jason Reitman, 2009); (f) *The Adjustment Bureau* (Georges Nolfi, 2011); (g) *The Ten Commandments* (Cecil B. de Mille, 1956); (h) *Exodus: Gods and Kings* (Ridley Scott, 2014).

Obviously, I have also been very interested in other alphabets, and other systems of writing—not all of them, lacking time and expertise.

Cinema has depicted the scene of the Tables of the Law in the biblical book of Exodus many times onscreen, notably in Cecil B. de Mille's *The Ten Commandments* (1956) and Ridley Scott's *Exodus: Gods and Kings* (2014) (**fig. 12.8g–h**). We know that in the first film the commandment is first announced by a deep male voice, this voice seeming to emit a column of fire that engraves the words in Hebrew characters on the stone by burning it. In the second, God expresses himself through a child's voice (a voice, thus, without a marked gender), and it is Moses himself, played by Christian Bale, who engraves the characters in stone, in consonantal Hebrew—a Hebrew that stopped being a spoken language for centuries before being re-created to become a common language in the state of Israel.

I have neither the time nor the knowledge to study the capital role of signs that are called "matres lectionis," which are used in a certain number of languages to signify the pronounced vowel indirectly. It is noteworthy that this is a feminine term. Hebraic letters in sacred texts are not supposed to touch, or be connected, being in masculine discontinuity and not in a continuity that is deemed feminine. Yet, the "matres lectionis," by calling for voice, could be considered to constitute an intrusion into this play.

Invented Writings

I have also been interested in the question of imaginary and invented languages in science-fiction movies, some of which do without writing (like *Avatar*) while others gradually develop writing, either in the films or TV series themselves, or in the video-game franchises that extend the universes of such films: for example, Klingon in the *Star Trek* series and the numerous films that bring it to the big screen; the writing of the Ancients in *Stargate*, a film whose success also inspired a TV series; Aurebesh in *Star Wars*, and the related video games, and so on. Almost always these invented forms are an imitation of our alphabetic writing, with the same distinction between consonants and vowels.

But these films also differ from one another. What is striking in the first version of the *Star Wars* trilogy, the three episodes of which were released between 1977 and 1983, is that there is almost no writing to be read in the background or on the screens of machines. The story imagined by George Lucas takes place a long time ago (relative to us) in a galaxy that is not ours, and we see flying spaceships and working robots, the functioning of which apparently required neither calculation nor writing. On the instrument panels, one can see arbitrary signs that could also be simple pictograms. In another area, the first episode of *The Hunger Games* saga, directed by Gary Ross and released in 2012, based on the novels by Suzanne Collins, depicts a universe in which there is no writing. This matters in *Star Wars* and *The Hunger Games*, because the presence of onscreen writing—besides the credits—would anchor the story in the English language and an Anglo-American frame. However, in these two series, the onomastics (the names of people) and the toponyms (place names) continue to preserve the symbolic vowel/consonant opposition.

Perspectives

As we have seen, I have not discussed the totality of world cinemas or world languages. What I can say is that the myth of an "oriental" writing, which would be entirely ideographic and nonlinear, as opposed to a "western writing," which would be entirely phonetic (subordinate to voice), linear and rational, is indeed a myth. If we only consider Japanese writing, for instance, we have an extremely complex and composite system; on the other hand, computers and internet connections have encouraged a predominance of the Western alphabetic system through the English language, a predominance that will probably universalize the consonant/vowel distinction.

This chapter, which is really more of a little exploration, poses a triple question: First, does the vowel/consonant distinction play a role in the dramaturgy of films in various languages that use Latin writing? The answer is yes. The second question is: Do films tell us the story of writing in general? On this point, I can hardly answer, since I have limited knowledge of Indian, Chinese, and other cinemas. . . . But I can put forth the hypothesis that it is perhaps a little senseless to try to construct a theory of writing in general, as Derrida claimed to do, and on the other hand to reduce alphabetic writing to a "linear" dimension. Finally, the third one: What about the "gendered" (sexual) consonant/vowel opposition? If we rely on the examples I have given, it remains very strong.

In some countries, it even becomes a bit of a caricature: in France, there is a very strong movement, coming from traditional and conservative groups, which opposes the introduction of "gender theory" in schools, as if it would lead to little boys being forced to play with dolls and pee sitting down. More than an anxiety about the loss of difference, there is a fear of panfeminism. There is a great deal of irrationality in this fear as it spreads through the world at large.

Notes

I would like to thank the Neubauer Collegium at the University of Chicago and all the members of the Voice Project who honored me with this invitation.

1. Michel Chion, *L'audio-vision: son et image au cinéma* (Paris: Nathan, 1990); 2nd ed. (Paris: Nathan, 2000); English translation as *Audio-Vision: Sound on Screen*, ed. and trans. Claudia Gorbman with foreword by Walter Murch (New York: Columbia University Press, 1994).

2. Michel Chion, *Film, A Sound Art*, trans. Claudia Gorman (New York: Columbia University Press, 2009), 468. (See "Glossaire" on www.michelchion.com.)

3. Michel Chion, *La voix au cinéma* (Paris: Éditions de l'Étoile, 1982), in English as Michel Chion, *The Voice in Cinema*, trans. Claudia Gorbman (New York: Columbia University Press, 1999).

4. Michel Chion, *L'écrit au cinéma* (Paris: A. Colin, 2013); English translation as *Words on Screen*, ed. and trans. Claudia Gorbman (New York: Columbia University Press, 2017).

5. Clarisse Herrenschmidt, *Les trois écritures: Langue, nombre, code* (Paris: Gallimard, 2007), 182.

6. Herrenschmidt, *Les trois écritures*, 182.

7. Herrenschmidt, *Les trois écritures*, 182.

8. Chion, *L'écrit au cinéma*, 110.

9. Novel by Anne Declos, published under the pen name Pauline Réage.

10. Alphabet soup is a symbol of the fact that in the domain of alphabetic writing, letters belong to the same world without differentiation of genre or function and seem to have the power to generate and transcribe all sounds, while in the domain of spoken language, letters often acquire distinct functions and revert to a binary difference with a "gendered" vowel/consonant. On the other hand, when the unpronounced letters of an "alphabet soup" start to combine into words, they are no longer undifferentiated; some of them become silent (like the "a" in the French pronunciation of the name "Jean"), while others are pronounced. According to the order of the letters, some fall into the unpronounced category (the "t" in the French word "port"—and, conversely, the "p" in the French word "trop") while others get pronounced. It differs for each language, according to its individual history of spelling and pronunciation.

11. Chion, *L'écrit au cinéma*, 200.

12. See http://www.slate.com/articles/news_and_politics/explainer/2010/01/avatar_in_spanish_or_french_or_german.html.

13. *Film, a Sound Art*, trans. Claudia Gorbman (New York: Columbia University Press, 2009), 179.

PART VI

Technology, Difference, and the Uncanny

13

The Prosthetic Voice in Ancient Greece

SARAH NOOTER

Early in Aristophanes's *Clouds*, a student of Socrates explains his teacher's view on the mechanics of gnat noise. After he describes how the breath of a gnat is pushed violently through its narrow intestine and out its ass, his interlocutor happily exclaims, "then the ass of gnats is a war-trumpet!"[1] As so often, the joke lies in the yawning juxtaposition of terms: the gnat is a tiny insect of no consequence; the war-trumpet, or *salpinx*, is a powerful instrument whose sound signifies both the terror of combat and divine force. In this essay, I look at places in Greek literature where the voice gets conceptualized as similarly, if less humorously, transformed through objects that may be thought of as prostheses for the vocalizing body and its abilities.

The particular objects under discussion here are a kind of oboe (the *aulos*) and the war-trumpet (the *salpinx*). In English, we would say these are two kinds of instruments, and would likely no longer notice the inert metaphor contained by the term "instrument," which means most literally "a means by which something of value is transferred, held or accomplished."[2] Our comfort with the term "musical instrument" allows us the ease of not asking *what* of value is "transferred, held or accomplished" by an oboe, for example (aesthetic experience? emotive expression?). For the duration of this essay, I ask that the reader suspend the use of the metaphorical term "instrument" for such objects as oboes and replace it with the term "prosthesis" in order that I may isolate a few aspects of how these objects get conceptualized in relation to the voice and body. If a gnat is said to contain a war-trumpet, it is a trumpet acquired strictly through the use of metaphor; its capability of being loud is inborn. An average Greek man, by contrast, could only shout with disproportionate volume—and thus terrify by way of sound—by way of an attachment crafted to fulfill precisely this function. He could cry out anguish or presumably use the *aulos* to mimic cries of anguish, perhaps with more affective power than he might through his own voice. What I discuss in the following pages is the perceived transformation of the boundaries of human voice and body that are summoned through the use of these musical prostheses.

The voice in these transformations becomes both an extension of ability and a displacement of identity by way of a new persona. This phenomenon is illuminated by Tracey Warr's recent description of certain contemporary works of art:

> Some of these prosthetic attachments provide an extension of the body that increases its ability to communicate, thereby creating a new hybrid body beyond the physical limits of the human scale. In other works the body is transformed into a tool or instrument.[3]

This passage describes the use by certain artists of extensions to their bodies to transform the way they are understood as people. When this kind of "extension" to the body takes the form of a vocal enhancement and seems able to reach much farther than the human voice, or boom more loudly, or ventriloquize too perfectly, an experience of the uncanny and inhuman is created, somewhat similar to the mechanical voice, as discussed by Mladen Dolar:

> The impersonal voice, the mechanically produced voice (answering machines, computer voices, and so on) always has a touch of the uncanny. . . . The mechanical voice reproduces the pure norm without any side effects; therefore it seems that it actually subverts the norm by giving it raw.[4]

One might imagine that the ancient Greek world, free as it was of voicemail, Auto-Tune, Apple's Siri, and Amazon Echo, would not have allowed for any experience of this form of "the vocalic uncanny,"[5] but I suggest here that we find the stirrings of this preoccupation in the Greek conception of musical prostheses that stand in for the voice. The experience of the uncanny points also to questions about the mimetic function of art: What is gained through the artificial construction of a likeness to ourselves? When mimesis is performed through a blurring of the boundaries between our voice and external sound, as well as of the boundaries between ourselves and bodily attachments, the uncanny aspect is heightened. This preoccupation also appears in the Hebrew mythology of the *shofar*, a cultural artifact made from a ram's horn. In both the Greek and Hebrew traditions, such prostheses show voice as accessing the pains of the body but also pointing to where the divine resides. Thus they serve as a locus for considering both the degradations of corporeality and the invincibly invulnerable.

I start by discussing the *aulos*, which Plato and others found problematic due to its ability to mimic human voices in lamentation and its literal interference with the ability of an *aulos*-player to express words.[6] From this perspective, the *aulos*—simultaneously a displacement and replacement for the human voice—signals a supplanting of rational identity by dangerously embodied expression, a fall that is amplified by the fact that the *aulos*, like the *shofar*, is also imagined as a mnemonic for the anguished cries of vanquished women from the indomitable perspective of the vanquishing force: the dangerous result is that these prostheses, affixed to the body, give voice to its lowest and most degraded part of human experience. I then move on to a prosthetic voice that produces the illusion of invulnerability, that of the *salpinx*, which is both imagined as the metallic voice of the gods and deployed in the context of war to silence and intimidate the enemy.

The *Aulos* and the Body

In classical Athens, the *aulos* became a focal point for reflection and anxiety on the role, powers, and physicality of the voice in song. As its technology was improved and innovated, allowing for ever greater aural versatility, it exacted ever more suspicion from musical purists and earned banishment from Plato's ideal city.[7] Like the voice itself, the existence and effects of the aulos are compounds of ethereal sound and bodily heft—a reconciliation of opposing forces that is itself recognized in Greek poetry. Two myths of the aulos, told during this time, involve the goddess Athena and make the corporeality of aulos-playing especially palpable. One has her rejecting it for herself because it deforms her facial features when she blows into it, calling it an "injury to [my] body" (σώματι λύμα).[8] The aspect of embodied effort necessary to *aulos*-playing and the unwillingness of the divinely unencumbered to undergo its humiliations are clear here. The other, more complex, tale is sung by Pindar in *Pythian* 12. To celebrate the victory of an *aulos*-player in a musical contest, the poet presents the story of Athena inventing the *aulos* to imitate the wailing of the Gorgons when their sister Medusa is killed by Perseus:

> But when from these labors, she had released this beloved man [Perseus],
> the Maiden created the all-voiced song of the *auloi*,
> so that whatever was forced from the swiftly-snapping jaws of Euryale
> she could imitate with arms [but often translated as "instruments"], the loudly screamed lament. (P. 12.18–21)

Athena ("the Maiden" above) creates the "all-voiced" (πάμφωνον) song of the *aulos* to literally mimic the cries of grief at the moment of the Gorgon's greatest vulnerability. Athena's own body is not an element of this story, but her creation of the *aulos* springs from her desire to maintain the vocal presence of the grotesquely embodied Gorgons, who are otherwise known by the horrible features of their bodies—snakes on the head of one and jaws snapping on another.[9] In Homeric epic, Athena arms for battle with many fierce accoutrements, including the Gorgoneion—the apotropaic head of the Gorgon—whose gaping orifice becomes permanently, if silently, incorporated into Athena's own visual identity.[10] Thus Athena kills the Gorgon but the Gorgon, in turn, shifts the shape of Athena; the act of mimesis becomes one of incorporation, with the *aulos* and its song extending and adjusting the powers of the goddess.

The poet then suggests that the *aulos* has an effect not just on a (mythical) goddess but also on the (actual) rituals and habits of men. For what follows from Athena's mimicking of the Gorgons' laments as embodied incorporation is a kind of social incorporation of the "tune of many heads" (κεφαλᾶν πολλᾶν νόμον) into an organized cultural context, the contests at Cephisus, as the goddess passes on the *aulos* to mortals:

> The goddess discovered it, but she discovered it for mortal men to have,
> and named it the tune of many heads,
> the glorious summoner of the crowded contests,
> often whistling through slender brass and reeds,
> the ones that dwell by the lovely-chorused city of the Graces,
> in the precinct of Cephisos, faithful witnesses of the dances. (P. 12.22–27)

Athena's giving of the *aulos* to men transforms it from "loudly screamed lament" into a civilizing tool that summons men into the institutions of society—contests and the choruses.[11] But Athena's intent to imitate the laments of the Gorgons also brings this version of the myth in line with a function of music itself: to give sonic analogues for emotional processes.[12] The actual object that is an *aulos* (and Pindar's poem draws its materiality into play, noting that it is made of "slender brass and reeds") becomes an enduring sign of corporeality in music, a physical extension of the voice. The *aulos* is also tasked with accompanying song in tragic performance, shifting the tenor of "lyric" passages from their tradition of lyre-accompaniment and marking the genre as one of a music more fully embodied (**fig. 13.1**).[13]

The danger, then, of the *aulos* to Plato, the imagined Athena, and the actual people who play and hear it is its purchase through artifice on mimicry of the embodied voice and the voice in grief in particular. It is an effective, perhaps uncanny, incorporation of suffering into the body and voice whose breaking of boundaries threatens to overrun control of the self.

FIGURE 13.1 Dionysus and the theater. Attic black-figure amphora, late sixth century BCE, J. Paul Getty Museum, Los Angeles.

The consonance between the body and the *aulos* runs deep and in both directions; thus Aristotle later compares the interior of the larynx to the workings of reeds within an *aulos*.[14] Such an analogy appears in Greek poetry also when the "breath" of an *aulos* is evoked, which is done quite casually at times. For instance, a character in Aristophanes's *Frogs*, on first hearing the chorus of initiates, asks: "Do you not hear it? . . . The breath of *auloi*" (*Ra.* 312, 313).[15] The analogy of breath (and breeze, also a meaning of πνοή) to the sound of an *aulos*, then, is not considered a difficult or intrusive one, but can be trotted out in direct and straightforward dialogue. And yet "analogy" is not really the word, for behind the description of the *sound* of the *aulos* as a breath or breeze is the physical act of blowing into one, so that the phrase seems to unite the act of giving voice to the *aulos* with its sonic effect. It is the *aulos* itself that is the analogy, a seeming imprint or extension of the vocal power of a person that also displaces that person's innate vocality.[16]

The use of the *aulos* as a prosthesis of human voice also points to another way that breath was imagined as a conduit for voice, with humans themselves as the prosthetic attachments through which gods might utter or sing. Perhaps the most suggestive form of such voicing is to be found in the image of the earth's breath as an oracular force that is heard through the prosthesis of a person. The voice of Apollo, likely the most relevant divine voice to the life of common Greek people, was at times configured as breathing through vapors that arise from a chasm in the mountains of Delphi, delivering truths that are transmitted through the voice of a priestess.[17] This envisaging of divine voice as breath echoes the Hebrew notion of *ruah*, as Adriana Cavarero has discussed:

> According to the Bible, God's power—which manifests itself to the people of Israel through creation and revelation—finds its expression in breath, *ruah*, and in the voice, *qol*. . . . As it comes from God, *ruah* also manifests itself as wind, breeze, storm, and, above all, as a creative force.[18]

The power of divine voice in the Hebrew tradition is also heard—and ritually reheard into eternity—in the blast of the *shofar*, the ram's horn that in Exodus rings out with crashes of thunder at the cataclysmic moment when the universe opens to reveal the Ten Commandments (19.16, 20.18) and that is sounded one hundred times every Rosh Hashanah. Like the *aulos*, the *shofar* extends human voice through breath into something so outsized as to be inhuman. As in Pindar's account of the sound of the *aulos*, the blasts of the *shofar* on Rosh Hashanah are mythically tied to the cries of a female who is mourning the downfall of her evil son—as Medusa's Gorgon sisters cry for her—and this cry of and for the vanquished is heard again in each triumphant blast.[19] The *shofar* is part of a larger discourse of divine breath (*ruah*) and voice (*qol*) within this tradition.

Although there are also obvious similarities between the divine vapors at Delphi and the equally celestial Hebrew *ruah*, there is a greater difference implicit in this comparison: in Greek culture, it is not the general divine voice but only the voices of particular deities that take on such palpable form, and they do so only when a human vessel is waiting to receive and deliver this voice to others, either as or through a prosthesis. Another example of this phenomenon in Greek literature is Hesiod's account in the *Theogony* of the Muses "breathing" inspiration into him, while also giving him a branch from a laurel tree and designating him a poet. The breath and branch work in conjunction to provide the voice that will sing as a god: through these enhancements, the shepherd becomes a poet. Yet the mortal poet is also the prosthesis through which the Muses communicate. In this scene, the Muses have announced their presence by hailing the narrator as (among other things) "merely a belly"

(*Th.* 26), thus summoning the body of the shepherd into play. It is made explicit that this body will now be changed by what the Muses provide. More implicit is the complementary entailment that the Muses have acquired such a "belly" themselves in order to bring their voice to men. The conception of gods' voices as breathing through men—and the corresponding notion of gods requiring the embodiment that men can provide—suggests a ream of possible metaphorical configurations whereby voice is an instrument that translates cosmic messages into human terms. In pushing the concept of instrument toward that of prosthesis, we begin to see what is at stake: an instrument can be picked up and put down; a prosthetic attachment becomes a part of the body and adjusts its contours. Which set of connotations is in play in this literature?

The use of Muses by men, and men by Muses, was a locus for poetic play and philosophical thought in antiquity.[20] One example that makes palpable the material difference thought to exist between divine and human voices is the full-throated invocation to the Muses that intrudes in the second book of the *Iliad*. Note the dichotomy traced by the poet between the voice of the Muses and the voice he wishes he had:

> Tell me now, Muses who have your homes on Olympus,
> for you are goddesses and are present and know all things,
> but we hear only legend and do not know anything:
> who were some leaders of the Danaans and their commanders?
> The multitude of them I could not tell nor name,
> not even if I had ten tongues, and ten mouths,
> and an unbreakable voice and heart of bronze within me,
> unless the Olympian Muses, daughters of aegis-bearing Zeus,
> should call to mind who came to Ilium.
> I will say anew the captains and all their ships. (*Il.* 2.484–93)

These lines follow a series of six extended similes on the vastness and dazzling display of the army[21] and precede the long and renowned catalogue of ships, a poetic feat that seems to require its own proem and invocation—practically a new start to the epic. The poet wishes to explain his inadequacy (that is, without the Muses) by suggesting that no quantity (ten tongues, ten mouths) or quality (a voice that is unbreakable, a heart of bronze) of physical attributes could allow him to tell what the gods know. His naming of lords, the dim transmission of glory (*kleos*), is nothing compared to the voice of the Muses: they sing with a clarity that rings forth out of their complete presence and knowledge, with a voice, however, that needs no great number of tongues, mouths, and metallic hearts.[22] The voice of the divine in this picture is immaterial, freed from all the baggage of the body, and yet the only way for the poet to imagine even approaching the power of their voice (if unsuccessfully) is through metallic enhancements. In reality, the poet does tell and name the very multitude he claims he cannot by constructing the image of a conceptual bridge of materiality that echoes the use of actual metal in the case of the *salpinx* to transmit a cry to multitudes.

The *Salpinx* and the Gods

Unlike the *aulos*, the *salpinx* is not imagined from the perspective of the player but from that of the listener. I have found no text where the body or mouth of the *salpinx*-player is imagined, nor any story of its invention.[23] Rather, it is always configured as fully formed and loudly blaring, often from some distance, and as inciting and connoting imminent destruction. In the world I am discussing—Greece in the eighth through fifth centuries BCE—a *salpinx* was likely to be easily the loudest sound that one person could produce without the architectural resources of a theater or odium. Its designation in translation as a *war*-trumpet points to the particular technological innovations that it offers: portability and durability. In the messy, crowded context of battle, whether by sea or by land, a *salpinx*, and only a *salpinx*, could be expected to be widely audible to thousands of listeners, a point emphasized by Peter Krentz in his study of the role of the *salpinx* in Greek warfare.[24] Even in this sense alone, the *salpinx* acts as a divine and invulnerable sonic force. As we have seen, divine voices were imagined in Greek culture as the source of prophetic knowledge and poetic inspiration, and yet they were more commonly thought of as a source of terror, especially in the context of war (**fig. 13.2**).

In these scenarios, such fearful sounds often were heard as precursors of destruction, as in the war scenes of the *Iliad*, where violent onslaughts are prefaced by terrifying "war cries" from the side that inevitably is victorious.[25] The most effective of all such cries is performed by Achilles, who at this point lacks armor and cannot fight. Yet he can shout:

> Standing there, he shouted and from afar Pallas Athena
> cried out. Then an unspeakable uproar arose among the Trojans.
> Like a ringing voice, or when a trumpet [*salpinx*] rings out
> beneath life-destroying enemies surrounding a town,
> like this was the ringing voice of the son of Aeacus. (*Il.* 18.217–21)

His inhuman power to annihilate is signified by the effect of his shout on the Trojans, as his voice is joined by Athena's own cry. Though the lines just

FIGURE 13.2 Warrior playing the *salpinx*. Attic black-figure lekythos, late sixth–early fifth century BCE, Museo Archeologico Regionale, Palermo.

quoted might be thought sufficient to portray the panic among the Trojans caused by this cry, the narrative pauses here still longer to add details and animate the experience of different Trojan hearers of this voice—the horses, the chariot drivers, the Trojans en masse once again, and then those who perish from fear:

> And when they heard the brazen voice of the son of Aeacus,
> the soul in every man was stirred up. Even the lovely-maned horses
> turned their chariots back. For they presaged grief in their souls.
> The chariot-drivers were panic-struck when they saw untiring fire,
> terrible, above the head of the great-souled son of Peleus,
> burning; the gleaming-eyed goddess, Athena, made it burn.
> Three times above the trench divine Achilles shouted loudly,
> three times the Trojans and their famous allies were stricken [with terror].
> And then and there twelve of the best men perished
> near their own chariots and spears. (*Il.* 18.22–31)

Great care is given to detailing the force and effects of Achilles's voice over the course of this passage: first it creates mere panic, then a simile is employed to tie its power to that of an enemy circling. Next the voice is called "brazen," or literally "of bronze" (ὄπα χάλκεον), a small metaphor that equates Achilles's quasi-divine voice with weaponry, much as the poet imagines a bronze heart would be required (yet insufficient) to sing his story. The threat of his voice, like an approaching earthquake, is first sensed by animals; it is supported by the optics of fire and, finally, the cry is repeated three times and, with marked anaphora, "three times" is repeated too, inflicting panic once again and finally causing death: twelve men (the "best" of them, no less) simply drop dead on the spot. As has been widely noted by scholars, Achilles's voice in the *Iliad* has a special role and status, aligned in some ways with that of the narrator and Zeus.[26] There is no more palpable display of such vocal distinction than its deadly effects.

To explain the frightening quality of this voice for an audience not accustomed to fighting on the field with the sons of gods, the poet poses the analogy of Achilles's voice to when a "*salpinx* rings out" (ἴαχε σάλπιγξ) as an enemy surrounds a town—a sound that signifies the onslaught of sacking and savagery. In the lives of real Greek people, the sound of the *salpinx* played exactly this role—a signal of triumph or annihilation in war that was so potent as to be associated with the divine and particularly with Athena, as a god of war.[27] Hence it follows that in Sophocles's *Ajax*, Odysseus likens the voice of Athena to that of a "bronze-mouthed bell of a Tyrrhenian trumpet" (16–17). Athena is at that moment in the process of crushing her enemy Ajax, whom she has driven mad, and thus the suggestion that her voice is awesomely destructive is fitting to the context and shows the power signified by the voice of the *salpinx*.

More normatively, a *salpinx* signaled the start of battle and came to signify the experience of battle itself. Xenophon's *Anabasis*, his first-person account of a large military expedition, is filled with instances of the *salpinx* sounding, often in conjunction with a paean being sung or a war-cry arising.[28] Inevitably in Xenophon's text, the Greeks are the ones blasting a *salpinx* and, soon thereafter, triumphing in battle. The *salpinx*, then, does not only signify war, but also a sort of invincibility that leads to victory in war. In Aeschylus's *Persians*, the full effect of such sound is exhibited when a messenger reports the launch of Greek ships in battle against much more numerous Persian forces ("the foreigners" here):

> And yet when day, with her white horses,
> had spread brilliantly over all the land,
> first then did a clamor peal out from the Greeks,
> like a song it rang out auspiciously, and shrilly at once

shouting back from the island crags
came an echo, and then fear was present in all the foreigners,
deprived of their judgment. For not as if in flight
were the Greeks singing their holy paean then,
but hastening for battle with strong-hearted courage.
A trumpet screamed and inflamed everything,
and straightaway met with the dashing of oars,
as they struck the salty deep, as commanded. (*Pers.* 386–97)

The story of this battle begins with a "clamor sounding" (ἠχῆι κέλαδος), which sounds like a song (μολπηδὸν εὐφήμησεν) and echoes against the landscape (ἀντηλάλαξε . . . ἠχώ); next comes the paean and, as a grand sonic finale, the blast of a *salpinx* incites the Greeks to strike the water with their oars, presumably in unison, since the practical effect of the *salpinx* was to signal the start of battle across a wide distance. We are told that the Greek sailors themselves shout and sing their paean altogether; this cohesion, vocal and otherwise, is a factor of their victory over the multilingual Persian forces.[29] But who plays the *salpinx*? No one, per se. The *salpinx* is the subject of its own verb of vocality ("it screams"—ἀυτῆι), an independent force that has set the world on fire (ἐπέφλεγεν). This sound from the trumpet is thus unauthored—nobody and no body is imagined as playing it—and divinely authoritative, with its sound figuratively inflaming the fleets just as flames leap from the head of Achilles as he shouts down the Trojans. It represents an expression, and perhaps an extension, of the power of the Greek fleet, without reference to the bodies that might be made vulnerable in such a battle scene if they were conjured in the first place.

By a kind of sonic simile, the sound of the *salpinx* made its way into the establishing of cultural institutions beyond war, as we see in another tragedy of Aeschylus. In his *Eumenides*, Athena's trumpet peals out to silence men and give them a new, divine form of law, an aetiological echo of the use of the trumpet to signal the start of legal proceedings at the law courts on the Areopagus.[30] Athena does not blow into the trumpet herself, perhaps in keeping with other representations of her attitude toward her own body. Rather, she has a herald do so, an otherwise silent character:

Be a herald, herald, and hold back the host,
or let the piercing Tyrrhenian
trumpet [*salpinx*], filled with mortal breath,
shine its voice at full pitch to the host.
For while this council hall is being filled,
it helps to be silent and to learn my laws
for the entire city for time immemorial
and for these people, so that justice may be decided well. (*Eum.* 576–83)

Athena commands the herald to quiet the crowd, and suggests he do this specifically by way of a *salpinx*.[31] She elaborates further, explaining that it is "filled with mortal breath" and that it will "shine," in an instance of pointed synesthesia also signaled by the metaphorical act of "inflaming" everything performed by the *salpinx* in Aeschylus's *Persians*. The likelihood that a blast of the trumpet customarily signaled the start of some procedures in the law courts implies that this enhanced vocality would have had ongoing resonance both through the present body of the actor and in the offstage lives of the contemporary audience.

But there is more to these lines. Rory Egan has argued that one particular verse of the passage, "for while this council hall is being filled" (which in Greek sounds like *plêroomenoo gar toode booleutêrioo*),[32] is unusually aurally expressive by virtue of its drumming repetition of "*oo*-sounds" that may themselves imitate the sound of a trumpet's blast, by "kinaesthetic imagery through which the actual movements of speech organs as they articulate sounds expressively mime, reflect, or correspond to the content or significance of the words uttered."[33] According to this interpretation, Athena's own vocalization and the particular vocal acts her actor would have employed in embodying her might have aurally aligned her speech and the sound of the trumpet. This is a compelling account of how vocality may have carried mimetic power in performance. I would add that if Athena's words sound somewhat trumpetlike, it is a fleeting sonic presence that also by and large underlines her active displacement of the act of sound-creation from herself to another, perhaps in an echo of her mythic refusal to let her body be distorted (i.e., her cheeks puffed) by the playing of the *aulos*. The herald, then, acts as a prosthetic attachment to make Athena's silencing sound out, but he himself must use a divinely empowered prosthesis to carry off this vocal feat.

The Robot and the Elephant

To accept this view of displaced vocality, one must understand that Greek thinking on voice (*phoné*) locates it as distinct from language (*logos* or *dialektos*) and also frames it as correspondingly embodied. Voice is the part of utterance that comes from the mouth but does not necessarily produce linguistic meaning. It is the individual stamp of vocal sound that can be heard in babble, humming, or sighs. Voice, as such, is a tool that people but also some animals are thought to possess, as Aristotle points out in the *Politics* (1253a). Elsewhere he elaborates further on this topic, introducing a number of distinctions that demarcate human voice (these include "soul" [ἔμψυχον], "breath" [πνεῦμα] and, evocatively, "imagination" [φαντασία])[34] and enumerating various kinds of sound-emissions—some vocal, some not—among nonhumans. He declares that birds, frogs, and dolphins are the few beasts that have an actual voice (*phoné*).[35] For him, the distinction between an animal sound that is voice and one that is not is strictly anatomical: Does the animal emit sound through a pharynx? a larynx? a tongue that is unhampered? lips that form consonants? The more of these boxes that can be checked, the closer to Aristotle's designation of "voiced" is that animal. Thus the sound of voice itself is a phenomenon that draws the body into play. The sound of voice produced by artifice seemingly attached to the body begs the question of the body's role in producing this voice and in the constitution of that body itself.

The examples from Greek literature in this essay suggest that the voice emitted through the artificial prosthesis of an *aulos* on the one hand or a *salpinx* on the other transmit meaning far beyond what their sound might in a different conceptual context. In this context, their sounds connote an undermining sense of vulnerability (on the one hand) and an ineluctable level of threat (on the other). There is a vast difference between these effects, but I would suggest that they exist on the same spectrum of the uncanny and, furthermore, that there are two similar and intersecting qualities that give them their connotative powers: one is the fact of their substituting for the human voice. In the case of the *aulos*, its capability to produce a nearly voice-like sound adds a note of the uncanny, a *frisson* of fear, to the myths and commentary surrounding it; in the case of the *salpinx*, it is the terrifying voices themselves that seem to take on the timbre and force of the horn. In both cases, there is an element of displacement of the actual voice that is in play. The other significant quality shared by the *aulos* and the *salpinx* is the physical fact of their being attached to the mouth of a player and thus appearing as extensions of flesh.

The combination of these two factors calls into play a particular kind of unease that attends upon prostheses of the body and simulations of the voice in our own culture as well. Thus an article in the *New York Times* from 2016 reports on attempts by computer companies to create a robotic voice that would not be "disturbing or jarring," a phenomenon reportedly known among software designers as "crossing the 'uncanny valley.' . . . They wanted a voice that was not too humanlike and by extension not creepy."[36] Dolar, in a passage quoted at the start of this essay, suggests the mechanical voice communicates the "pure norm" and that the lack of "side effects" is what causes the uncanny effect, but in cases ranging from the cry heard in the melody of an *aulos* to the tones of a robotic voice that is "too humanlike," it may perhaps be the sound of mimicry straining to successfully conceal its mimetic nature that disturbs—the sound of artifice taking root in our selves.

Aristotle ends his discussion on the sounds and voices of animals with a point about the dual voices of an elephant:

> When an elephant utters without its trunk but just with its mouth, it makes a wind-like sound, like when a man exhales or wails [literally: "cries *aiai*"], but with its trunk it is like a savage war-trumpet.[37]

The philosopher locates two vocal modes for the elephant and uses the linguistic prosthesis of a simile in both cases. His explanatory act is, in this way, not dissimilar from Aristophanes's flippant metaphor on the ass of the gnat as a trumpet. Likewise, the elephant is imagined by Aristotle as if in command of two modes of human expression: when the elephant uses just its mouth, it sounds like a person who is inarticulate (exhaling) and sad (crying *aiai*). (One might note that this untrumpeting elephant sounds rather like Sophocles's tragic hero Ajax, *Aias* in Greek, who self-consciously cries *aiai*.)[38] When the elephant employs its trunk, however, its voice transforms into the savage sound of the *salpinx*, whose terrifying effect Aristotle feels no need to explain. The use of the trunk, then, with all its sonic effect, transforms the voice of the elephant, but the transformation is inborn in the elephant; this vocal duality is in fact a constitutive ingredient of elephantness. To explain the noise of gnats and elephants in terms of the human artifice of vocal prosthesis is to underscore the hard work performed by humans, and humans alone, to sound just like ourselves and, in so doing, to make ourselves different selves.

Notes

I gratefully acknowledge the influence and inspiration of everyone involved in the Voice Project, generously sponsored by the Neubauer Collegium, and especially Martha Feldman, David Levin, and Judith Zeitlin for bringing it to life.

1. σάλπιγξ ὁ πρωκτός ἐστιν ἄρα τῶν ἐμπίδων (*Nu.* 165). A scholiast on this passage expands upon the analogy as a matter of shape, picking up on the student's prior description of Socrates's views on gnat-noise, with the upper part of the insect being "narrow" (στενή), and the lower part being "hollow" (κοίλη). Cf. Kenneth J. Dover, *Aristophanes: Clouds* (Oxford: Oxford University Press, 1970), 85, on how this passage may refer to the auditory theories of Alcmaeon. See also a similar sort of joke in the *Batrachomyomachia*: "and then mosquitoes, bearing great war-trumpets, trumpeted the terrible clash of war" (καὶ τότε κώνωπες μεγάλας σάλπιγγας ἔχοντες / δεινὸν ἐσάλπιγξαν πολέμου κτύπον [198–99]). This is more clearly a mockery of certain loud passages of war from the *Iliad*, which feature war-trumpets, as we will see below. Cf. Peter Krentz, "The *Salpinx* in Greek Battle," in *Hoplites: The Classical Greek Battle Experience*, ed. Victor Davis Hanson (London and New York: Routledge, 1991), 110–20; and Thomas J. Mathiesen, *Apollo's Lyre: Music and Music Theory in Antiquity and the Middle Ages* (Lincoln: University of Nebraska Press, 1999), 230–34, on our evidence for the physical construction of the *salpinx*, which was generally shaped from bronze.

2. In classical Greek, musical instruments are not often grouped as a general category (individual instruments are much more frequently mentioned), but to the extent that there is a bracketing term, it is *organon*—"*an organ, instrument, tool, for making* or *doing* a thing" (Liddell and Scott's *Greek-English Lexicon* [Oxford: Oxford University Press, 1999], 565). This term is used in many other ways as well (much like the word "instrument"), but its relation, or possible use, as part of an organic being, and indeed its afterlife into the English words "organic" and "organ," point to a more embodied mode of considering musical instruments than does our own term.

3. Tracey Warr, ed., *The Artist's Body* (London and New York: Phaidon, 2012), 178.

4. Mladen Dolar, *A Voice and Nothing More* (Cambridge, MA: MIT Press, 2006), 22.

5. Cf. Steven Connor, "Echo's Bones: Myth, Modernity, and the Vocalic Uncanny," in *Myth and the Making of Modernity: The Problem of Grounding in Early Twentieth-Century Literature*, ed. Michael Bell and Peter Poellner (Amsterdam and Atlanta, GA: Rodopi, 1998), 213–35; and Yoshiki Tajiri, *Samuel Beckett and the Prosthetic Body: The Organs and Senses in Modernism* (Basingstoke, Hampshire, and New York: Palgrave Macmillan, 2007), 139.

6. A point made by Aristotle, though he is naturally concerned about the prevention not of *phoné* but of *logos*: "*aulos*-playing prevents the use of *logos*" (τὸ κωλύειν τῷ λόγῳ χρῆσθαι τὴν αὔλησιν [*Politics* 1341a25]). Cf. Eric Csapo, "The Politics of the New Music," in *Music and the Muses: The Culture of Mousike in the Classical Athenian City*, ed. Penelope Murray and Peter Wilson (Oxford and New York: Oxford University Press, 2004), 217–18. Plutarch pointedly notes that the sound made through an *aulos* is as if "through another's tongue" (δι᾽ ἀλλοτρίας γλώττης), *Advice to Bride and Groom* (142 D).

7. The *aulos* was associated with New Music (particularly when not accompanying vocal performance) and viewed as a threat to the old guard of music and musicians (theoretically pitted against the more elegant *kithara*), as well as a potential political threat. It was also utterly ubiquitous in fifth-century Athens, the "instrumental motor driving dozens, if not hundreds, of choral performances in the city and countryside of Attike every year." Peter Wilson, "The *Aulos* in Athens," in *Performance Culture and Athenian Democracy*, ed. Simon Goldhill and Robin Osborne (Cambridge: Cambridge University Press, 1999), 58–95, 75. Cf. also Richard Martin, "The Pipes Are Brawling: Conceptualizing Musical Performance in Athens," in *The Cultures within Ancient Greek Culture: Contact, Conflict, Collaboration*, ed. Carol Dougherty and Leslie Kurke (Cambridge: Cambridge University Press, 2003), 153–80; Csapo, "The Politics of the New Music," 207–48; Deborah Steiner, "The Gorgons' Lament: Auletics, Poetics, and Chorality in Pindar's *Pythian* 12," *American Journal of Philology* 134, no. 2 (Summer 2013): 173–208; and Pauline LeVen, *The Many-Headed Muse: Tradition and Innovation in Late Classical Greek Lyric Poetry* (Cambridge: Cambridge University Press, 2014), 83–86 and 105–12. Plato crystallizes one side of the debate with his proscription of players and makers of *auloi* from the ideal city on the grounds that the *aulos* is the most "many-chorded" (πολυχορδότατον) of all instruments (πάντων ὀργάνων), which even the most "all-harmony-ed" (παναρμόνια) of stringed instruments imitate due to its multiplicity of voicing—to the detriment of all involved (*Republic* 399d–e).

8. This is the earliest version of this myth, found in Melanippides, Fr. 758, Denys Page, *Poetae melici Graeci*, (Oxford: Clarendon Press, 1962). Cf. Peter Wilson, "The *aulos* in Athens," 60–65.

9. LeVen, *Many-Headed Muse*, 110, suggests that "Athena's body is conspicuous by its absence," given the prevalence both of other "maidenly" bodies in the poem and the presumed ubiquity of the other tale of Athena and the *aulos* in Greek culture. Françoise Frontisi-Ducroux, "In the Mirror of the Mask," in *A City of Images: Iconography and Society in Ancient Greece*, ed. Claude Bérard, Christiane Bron, Jean-Louis Durand, Françoise Frontisi-Ducroux, François

Lissarrague, Alain Schnapp, and Jean-Pierre Vernant, trans. Deborah Lyons (Princeton, NJ: Princeton University Press, 1989), 151–65, argues that the horrible sight of the Gorgons and the purportedly maddening sound of the *aulos* always imply one another: "The mask of Gorgo, by its monstrosity, renders visible to humans the radical otherness of night, which blurs and mixes categories distinguished by the world of the living. The bestial mixes with the human. . . . To this horrifying vision is added an aural dimension emphasized by the literary texts. No articulate voice, however, issues from the gorgon's distended mouth. There are instead indistinct gurgles, the grinding of teeth, the gnashing of jaws, all dominated by the hissing of snakes. It was to imitate these piercing cries that Athena invented the flute [*aulos*]" (158–59).

10. *Iliad* 5.741. According to Socrates's joke in Plato's *Symposium* 198b, the Gorgoneion causes silence too, as he notes in his joke that a Gorgianeion (as in the orator Gorgias) will turn him to "stone" (λίθον) and render him "speechless" (τῇ ἀφωνίᾳ).

11. Cf. Charles Segal, *Aglaia: The Poetry of Alcman, Sappho, Pindar, Bacchylides, and Corinna* (Lanham, MD: Rowman & Littlefield, 1998), 85–104; and Martin, "The Pipes Are Brawling," 161–64.

12. Cf. Lawrence Zbikowski, "Music, Language, and What Falls in Between," *Ethnomusicology* 56, no. 1 (Winter 2012): 125–31: "Music, through providing sonic analogs for emotional and psychological processes, provides an ideal means of sharing attitudes and feelings among the members of a group; language can certainly do this as well . . . but without the immediacy and potential for corporeal engagement of music" (129).

13. Cf. Peter Wilson, "The *aulos* in Athens," 76, on the close association between tragedy and *aulos*-playing: "In Attic iconography, the presence of an 'official' *aulêtês* among tragic figures is one of the securest signs of a 'theatrical' context or connection. This testifies to his importance as the mediator between the world of tragedy and the ordinary world, and *visually* establishes him as the 'introducer of alterity.'"

14. Cf. Aristotle, *De Anima* 420b14–421a7, for a rather baroque description of the role of air in the production of voice. The origin of the word "larynx" itself is a mystery, but according to the *Suda* (132), it was sometimes interchanged with the word "pharynx" to denote the whole throat. As in English, the word "throat" could be used metonymically to mean "neck," and at times had little to do with the production of voice (e.g., Aristophanes, *Knights* 1363). Cf. Steven Connor, *Beyond Words: Sobs, Hums, Stutters, and Other Vocalizations* (London: Reaktion Books, 2014), 35–36, for some inspired comments on the implications of thinking of voice as breathed.

15. Also, for example, Aristophanes, *Frogs* 154; and Euripides, *Bacchae* 128.

16. Martin West, *Ancient Greek Music* (Oxford and New York: Clarendon Press, 1992), 81–109, emphasizes that a player of pipes does not merely blow, but must "set . . . up vibrations in air that is enclosed in a pipe or pipes," so it is not simply the presence of breath/air that is critical but the vibrating envelope through which the air must pass. Ps.-Aristotle, *De Audibilibus* 803b19, 804a9, on the audio effects of different quantities of breath in the *aulos*, makes clear that the breath used in the activity was considered (cf. Steiner, "Gorgons' Lament," 192, on these passages), but actual Aristotle makes it clear that it is not "voice" (*phoné*) emitted by an *aulos*, except in the realm of analogy, or "likeness" (καθ᾽ ὁμοιότητα), since things "without souls" (ἀψύχων) cannot produce voice. Martin, "The Pipes Are Brawling," 167, theorizes that the *aulos* is actually viewed by some ancient artists as "inhuman," meaning animalistic.

17. Cf. Peter Green, "Possession and Pneuma: The Essential Nature of the Delphic Oracle," *Arion*, Third Series 17, no. 2 (Fall 2009): 27–47, for more detail on the sources of this idea.

18. Adriana Cavarero, *For More Than One Voice: Toward a Philosophy of Vocal Expression*, trans. Paul A. Kottman (Stanford, CA: Stanford University Press, 2005), 20. Steven Connor,

Dumbstruck: A Cultural History of Ventriloquism (Oxford and New York: Oxford University Press, 2000), 49–59, takes the Delphic oracle as an early locus of meaningful ventriloquism: "[t]he association between prophecy and ventriloquism at Delphi arises out of the new fascination with the nature of the physical process whereby the god spoke in the priestess" (51). Connor looks at the role of the earth, breath, and frenzy in his account.

19. In the case of the *shofar*, the female is the mother of Sisera, who is imagined as crying when her brutal son, enemy of Israel, is finally killed (*Judges* 5.28–30). Sol Finesinger, "The Shofar," *Hebrew Union College Annual* 8/9 (1931–1932): 193–228, argues that there is an inherent ambiguity in the intended sonic effect of the *shofar*: it expresses an entreaty to God but also has an apotropaic function directed toward Satan. It is also used in the Bible to announce the inauguration of a king, as a signal to start or stop a battle, to call people to assemble, and so on. It thus shares certain qualities with the *salpinx*, as well as with the *aulos*. Cf. David Wulstan, "The Sounding of the Shofar," *Galpin Society Journal* 26 (May 1973): 29–46.

20. For example, Plato's Socrates suggests that the Muse invests poets with divine inspiration as a magnet lends attraction to stones (*Ion* 533e).

21. The army is compared here to a forest fire, geese and cranes, leaves and flowers in spring, insects swarming over milk, goats and their herders, and finally gives way to a simile in which Agamemnon, their leader, is compared to Zeus, Ares, and Poseidon, and an ox among lesser cattle (*Il.* 2.455–83).

22. Andrew Ford, *Homer: The Poetry of the Past* (Ithaca, NY: Cornell University Press, 1992), 174, reads the poet's disavowal of such a solid voice and heart as a cry of freedom "figured in the poems as a liquidity of voice, against which is set the fixity and solidity of things made." I see here also an acknowledgment of the passing, the inevitable loss, of such a voice.

23. The lack of "creation myth" for the trumpet is explored by John Ziolkowski, "The Invention of the Tuba (Trumpet)," *Classical World* 92, no. 4 (1999): 367–73, who concludes that the instrument's association with death, by way of its use in war and at funerals, discouraged poets from framing a myth. This does not strike me as a convincing explanation, given the willingness of Greek poets to explore death and death-related phenomena in many contexts. I would tend to think that the *salpinx* lacks an origin story in part because it is not conceived of as strictly *musical*, so much as sonic, much as it is not thought of as being played so much as heard. Martin West, *Ancient Greek Music*, 118, demarcates it as nonmusical; and Gullog Nordquist, "The Salpinx in Greek Cult," in *Dance, Music, Art, and Religion*, ed. Tore Ahlbäck (Stockholm: Almquist & Wiksell International, 1996), 241–56, 242, explores the physical limitations of its form that would also have kept it from offering much in the way of melodic variation.

24. Cf. Krentz, "The *Salpinx* in Greek Battle," 110, on how the *salpinx* was able to "overcome both aural and visual obstacles."

25. For example, one battle scene begins with the cry of Strife (Eris), "great, terrible and shrill" (μέγα τε δεινόν τέ / ὄρθι [*Il.* 11.10–11]), which "puts strength into the hearts of the Achaeans" (11–12) and leads quickly to the war cry of Agamemnon (15). Next comes his arming with, among other things, a shield covered with the face of the terrifying Gorgon (36–37), terrifying in face *and* voice, as we know, and finally a god-sponsored crash of thunder around him (45) that signals his power to wreak destruction on his foes. Not all war cries are created equal, however: in one case, the Trojans rush to war clamoring like fowl, while the Achaeans approach in dignified silence (*Il.* 3.1–9). Cf. Sean Gurd, *Dissonance: Auditory Aesthetics in Ancient Greece* (New York: Fordham University Press, 2016), 27–32, on sounds, war, and destruction in the *Iliad*. Voice can also play a different role in war, as in Herodotus 8.65, where a disembodied and sourceless

voice (φωνῆς) indicates what direction the battle will take, with its true meaning (the Iacchus cry) only heard and understood by the right listener.

26. Cf. Paul Friedrich and James Redfield, "Speech as a Personality Symbol: The Case of Achilles," *Language* 54, no. 2 (June 1978): 263–88; Richard Martin, *The Language of Heroes: Speech and Performance in the Iliad* (Ithaca, NY: Cornell University Press, 1989); and Sarah Nooter, *When Heroes Sing: Sophocles and the Shifting Soundscape of Tragedy* (Cambridge: Cambridge University Press, 2012), 22–24. Yet these works all discuss Achilles's patterns of speech more than his actual voice.

27. Cf. Anastasia Serghidou, "Athena *Salpinx* and the Ethics of Music," in *Athena in the Classical World*, ed. Susan Deacy and Alexandra Villing (Leiden, Boston, and Köln: Brill, 2001), 57–74, who sees Athena's preference for the *salpinx* over the *aulos* as being connected to her affiliations with both war and the *polis*. She comments also on the lines quoted from *Ajax*, noting that the sound of Athena persists although the goddess herself "remains invisible and distant," 67. In this sense too, the sound of the trumpet is once again imagined in terms that do not conjure the physical presence of a trumpet player.

28. Cf. *Anabasis* 3.4.4, 4.2.7, 5.2.14, 6.5.27, and 7.4.16.

29. This is described as the "noise of the Persian tongue" (Περσίδος γλώσσης ῥόθος [*Pers.* 406]).

30. Cf. the scholiast on 566 and Rory Egan, "The Assonance of Athena and the Sound of the Salpinx: *Eumenides* 566–71," *Classical Journal* 74, no. 3 (February–March 1979): 203–12, at 211. The *salpinx* was also used in athletic competitions and contests, funerals and cultic activities, on which see Nordquist, "The Salpinx in Greek Cult."

31. Anastasia Serghidou, "Athena *Salpinx*," 68, notes that "the trumpet, unlike other musical instruments, is endowed with the specific skills of the herald." She sees this herald-like skill as allowing the trumpet, unlike the *aulos*, the authority to enter political space. She views the comparison as rooted in the *practice* of using the trumpet to send signals in the way of a herald, a use to which the *aulos* (for example) was never put. This derivation, again, relates most basically to the capability of the instrument to be inhumanly loud.

32. πληρουμένου γὰρ τοῦδε βουλευτηρίου (*Pers.* 580).

33. Cf. Rory Egan, "The Assonance of Athena," 207–8; and Walter Porzig, *Aischylos: Die attische Tragödie* (Leipzig: E. Wiegandt, 1926), 85, on this passage. This is not the only place where Athena is clearly using soundplay to reinforce the content of her words. The line "calm the bitter passion of the black breaker" (κοίμα κελαινοῦ κύματος πικρὸν μένος [832]), spoken as she tries to soothe the Erinyes's anger later, is an instance of emphatic alliteration, presumably here to create a calming effect.

34. Cf. Aristotle, *De Anima* 420b6, 420b32, 420b14–421a7, and 420b32–33. These requirements accrue to the fact that "voice is a sound with meaning" (σημαντικὸς γὰρ δή τις ψόφος ἐστὶν ἡ φωνή [420b33]), a statement which points back toward *logos*.

35. *Historia Animalium* 535a27–536b23.

36. John Markoff, "Creating a Computer Voice That People Like," *New York Times*, February 14, 2016.

37. ὁ δ' ἐλέφας φωνεῖ ἄνευ μὲν τοῦ μυκτῆρος αὐτῷ τῷ στόματι πνευματῶδες ὥσπερ ὅταν ἄνθρωπος ἐκπνέῃ καὶ αἰάζῃ, μετὰ δὲ τοῦ μυκτῆρος ὅμοιον σάλπιγγι τετραχυσμένῃ (Aristotle, *Historia Animalium* 536b20–23).

38. As Sophocles's Ajax says: "*Aiai* [αἰαῖ]: who would have ever thought the name I was named would so agree with my troubles? For now it is time for me to cry *aiai* [αἰάζειν] even twice, and a third time" (*Ajax* 430–33). Cf. Sarah Nooter, *When Heroes Sing*, 40–41, on these lines.

14

The Duppy in the Machine: Voice and Technology in Jamaican Popular Music

ANDREW F. JONES

In April 2014, after the longest and most closely watched jury trial in Jamaican history, the dancehall star Vybz Kartel was convicted of murder and sentenced to thirty-five years of hard labor. The drama of Vybz Kartel's rise and fall continues to polarize Jamaican society. Vybz Kartel has been widely excoriated as a musical proponent of sexually explicit "slackness," gangsterism, and gun violence. Vybz Kartel has constructed over a number of years a persona exquisitely calibrated to jab at the island's sorest social contradictions, while also unabashedly generating attention and revenue for his own brand. He has offended the established Church with his open questioning of organized religion, and is perceived to have profaned Garveyite principles of Black pride with his controversial embrace of skin bleaching and tattoos. At the same time, his fierce condemnations of the Jamaican political order have earned him a series of adulatory epithets: born Adidja Palmer, he is apostrophized as "Adi the Teacher" and celebrated as the "Worl' Boss," presiding over his ghetto community in the Kingston suburb of Portmore—a neighborhood pointedly referred to as "Gaza." My point of departure for this paper, however, is his self-styled role as *The Voice of the Jamaican Ghetto*—as the title of his 2012 prison memoir would have it.[1]

This rhetorical claim to political representation, predicated on the singularity of a "voice," even as it ventriloquizes the speech of a silent multitude, seems familiar, almost self-evident. Vybz Kartel, of course, is far from the only one to have claimed this sort of equivalency, or to have laid claim to the power and legitimacy it offers. Yet what does it mean when the "voice" in question—the voice manifested in the musical practice of Vybz Kartel as well as many other artists—is itself the product of a complex series of technological mediations? The voice of Vybz Kartel—as even a casual listen to his recorded output will attest—is anything but singular, far from "organic," and lays no claim to an unretouched authenticity. It is invariably and unmistakably digitally processed. To an extent arguably unheard of even in R&B and hip-hop in the United States, dancehall has for the past decade been saturated by the "distorted," "robotic," and patently processed vocal timbres produced by the creative misuse of the software plug-in Auto-Tune.

The widespread use of such digital manipulation has often been lamented as a marker of dancehall's ethical and aesthetic degeneracy with respect to the golden era of conscious roots reggae and dub music of the 1960s and 1970s. This is a false dichotomy, one that gives short shrift to the continuities that bind the two eras together. Principal among these continuities is precisely the use of electronics as a sonic attraction, foregrounding the technical virtuosity with which artists, sound systems, and studio engineers create novel timbral effects and forms of bodily and affective experience. Much of the attraction, moreover, lies in the *semantic* power of timbre, for these effects speak to and embody the dialectic of black working-class dispossession and liberation that has been central to Jamaican popular music since the 1960s. Whether in the now-classic work of the reggae artist Burning Spear or the dancehall anthems of Vybz Kartel, the electronic mediation of the voice enables new forms of mediumship, opening channels through which other voices, be they ghostly revenants (or "duppies") from the days of slavery, or dehumanized ghetto people in the neoliberal present, demand to be heard. These voices—attenuated by high-pass filters, floating disembodied across the stereo soundstage, drenched in reverb and delay, or defamiliarized by pitch-correction software—haunt the perpetual present of the recorded musical artifact.

Let me rewind a bit and situate these claims in the social and technical history of the voice in Jamaican popular music. The music that began to emerge from the ghettos of Kingston in the immediate and exuberant wake of independence from the United Kingdom in 1962 manifested, from the very start, an insistent interest in the voice as a marker of working-class tribulation and postcolonial aspiration. This music, known as ska, was inspired by jazz, doo-wop, rhythm and blues, and soul records, imported by Jamaican migrant laborers to be played by deejays at dance parties, or picked up on the AM band from 50,000-watt transmitters broadcasting from as far away as New Orleans and Nashville.[2] Aspiring musicians, many recently arrived in Kingston from the countryside, enamored of groups like the Moonglows, the Drifters, and the Impressions, and lacking the resources to purchase musical instruments or studio time, adopted the vocal trio as a format. The concrete gullies running from the surrounding hills down to Kingston harbor proved to be suitably resonant spaces in which to practice new tunes, which might in turn be pitched to record producers like Coxsone Dodd of Studio One. Bob Marley's first harmony trio, formed in the slums of Trenchtown in 1963, were the Wailers, and their first long-playing record for Studio One in 1965 was titled "The Wailing Wailers." This adjectival reduplication speaks to the way in which the project was predicated on the affective resonance generated by particular vocal timbres, by voices that keen, moan, groan, weep, or wail in response to poverty and "sufferation."

Even more crucial was the auditory medium through which these voices, more often than not, resonated. The Jamaican sound system—portable assemblages of audio equipment set up to play records for outdoor dance parties—has shaped the aesthetics not only of reggae, but also of subsequent popular genres from hip-hop to electronic dance music. As Julian Henriques puts it, sound systems since the late 1950s have served as "sonic war machines, vehicles for cultural expression, vessels for identity and pleasure, economic engines, commercial ventures, instruments for musical production, institutions for artist's training, multimedia communication systems, test-beds for technological innovation . . . [and] laboratories for sonic science."[3] Operating within the violently contentious territory of the garrison communities of West Kingston, or touring the Jamaican countryside, the competition between rival "sounds" (as they are colloquially referred to) not only generated ritualized "sound clashes" between operators, but also led to the improvisatory invention of vernacular audio technologies. As early as 1947, self-taught audio engineer Hedley Jones, using hand-wound transformers and a proprietary pre-amplifier circuit, had cobbled together a sound system for a dance promoter named Tom Wong (aka Tom the Great Sebastian), consisting of homemade "bass reflex baffles, mid-range speakers, and high range tweeters," replacing an old RCA public address system incapable of delivering adequate frequency response.[4] Jones's innovations triggered a kind of arms race over the following two decades, as local engineers vied to construct and aggregate ever more massive stacks of homemade speaker boxes, driven by powerful hand-built amplifiers. These systems were designed with the aim of propagating bass-heavy music with such authority that what Henriques calls a physically immersive "sonic dominance" could be established, not only over competing sounds, but over the bodies of the dancers as well.[5]

This "dancehall space" (as it is now colloquially known) also shaped the Jamaican record industry and drove its hugely influential innovations in studio craft. The music began to reach toward frequency extremes unheard of in Anglo-American popular music. These lower lows and higher highs were the result of a kind of audio bricolage. Sylvan Morris, a recording engineer at Studio One, for instance, took to various creative misuses of his equipment to cater to the sound systems' voracious appetite for new sounds. He experimented with tape delay to generate cavernous echoes, and recorded electric bass by cutting holes in the back of a speaker cabinet, and placing two microphones directly inside the enclosure to derive ever more cavernous low-frequency reverberations. When one of the ribbon microphones in the studio broke, he fashioned a new ribbon from the silver tabs at the end of a reel of two-track tape reels that would selectively pick up lower frequencies, yielding an even "rounder bass."[6]

Perhaps the most crucial innovation, however, came as Jamaican studio engineers took to cutting exclusive "dubplate" versions of popular songs with the vocal tracks removed. Dubplates facilitated not only dancing, but also the chatting of dancehall deejays over the underlying bass and drum patterns. Dub is in this sense a radical deconstruction of popular musical protocol, eliminating the lead singer (and often vocal harmonies as well), precisely in order to open up a space for other voices. If dub versions sound spacy, this is in large part because they evacuate the midrange, often dispensing even with the propulsive interlocking rhythm guitar and electric piano parts that typify reggae as a genre. Dub pulls apart the frequency band, accentuating its extremes, and opening up an expansive aural space between the hi-hats and rimshots of the drum kit and the low rumble of the kick drum and electric bass. This audio space caters to the physical and technical specifications of the sound system, in which, in the words of music critic Klive Walker, "woofers pushed out bass thunder with such benevolent force that the zinc sheets fencing the perimeter of the large outdoor dancehall would hum . . . [while] steel horns—sometimes perched high in the branches of trees—produced piercing treble sounds . . . in counterpoint to the rich baritone offered by the speaker boxes."[7] The sense of a spatial enclosure was further emphasized by the use of two or sometimes three separate stacks of speakers, allowing for sound effects and vocals to swoop from channel to channel in a circle around the assembled dancers. By the late 1970s, these stacks were piled in pyramid-like configurations rising up to twenty feet tall, with bass-reflex boxes at the bottom, followed by low and high midrange units, and tweeters and super-tweeters on top. Such speaker arrays also necessitated the invention of proprietary crossover circuits to split the frequency band and route the audio signal through to the correct speaker driver, and thus, as the parlance goes, "voice" the system as a whole.[8]

As Michael Veal has convincingly argued, pioneering studio engineers like Morris, King Tubby, and Lee Perry had by the mid-1970s transformed dub plate versions into an improvisatory yet exacting vernacular modernist practice, appropriating and reconfiguring outdated and rudimentary studio equipment so as to develop an aesthetic in which pop song structures were shattered, replaced by evanescent, evocative, and abstract soundscapes.[9] The efflorescence of dub as a genre unto itself—with its ever more self-conscious experimentation with echo, reverb, and delay units, idiosyncratic and extreme equalization effects at both ends of the frequency spectrum, and hard pans across the soundstage—coincided with the emergence of a "conscious" reggae dedicated to anticolonial critique, historical self-representation, and Rastafarian spiritual ideals. And it is in this context that electronic crossover circuits also became a ritual space for the evocation of the Middle Passage and the lingering echoes of the days of slavery in the postcolonial era.

The work of Burning Spear—born Winston Rodney in 1948 in Marcus Garvey's hometown of St. Ann's Bay, Jamaica—embodies this form of mediumship. Renowned since the early 1970s for his advocacy of Garvey's Pan-Africanist vision, as well as for the oracular power of his live performances, Spear began his recording career fronting a vocal harmony trio at Studio One at a time when both his open avowal of his Rastafarian faith and his approach to vocal production were still seen as highly unorthodox. His second long-player for Studio One, "Rocking Time," featured a song entitled "Weeping and Wailing," and his approach to vocal production was of a piece with the title. Klive Walker has written that Spear's voice, with its "hollow emotional rasp" and "moaning scat improvisations," sounds "like an ancient cry channeling the spirits of African-Jamaican freedom fighters."[10] Walker further suggests that "Burning Spear has a chasm in his voice," a chasm through which these spirits travel.[11] That chasm may not be so much an inherent property of Spear's tenor as a product of the breach between the low bass and high treble characteristic of the genre.

At the same time, as Walker implies, Burning Spear's work draws self-consciously on Jamaican folk religion and its rituals of spirit possession. Revivalist practices such as Pocomania (also referred to as Pukkumina or Poko), Kumina, and Zion, dating back to at least the mid-nineteenth century, centered around the musical invocation of powerful "myal" spirits through hypnotic and communal acts of drumming, dancing, foot-stamping, rhythmic chants, groans, and heavy breathing, referred to as "laboring." With the mass migration of country folk to the capital in the 1960s, these largely rural traditions also came to inform everyday life in the residential yards and shantytowns of West Kingston, with revivalist "sessions" resonating alongside sound systems and record shacks advertising their wares.[12] The early Rastafarian congregations of East Kingston, moreover, had long since adopted African-derived *burru* drumming and the "country" kumina chants of neighboring St. Thomas parish into their devotional repertoire.

By 1975, when Burning Spear left Studio One to pursue an independent path as a producer in partnership with the Ocho Rios sound-system operator Jack Ruby, these revivalist residuals were incorporated into an explicitly Garveyite project of racial and historical consciousness-raising.[13] Anchored by the Poko-inflected pulse of Leroy "Horsemouth" Wallace's drum kit, songs like "Marcus Garvey" (originally recorded as an exclusive for Ruby's Hi-Power sound system) and "Slavery Days" quickly won Burning Spear island-wide fame, and a recording contract with the Jamaican entrepreneur Chris Blackwell's London-based Island Records.[14]

As Nadia Ellis has written in an insightful analysis of the classic 1976 album *Marcus Garvey*, Burning Spear's vocal performance takes him "inside and out of several subject positions," as he alternatively inhabits the role of a heraldic scribe, of the suffering masses, and of Marcus Garvey himself ministering to his flock.[15] To inhabit these roles is also to be inhabited, as Spear himself has suggested in speaking of his own compositional process: "The man just show himself to I through the music and the vibration and the vibes, but you know, physically, him don't show himself. So, I myself don't even know who is the man . . . But, the man speak I through the music, and I sing the lyrics what him speak I . . ."[16]

In Burning Spear's "Slavery Days," this collapse of the boundaries between subject positions is also a temporal collapse, initiated by a haunting refrain—"Do you remember the days of slavery . . . And they beat us . . . And they work us so hard . . . And they use us . . . until they refuse us"—that insists that we inhabit the laboring, terrorized bodies of the enslaved in the present tense, even as they continue to inhabit us. "Possession," as Ellis puts it, "becomes the sign and the redress for historical dispossession" (**web. ex. 14.1**).[17]

Burning Spear's 1979 dub "Children of Today" is similarly haunted by the sufferation of spirits whose voices continue to reverberate in the present.[18] The original seven-inch single from which this dub was versioned is titled "The Whole a We Suffer," invoking the commonality not only of black people "today," but also linking the plight of the living with that of the dead. "The Whole a We Suffer" is also the first-person plural refrain that threads the song together. Midway through the song, Burning Spear directly apostrophizes the prophet, "Marcus Garvey say," and with this ritual preliminary achieved, assumes Garvey's persona. Yet in the dub version, the lead vocal is almost entirely missing, and all that remains is an invocation of the prophet's name, subject to electronic delay so that it shimmers and then shudders to a stop, surrounded by the wrenching, wretched howls and cries of those who have and will continue to suffer. The spectral quality of those voices is, of course, a deliberate effect, secured not only by their placement toward the back of the mix, but their seemingly disembodied diffusion across the soundstage. More important, their spectrality is a product of the electronic recalibration of the frequency spectrum, for in channeling the human voice through high-pass filters that block out the low end of the audio waveband, the studio engineer Sylvan Morris has subtly transformed living voices into shades.[19] The liberal use of delay—applied not only to voices but also to the drum kit and the heraldic blasts of the horn section—also functions as a searingly self-reflexive historical commentary. Sonic fragments skitter at different tempi across the underlying beat, their echoes and repetitions and attenuations mimicking the fearsome loops yoking Burning Spear to his ancestors, and postindependence Jamaica to its colonial past (**web. ex. 14.2**).

I want now to circle back around to Vybz Kartel and the contemporary Jamaican "dancehall space." While some of the invective directed at figures like Kartel has to do with their failure to hew to and honor historical memory, I want to suggest that it may be precisely in their creative "misuse" of pitch-correction software like Auto-Tune that their music continues to speak to questions of possession and dispossession in Jamaica's current sociopolitical dispensation. Auto-Tune—originally developed by an Exxon engineer named Andy Hildebrand who realized that algorithms used for sonically mapping subterranean topographies could be repurposed as a pitch-correction device for digital recordings—is widely reviled for its inauthenticity, but for all that has become an indispensable element of contemporary popular music production. By the late 1990s, engineers had already discovered that by adjusting the program's "retune speed" setting to zero (as opposed to say 20 to 50 milliseconds), the rapidity of the resultant pitch modulation created an unusual effect, as vibrato (natural, continuous variation on a given pitch) and portamento (the glide from pitch to pitch) are completely eliminated. Sometimes dubbed the "Cher effect," because of its conspicuous use in her 1998 smash "Believe," the resultant vocal timbre leaves a distinctly robotic impression. In this respect, Auto-Tune picks up where the vocoder, an analog device popularized by the German quartet Kraftwerk on their 1978 album *The Man-Machine*, left off.[20] It also occupies similar semantic territory at the fraught border between the organic and the prosthetic, the human and the not-quite human, and between self-possession and dispossession. Indeed, the lyrics of Kraftwerk's initial foray into vocoder technology self-consciously mined the critical potential of this ambiguity, riffing on the etymological link between the Czech "robota" (meaning slave or forced laborer) and robot.

In Jamaican dancehall, as in US R&B and hip-hop acts, Auto-Tune has been pressed into service in ways that the inventor of the algorithm certainly could not have anticipated.[21] The effect was initially marshaled as a sonic attraction, calling attention to technical apparatus behind the production of popular music, rather than smoothing it over by way of unobtrusive correction of vocal faults, as was originally intended. In the work of US artists like Kanye West and T-Pain, its timbral effects have famously been used to craft hooks, fashion a unique sonic signature, and project a sense of alienation and dysphoria.[22] And because the program allows for the precise and even real-time manipulation of practically any sonic parameter, from pitch to tempo to vibrato to timbre, it has also become a kind of second-order "instrument" for playing the voice.

In the competitive environment of the Jamaican dancehall, this sort of experimentation has been especially unhinged from traditional pop musical structures, producing an almost unprecedentedly elastic sense of the human voice and its possibilities.[23] The dancehall deejay Beenie Man is said to have been among the first dancehall artists to adopt the technology, utilizing Auto-Tune's characteristically flat-lined timbre as a kind of sonic tagline punctuating the refrain of his 2004 single "Dude." More than a decade later, pitch-correction software is close to ubiquitous in Jamaica, utilized not just as an added frisson or fleeting effect, but as an integral component of melodic and rhythmic architecture of the music. In the work of Vybz Kartel, as well as the younger cohort of performers such as Popcaan and Alkaline, Auto-Tune-less voices are the rare exception to the rule, and the technology is used to create a panoply of novel effects. Voices warble as they toggle helplessly between semitones, leap cartoonishly across several octaves only to plunge back down again, abruptly accelerate or decelerate in front of or behind the beat, or, chameleon-like, take on the coloration and pulse of an underlying rhythm track.

The playfulness and plasticity of recent dancehall vocal tracks seem to speak to larger questions of how a globalized neoliberal economy is experienced on the margins of that system. In Jamaica, as elsewhere, labor markets have become increasingly precarious. High rates of unemployment and governmental retreat from the public sector, prompted by foreign debt in excess of 140 percent of GDP, have compelled substantial portions of the population to cobble together a living as flexible "urban improvisers" in the informal economy.[24] The formal economy is increasingly reliant on the service sector, representing some 70 percent of GDP, in which employees are called upon to retool and reinvent themselves in tune with the rapidly shifting demands of a globalized market and the increasing importance of affective, rather than manual, labor. Thirty percent of GDP is associated with the tourism sector; and customer service call centers and BPO (business process outsourcing) for North American clients are among the very few growth industries.[25] In contrast to the collectivist ethos of Michael Manley's "democratic socialism" of the 1970s, an aspirational cultural style, celebrating fluid, shape-shifting identities, entrepreneurship, fierce competition, and conspicuous consumption, has flourished in the dancehall in recent decades. This style echoes in some respects what Sianne Ngai has called the "zany": an aesthetic "highlighting the affect, libido, and physicality of an unusually beset agent" whose "strenuous relation to playing seems to be on a deeper level about work."[26] Of course, dancehall's "strenuous relation to playing," with its competitive barbs and factional rivalries, sometimes plays out in a deadly serious manner, given its origins in communities beset not just by the escalating demands of the post-Fordist economy, but also by gangs and gunplay. On the aggressive "diss" tracks that inflame sonic "clashes" between rival deejays and their fan bases, Auto-Tune often is used as a kind of sonic armor, a hardened timbral sheath rendering the voice of the performer invulnerable to attack. Yet it is also in moments of Auto-Tune-assisted levity, when the voices of performers fly improbably free of limitations, urging dancers ever upward, that this aesthetic stages a momentary mutiny against the forces of socioeconomic gravity.

Vybz Kartel's stage name, of course, knowingly conflates organized crime and the retailing of affect so central to both tourism and the music industry. His songs provide listeners with a variety of personae and possibilities, from the rhetorical hyperviolence of his thug tunes to the hypermasculinity of his paeans to sexual pleasure.[27] Given the Protean nature of those personae, it should not come as a surprise that he is also able to seamlessly morph from playing the remorseless "bad man" to "Adi the Teacher," mobilizing "conscious" lyrics to the task of ministering to the political and economic misery of his ghetto constituency.

As I suggested at the outset, this form of musical labor involves taking possession of the voices of ghetto people, and in turn, being possessed by them. Kartel's own description of live performance suggests something of the ritual nature of such occasions: "More time when mi deh pon stage an do mi girl or thugs tune, I can barely hear myself because the crowd goes into a frenzy. The girls get wild and di man dem bawl 'fawud' [Forward!]. When I sing a conscious song . . . dem ah feel di ting to dem heart . . . the entire crowd sings with me, with their eyes closed and their hands pointing to the sky . . . like a mini-prayer."[28]

Kartel's reflection on the "Life We Living," from his 2010 *Pon di Gaza 2.0* album, is one such prayer, and as with the music of Burning Spear relies on the electronically altered vocal timbre for its affective and semantic impact:

[Spoken]
Jamaica, we need a way

[Sung]
Tell mi, how mi youth fi survive
How me fi send him to school in dis time
If mi don't mek money
Di politician come pon TV
A show we dis big pretty smile
Nothing nuh funny

[Refrain]
Look pon di life we living
Is a better way we seeking

Mi haffi hide from the landlord
Becah mi owe bout four months rent
Weekend a come mi nuh have a red cent
Cry mi cry when mi hear mi son she
Daddy can you please buy mi a Nike Air
And di likkle money weh mi have done spend
Di last grand mi have mi pay di light
but Water Commission cut mi pipe again

Di garrison need a betta way
And a betta life (fi we pickney dem)
Society, please don't condemn di ghetto to hell
Just look pon di life we living
Is a better way we seeking

Nothing nah gwaan
Ghetto youth haffi sit down pon di corner
Some a we a hustle
Some a beg chump change
Society please mek dis betta days
Mi go fi buy a bagga frass but cigarette raise
All we a cry dem a give we deaf ears
Then if di times so hard right now
what ago gwaan inna dis country in another ten years

Look pon di life we living
Is a better way we seeking

As in the earlier examples from Burning Spear, the song's rhetoric is built around apostrophe and the subsequent assumption of a persona. This is a crucial point of inflection. Kartel begins the song unaccompanied, addressing his constituency directly, in a resonant yet natural spoken voice, his proper voice: "Jamaica, we need a way out." Yet as soon as the song proper begins, the spoken voice is possessed by the voice of the ghetto sufferer and supplicant, asking not to be relegated to an inhuman existence. That very inhumanity, and the inhuman refusal of "Society" to see or lend an ear to "all we a cry," is allegorized by the haunting otherness of the wailing, distorted vocal timbre that prevails for the rest of the recording. Auto-Tune is vital to not only the musical phrasing, but also the ideological and ritual structure of the song, for with each repetition of the last word of the refrain, "Look pon the life we *living*," the sustained plateauing of the pitch acts as a kind of italicization, slanting forward across the beat, and casting us down into an uncanny valley in which it seems difficult to distinguish between the human and the drone, the living and the dead (**web. ex. 14.3**).

In the wake of Vybz Kartel's murder conviction, the prominent dancehall scholar and *Jamaica Daily Gleaner* columnist Carolyn Cooper editorialized that Jamaican society had "perversely refuse[d] to concede the possibility that 'Vybz Kartel' is a persona, a mask worn by an actor to project a fabricated character."[29] Had jurors, she wondered aloud, also failed to distinguish between the man and the mask, so that the association of Adidja Palmer with Vybz Kartel's gun-toting gangster persona proved prejudicial in his conviction? The answer to Cooper's question is imponderable. What is perhaps more interesting is that this split identity—and its production of a politically resonant "Voice of the Jamaican Ghetto"—was in large part a technologically mediated timbral effect. The rap against Auto-Tune, from its inception, has been its inauthenticity. In pitch-correcting wayward notes, eliminating human error, and papering over those precarious moments in which the voice shows itself to be most prone to limitation and failure, Auto-Tune prevaricates, confusing the genuine for the counterfeit, the human with the machine. That confusion can bring a dangerous blurring of boundaries, or even the sort of conflation Cooper cautions against. But recording technologies, whether in the digital present or the analog past, also afford new artistic and political potentialities, as otherworldly vocal timbres allow us a medium to imagine, if only for a moment, that we can hear the voices of the vulnerable, the silenced, and the dead.

Notes

1. See Adidja Palmer and Michael Dawson, *The Voice of the Jamaican Ghetto* (Kingston: Ghetto People Publishing, 2012).

2. For the early history of reggae, see Lloyd Bradley, *Bass Culture: When Reggae Was King* (London: Penguin Books, 2001). For the role of American records and radio, see Timothy White, *Catch a Fire: The Life of Bob Marley* (New York: Henry Holt, 2000), 17–18.

3. Julian Henriques, *Sonic Bodies: Reggae Sound Systems, Performance Techniques, and Ways of Knowing* (New York: Continuum, 2011), 3.

4. See Hedley Jones, "The Jones High Fidelity Power Amplifier of 1947," *Caribbean Quarterly* 56, no. 4 (December 2010): 105.

5. Henriques, *Sonic Bodies*, 85.

6. See David Katz, *Solid Foundation: An Oral History of Reggae* (New York: Bloomsbury, 2003), 121.

7. Klive Walker, *Dubwise: Reasoning from the Reggae Underground* (Toronto: Insomniac Press, 2005), 120–21.

8. See Henriques, *Sonic Bodies*, 68–87.

9. See Michael E. Veal, *Dub: Soundscapes and Shattered Songs in Jamaican Reggae* (Middletown, CT: Wesleyan University Press, 2007), 38–42. Veal argues convincingly that dub needs to be considered as experimental and avant-garde alongside canonical classical composers such as Karlheinz Stockhausen or Pierre Schaeffer. Indeed, I would argue, following Miriam Hansen, that dub, in transforming the limits of the audible by locally repurposing and re-inflecting recording practices from the metropole, represents a form of "vernacular modernism." See Miriam Hansen, "The Mass Production of the Senses: Classical Cinema as Vernacular Modernism," in *Modernism/Modernity* 6, no. 2 (1999): 59–77.

10. Walker, *Dubwise*, 225.

11. Walker, *Dubwise*, 275.

12. See Clinton Hutton and Garth White, "The Social and Aesthetic Roots and Identity of Ska," *Caribbean Quarterly* 53, no. 4 (December 2007): 81.

13. The impact of this intervention into a mainstream culture still very much informed by colonial pedagogy and the disavowal of Africanisms was immediate and palpable. As writer and sociologist Erna Brodber recalled of that period: "Burning Spear . . . was singing through the amplifiers of the record shops in tones similar to Bambi's: 'Do you remember the days of slavery?' 'Do you remember the days of slavery?' It was as if a river of sentiment that had been running underground for decades had suddenly surfaced. I and my kind of Afro-Jamaican knew only the silence of that sentimental river. Nowhere in elementary school, in high school or in university had I and my agemates in the scribal tradition seen or heard that river. We were glad to hear this new sound. It relaxed us. We took off our make up; we washed our hair and left it natural; we took off our jackets and ties and made ourselves comfortable in our shirt jacks. And we understood at a personal level that for us Black Jamaicans, there were two orientations: a mulatto-orientation and an Afro-orientation, the latter having been submerged in our consciousness. The persistent reggae beat—and the lyrics it carried—was partly responsible for awakening this consciousness." See Erna Brodber, "Black Consciousness and Popular Music in Jamaica in the 1960s and 1970s," *Caribbean Quarterly* 31, no. 2 (June 1985): 54.

14. For Leroy "Horsemouth" Wallace's background in pocomania, see Katz, *Solid Foundation*, 156.

15. See Nadia Ellis, *Territories of the Soul: Queered Belonging in the Black Diaspora* (Durham, NC: Duke University Press, 2015), 156.

16. See Carter Van Pelt, "Burning Spear: African Teacher," at http://incolor.inetnebr.com/cvanpelt/spear.html, accessed July 1, 2016.

17. Nadia Ellis, *Territories of the Soul*, 163.

18. The song appears on Burning Spear's 1979 release, *Living Dub, Volume 1*, which is a dub version of the 1978 studio album *Social Living*, on which "The Whole a We Suffer" is entitled "Marcus Children Suffer."

19. For an introduction to and analysis of Sylvan Morris's work, see Veal, *Dub*, 95–107. See also Paul Sullivan, *Remixology: Tracing the Dub Diaspora* (London: Reaktion Books, 2014), 32–34.

20. The refrain of Kraftwerk's "The Robots" reads "Ja tvoi sluga (I'm your slave) / Ja tvoi rabotnik robotnik (I'm your worker) / We are programmed just to do / Anything you want us to / We are the Robots." For an entertaining and idiosyncratic history of the vocoder and its origins in military voice encryption technology, see Dave Tompkins, *How to Wreck a Nice Beach: The Vocoder from World War II to Hip Hop* (Chicago: Stop Smiling Books, 2011).

21. Alexander G. Weheliye has addressed the use of vocoder technology and futurist tropes in American rhythm and blues in his groundbreaking theoretical critique—from the standpoint of black critical inquiry—of the provinciality of any articulation of the "posthuman" which does not take into account the status of those who have been denied full access to humanity within the historical dispensation of modernity. See Alexander G. Weheliye, "'Feenin': Posthuman Voices in Contemporary Black Popular Music," *Social Text* 71, vol. 20, no. 2 (2002): 21–47. This line of inquiry is echoed and extended in the interdisciplinary work—encompassing black popular music, science fiction, and afro-futurist aesthetics—of Louis Chude-Sokei. See Chude-Sokei, *The Sound of Culture: Diaspora and Black Technopoetics* (Middletown, CT: Wesleyan University Press, 2016).

22. See Ragnhild Brøvig-Hanssen and Anne Danielsen, "Autotuned Voices: Alienation and 'Brokenhearted Androids,'" in *Digital Signatures: The Impact of Digitization on Popular Music Sound* (Cambridge, MA: MIT Press, 2016), 120–32.

23. For an outspoken piece on what distinguishes the Jamaican use of Auto-Tune from that of mainstream popular music, see Neil Kulkarni, "Why Only Jamaicans Should Use Autotune," *The Quietus* (March 3, 2010), at http://thequietus.com/articles/03828-this-month-in-dancehall-by-neil-kulkarni, accessed July 1, 2016.

24. For "urban improvisers" and the relation between neoliberal economics and dancehall in Jamaica, see Anne Galvin, *Sounds of the Citizens: Dancehall and Community in Jamaica* (Nashville: Vanderbilt University Press, 2015), 5–6.

25. For economic statistics, see the World Factbook, at https://www.cia.gov/library/publications/the-world-factbook/geos/jm.html, accessed July 1, 2016. For BPO, see Ingrid Brown, "BPO Explosion," *Jamaica Observer*, August 5, 2015, at http://www.jamaicaobserver.com/news/BPO-explosion_19222249, accessed October 1, 2015.

26. See Sianne Ngai, *Our Aesthetic Categories: Zany, Cute, Interesting* (Cambridge, MA: Harvard University Press, 2012), 7.

27. These personae, however, are more complex than they may seem at first blush, and are often tightly and reflexively linked to the conditions of contemporary life. Vybz Kartel's 2008 smash-hit duet with dancehall diva Spice, "Romping Shop"—banned by the Jamaica Broadcasting Corporation for obscenity upon its release—consists of Vybz and Spice trading explicit boasts and bluster through the course of a steamy sexual encounter. The flattened contours of their Auto-Tuned voices suggest not so much unfeeling or dehumanized androids as beings possessed of the capacity for superhuman potency and pleasure. Yet pleasure constantly threatens to revert to hard work, to be exposed as strenuous performance. Indeed, the song plays on the congruence between the two realms, as accoutrements of the globalized communications economy are pressed into service for a more intimate sort of connectivity: Spice gyrates atop Vybz like a "satellite dish" and assures him at the moment of his climax that when "mi two phone a ring . . . mi nuh answer none." Appropriately, it is also at this moment of hilarity (and human vulnerability) that their voices are the least processed.

28. See Palmer and Dawson, *The Voice of the Jamaican Ghetto*, 233.

29. See Carolyn Cooper, "Kartel: Beyond Reasonable Doubt?," *Jamaica Daily Gleaner*, March 16, 2014.

15

The Actor's Absent Voice: Silent Cinema and the Archives of Kabuki in Prewar Japan

JONATHAN ZWICKER

In April 1897, just a few months after Edison's vitascope and the Lumière Brothers' cinematograph had been exhibited in Japan, a short pamphlet on *The Art of the Moving Picture* (*Jidō shashin jutsu*) was published by an obscure novelist, Okamura Shōkei.[1] Although ostensibly an introduction to the cinematograph as both technology and medium, *The Art of the Moving Picture* also included, as an appendix, a short story titled "The Moving Picture: A Story" (*Shōsetsu jidō shashin*). The story—which runs only seventeen pages but is longer than the book's exposition of the cinematograph—is set one year in the future (1898) and imagines a world in which cinema has already come to occupy a central place in public entertainment.

Okamura's story opens with an imagined scene set outside a kabuki theater in Osaka: here, a crowd has gathered for a showing of the first film ever to be made entirely by Japanese. As we linger among the audience—"the mountain of people before the entryway"—we hear different voices, anonymous and disembodied, discussing the program. Presently, we follow these voices into the theater and overhear the following exchange centered on the great kabuki star Ichikawa Danjūrō IX playing the role of the Qing Admiral Ding Ruchang in a filmed scene of a play set at the end of the Sino-Japanese War in 1895: "During the final soliloquy—so full of bravura—that Danjūrō gives as Ding Ruchang just before he drinks the morphine, although we cannot hear his voice . . . it seemed as if he were there upon the stage before our very eyes." "It was great," replies his interlocutor, "just as if we were watching him in reality."[2]

Here, at the same moment as the cinema begins to appear in Japan, we have a story that makes voice central to the ontology of the moving picture. Indeed, the scene turns on two rather different intuitions of the voice. On the one hand, there is the conceit that the reader is overhearing a conversation, voices heard but bodies not seen; on the other, there is the fact that for the characters within the story, the opposite is true: they see the actor but cannot hear him.

In Okamura's story, however, the disembodied voice of the fictional dialogue—a familiar device because so widely used[3]—stands in sharp contrast to the absent voice of the embodied actor, an absence around which this dialogue turns and which marks the novelty of the cinema. But the absence of the voice, here, far from troubling the sense of the presence of the actor, becomes a marker that authenticates film's capacity to make present that which is absent by suggesting a kind of limit which the image is able to overcome. This is really the role of the concessive structure of Okamura's sentence: even though we cannot hear Ichikawa Danjūrō's voice, he seems present; I know that Danjūrō is not standing before me onstage, the imagined viewer tells us, and his absent voice makes this perfectly clear—*and yet* I believe him to be present.

Here we find embedded in one of the earliest attempts to make sense of the technology of the moving image a literal enactment of the fetishistic disavowal that Slavoj Žižek has placed at the heart of his analysis of ideology: "I know very well, but nevertheless. . . ."[4] The moving image does not trick the viewer; rather, the viewer willingly suspends disbelief to participate in the illusion. And this structure would be central to apprehensions of early cinema in Japan whether they focused on the actor's absent voice or the presence of the actor's body and would continue to play an important role in how the archival technologies of film were imagined well into the twentieth century.

Nor should we be surprised to find embedded in one of the first responses to the motion picture in Japan a meditation on the problem of fetishistic disavowal. For disavowal is, in its own way, central to the cinematic enterprise: "It is understood that the audience is not duped by the diegetic illusion, it 'knows' that the screen presents no more than a fiction. And yet it is of vital importance for the correct unfolding of the spectacle that this make-believe be scrupulously respected . . . that everything is set to work to make the deception effective and give it an air of truth."[5] But in the entirely fictional scene which *stages* the mechanics of the process of disavowal, there is an additional turn: it is not the diegetic illusion on which the dialogue turns—the characters do not believe a reanimated Chinese admiral is before them; rather, it is the staging of the filmed play by live actors which becomes a central problem for cinematic illusion. Indeed, this would continue to be a very common response of audiences to seeing films of kabuki stars into the twentieth century.[6]

In this way, and to judge from its immediate aftermath, Okamura's novel was strangely prophetic: two years after its publication, the actor Ichikawa

Danjūrō IX was in fact recorded on film by a Japanese cameraman, Shibata Tsunekichi, in what is the oldest surviving Japanese film, in two sequences from the dance play *Maple Viewing* (*Momijigari*). But despite this convergence of art and life, there are two rather interesting differences between the film that was made in 1899 and the one that was imagined by Okamura in 1897.

The first difference is that while the film in Okamura's story *The Moving Picture* is imagined as part of a commercial program at a busy theater, *Maple Viewing* was in fact made primarily for archival purposes.[7] When the film was shot, it was on condition that one print would be left with the Kabukiza Theater "to preserve for posterity," and that the film would not be shown publicly while Danjūrō was alive.[8] The film was shown in 1899 in private at Danjūrō's residence and not again until 1903 in place of a live performance by the actors at Osaka's Nakaza Theater in conjunction with that year's Fifth Industrial Exposition. By that time, Danjūrō was on his deathbed and his costar, Onoe Kikugorō V, had already died.[9] In life as in fiction, the film seemed to bring the actor to life before the eyes of the audience: "It felt as if [the actors] were there and as if we were watching their extraordinary skill," wrote a reporter for the Osaka *Asahi Newspaper*.[10]

The second difference is the film's subject matter. For histories of cinema, the play itself has been incidental: it is treated almost as a kind of actuality, a happening that gets caught on film.[11] But the film was, of course, *staged*, and part of that staging was the idea that what was filmed would be preserved in perpetuity, a document of the two great actors of the age but also a document of kabuki at the fin-de-siècle. In this context, the pseudoclassical *Maple Viewing*, invoking the dramatic heritage of the nō theater, casts a rather different afterimage than might a contemporary war play like that conjured up by Okumura Shōkei in *The Moving Picture*. Indeed, the fictional play within *The Moving Picture*—a play about the 1894–1895 Sino-Japanese War with Danjūrō performing the suicide of the Qing Admiral Ding Ruchang—provides an interesting counterpoint to the dance sequence of *Maple Viewing*. *Maple Viewing* was an adaptation of the late-fifteenth-century playwright Kanze Nobumichi's nō play that told the story of the warrior Taira no Koremochi's hunting excursion among the autumn foliage used as a premise to vanquish the demon appearing in the guise of the beautiful Sarashinahime. In contrast, war plays like that imagined by Okamura in *The Moving Picture* represent what the theater historian Kamiyama Akira has called "a completely forgotten genre of the Meiji Period": until the Sino-Japanese War, contemporary plays which took war and other current events as a central subject and which performed a kind of reportage-like function were a mainstay of the kabuki theater.[12] But the unprecedented commercial and critical failure of the Sino-Japanese War play *Our National Flag Victorious on Land and Sea* (*Kairiku renshō nisshōki*) staged in 1894 starring Danjūrō and Kikugorō opposite one another became a turning point. As Hyōdō Hiromi has argued, "it can even be said the transformation of kabuki into a classical theater was brought about by the failed staging of . . . Danjūrō's Sino-Japanese War play."[13]

In this context, *Maple Viewing* can be seen as belonging to a contested moment in the history of the struggle over the nature of kabuki's identity as a representational medium. Written for kabuki by Kawatake Mokuami in 1887, *Maple Viewing* was from very early on part of an effort to "preserve" kabuki: in 1889, it was included in a program of plays by the Japan Entertainment Society (Nihon Engei Kyōkai), which had adopted the concept of preservation or *hōzon* from work being done on the history of Japanese art by figures like Okakura Tenshin and Ernest Fenollosa.[14] The play itself, the object of preservation through the cinema, was thus intimately bound up with the *idea* of cultural preservation and so becomes almost a kind of overdetermined object of the impulse to preserve. It both emphasizes kabuki's place as a "traditional" art form and, through this, anchors the new photographic technology of the cinema within a broad cultural framework imbued with a sense of tradition.

Equally critical to the choice of *Maple Viewing* is that as a dance sequence, there is no dialogue and so no voice: the problem of the actor's absent voice disappears. It becomes, in a sense, naturalized, no longer the mark of a lack in the cinematic medium but a constituent element of a dramaturgy of the gesture. Even though the film could be, and was, accompanied by vocal music—both live and, later, recorded—the question of preserving the actor's voice was immaterial.[15] To be sure, the foregrounding of gesture over speech as an object of preservation makes sense: gesture, after all, is what early cinema could capture, and it could do so in ways markedly different from anything that had come before. When early spectators remarked about film's power to give life to the dead, this is what they meant.[16] And the earliest films shot in Japan by the Lumières—and of Japanese subjects outside Japan, like Edison's 1894 "Imperial Japanese Dance"—all focused similarly on the gestural: swordplay or dance, foreshadowing the rise of the great period pieces that dominated Japanese cinema during the silent era.[17]

When film as a medium came to be theorized in Japan in the early twentieth century, this absence of the voice became—uncannily—also a guarantor of the future archival potential inherent in filmic technology. The philosopher Nakagawa Shigeaki, for example, writing in 1911, argued against film as an aesthetic medium because it was, for him, purely documentary, though as yet incomplete because it still required the integration of sound technology to produce a kind of total archive. Nakagawa imagined a future in which the phonograph would be combined with the motion picture to capture "social events," thus becoming what he called "an indispensable tool for the historian through which events would be passed just as they are to later generations, presenting themselves directly to the eyes and the ears."[18]

Nakagawa was writing at a moment when sound recording was just beginning in Japan. The earliest recordings of kabuki actors were made in 1907 by Beka and Columbia, and roughly six hundred recordings of kabuki were made in the period between 1909, when the first domestic records were produced in Japan, and the end of World War II.[19]

It seemed plausible in 1911 to imagine something like a total archive of kabuki as a performing art that would combine sound recording with film, and that such an endeavor would occupy a central place within the historiography of this dramatic form. But this is not what happened. Indeed, in the century since the first recordings of the actor's voice, these SP records have largely been forgotten by historians of kabuki or seen as lying outside the ken of theater history, and it has only been in the last decade that the work of historians and collectors like Iijima Mitsuru and Ōnishi Hidenori has begun to conceive of these recordings as an archive.

In the twentieth century, the writing of kabuki's history took a different tack, profoundly shaped by the enormous but unacknowledged influence that the cinematic regard would have on the historiography of Japanese theater. At the first level, this had to do with the impact that early cinema as an archiving technology had on kabuki in the decades after *Maple Viewing*. "The significance of cinema, in this context," Mary Ann Doane has written, "lies in its apparent capacity to perfectly represent the contingent, to provide the pure record of time," and thus for performance the promise of archiving ephemerality itself.[20] Indeed, the "archival desire" that accompanied the emergence of cinema—"the drive to fix and make repeatable the ephemeral"[21]—plays out in Japan not only as an almost utopian intuition of the film as a not-yet-realized medium of the total archive, but also as a way that allowed historians of the theater to reimagine the visual record of kabuki's past as protocinematic. This historiographical stance in turn shifted the focus toward gesture as that which was preeminently archivable, and thus paradoxically provided kabuki with the very archive it seemed to lack. If there were no *films* of kabuki's first three centuries, there was an extensive visual record which could be—and was—reimagined within the context of a utopian understanding of the medium of cinema as a protofilmic archive. In this process, the voice was emblematically absent: not just in the archival materials to which historians turned, but also as a historical problem that required attention.

Tsubouchi Shōyō and the Theater Archive as Protocinema

The central figure in this reconceptualization of the archives of kabuki from the perspective of filmic technology was Tsubouchi Shōyō (1859–1935). Although Shōyō is now best remembered for his 1885 essay on the essence of the novel (published when he was twenty-six and a work which would become a key document in introducing Western conceptions of fiction to a generation of writers), in his own lifetime Shōyō was better known as a playwright, critic, translator of Shakespeare, and pioneering historian of Japanese drama. In 1928, to celebrate the completion of his translation of Shakespeare's complete works, Waseda University opened its Theatre Museum, one of the earliest museums of theater history in the world and still one of the most important archives of theatrical material in Japan.

Shōyō first mentions the idea of creating a theater museum in 1916, in a note about ideas for future projects.[22] And beginning around this time, Shōyō would become increasingly interested in woodblock prints—theater prints and actor prints, but also block-printed illustrated fiction—as a set of documents providing what he called historical or documentary evidence of theatrical history. It was a unique archive, Shōyō argued, completely unlike anything that existed for other theater cultures elsewhere and, indeed, an enormous collection of theatrical prints—many from Shōyō's own collection—formed the core of the Theatre Museum's collection when it opened a decade later. Central to Shōyō's conception of these prints was the idea that they constituted a kind of cinematic or protocinematic archive, an idea to which he would return repeatedly in the 1910s. Such prints, Shōyō would later write, "reanimate what really happened on stage like a Kinemacolor film."[23]

It was in 1915, a year before he began to imagine a future museum of the theater, that Shōyō first conceptualized the nature of the printed archive of theater images as cinematic in an essay he published on "Motion Pictures and the Past of Japanese Drama" ("Katsudō shashin to wa ga geki no kako"). In explaining the emergence of long-form illustrated fiction that used actors' images, for example, Shōyō argued that "From at least a hundred and thirty or forty years ago, production of a kind of film that we could consider a primitive motion picture began in Japan, and gradually the scale was increased so that roughly a century ago even extremely long-form films began to be produced."[24] This is the printed page reimagined as filmic print. But what is most important about this conception of theatrical history in which theater prints become a protocinematic archive is that it flattens kabuki out in a particular way. If this archive is able to capture the history of kabuki in an essentially documentary fashion, it is able to do so, Shōyō argues, because kabuki was primarily gestural: "In the case of Japanese drama, it goes without saying that for the puppet theater and kabuki . . . with the exception of certain instances from the puppet theater, there is very little that needs to be heard with the ears."[25] This is because, Shōyō explains, kabuki placed importance on "appealing directly to the eyes."[26] Here, not just the actor's voice in both spoken dialogue and dramatic recitation (*tsurane*) but also vocal and instrumental music fade into the background as inessential elements of a drama that would come to be literally embodied in "frozen moments" (*mie*), the dramatic poses and gestures that have come to define the way kabuki has been imagined as a dramatic art.

While the silent cinema of the 1910s, and especially the rise of period pieces that employed kabuki actors and relied heavily on stylized swordplay, is the immediate backdrop to Shōyō's essays, it should be noted that this intuition of printed images as protocinematic also coincides with the early history of animation in Japan. Foreign films, including the work of Emile Cohl, were shown in Japan beginning in 1911, and Japanese animated films began to be produced in 1917, years which bracket Shōyō's earliest conception of the cinematic nature of illustrated fiction, the pages of which in some respects *look* like a form of animation.[27] Indeed, it is not difficult to imagine that in the process of flipping through these books—which Shōyō had read since his childhood—he noticed something like a zoetrope effect, as the characters, drawn with actors' likenesses, appeared to move on the page.

It is within this context, then, that we need to situate a turn in Shōyō's work toward the gestural as the defining element of kabuki, a turn which has had profound impact not only for the historiography of kabuki—which was largely shaped by Shōyō and his students—but also for the very nature of the archive of kabuki which has, since the 1910s, foregrounded the visual record.[28] Moreover, the conception of these prints as somehow protofilmic and as essentially documentary has meant that a literalism has pervaded the scholarly approach to this material with questions centered on *what* is represented in these prints and what they can tell us about performance rather than on *how* these prints represent their purported object and how the relationship of stage is mediated on or by the page. All this despite the fact that we know that most representations of actors onstage and in character were made before the performances took place. They were made as advertising, a fact that is most easily grasped by the many instances of actors withdrawing from roles due to illness and their heads being literally dug out of the printing blocks and new faces added in their stead.[29]

But there is another context for understanding Shōyō's conception of theater prints as protocinematic and his turn away from the ear and toward the eye: the emergence of sound recording in Japan. Indeed, Shōyō's disregard for the voice and for sound more generally—kabuki, after all, was a dramatic art that incorporated both vocal and instrumental music—and his turn toward gesture and movement that "appeals directly to the eye" as the defining elements of kabuki's dramaturgy comes, paradoxically, at precisely the moment when an archive of the actor's voice became thinkable for the first time. By the 1910s, kabuki records were being produced in Japan by Menophone, Tokyo Record, Orient, Sphinx, and Nipponophone, the forerunner of Columbia Japan, and it became possible to imagine the question posed in 1921 by an advertisement by Nipponophone for its kabuki recordings: "Is theater meant to be seen? Or to be heard?"[30]

Despite this abundance of recordings during the 1910s and 1920s—not just of actors but also of the vocal music of kabuki (*nagauta*) and of chanters from the puppet theater—Shōyō seems curiously blind—or, rather, deaf—to the possibilities this material might hold both for imagining a history of kabuki in sound and for archiving the actor's voice in the 1910s and 1920s.

There are several reasons for this seeming divergence between how film came to be imagined as an archiving medium for the theater while sound recording realized no similar potential. The first is the very nature of what was recorded: since there were no recordings made of live performances of kabuki during the prewar period, what was recorded on SP records were recitations of play scripts made by actors in recording studios. Thus the historian is immediately faced with a question of the ontology of this material: What, exactly, does it preserve? The voice of the actor, of course, but not a performance as such. Or a performance, but something very different from what transpired onstage in front of an audience. As Jonathan Sterne has written about early sound recording, "performers had to develop whole new performance techniques in order to produce 'originals' suitable for reproduction."[31] In the case of kabuki, actors would stand, stationary, in front of a horn—and, after 1925, a microphone—and recite their lines. It was, in many ways, the opposite of the silent film: the voice was preserved, but all movement and gesture was excised.[32]

The second reason these recordings have largely been ignored is that they serve as an archive of a period in kabuki's own history when the tradition was seen by contemporary observers to have largely fallen into decline, a subject about which Shōyō himself wrote on numerous occasions.[33] What this material served as a record of was a moment in kabuki's history that was largely thought not *worth* preserving.

Perhaps most important in shaping our approach to Japan's historical past is that while Shōyō was able to reimagine the huge body of theatrical prints and printed fiction as protocinematic, there is no comparable body of work that could extend the auditory archive back a century or two into the early nineteenth or late eighteenth century. Or Shōyō and his contemporaries were unable to imagine how what did remain—books of vocal music, for example, or books used for mimicking the voices of famous actors (kowairo) that began to appear in the 1830s and 1840s—might be reimagined as an archive of kabuki's soundscape before the advent of sound recording per se. For Shōyō it was the absence of the voice, in contrast to the presence of the image, that weighed on how he imagined theater's (incomplete) archive. In his preface to a collection of historical photographs of the actor Ichikawa Danjūrō IX (died 1903) published by photographer Abe Yutaka in 1923, what the actor's two-decade-long photographic survival made most pronounced was that his voice, so central to his presence on stage, had been lost to history:

> Imagine if Danjūrō IX had recorded that clear voice of his, that controlled intonation, onto a gramophone and we could hear it today just as it was. Oh, that clear voice. That famous style of his that would reverberate with such vigor and such force to every corner of the boxes on the balcony until the early 1890s.[34]

During his lifetime, Danjūrō had been photographed and even captured on film, but his voice had never been recorded, so here the voice becomes a marker of that which has not been preserved, that element of performance that has been lost to the archive and can be recalled only in the mind of those who heard it. In this sense, the voice becomes a symptom of a much larger problem, a problem felt keenly by Japanese intellectuals in the late teens and early twenties: What becomes of the past that is not preserved?

It was only toward the end of his life that Shōyō himself turned directly to the subject of the actor's voice. Shōyō had an early interest in techniques of elocution dating to the 1890s, but to my knowledge, in his voluminous writings on the theater, Shōyō only once addressed the role of the voice on the stage directly, in a late essay on acting technique written in 1933 at the age of seventy-four, two years before his death.[35] "What moves the spectator," writes Shōyō, "is the face, it is the expression; no, it is the voice. The voice is anger itself, it is sorrow itself, it is anguish, it is rhapsody. The voice is music. Thus it directly touches our sentiments. And yet for some reason, playwrights and actors and directors are indifferent or completely disregard this facet."[36] We might add to Shōyō's list of writers and actors and directors *historians*, who long disregarded the voice as an object of inquiry for the history of the theater—including Shōyō himself.

There is a kind of phantasmagoric element in Shōyō's almost-too-late recognition of the voice. It was, Shōyō writes in this essay, in the context of the emergence of the phonograph, the talkie, and the radio that he realized that we must "pay attention" to the voice. That is to say that the voice, for Shōyō, seems to emerge as a problem only once the moment that augmented and reproduced it had passed into the realm of the archivable, which in turn posits the possibility of the voice as authentic locus of meaning of which the recording becomes a kind of trace.

How are we to understand this trace? Shōyō had maintained an ambivalent relationship to the technologies of sound since the 1920s. In July 1925, Shōyō's kabuki play *A Paulownia Leaf* (*Kiri hitoha*), which he had written between 1894 and 1895 and which was first staged in 1904, became the first radio drama broadcast in Japan. And in the early 1930s, Shōyō had, on several occasions, recorded his own voice. First, in 1930, Shōyō had recorded the text of his children's play *The Hat Maker and the Monkey* (*Eboshi ori to saru*) for Polydor Japan, an SP record that was intended to accompany an animated film of the play that the manga artist Kanei Kiichirō was producing. Shōyō also recorded for Polydor the opening and grand finale of his kabuki play *The Setting Moon and the Fall of Ōsaka Castle* (*Kojō no rakugetsu*), a sequel to *A Paulownia Leaf*, which was written in 1897 and first staged in 1905.

But the immediate context for Shōyō's reflections on the actor's voice in his 1933 essay was his experience that year of recording two dramatic recitations of his own translations of Shakespeare for Columbia Records, the soliloquy of Hamlet and Antonio's trial from *The Merchant of Venice*. Shōyō was reluctant to make these recordings and, in an essay written in the months after the recordings were made, he would describe the experience as one of great "shame."[37] "For me, for whom canned food has been for some time strictly off limits, the canned voice is similarly distasteful."[38] Shōyō was not the first to draw this analogy between the preservation of sound through recording and the preservation of food through canning, and his skepticism toward the value of preservation as such is part of a broader set of misgivings both about the nature of what was being preserved as well as the altered nature of the object that had been subjected to these new methods of preservation.[39]

Indeed, Shōyō is keenly aware of the question of authenticity as it relates to such techniques of preservation. In his reflections on recording his own voice, Shōyō describes how the recording would stop and start again due to the "interference" of various external sounds: a motorcycle, the bark of a dog, the cries of a tofu peddler.[40] This "interference" needed to be eliminated for the voice to be preserved in its purity, and this experience only highlights the artificial nature of the recording from which all exogenous elements had to be excised. If, two decades earlier, the philosopher Nakagawa Shigeaki had imagined sound recording as part of a total archive of reality as it unfolded, here, recording as preservation was premised on an artificiality of circumstance.

But the very artificiality of this circumstance, and Shōyō's recognition of how this, in turn, changed the nature of the archive, might give us pause. For the *overtly* artificial, the canned nature of sound recording is itself but a repetition of the artificial nature of other archiving technologies even when they might seem—even when for Shōyō himself they *did* seem—more natural, less mediated. For if the 1899 film of Ichikawa Danjūrō and Onoe Kikugorō in *Maple Viewing* seems to preserve a moment lost to history, this document which was shot in a temporary studio set up in the garden of a teahouse behind the Kabukiza Theater is no less artificial than the sound recording of Nakamura Shikan V and Ichikawa Komazō VIII reading from Kawatake Mokuami's 1881 play *Dawn at the Hunting Field after the Sogas' Night Attack* (*Youchi Soga kariba no akebono*) made by Beka in 1907. And the same can, of course, be said for the images of the great actors of the early nineteenth century—Ichikawa Danjūrō VII, Matsumoto Kōshirō V, Iwai Hanshirō V—drawn in character by Utagwa Toyokuni and his school in the 1810s and 1820s that Shōyō would imagine as protocinematic, a documentary record of kabuki before the advent of film (see **fig. 15.1**).

In his own way, Shōyō himself seems to have recognized this. In an introductory essay he wrote in 1919 to a catalogue of theater prints, Shōyō invoked the role of the historian: if images in the catalogue spanning two centuries from the 1670s to the 1870s represented "a motion picture of the nation's theatrical history," it was the historian, Shōyō wrote, who served in the crucial role of the *benshi*, the narrators who accompanied silent films and who often became stars in their own right.[41] The historian, that is, literally speaks for—gives voice to—these silent images.

In these visual media—the woodblock print, the silent film—the actor's voice is, emblematically, absent. But what of the presence of the actor's voice today? Not only have many recordings from early SP records been restored, remastered, and reissued, but increasingly the soundscape of early twentieth-century Japan has become available via the web through the National Diet Library's Historical Recordings Collection, which includes not only a range of dramatic works but also Shōyō's own Shakespeare recordings for Columbia.[42] Shōyō's recordings live on, stored on servers in central Tokyo but available anywhere in the world, notwithstanding his own view of them as great failures.

But these recordings, no less than the mute images of actors in roles that document kabuki's first three centuries, still need to be spoken *for* by the

FIGURE 15.1 The actor Onoe Matsusuke playing the ghost of Kohada Koheiji's wife in the play *Eiri otogizōshi* at Edo's Ichimura Theater. Utagawa Toyokuni, 1805. Tsubouchi Memorial Theatre Museum, Waseda University.

historian. If the actor's absent voice has now returned, and if it seems possible at this moment to imagine an archive for kabuki that accounts more fully not only for the presence of the voice but for the entire rich sound ecology in which kabuki has always been embedded, we are still no closer to the utopian fantasy of a total archive that the philosopher Nakagawa Shigeaki imagined a century ago.

Part of this has to do with historiography's turn away from totality itself as an idea and an ideal and the recognition that the object of history is not the reconstitution of the whole but an understanding of the interrelation of strata or series.[43] But part of this too has to do with the nature of an archive that is itself fractured and fragmentary. We can now mix sound with woodblock prints or still photographs or silent film or, more recently, with virtual recordings made with motion-capture software,[44] but we are under no illusion that we are any closer to a total record of the ephemeral performance, let alone to the recording of reality "just as it is," as Nakagawa had hoped.

Rather, the voice stands as a historical problem in its own right, and Shōyō's recordings from the 1930s are suggestive of the contours of that problem. For these are strange historical documents indeed. What is etched on these records, what we can now hear streamed over the internet, is both a rendering of Shakespeare's lines in mid-century Japanese but also a remainder that exceeds the literal meaning of the recorded soliloquies; and it was, we might imagine, this remainder over which Shōyō felt shame.[45] The sounds of motorcycles, of barking dogs, of tofu peddlers, have been eliminated, and what we have is a single and singular voice speaking to us from the grave, contemplating its own being. But how do we describe and interpret this remainder? It is, on the one hand, the frail voice of a man in his seventies, only two years from his own death. But on the other, for anyone who knows of Shōyō's lifelong engagement with Shakespeare and his complex relationship with European Orientalism, the voice seems pregnant with myriad meanings.[46] Shōyō had first heard Hamlet's soliloquy at age sixteen in 1875, recited by his American English teacher, and he would recall, half a century later, that the scene was "strangely still lingering in my eyes and in my ears."[47] In 1881, as a student at Tokyo University, he would fail an exam on *Hamlet* administered by Ernest Fenollosa and lose his scholarship.[48] Thirty years later, Shōyō would stage a version of *Hamlet* with a Japanese cast based on his own translation, an event about which he felt great pride but also a measure of ambivalence, even embarrassment.[49] Another two decades on, Shōyō would sit in the Hibiya offices of Columbia Japan with an upset stomach and record the soliloquies repeatedly, a dozen times, over the course of four hours.[50] In some ways, the recording is emblematic of his long, tortured history with Shakespeare, fraught with anxiety and a sense of failure. But what of this can be heard in that "canned" voice over which he felt such shame, and what of it is projected onto the empty signifier of the voice by the historian's own desire to make it significant (see **fig. 15.2**)?

For the last several decades, the historicist project has been intimately bound up with a desire to speak with the dead.[51] To call this a desire is to recognize its essentially asymptotic nature: though we may become more attuned to the past, and make more sense of its mysteries, we can never really speak with the dead. In many ways, historicism is itself an exercise in a kind of fetishistic disavowal: I know that I will never speak with the dead, I know that I cannot really hear their voices, and yet. . . . "And yet" is in some real way a kernel—perhaps *the* kernel—of historicist work: despite the fact that we cannot hear the dead, we nevertheless try to make the dead speak, perhaps even against their will.[52] The audible past is now more present than ever, offering

FIGURE 15.2 Hamlet's soliloquy with Dohi Shunsho as Hamlet and Matsui Sumako as Ophelia in Tsubouchi Shōyō's staging of *Hamlet* at the Imperial Theater, 1911. Tsubouchi Memorial Theatre Museum, Waseda University.

entirely new opportunities for historical work and yet caught within the same contradictions that have always been posed by the archive: to make sense of its "tracks" requires a recognition of the essential distance of the past—"I know the past is not here before me"—and at the same time such work must be premised on a disavowal of that unbreachable distance—"nevertheless. . . ."

Notes

1. Daitōrō Shujin [Okamura Shōkei], *Jidō shashin jutsu* (Osaka: Nishida Teiichi, 1897).

2. Shujin, *Jidō shashin jutsu*, 25.

3. The trope of the reader overhearing a conversation is an old one in fiction: in Japan, this tradition goes all the way back to the eleventh-century *Tale of Genji*, in which various forms of overhearing, sometimes embodied by eavesdropping characters, play an important role in the narrative. Nor is this structure limited to Japan; as the work of scholars like Paize Keulemans and Ann Gaylin has shown, overhearing is a common device in the fiction of late Imperial China, for example, and in the European novel. See Paize Keulemans, *Sound Rising from the Paper: Nineteenth-Century Martial Arts Fiction and the Chinese Acoustic Imagination* (Cambridge, MA, and London: Harvard University Asia Center, 2014); Ann Gaylin, *Eavesdropping in the Novel from Austen to Proust* (Cambridge and New York: Cambridge University Press, 2003).

4. Slavoj Žižek, *For They Know Not What They Do: Enjoyment as a Political Factor* (London and New York: Verso, 1991), 248.

5. Christian Metz, *The Imaginary Signifier: Psychoanalysis and the Cinema* (Bloomington: Indiana University Press, 1982), 72.

6. On this point see, for example, Manabu Ueda, *Nihon eiga sōsōki no kōgyō to kankyaku: Tōkyō to Kyōto o chūshin ni* (Tōkyō: Waseda Daigaku Shuppanbu, 2012), 175–77.

7. See the newspaper clipping "Katsudō shashin," in the scrapbooks of the *benshi* Komata Kōyō, now housed at the Waseda University Theatre Museum. "Katsudō shashin," Engeki Hakubutsukan, http://www.enpaku.waseda.ac.jp/db/ref/komada/large/EK360125.jpg, accessed November 28, 2018.

8. See "Katsudō shashin."

9. See Ueda, *Nihon eiga sōsōki no kōgyō to kankyaku*, 175–77.

10. Quoted in Ueda, *Nihon eiga sōsōki no kōgyō to kankyaku*, 176.

11. On this point, see the excellent analysis by Komatsu Hiroshi, "Questions Regarding the Genesis of Nonfiction Film," *Yamagata International Film Festival: Documentary Box #5*, 1994, http://www.yidff.jp/docbox/5/box5-1-e.html.

12. Kamiyama Akira, *Kindai engeki no raireki: kabuki no "isshin nisei"* (Tōkyō: Shinwasha, 2006), 166.

13. Hyōdō Hiromi, *Enjirareta kindai: "kokumin" no shintai to pafōmansu* (Tokyo: Iwanami Shoten, 2005), 67. See also Kamiyama, *Kindai engeki no raireki*, 168.

14. See Kamiyama, *Kindai engeki no raireki*, 94–108.

15. See Ueda, *Nihon eiga sōsōki no kōgyō to kankyaku*, 175–87. For a broader discussion of sound accompaniment to early cinema in Japan, see Kentarō Imada, "Katsudō shashin kōgyō to sono shichō taiken no shosō," *Firogaria* 21 (2004): 15–34.

16. This was the reaction of Maejima Toyotarō, who witnessed one of the earliest screenings of a film in Japan in 1897 in Shizuoka. See Akiko Takeyama, "Kan katsudō shashin ki," *Mediashi kenkyū* 8 (1999): 97–101.

17. On the "spectacle" of swordplay in Japan's silent cinema, see Iwamoto Kenji's introduction to Kenji Iwamoto, *Jidaigeki densetsu: chanbara eiga no kagayaki* (Tōkyō: Shinwasha, 2005), esp. 14–17.

18. Nakagawa Shimei [Nakagawa Shigeaki], *Shokuhai Bigaku: Keiji Shinin* (Tokyo: Hakubunkan, 1911), 159, http://dl.ndl.go.jp/info:ndljp/pid/875135.

19. See Iijima Mitsuru, "Kabuki SP rekōdo no yukue," *Kabuki: kenkyū to hihyō* 38 (2007): esp. 6–7. While a complete catalogue of prewar recordings of kabuki actors in role is still a work in progress, Ōnishi Hidenori has estimated that there were likely around six hundred SP records made. See Ōnishi Hidenori, "Kabuki SP rekōdo disukogurafi (senzenhen miteikō)," *Kabuki: kenkyū to hihyō* 38 (2007): 29–67, at 30. Kerim Yasar has identified earlier recordings of actors which are no longer extant but which were exhibited in public as early as 1890, almost a full decade before Shibata's film of *Momijigari* was shot. See Kerim Yasar, *Electrified Voices: How the Telephone, Phonograph, and Radio Shaped Modern Japan, 1868–1945* (New York: Columbia University Press, 2018), 87–89.

20. Mary Ann Doane, *The Emergence of Cinematic Time: Modernity, Contingency, the Archive* (Cambridge, MA: Harvard University Press, 2002), 22.

21. Doane, *The Emergence of Cinematic Time*, 22.

22. See Morishige Noburō, "Wagakuni hatsu honkakuteki daigaku hakubutsukan no tanjō ni tsuite," *Nihon daigaku daigakuin sōgō shakai jōhō kenkyūka kiyō*, no. 11 (2010): 131.

23. Tsubouchi Shōyō, "Shibai-e to toyokuni oyobi sono monka," in *Shōyō senshū*, ed. Shōyō Kyōkai, vol. 7 (Tokyo: Daiichi shobō, 1977), 7.

24. Shōyō, "Katsudō shashin to wa ga geki no kako," in *Shōyō senshū*, 302.

25. Shōyō, "Katsudō shashin to wa ga geki no kako," 300.

26. Shōyō, "Katsudō shashin to wa ga geki no kako," 300.

27. On the earliest Japanese animation, see Frederick Litten, "Some Remarks on the First Japanese Animation Films in 1917," http://litten.de/fulltext/ani1917.pdf, accessed August 3, 2016; Frederick Litten, "On the Earliest (Foreign) Animation Films Shown in Japanese Cinemas," http://litten.de/fulltext/nipper.pdf, accessed August 3, 2016; and Yukari Hagihara, *Masaoka Kenzō to sono jidai: "Nihon animēshon no chichi" no senzen to sengo*, (Tōkyō: Seikyūsha, 2015), 19–25.

28. When the Tsubouchi Memorial Theatre Museum opened at Waseda University in 1928, for example, the overwhelming majority of the objects it housed were early modern block-printed images. According to a newspaper account of the opening, the museum had some thirty thousand prints, over half of which Shōyō had himself donated. See "Kyō kaikanshiki no Engeki Hakubutsukan," *Yomiuri shinbun*, October 27, 1928, 11.

29. See Akane Fujisawa, *Utagawa-ha no ukiyoe to Edo shuppankai: yakushae o chūshin ni* (Tōkyō: Bensei Shuppan, 2001).

30. Nipponophone, advertisement, November 10, 1921, *Yomiuri shinbun*. Among the records listed in the advertisement was a recording of two scenes from Tsubouchi Shōyō's play *A Paulownia Leaf* (*Kiri no hitoha*).

31. Jonathan Sterne, *The Audible Past: Cultural Origins of Sound Reproduction* (Durham, NC: Duke University Press, 2003), 26.

32. Iijima Mitsuru, "Kabuki SP rekōdo no yukue," 8.

33. On this point, see especially Shōyō's essay on kabuki's "senility" written in 1933, in which he discusses not only his own "diagnosis" but also the prevailing attitudes of other "doctors." Tsubouchi Shōyō, "Rōsui no kabuki no chindansuru," in *Shōyō senshū*, supplementary vol. 4 (Tokyo: Daiichi shobō, 1977), 653–70.

34. Tsubouchi Shōyō, "*Butai no Danjūrō* jo," in *Shōyō senshū*, 296.

35. On Shōyō's early interest in elocution, see Yoshie Hara, *Koe no bunkashi* (Tokyo: Seibundō, 2016), 249–62.

36. Tsubouchi Shōyō, "Haiyūjutsu," in *Shōyō senshū*, supplementary vol. 4 (Tokyo: Daiichi shobō, 1977), 642–43.

37. Shōyō's essay, which was written in January 1934, was titled "Rōdoku fukikomi zanki," or "The Shame of Recording My Readings."

38. Tsubouchi Shōyō, "Rōdoku fukikomi zanki," in *Shōyō senshū*, supplementary vol. 4 (Tokyo: Daiichi shobō, 1977), 743.

39. See Sterne, *The Audible Past*, esp. 292ff.

40. Shōyō, "Rōdoku fukikomi zanki," 744.

41. Tsubouchi Shōyō, "'Shibai nishikie shūsei' jo," in *Shōyō senshū*, 291.

42. For an outline of the collection's recordings of drama, see Ōnishi Hidenori, "Historical Recordings Collection (Rekion)—Introductory Guides to Historical Recordings—'Listening' Drama," http://rekion.dl.ndl.go.jp/en/ongen_shoukai_08.html, accessed August 4, 2016. To hear the recordings, go to http://rekion.dl.ndl.go.jp/info:ndljp/pid/1316207/1; http://rekion.dl.ndl.go.jp/info:ndljp/pid/1316207/2; http://rekion.dl.ndl.go.jp/info:ndljp/pid/1316207/3; and http://rekion.dl.ndl.go.jp/info:ndljp/pid/1316207/4 (Tsubouchi Shōyō, *To Be or Not to Be* [Columbia, 1933], Historical Recordings Collection, National Diet Library, accessed August 4, 2016).

43. Michel Foucault, *The Archaeology of Knowledge and the Discourse on Language*, trans. A. M. Sheridan Smith (New York: Vintage, 1982), 9–19.

44. On the use of motion-caption software for creating a digital record of traditional performing arts in Japan, see Akama Ryō et al., eds., *Bunka jōhōgaku gaidobukku* (Tokyo: Bensei Shuppan, 2014), 103–36.

45. On the problem of the remainder in relation to the voice, see Mladen Dolar, *A Voice and Nothing More* (Cambridge, MA: MIT Press, 2006), 19–20.

46. I explore Shōyō's ambivalent relationship with the West in "Curio Fever: Tsubouchi Shōyō, Lafcadio Hearn, and the Cultural Politics of 'Collecting Japan' in the Age of Empire," in Jyotsna Singh and David Kim, eds., *The Postcolonial World* (London: Routledge, 2017), 274–87.

47. Tsubouchi Shōyō, "Gakusei jidai no tsuioku," in *Shōyō senshū*, vol. 12 (Tokyo: Daiichi shobō, 1977), 48; quoted in Minokamo City Museum, *Jōnetsu no hito: Tsubouchi Shōyō* (Minokamo City, Gifu Prefecture: Minokamo City Museum, 2005), 40.

48. See Minokamo City Museum, *Jōnetsu no hito*, 10.

49. Tsubouchi Shōyō, " 'Hamuretto' no kōengo no shokan," in *Shōyō senshū*, vol. 12 (Tokyo: Daiichi shobō, 1977), 667–73.

50. There is a detailed description of this experience in Shōyō's diary entry from October 7, 1933. Shōyō Kyōkai, *Mikan Tsubouchi Shōyō shiryōshū* (Tokyo: Shōyō Kyōkai, 2003), 171.

51. Most famously, of course, this was articulated by Stephen Greenblatt in his *Shakespearean Negotiations: The Circulation of Social Energy in Renaissance England* (Berkeley: University of California Press, 1988).

52. Marc Bloch, *The Historian's Craft* (New York: Knopf, 1953), 64.

16

A Voice That Is Not Mine: Terror and the Mythology of the Technological Voice

TOM GUNNING

In Roberto Rossellini's extraordinary 1948 film *Germany Year Zero*, filmed in the ruins of Berlin soon after the defeat of the Third Reich, the film's protagonist, Edmund, a young German boy struggling to provide subsistence for his family through black-market dealing, attempts to sell a recording of Hitler's speeches to some British soldiers. Using a portable gramophone, he plays the recording among the ruins of the German Chancellery. In a sequence powerful for both its neorealist aspects (shot among the actual ruins) and its nearly allegorical juxtaposition of a voice with its aftermath, we hear the unmistakable voice of the dead dictator announcing, "Victory will be ours" as the camera pans the ruins and a passerby with a small child seems to react fearfully to this ghostly rhetoric. Whose voice is this that echoes so loudly? To whom, we might ask, does this voice belong?

The power of this sound/image articulates a historical moment in its deepest sense, and captures the dynamics of the voice in the age of its mechanical reproducibility. In a previous essay, I stressed that the ability to record and play back the human voice offered by Edison's phonograph when it first appeared in 1877 not only enabled the capturing of sound (the voice, instrumental music, or other sounds), but equally importantly allowed the recording and replay of a specific moment of unrolling time.[1] But if the technology of recording serves to preserve the voice, it also transforms it fundamentally, not the least through its power of abstracting it from its embodied instance. Separated both from its human bodily source and the moment of its origin, the recorded voice becomes an alien entity, free-floating and replayable, belonging in effect to no one, or perhaps clinging to whoever hears it. As a number of commentators have noted, this detached voice transcends not only the fact of embodiment, but the physical condition of mortality.

Hitler's voice echoing through the ruins (replayed on the very location of his final bunker) survives his death and the destruction of his Reich, and serves simultaneously as a *memento mori* and as an eerie hint at the possible survival of its message of hate and war.

If the disembodied voice becomes immortal through its technological reproduction, can it ever be killed? And if the recording seems to possess a certain immortality, does its absolute separation from the human body or context of enunciation make it an emblem of the abstract and inhuman? Paradoxically, more than a survival, does the mechanical immortality that sound recording offers become the voice of death itself? As theorists (such as Roland Barthes in his late essay on photography *Camera Lucida*)[2] have traced the link between photography and death, does the aural equivalent forge a similar connection? Sound theorist Allen S. Weiss describes this new uncanny ontology of the technological voice as mixing our categories of life and death: "Sound recording and broadcast offered radically new discursive formations at the inception of modernism . . . the perpetuation of the voice beyond the grave radically changed our relation to disembodiment, death, and nostalgia."[3] Weiss stresses "the voice of the century's newly imagined sound recording and broadcast technologies, of acousmetric voices without origin or telos, of the inmixing of voices of the living with those of the dead."[4] In this way, the technological voice recalls and perhaps gathers the energies of the ancient desire to speak with the dead, to summon a voice from beyond the grave, which the nineteenth-century movement of Spiritualism with its mediums and séances modernized by relating such communication to new technologies such as photography and telegraphy. As Weiss, Lawrence Rainey, and especially Jeffrey Sconce have shown, the connections between this nineteenth-century metaphysical movement of speaking with the dead and the emergence of modern technologies of communication, from telegraphy to television, have been constant.[5]

But the issue subtending communication with spirits of the dead is not simply demonstrating the survival of the soul after death, but the possibility of the living receiving a voice coming from the position of death. In his writings on this technologically "breathless" voice, Weiss repeatedly claims "that archetype of impossible locutions 'I am dead' takes on a disquieting new meaning."[6] The disembodied voice has long been an indication of the beyond-human, whether the ghostly, the demonic, or the divine. After 1877, the disembodied voice could also be taken as the voice of modern technology, and more specifically as the enunciation of a new mechanism of storage, archiving both the voice and the moment. As the replaying of a moment, voice recording could be described as embalming of the voice; but again we must ask, does this recorded voice belong to the living or to the dead?

The phonograph and the wireless or radio became essential elements in the disembedding of experience that occurs in modernity as described by Anthony Giddens, as face-to-face interactions give way to transactions that are technologically mediated and in effect become liberated from traditional constraints of space and time.[7] At the turn of the nineteenth to the twentieth century, the discovery of Herzian (later known as radio) waves not only confirmed Michael Faraday's theory of the unity of electricity and magnetism, it announced the possibility of using these waves to transmit information without wires.[8] Wireless telegraphy, pioneered commercially by Guglielmo Marconi in the beginning of the century, not only liberated telegraphic messages from physical cables, but carried wave-borne messages over geographic barriers, such as mountains or rivers, and eventually circulated around even the curvature of the earth. Whereas communication by wire, whether by telegraph or telephone, formed a circuit between specific senders and receivers, radio waves by nature radiated broadly out from a point and therefore could be accessed by multiple and unspecified receivers. The broadcast radio message did not have a specific addressee. Radio signals not only transcended material circuits as waves carried through the air; they were unaffected by material barriers. As an immaterial signal broadcast to the airwaves, indifferent to its ultimate receiver, radio, and hence the wireless, transforms the experience of space and time.

During World War I, wireless messages played important tactical roles in military communication, since such messages could leap over battle lines and did not require laying cables in dangerous circumstances; however, wireless transmissions could also be intercepted easily. These tactical concerns motivated military research into tracking down and accessing radio signals that in turn led to the fine-tuning of radio waves. With the coming of peace, such technical refinements allowed radio signals to carry not only electronic signals but recognizable voices and music. This innovation marked the transition from wireless telegraphy (which employed a coded system of abstracted electronic signals, as telegraphy had) to radio as the carrier of sound rather than simply code and noise. Sound recording had liberated the disembodied voice from the temporal constraints of immediacy; radio broadcasting liberated the voice from a limited range in space. Yet, as opposed to sound recording, radio transmission would seem to carry a force of immediacy, tied to the instant of its delivery, hence radio's liveness of transmission rather than the phonograph's possibility of storage. But the voice that issues from the radio remained phantasmatic, ungraspable. The union soon forged between sound recording and radio allowed for a new sound environment in which sound and the voice could operate within a free range of both space and time.

The voice on the radio also generated a revolution in the way the voice sounded. Not only did national broadcasting systems announcers generate a nonregional manner of speaking that maximized clarity, but radio broadcasts began to influence the daily speech of listeners. In the novel *Thumbprint*, written in 1936 by the Swiss mystery writer Friedrich Glauser, the protagonist detective Sergeant Studer, while investigating a murder in the small Swiss village of Gerzenstein, notices that these rural folk now sound like the announcers and performers on the radio. "What had these people done with their own voices? Had they been infected by the radio? Had the wireless sets in Gerzenstein triggered off a new epidemic: voice-swapping?" He concludes later, "it was the wireless that controlled Gerzenstein. Didn't the mayor speak with the voice of an announcer?"[9] In contrast to the thumbprint left on the murder weapon, the archetypal clue that could identify a single unique culprit, the new technology of radio had homogenized the speech of the village populace through omnipresent radio broadcasts. "Voice-swapping" conjures a situation in which voices can be exchanged over the airwaves and even function as a sort of contagion in village life, placing both regional and personal identity in some ambiguity.

While radio was jump-started by the battlefield tactics of World War I, it was during the 1930s that its political possibilities were recognized, theorized, and exploited. FDR's "fireside chat" radio broadcasts beginning in 1933 created what Jason Loviglio has called an "intimate public," a sense of community headed by a benevolent but indispensable leader.[10] In Italy, Germany, and Japan, radio played an essential role in the address of fascist leaders to their publics. Although the complexities of fascism and mass media exceed the confines of my essay if one is to go beyond clichés, I want to touch upon the relation between the technological voice and the ideology of fascism, especially its popular mythology, in order to capture the psychological and social roles the technological voice began to play.

The political ambivalence of the popular mythology of radio must be stressed. Radio's ability to range freely across space, crossing borders and penetrating barriers, could lead to utopian fantasies of a unified transnational world. Rudolph Arnheim's 1936 study *Radio* expresses this ideal:

> Wireless is equally available on either side of the frontier. Nor is it like a letter, message, telegram or telephone conversation which can be suppressed or stopped at the frontier; it passes all customs-officers, needs no cable, penetrates all walls and even in house raids is very difficult to catch.[11]

And yet this ghostlike ability to penetrate anywhere, radio's inability to be shut out, can also generate fear of submission to an all-powerful voice, a fear that corresponds to psychoanalytical descriptions of fantasies of persecution both paranoid and schizophrenic, as well as recalling actual techniques of surveillance and propaganda by modern political entities.

The free penetration of radio makes it a powerful model for the "loss of ego boundaries" described by Freud's disciple Victor Tausk in his famous essay on the fantasy of "the influencing machine."[12] In this delusion, patients described their persecution and control via an elaborate apparatus that submits them to an alien will that "produces as well as removes thoughts and feelings by means of waves or rays or mysterious forces which the patient's knowledge of physics is inadequate to explain."[13] Both Tausk's patient and the psychotic Dr. Schreber discussed by Freud saw themselves as tortured physically and mentally by invisible rays and powerful influences against which they had no defense. Alien wills, thoughts, and feelings were in effect projected into them by powerful personalities, including, as in Schreber's case, God himself.

These psychotic fantasies have some similarity to the ambitions that fascists had of controlling populations through the medium of radio. Soon after the Nazi election victories in 1933, control of the Reich's radio was placed under Goebbels's Ministry of Propaganda. Goebbels in 1938 famously claimed that "It is no exaggeration to say that the German revolution, at least in the form it took, would have been impossible without the airplane and the radio."[14] Beyond its modern nature in overcoming space and time, radio, Goebbels proclaimed, was the medium of the spiritual power of the Nazi revolution. "The radio is the most influential and important intermediary between a spiritual movement and the nation, between the idea and the people."[15] Goebbels's control of radio made it the organ of Nazi propaganda; as he announced in 1933: "We will place the radio in the service of our ideology and no other ideology will find expression there."[16]

Eugen Hadamovsky, executive director of the Reich Broadcasting Corporation, described radio in terms that blend its mastery of space with psychological control: "A miraculous power—the strongest weapon ever given to the spirit—that opens hearts and does not stop at the borders of cities and does not turn back before closed doors; that jumps rivers, mountains and seas; that is able to force people under the spell of one powerful spirit."[17] Of course one should not take such political rhetoric, any more than psychotic fantasies, for actual fact. After a year of aggressive political broadcasting, Nazi radio managers realized that this was not the way to maintain the broad popular audience they sought, and returned to a primarily entertainment-based programing.[18] But both rhetoric and fantasies reflect what I am calling the popular mythology of the technological voice and reveal its role in merging the psychological and the political, thereby generating both intimacy and terror. Voices that penetrate and influence, and whose source remains ungraspable.

Few figures have dealt as deeply with the resonance of the technological voice as the Austrian-German film director Fritz Lang. His masterpiece *M* from 1930 demonstrated an early grasp of the dynamics of film sound, capturing the grain of the voice in its use of an everyday vernacular with an unmistakable Berlin accent, thus anchoring its plot in a specific realist environment. But Lang also explored the range of spatial relations that voice and sound could have to the image onscreen. Throughout *M*, the voice not only syncs with the image onscreen; it often asserts its independence by taking place offscreen (opening the space beyond the frame). The film's opening in which the voice of Mrs. Beckmann echoes across space, attempting to call home her daughter who has been the victim of a serial killer, remains one of the most poignant uses of voice in the history of cinema.[19] But, as Michel Chion has shown, it is perhaps Lang's second sound film, *The Testament of Dr. Mabuse*, that plays most daringly with the disembodied voice (a phenomenon Chion has dubbed the "acousemêtre"). In this film, Lang explores the power rather than the poignancy of the voice separated from its embodied source, especially the liberation of voice from its original source through technology (recording and broadcast) and hallucinatory fantasy.[20]

The "testament" of Dr. Mabuse consists of written plans for establishing the "Empire of Crime," which psychiatrist Dr. Baum inherits from the insane gangster and terrorist Mabuse after he dies while an inmate in Baum's asylum. Mabuse was admitted to the asylum, mute and nearly catatonic. Staring blankly before him, Mabuse's only physical movement is to fill page upon page mechanically with what seem at first pointless scribbles. Eventually Baum realizes these seemingly random marks actually form a complex interweaving of text and image. Mabuse functions as a sort of writing machine, performing automatic writing without pause or reflection. These hieroglyphic texts outline Mabuse's "Herrschaft des Verbrechens," the empire of crime, a plan for total control stemming from a series of terrorist attacks, destruction of public services, such as railways, water and gas works, and the manipulation of currency. The testament calls for crimes "which profit no one, whose only objective is to inspire fear and terror."

In the film's central scene, Dr. Baum reads these words from Mabuse's testament soon after his death. Baum lifts his head from the paper toward the camera and closes his eyes as if going into a trance as the camera moves in on him. On the soundtrack, the reading of the text continues ("the only purpose of crime is to establish the endless empire of crime, a state of complete insecurity and anarchy") but is taken over by an entirely different voice than Baum's—harsh, raspy, and whispering—very closely miked, high in pitch in contrast to Baum's deep bass. We also hear on the soundtrack a high-pitched continual chord. This moment has a strong resonance with Lang's previous silent Mabuse film *Dr. Mabuse the Gambler* from 1923, in which Mabuse exerted his control over victims primarily through hypnosis. In the earlier film, Mabuse's demonic mind control was imaged as an intent stare that Mabuse directed at a victim. The power of this hypnotic gaze was conveyed through a direct 180-degree shot/countershot editing pattern. In its most powerful instance, Lang combines this editing with track-in on Mabuse, which seems to greatly enlarge his face against a black background. The track-in to Baum in *Testament* seems to reference Mabuse's hypnotic power from the earlier film, but instead of conveying the power of a gaze, it is a whispering and eerie voice that dominates the shot. The sequence seems to portray Baum's autohypnosis, or even his possession by Mabuse's plan (or the spirit of the dead madman).

The next shots follow the pattern of shot/reverse shot of the earlier Mabuse film, alternating between Dr. Baum and the wraith-like figure of Mabuse, but work in a much more ambiguous manner, exceeding the role of indicating an exchange of glances. As Baum's eyes suddenly pop open, we cut to the source of the whispering voice, the Mabuse figure sitting across from Baum at the table. But, as opposed to the enlarged close-up of Mabuse's hypnotic stare from the first Mabuse film, Mabuse appears as an odd phantom, resembling a revenant from the silent Weimar cinema. This semitransparent and heavily made-up Mabuse stares through opaque artificial eyes that almost eliminate the pupils, making him resemble a Sumerian idol with an apparently exposed brain. The whispering voice continues its rant: "When humanity, subjugated by the terror of crime, has been driven insane by fear and horror, and when chaos has become supreme law, then the time will have come for the empire of crime." Lang intercuts close-ups of Baum staring directly into the camera as the Mabuse phantom speaks. As the voice ends, Lang cuts to a long shot showing the phantom and Baum seated on opposite sides of the table. The Mabuse phantom splits, as a transparent double rises from the seated phantom, and then appears beside Baum. After placing the manuscript pages before him, this double sits down in Baum's chair and seems to be absorbed by Baum's body.

This use of superimposition portrays a psychotic possession visually, as Baum absorbs this alien personality into his body. But on the audio track, this process of surrender to an alien of personality is conveyed through the modulation of the voice in both performance and recording. The voice of Mabuse (who never speaks in the film until after his death) does not have the timbre or cadence of a spoken voice occupying shared space, but rather the whispering intimacy of an interior voice, the sort of voice heard by Tausk's patients or Dr. Schreber: an alien will be issuing commands and threatening punishment.

Now serving as Mabuse's mouthpiece, Baum becomes the hidden mastermind of a gang of criminals. Baum/Mabuse makes use of the technologies of the voice to fulfill the testament of the dead criminal and establish his empire of crime. His communications with the gang that carries out the crimes described in the testament is always mechanically mediated, whether through typewritten notes bearing the name of Mabuse or ordered over the telephone. When the gang members gather in a group to take their orders, they hear Mabuse's voice issuing from behind a curtain on which the silhouette of a man appears as a shadow. When later in the film a rebellious member of the gang fires into this curtain, he discovers the silhouette to be only a pasteboard cutout as the voice issues from the speaker horn of a radio. Even after being riddled with bullets, the electronic Baum/Mabuse continues to broadcast his orders from this horn, exemplifying Chion's concept of the disembodied acousmetric voice.

Toward the end of the film, detective inspector Lohmann presents Baum to the captured members of the Mabuse gang, but none of them can identify him as their leader due to his previous visual camouflage. Identification of Baum with the master criminal Mabuse only occurs when Kent, the rebellious member of the gang, finally recognizes Baum's voice as the one heard coming from behind the curtain. Significantly for Lang's conception of the power of the technologically mediated voice, it is only when he hears a *phonograph recording* of Baum's voice that Kent can make the identification. The voice of the terror plot is not that of the *living* Baum, any more than it is simply the voice of the dead Mabuse. Rather, it is this voice absorbed, "swapped," through the dual process of physical death and mechanical reproduction. The work of death and the technological voice, as Weiss claimed, together allow a new articulation of the voice, either transcending death or, like Edgar Allan Poe's M. Valdemar, suspended within the space between life and death.[21]

The Testament of Dr. Mabuse was the last film Lang directed in Germany, after which he emigrated, serving most of his remaining career in Hollywood. He later, somewhat self-servingly, described *Testament* as an allegory of the Nazi takeover, and indeed, the Nazis banned the film in 1933. Besides the numerous films Lang directed in the United States, he also wrote a number of unproduced scenarios and treatments during this period. One of these, *LB 2*, brilliantly weaves together and articulates a number of the themes that make up the popular mythology of the appropriated voice of technology, its mass address, and its association with the voice of death and terror.[22]

In *LB 2*, an American businessman (Lang describes him as an entrepreneur marketing chewing gum or sewing machines) investigating business opportunities in Europe after the end of World War II becomes embroiled in a plot to revive Nazism. The businessman appears on the streets of Brussels unwittingly wearing a tie that is meant to serve as the secret insignia of a clandestine group. As he strolls along, strangers approach him and surreptitiously slip him money and valuables. Approached by the secret service of the United Nations, the businessman learns that he involuntarily has become an agent of an effort to raise money for the return to power of Adolf Hitler. The center of this plot is a series of shortwave broadcasts that have popped up in Europe from a station that identifies itself as LB 2, in which the voice of Hitler is heard announcing, "The Führer speaks to you." Hearing this "cursed" voice, auditors, Lang tells us, react with "fear, anger, consternation and in certain cases, joy."

The voice of Hitler announces that, contrary to false Allied reports, he remains alive and will soon return to power. The voice asks fascist sympathizers throughout Europe to offer financial support to his undercover agents, who will be walking the streets of European cities bearing a secret insignia. The United Nations agents try to track the source of the broadcasts and identify the voice, which is confirmed by experts in phonology to be Hitler's. It is first suspected that the voice may be the product of a montage of Hitler's previous speeches, but constant references to current events in the broadcasts belie this thesis. Attempts to locate the point of the broadcast are unsuccessful, and station LB 2 remains, as Lang says, "ungraspable." It broadcasts, we learn, from a mobile unit, moving through the streets of European cities disguised variously as an ambulance, a grocery delivery truck, or a moving van. A suspenseful chase narrative follows, which Lang explicitly modeled on a Hitchcock thriller, moving through settings in various countries and all levels of society and including both comedy and romance. The mobile radio unit is finally located during a broadcast. Searching the van, the UN agents cannot locate Hitler. Instead, the source of the voice is revealed to be not a resurrected Führer, but an unemployed former Hungarian vaudeville performer who had earlier made a career imitating Hitler's speeches. The plot for the revival of fascism in Europe turns out to be a simple confidence scam in which the organizers were lining their own pockets with contributions from Nazi sympathizers.

The return of the Führer that had inspired terror or joy is revealed, then, as a voice and nothing more. This confluence of the popular entertainment of a vaudeville voice imitator using broadcast technology within an atmosphere of terror spawned by recent historical events makes Lang's yarn a powerful condensation of the mythology of the technological voice. This voice can be addressed to everyone ("The Führer speaks to you"), yet can be deceptive about its source. Its source seems to be recognizable, yet it remains elusive to grasp or locate. Lang ends his rather brief treatment with this statement:

> The world learns the identity of the self-proclaimed Führer. The legend of Hitler is destroyed. The entire world heaves a collective sigh of relief. The entire world breaks into a Homeric burst of laughter.

Lang reassures the entire postwar world, still haunted by the echoing voice of Hitler mediated by technology, through a burlesque act of stripping away false facades. In the end, carnivalesque laughter dispels terror. But it is perhaps worth noting that the voice still plays a crucial role in this expression of comic inversion: the collective sigh, the Homeric guffaw of the entire world, invokes precisely that element of breath that the technological voice can never possess (hence Allen S. Weiss's canny title for his book on sound recording and disembodiment, *Breathless*). Yet one might wonder what the medium for this concluding expression of forced breath and laughter of the "entire world" might be. And how in fact might it be broadcast—and how will it be heard?

Notes

1. Tom Gunning, "Doing for the Eye What the Phonograph Does for the Ear," in *The Sounds of Early Cinema*, ed. Rick Altman and Richard Abel (Bloomington: University of Indiana Press, 2001), 13–31.

2. Roland Barthes, *Camera Lucida* (New York: Hill and Wang, 1982).

3. Allen S. Weiss, *Breathless: Sound Recording, Disembodiment, and the Transformation of Lyrical Nostalgia* (Middletown, CT: Wesleyan University Press, 2002), xiii.

4. Weiss, *Breathless*, 19.

5. Jeffrey Sconce, *Haunted Media: Electronic Presence from Telegraphy to Television* (Durham, NC: Duke University Press, 2000); and Lawrence Rainey, "Taking Dictation: Collage Poetics, Pathology, and Politics," *Modernism and Modernity* 5, no. 2 (1998): 123–53.

6. Weiss, *Breathless*, 19.

7. Anthony Giddens, *The Consequences of Modernity* (Stanford, CA: Stanford University Press, 1990), 21–28.

8. Timothy C. Campbell, *Wireless Writing in the Age of Marconi* (Minneapolis: University of Minnesota Press, 2006), 1–30, offers a summary of Guglielmo Marconi's invention.

9. Friedrich Glauser, *Thumbprint* (London: Bitter Lemon Press, 2004), 87, 109.

10. Jason Loviglio, *Radio's Intimate Public: Network Broadcasting and Mass-Mediated Democracy* (Minneapolis: University of Minnesota Press, 2005).

11. Rudolph Arnheim, *Radio* (London: Faber and Faber, 1936).

12. Victor Tausk, "On the Origin of the 'Influencing Machine' in Schizophrenia," in *Sexuality, War, and Schizophrenia: Collected Psychoanalytic Papers*, ed. Paul Roazen (New Brunswick: Transaction Publishers, 1991), 185–219.

13. Tausk, "On the Origin," 187.

14. Joseph Goebbels, "The Radio as the Eighth Great Power" (1933), German Propaganda Archive, Calvin College web archive, http://research.calvin.edu/german-propaganda-archive.

15. Goebbels, "The Radio as the Eighth Great Power."

16. Quoted in Corey Ross, *Media and the Making of Modern Germany: Mass Communications, Society, and Politics from the Empire to the Third Reich* (Oxford: Oxford University Press, 2008), 281.

17. Martin A. Doherty, *Nazi Wireless Propaganda: Lord Haw-Haw and British Public Opinion in the Second World War* (Edinburgh: Edinburgh University Press, 2000), 4.

18. Ross, *Media and the Making of Modern Germany*, 331.

19. Tom Gunning, *The Films of Fritz Lang: Allegories of Vision and Modernity* (London: British Film Institute, 2000).

20. Michel Chion, *The Voice in Cinema*, trans. Claudia Gorbman (New York: Columbia University Press, 1999), 31–44.

21. Edgar Allan Poe, "The Facts in the Case of M. Valdemar," in *Poe: Poetry and Tales* (New York: Library of America, 1984), 833–42. Weiss's *Breathless* begins with a brilliant discussion of this tale.

22. Fritz Lang, *LB 2*. Although Lang wrote this unproduced scenario treatment in English, it has never been published in this language, so I relied on the French translation by Christine and Jacques Rousselet in *La montagne des superstitions et autres histoires*, ed. Cornelius Schnauber (Paris: Pierre Belfond, 1991), 11–24.

AFTERWORD

Voices That Matter

MLADEN DOLAR

Verba volant, scripta manent, says an old Latin adage. Spoken words fly away, written words remain. Lacan remarks somewhere that actually quite the opposite is the case: written and printed words fly around and make the whirlwind of history, the swiveling chaos of its traces, while spoken words remain on the spot where they were emitted, never leaving their birthplace which coincided with their deathbed, available only to the people who happened to be there to hear them, then entrusted to the unreliable vestiges in their memory.

So my memory takes me back to the outstanding days in November 2015, the days of the voice conference at the University of Chicago, a very happy occasion, an exceptional congregation of very committed scholars, some of them dear friends and colleagues, some of them people I met for the first time on that occasion and instantly engaged with, a generous exchange of ideas, excellent scholarly achievements, a very attentive and competent audience, excellent organization (thank you again, Martha Feldman and Judith Zeitlin), a most memorable event. The occasion cried out for a publication, a collected volume that would no doubt represent a new landmark in the budding field of voice studies and across the disciplines. The spoken words remained there, as voices do, and the volume is now ready to enter the whirlwind, and one hopes that it will capture something of that moment. Which brings us immediately to the topic of the voice and its nature, its treacherous retention by writing, where one would have to avoid the twin traps of mourning the live presence of the voice never to be recaptured, a melancholy loss, and on the other hand the deconstructive proliferation of traces without a foothold. Can there be a voice as "something more" beyond this dilemma?

Having been invited by the editors to write an afterword, I find myself confronted with an impossible task. I was very honored that the title of the conference, "A Voice as Something More," was a paraphrase of the title of my book on the voice, *A Voice and Nothing More*, and a most apposite paraphrase: it was on the one hand a token of recognition, and of course I greatly appreciate it, yet not at all confined to a gesture of an homage, for the point was and is precisely to make "something more" out of it, to take it in other directions, to do something else and different and possibly even opposed to it. What more could an author wish for than to have his work serve as an inspiration and a tool to produce something beyond it, something exceeding its scope? I am glad that my book has become a point of reference, but even more glad that it has contributed to inspiring work that extends and transcends it and explores dimensions beyond its span.

The papers in this collection point in many different directions while having the same problem at their core, tackling it in a vast variety of ways. Are they diverse pieces of a mosaic that in the end add up to a picture, a design, an overall theory? Hardly, but the heterogeneous and nonunified picture they present is perhaps the best way to be true to this multifaceted, elusive object, the object-voice, and the common thread they have at their core is never quite "the same problem." It evolves, it alters and expands through its manifold treatments. There is no way to do justice to all these approaches, all very competent and inspiring in their very different ways, so my few reflections can only be uneven, focusing on some issues that are closer to my own concerns and expertise, while unjustly leaving aside some areas where I lack competence and can only learn myself. And perhaps it is not inappropriate if I take this as an occasion for reflection on my book and its topic from the distance of more than a decade, to deal with some aspects that in retrospect seem unsatisfactory and some aspects that were not dealt with and that ample subsequent work by others has brought to the fore.

One of the recurring criticisms of my book turns around the absence of a chapter that would deal specifically with the aesthetics of the voice, and hence more pointedly with music. The book dealt with the voice under the headings of linguistics, metaphysics, "physics," ethics, and politics, and also dealt with the voice in Freud and Kafka, all oriented by the background insights of psychoanalysis. But what of the voice as an aesthetic object per se, an object of aesthetic enjoyment, with its inherent deployment in music? The way that I presented my case from the outset seemed to imply that there is something wrong and flawed with treating it under the auspices of the aesthetic. "The aesthetic concentration on the voice loses the voice precisely by turning it into a fetish object," as I state at the very opening.[1] Or, to take the even more forthright pronouncement by Jacques-Alain Miller that I quote in the book:

"If we make music and listen to it . . . it is in order to silence what deserves to be called the voice as the object *a*."[2] So the position seems to be clear-cut, and the implied alternative may be spelled out like this: either the music or the voice. If we concentrate on music as an aesthetic experience, then we run the risk of losing the object-voice, the singular dimension of the voice that the book tries to pursue, and that is ultimately to be divorced from sonority. Music would thus ultimately serve as the domestication or an obfuscation of this extraordinary dimension, a way of taming its paradoxical nature. There is definitely something wrong with this alternative.

The title "a voice and nothing more" was obviously meant ironically, for the point of the book could also be summed up, in a makeshift way, by the thesis that there is no such thing as a voice and nothing more. The voice as the paradoxical object of pursuit "exists" only as entangled in the various aspects that the book proposes, linguistic, ethical, political, and so on; it doesn't inhabit a domain of its own, separate from other domains, "out of this world," an autonomous area of study, a voice in its purity untainted and unaffected by other concerns and interests, or even by materiality. There is no such thing, for the object-voice always sticks to the materiality of the worldly experience and its different facets, persevering in them and through them, yet possessing the capacity for the break, for producing a gap in this experience, for introducing a negative aspect, as it were, in its glittering positivity. The object-voice is not an immaterial entity, yet it cannot be quite reduced to the materiality that sustains it, yet what seemingly transcends this materiality can never be isolated as such, as some realm apart. The pursuit and the investigation of this object can never be spared the patient engagement with a variety of experiences that evoke it, and its research is necessarily bound up with heterogeneous fields of research and with an inherent hybridity. Or, to frame this using another simple opposition: one could study it as a separate area if it had an existence of its own, but it doesn't quite; it rather insists on a variety of existing practices and domains. (But I guess the opposition existence/insistence, helpful as it is, also presents its own dangers, for example, of assuming that there is such a thing as an unambiguous existence.)

The argument against the treatment of the voice under the heading of the aesthetic would then hinge on pointing out that the aesthetics of the voice by definition sins against the nature of the object-voice precisely by isolating the voice and considering it as something extant. The moment one isolates it as a separate entity, it turns into a fetish, which by its fascination with its gleaming presence, by aesthetic enjoyment and veneration, presents a rampart against the dimension of the object. And the minimal assumption of an aesthetics of the voice would seem to be that its object exists and can be studied as such.

Still, I was wrong in too quickly dismissing the aesthetics of the voice.[3] Is it really doomed to the fetish by virtue of its nature, which turns a "negative entity" into the deceptive positivity that can be both revered and scrutinized? There is something paradoxical about the very idea of aesthetics and the supposition of it being a "discipline." I rather think that it has the makings of a retroactive fantasy—a "discipline," or an area of study, which would simply deal with "the beautiful" and would hence solidify and fetishize its objects, betraying their ambiguous, uncanny, disturbing, split, wavering nature through the very way of espousing and promoting them. Such an aesthetics may well be a modernist myth, a retroactively imagined and constructed springboard against which modernism could establish its program. The modernist heroic narrative proposed an art that would leave behind the representational and mimetic constraints of the traditional art, an art that could freely espouse its content and its form, autonomously constructing its own rules beyond prescriptive fetters (in the case of music, which always occupied a special position in this regard, abandoning the framework of harmony and tonality that largely ruled its history). The heroic narrative posits (to boil things down) that once there was an era of art where mimesis, representation, fetish, aura, aesthetics, and so on reigned supreme, and then modernism came along and intrepidly bid farewell to all this, inaugurating a new era and opening new horizons, hitherto inconceivable. But was there ever such an era, was there ever such an art? Shouldn't one rather raise the suspicion that this narrative involves a certain homogenization, bringing things down to a handy common denominator that cannot be homogenized or unified?[4] Isn't it rather a myth of an art and its aesthetics that was needed for modernism to be launched? Something was obfuscated in the modernist heroic saga (at least in its widespread vernacular version), something that concerns the simple opposition, at minimum between the fetish and the object (to stick to our problem of the voice and leave aside such wider issues as mimesis).

In my book I briefly evoked Adorno, in connection with two iconic modernist moments, Munch's *The Scream* and Schoenberg's *Erwartung*, pointing out a possible hidden connection between the two in something that could be called "anti-voice." From there, I proposed a formula for a minimal program of modernism: "It hinges on the tenet that *there must be an object other than the fetish*."[5] The program was perhaps most succinctly spelled out in Adorno's famous essay "On the Fetish-Character in Music and the Regression of Listening" (1938).[6] At face value, the proposed formula espouses precisely this understanding: there once was a kind of musical experience largely ruled by the fetish, and modernism provided the path to another experience which offers and pursues an opening to the object-voice beyond the fetish.[7] But perhaps it's all too easy to set up such aesthetics as a straw man, and indeed, since there has always been a discontent, a malaise attached to the very use of this term (to use Rancière's parlance),[8] perhaps aesthetics was always conditioned by an impossibility of aesthetics. After Hegel, aesthetics was doomed to live its afterlife, without ever quite enjoying its life, for Hegel, who largely inaugurated the area (after Baumgarten) with his monumental *Aesthetics*, in the same breath proclaimed its demise, the end of art such as it was supposedly ruled by traditional assumptions. Thus the proper object of aesthetics could perhaps best be epitomized by the split fetish/object; its object is rather the very bar or the gap between the two. This means that one can never simply relegate traditional music and its aesthetic assumptions to the other side of the bar. The fetish function may well serve to cover up the crack, ultimately "the wound of castration," yet it cannot do so without evoking it, its operation is never unambiguous, and we are never confronted simply with one or the other, the fetish or the object; it is the bar between the two that presents a constant task of negotiating their tension.

Several essays in this volume touch upon this. Marcelle Pierson's essay addresses the opposition of modernism to the voice, indeed points up its "rejection of voice,"[9] its struggle against an ingrained vocal aura and the fascination it holds. It explores the opposed strategies by Nono and Stockhausen which, in the argument of the essay, translate into the split epitomized by ultimately sustaining the "human" or "inhuman" voice. The split fetish/object is transposed or elaborated into another split and places the voice, at the heart of modernist concerns, at the verge of human/inhuman which is inherent in it. Martha Feldman's essay points in this direction already by its title "Voice Gap Crack Break": it explores the instances of willed and yet not quite calculable failure as a strategy of bringing forth "the voiceness of the voice," pointing out the enormous discipline and training required of composers and performers in order to paradoxically bring forth the failure, the crack and the excess of jouissance, and it very lucidly points out the dangers not merely of fetishizing the voice but rather of fetishizing the gap, the break, the crack itself. David Levin carefully studies Zemlinsky's *Der Zwerg*, another modernist crux, and its way of tackling the "dwarfed" voice, highlighting the aria of the Dwarf as "an aria of and as the wound," bringing forth "the voice of castration." Seth Brodsky's essay explores the modernist composer's voice (through the instances of Lachenmann, Nono, and Berg) and its paradoxical absence, the strategies of rejection of the authorial voice which is nevertheless pervasive in its absence ("the modernist composer's voice . . . emerges through fantasizing the silence opened up and laid bare in the effort to disintegrate the fantasy of voice"). I cannot do justice to the complexities of the arguments in these essays (and several others which also touch upon this); these are just some instances that pointedly display and magisterially practice advancements in an area of investigation that my book left aside, and what in retrospect I see as its shortcoming. It was based on the assumption that taking the object-voice head-on would necessarily miss it, solidify it, fetishize it, and so on, so that the proposed strategy was that of tackling it sideways, indirectly, through the lenses of linguistics, physics, ethics, and so forth, by displaying how it is irreducible to them. But taking head-on the voice as a musical or more widely aesthetic object actually necessarily leads to taking on its split and the way it is never simply itself, singling out the points where the split is inscribed in its singularity and materiality, through the instances of failure, crack, distortion, silence. . . . By discarding or leaving aside the aesthetics of the voice, I was tacitly still prey to the modernist myth, and I rejoice in the fact that so many of the essays in this volume largely fall into this category, and that they amply display various possibilities for how this is to be done.

In several places in my book, I used the handy demonstrational device of the intersection of two circles.[10] In Seminar XI, Lacan famously used that intersection to illustrate the logic of alienation and separation[11]—although "illustrate" is not quite the right word, for there is no simple illustration that would just innocently clarify and illuminate what was put forth by words, and particularly with Lacan one could see how the topological devices that were initially meant just to illustrate that gradually acquired a dimension of the real and became themselves the privileged objects of theory. The illustration necessarily involves more than what one bargained for. Although the intersection of two circles seems to be the simplest and the most obvious of these devices, its simplicity is treacherous. The way I used it certainly takes liberties with respect to Lacan's intentions in Seminar XI, yet I believe remained faithful to his general thrust.

The basic point I was trying to make (and the intersection of two circles looks like the simplest and most forceful way to demonstrate this) concerned the paradoxical topology of the voice caught between the body and language. The voice doesn't pertain to the body, nor to its stout physical presence; it is a missive and a missile that departs from the body, it emanates from the body's unfathomable interior and extends into the outside world, its "nature" pertains to crossing the boundary inside/outside. The voice evokes a spectral body that cannot be counted as a bodily part. On the other hand, it is also not simply part of language since the linguistic dissection of the voice, the crucial vehicle and ingredient of language, turns the voice into the signifier and cannot tackle it in its dimension of the object, the remainder of the linguistic operation. But this can easily lend itself to a misunderstanding, namely that there are such preexisting entities as "bodies and languages" as two separate areas; the assumption, in other words, that we may well know what a body is and what language is such that we can study these two areas separately following the laws of physiology and linguistics as the established disciplines that deal with them (with a number of adjoining disciplines that provide additional shadings, social, cultural aspects, and so on). So the assumption is that there is hard evidence about the functioning of the body and hard evidence as to the functioning of language, that they follow very different trajectories with no common ground between, say, the somatic and the signifier. Following this, the argument is that the voice provides the paradoxical link that both these separate areas entail and that the voice is the element providing a connection, a tie between the two. The misunderstanding that easily arises is that first we have bodies and languages and then in a second stage we have to figure out their link, their intersection, which is to be found in the voice. But what if the intersection comes first, as it were?[12] What if we are never dealing with some primary givens, seemingly established in themselves, incommensurate in their functioning? Perhaps the experience of the voice ultimately implies that we can never totalize the two areas of bodies and languages as simply separate areas, and once we posit them as separate and incommensurate we can only do so at the price of an obfuscation or repression. When one establishes two neatly separate domains, a repression has already taken place, the repression of their paradoxical interface and intersection. Thus voice would not be the linkage of two preexisting domains, self-evidently given in common experience and pertaining to separate scientific disciplines, but rather the operator of both their linkage and their separation, hence a process, a becoming, a negotiation of a constantly shifting line, a wavering demarcation, a demarcation never to be completed or safely ascertained and recognized. Thus too the experience of the voice, if pursued far enough, would ultimately lead to the experience of an ontological incompleteness and uncertainty, the shattering of common boundaries and separations that we take for granted.[13] As opposed to the totalization of two domains, the voice would rather be the agent of their detotalization.

The essay in this collection that comes closest to this concern—and I was uneasy about this point for a long time, having the impression that I didn't present it clearly enough—is the one by James Q. Davies that addresses the issue directly, although framed in a different way. Already the subtitles in his essay, the first one and the last one, are telling enough: "What comes first: Voice or body?" and "There is no before and after." Davies thus speaks of "the phantasm we call 'the body,'" adding "Bodies, our materialities, are never *just there*."[14] He claims in conclusion that "essences are formed in voice," never simply preceding it, and that "there is no necessary before and after when it comes to voice." To be sure, my contention above that "the intersection comes first" was rather a provocation to call into question the assumptions of usual temporality and causality. Indeed, there is strictly speaking no before and after, and the proposal of an inversed temporality is a tool to help us change any such perspective. And even when Davies presents his reservations and criticism in regard to psychoanalysis, speaking ironically of "fracture, interruption, schizophonia, rhizophonia, breakage, rupture, absence, some fearful modernist break," I tend to go along with his claims "that vocal aura is less a byproduct of voice's detachment from the world than an effect of voice's deep connection to that world," and that voices are "in fact involved in placing matters in the world, and making worldly presence available and known to us." It is precisely because there is no priority given to bodies, and palpable social entities, as opposed to the detached voice, that the voice in its spectral materiality is placed at the core of the material and of the social fabric. Its detachment, more precisely the way it is not deducible from nor reducible to materiality, doesn't relegate it to some immaterial place apart, but rather places it at the principle of the very torsion that inhabits the material entities from inside and conditions their presentation. The break, the rupture, the gap is never simply an operator of detachment, but rather an operator of a "closer" attachment, as it were, to the entities from which it is supposedly detached, and it is this "too-closeness" rather than the extrication that presents the problem. But this also means that the claim that there is no before and after, that there is no ontological priority, doesn't entail a world of coalescence and unproblematic coexistence of bodies and voices, say, enhancing each other in the intermingling and the mixture, but this is a world still based on a break and antagonism.[15]

This brings me to a further consideration on matter and on materialism. The subtitle of the collection is "Essays Toward Materiality," which frames the volume in the direction of seeking and promoting materiality, ultimately of espousing materialism. Of course there is the great danger of idealizing the voice, and this may well have been one of the major levers of idealism (cf. Derrida's notion of phonocentrism as the key to metaphysics); there is also the danger that in opposing this "spontaneous" idealist tendency inscribed in the voice and its spectrality, one would espouse an "indirect" idealism through the roundabout of a more sophisticated argument that would sustain it in a circuitous way. But let me state my position clearly: just as there is no "voice and nothing more," for the voice (as with all instances of the object *a* in psychoanalysis)[16] is always attached to the body and in a wider sense to materiality rather than inhabiting some separate realm detached from "reality," so there is no such thing as "matter and nothing more," a matter that would coincide with itself and would form the firm basis of our reality and experience. (As stated above, bodies and materialities are never just there, which may be the simplest way of putting it.) Voice and language, *objets a* and structures, only exist through their material "manifestations," but they are neither deducible from positive material properties nor reducible to them—but this doesn't call for a dualism (two separate realms or substances) nor does it amount to monism (matter as the single substance). This is the difficult thing with matter and materialism: to take into account "*more than one*" (the matter not coinciding with itself always involving a lack/surplus, the surplus at the point of a lack) as well as "*less than two*"—for there is no other dimension to which one could relegate what is not accountable through matter alone. In other words, matter is not a substance, and what is wrong with so many varieties of materialism is not that they swear by matter, but that they turn it into a substance—which is precisely a move that structurally espouses an idealist perspective.[17]

The same goes for the body, and the common move of extolling the body seems to be the touchstone of materialism. What could be more palpably and viscerally present than bodies, their palpitating and throbbing flesh, their pain and jouissance? Those bodies that have been neglected and demoted to a secondary rank by virtually the whole philosophical tradition, which preferred to speak about ideas, so that materialism would have to firmly assert them? Yet, there is the danger of the mystification and even the spiritualization of the body in this move (palpably present in many versions of the current vogue for new materialisms), and there is the danger of adopting the all-too-easy stance of what Badiou termed "democratic materialism,"[18] based on the adage that "there are only bodies and languages" (in which Badiou sees the unwitting idealism of our times). There is the danger of extolling the voice as an extension of the body and its flesh, most famously present in Roland Barthes's notorious formula of "the grain of the voice" as "the body in the singing voice,"[19] celebrating the grain of the body, its recalcitrant remainder, as the crux of what appears as disembodied.[20] In regard to all these dangers and what I see as possible pitfalls, I continue to follow the basic psychoanalytic line: to put it simply, body is in fact the cut in the body.[21] There is no body without a cut, without a wound, and the voice is the indicator of this cut, this wound, not simply of the visceral presence of the body in its multiple forms. This is why I proposed the extreme formula of envisaging a voice deprived of sonority, of all its material properties (epitomized by the silent voice), an utter reduction of the body in the voice—not in order to arrive at some disembodied pure ideal entity of a voice beyond all audible voices and sonorities, but in order to push the logic of the cut to the extreme, thus not to turn the *objet a* into a bodily remainder, however fragmented, distorted, distilled, or maimed. The point is not to place the voice somewhere beyond bodies and materialities, but at their core, with the insistence on the cut which disrupts them at that core. There is no such thing as a pure voice that one would have to extricate from the messiness of the bodily and the material, for the cut that conditions the voice runs through their core and has no other location, so that one is always stuck with closely scrutinizing and passionately investigating the inherent impurity of the voice, its "cut-value" being internal and not external to "bodies that matter." Is materiality and "carnality" that which constitutes the "something more" in the title slogan "the voice as something more"? I don't believe so, for there is no simple way of espousing materiality and "carnality," for the reasons I have tried to briefly develop here.

One more remark of a different tenor, inspired by Judith Zeitlin's remarkable essay. I lack any competence in Chinese studies, so the remark goes in the direction of the possible repercussions of her survey of the multiple uses of the voice in Chinese culture and history on "our" own assumptions. I have used the device of the intersection of two circles also for the intersection between *phone* and logos,[22] to "illustrate" the way that Aristotle set up their opposition, in a passage (at the beginning of his *Politics*) foundational to so many presuppositions and ramifications of Western political philosophy and anthropology. We take for granted the divide between *phone* and logos, which has informed our tradition, and it is difficult for us to adopt another perspective. But is this divide obvious, self-evident, unambiguous, and clear-cut? (I mean clear-cut as an assumption that my argument then tries to dismantle by the intersection.) The way that Zeitlin presents the multifaceted uses of the voice in the Chinese culture (to the point that there is no single and simple word for the voice in Chinese) entails a reflection on or a questioning of its seeming givenness. One has to envisage a constellation where there is no massive opposition between *phone* and logos (or between the voice and the signifier),[23] but rather a series of "weak differences," which don't amount to and cannot be summed up by this massive opposition. The cut may have different faces that are heterogeneous and irreducible to *phone*/logos. Does this also call into question in a more general way the use of the intersection of two circles as a simple demonstrational scheme? Does it call for some different and more refined instruments and different topologies? The questions must remain suspended here, for they require further investigation.

In my book, I recurrently used the mechanism of the echo, briefly dealing with the Narcissus and Echo story in Ovid, pointing out the echoes and reverberations in homonymies and similarities within what Lacan called *lalangue*, and finally dealing with the soundless echo produced in the Other, returning the message to the sender in an inverted form, and one that may well stand at the core of the psychoanalytic endeavor.[24] Still, these uses were scattered and limited, not taken far enough, and the remarkable essay by Shane Butler amply reminds us of this and extends their scope. I have some basic disagreements with it, but this in no way affects my appreciation.

One particularly poignant way to display the split, the cut that conditions the voice, is by way of the echo, the mechanism of the split as the minimal redoubling of the voice. The voice is something that produces an echo, and one could ultimately claim that there is no voice without an echo, that it necessarily entails an echo—no voice without a strange appendix, which links our topic of the voice (as partial object, object *a*) to another paramount topic of psychoanalysis, that of repetition. To put it in a nutshell, in repetition between one occurrence and the next, which seems but to repeat the same, there is a gap, and through this gap the second time is never the same as the first one. The voice is echoed, and the echo, far from being the fading of the voice, its extenuation, more of the same only less so, is the way that repetition produces a novelty. Instead of revisiting Ovid, let me take a quote from Kierkegaard to elaborate on this point. Kierkegaard, who was so attached to reflections on irony and who also wrote a wonderful small book on repetition, saw the simplest lever of both in the echo. For irony, one can rely on common experience: if one merely echoes the proffered words by literally repeating them, this inevitably fills them with irony and undermines their authority and the speaker's intent. Everything can be submitted to irony merely by being echoed. Here is how Kierkegaard puts it:

> Oh Echo, yes Echo, thou great master of irony! You who parody in yourself the highest and deepest on earth: the Word which created the world, since you merely give the contour not the fullness. . . . Yes, Echo, you whom I once heard chastise a nature lover when he exclaimed: "Hear yonder, the lonesome flute tones of a lovelorn nightingale" [*Nattergal*]—and you answered: "Mad" [*gal*].[25]

The romantic poet wanted to praise the nightingale (which echoes Shane Butler's argument), but the echo ironically pointed out his madness by merely repeating the last bit of his elated speech (this only works in Danish). Kierkegaard's example of course echoes the *locus princeps* in Ovid, the nymph Echo who could only repeat what was said, but managed nevertheless to say everything just by echoing, filling every utterance with irony. The voice is answered by the echo, and it seems that the echo brings only a contour, a pale shadow of the original, yet in that shadow there is nevertheless a surplus, something that has the form of an unexpected answer, there being more in the echo than in the voice echoed.[26] The voice obtains a "supplement" in the echo, which merely repeats it, but thereby displaces and transforms it, producing more than what was enclosed in the original. This is the irony of repetition: one merely repeats the same, yet the repeated thing alters with repetition—it brings new and unexpected meaning by just echoing, like *gal*—but this is a way in which the echo cashes in, as it were, on this surplus by turning it into a new meaning. Yet what is at stake (and here both Ovid's and Kierkegaard's examples may be misleading) is not just the production of a new and unexpected meaning through the echo, but rather circumscribing a gap in meaning, a gap that insists through repetition; and its counterpart is an excess which is as if produced by it, between the occurrence and its echo.

There is more. Kierkegaard's fragment from *Papirer* begins like this: "Each time I wish to say something there is another who says it at the very same moment. It is as though *I thought double*, and my other self continually stole a march on me." This is where this passage is really astounding. To follow this line, the echo is not produced only in the aftermath, it is already interior to what is said. It is tacitly inscribed in its first occurrence, the utterance is in itself already inextricably intertwined with its own echo, and my voice is redoubled with the echo from the outset, hence the voice is "always already" a split voice. This too one can extend: the echo would thus always be the echo of an echo, repeating the repetition that secretly accompanied it already the first time, making explicit that the first occurrence was not equal to itself, or contemporary to itself, that it was already the echo of itself and in itself. The moment I speak, another voice intrudes into mine, like an alien that I myself produced but cannot control, not quite another self, but an unintended echo of the self, at the kernel of my selfhood. The moment I think, another thought encroaches on mine, as if I were thinking double. Thus, repetition would only repeat the initial split of the supposed original, bringing forth a real that emerged in it and which is not reducible to an identity or to a (positive) difference, irreducible to the difference between the original and its echo. Following this line, the voice would thus be "a voice within a voice," indeed "a voice as something more," emerging the moment one tries to isolate the simplest voice.

What Lacan called the object-voice doesn't coincide with any voice one can hear, but at the same time it cannot be placed somewhere apart; as an otherworldly extraterrestrial voice of some beyond, it cannot be disentangled from the voices produced and heard, but rather inhabits them as their inaudible appendix. The echo is perhaps a privileged way to approach this dimension and to render it palpable—the echo as precisely the agent of the split. The echo, by seemingly being a mere shadow, throws a shadow on what it is the shadow of. It doesn't merely repeat the voice in an extenuated (or amplified) form; it exhibits the split that was already there in the supposed original, and the object-voice can only make a shadowy appearance between the two. Perhaps saying "voice" already implies "two voices," not coinciding either with the original voice or with its echo.

Following this logic of the echo, one can propose a subjective position that goes along with it, or to use a stronger word, an ethical stance. One could call it the ethics of the echo—to make oneself an echo, or to turn into echo. From there, one can make a quick short-circuit to psychoanalysis: seen in this light, what else is the position of the analyst but the stance of turning oneself into a soundless echo of what is said, and thereby transforming it? Isn't the position of the analyst akin to Ovid's nymph Echo in relation to the Narcissus of the analysand? Maybe the minimal wager of psychoanalysis is not unrelated to the minimal move of irony, such as Kierkegaard describes it—not as the smiling conceit or the self-congratulatory cleverness, but as the force of insistent negativity, joining forces with the minimal move of repetition. The echo presented in analysis, the silent yet unrelenting echo, doesn't go in the direction that both Ovid's and Kierkegaard's examples point to, the direction of producing a surplus meaning, finding unexpected meaning in the mere echoing of what is said, but rather in the direction of flaunting the gap in meaning that echo brings to the fore, by merely formal and structural means. Its aim is not filling in the gaps in view of a seamless restoration of meaning, the recovery of some lost or deeper meaning, but leaving the gap open where a truth can emerge.

Another point can be stressed (or restated) in this context. The logic of the echo is all-pervasive in the Lacanian notion of *lalangue*, which can be seen as a massive web of echoing within language as the web of signifiers. One could say: ultimately there is no signifier without an echo, although the implication here is rather different from "no voice without an echo." For the signifier is in itself a mere disembodied web of differences, "with no positive terms," as Saussure insisted, divorced from any materiality or bodily presence. Yet, signifiers can only be there through their material manifestations—the notion of a pure signifier is a pure fantasy, it has no hold, and the moment it is attached to a voice (or writing), it enters the universe of reverberations and echoes. The moment one can hear (or see) a signifier, it becomes endowed with contingency, and the subject is attached not just to the signifier but essentially to these linguistic contingencies. No language without homonymy, which entails a massive psychoanalytic consequence: no unconscious without homonymy, which is ultimately based on the mechanism of the echo. One could thus maintain: no unconscious without an echo. For the scandalous thing with the Freudian unconscious is that it is not based on pursuing a hidden or repressed meaning, but utterly depends on the contingent encounter of words and sounds. It is based on the capacity of language for punning, not on the differentiality of the signifier. Nobody is Saussurean in their unconscious,[27] everybody is rather a Cratylian (to evoke Plato's curious dialogue *Cratylus*, which can be read as a sheer exercise in *lalangue*, language under the auspices of the nonarbitrary). The echo, in this large sense, is the condition of the unconscious, for the unconscious depends on the sonority of the nonsonorous signifier, yet is irreducible to the sonorous effects as well as to the effects of meaning, instead inhabiting gaps and cracks, so that one can never meet it in person, as it were, only through dislocations, distortions, and echoes.

I have limited my (admittedly dense) comments to these three aspects, the question of the aesthetics, the nature of intersection, and the mechanism of the echo, all of which call for reflections about what I see as shortcomings in my book. These three aspects touch upon a number of essays in this volume, and I regret that I couldn't engage with other essays that equally deserve further reflections and response: Neil Verma's and Tom Gunning's lucid dives, from very different angles, into the "radio voice," which by way of the haunting technological "roundabout" comes so close to the strange nature of voice itself; Steven Rings's persuasive exploration of the thin (always already crossed?) line between speech and song; Robert Polito's luminous reflections on the voice in poetry, both the inevitability and the impossibility of its status and metaphor (and I am very grateful for being introduced to the wonderful poetry of James Merrill that I was not familiar with before); Laurie Stras's vivid presentation of the three black women blues singers, on the thin line between mimicry, de-individualization, and asserting an identity; Andrew Jones's powerful exposition of "the voice of the Jamaican ghetto" on another thin line between the voice and its technological transformation/"distortion"; Jonathan Zwicker's fascinating glimpse into a very particular Japanese historic juncture involving a critical moment of the voice. This is but a patchy list giving some very short snippets of a vast variety of cues that would demand extensive reflection.

As to the shortcomings of my own work, of course there are more, and I am glad that the work presented in this volume has substantially extended the scope of my book in new directions and in many ways superseded its span. I rejoice that the area of voice studies has expanded beyond anything I could imagine a decade ago, and that this volume is part of a vigorous collective effort and engagement to be pursued.

Notes

1. Mladen Dolar, *A Voice and Nothing More* (Cambridge, MA: MIT Press, 2006), 4.

2. Dolar, *A Voice*, 31.

3. I didn't simply dismiss it, I actually amply wrote about some of its aspects in the book devoted to opera, Slavoj Žižek and Mladen Dolar, *Opera's Second Death* (New York and London: Routledge, 2002). But the framework and the ambition of that book were quite different.

4. To take two paradigmatic instances of modernity: first, the Brechtian notion of estrangement, *Verfremdungseffekt*, which, at least in its naive form, relies on a foundational narrative that there once was the Aristotelian theater based on empathy and identification, and then Brecht undermined its presuppositions by the effect of estrangement. But did such a theater ever exist? One could oppose this narrative by means of two simple theses: first, there never was a theater which would simply fit that description, and second, the Brechtian estrangement didn't quite dismantle it in any case. Second, the narrative of Benjamin's famous piece is usually spelled out like this: there once was the auratic art that the advent of mechanical reproduction then dismantled. Against this, one should perhaps maintain: first, there has never been such a thing as an auratic art, not in its usual description, and second, nevertheless mechanical reproduction failed to dismantle it, though it may have rendered it more intractable (as Adorno was quick to point out). But all this would lead us too far astray.

5. Dolar, *A Voice*, 69.

6. Theodor W. Adorno, *Essays on Music*, ed. Richard Leppert, trans. Susan H. Gillespie (Berkeley and Los Angeles: University of California Press, 2002).

7. Adorno, to be sure, massively warns against the fetish character being increased and reinforced with modernity, and argues for "structural listening," which works against the fetish character already in traditional music.

8. Jacques Rancière, *Aesthetics and Its Discontents* (Cambridge: Polity Press, 2009).

9. Cf. "It may seem as though a simple rejection of voice would be the best course of action for a modernist, but . . . the results of this meeting between voice and modernism are much more complicated and contradictory than that."

10. Dolar, *A Voice*, 73, 103, 121.

11. Jacques Lacan, *The Four Fundamental Concepts of Psychoanalysis*, ed. Jacques-Alain Miller, trans. Alan Sheridan (London: Penguin, 1977), 211–12.

12. An analogous point can be made about the division into the interior and the exterior of the body. Voice inhabits the passage between the two; it is "nothing but" the passage in its emission and its reception, but the two areas do not simply preexist the divide. Rather, it is by negotiating this divide through the passage that they can be treated as separate—and the experience of the voice is such that the boundary is always wavering, to the point that the question can

be raised whether one can conceive of the very notion of an interior and its exterior counterpart without a reference to the voice (or more generally to the partial object).

13. This point has further far-reaching consequences concerning the status of some key psychoanalytic entities on the verge between nature and culture. Thus Freud describes the drive as the representative of the somatic in the psychic, placing it precisely on the interface between nature and culture. The analogous argument can be made that ultimately the interface, the intersection, doesn't come second in relation to two preexisting realms (of nature and culture), but actually undermines their seeming givenness and renders their totalization (setting them up as two opposed totalities) impossible. The drive is neither simply natural nor simply cultural, nor does it inhabit some other location. I have developed this further in "Of Drives and Culture," *Problemi International* 1, no. 1 (2017): 55–79.

14. Martha Feldman in her essay speaks of "not-quite-thereness" of the voice as the partial object, but this "not-quite-thereness" has repercussions for the "not-quite-thereness" of bodies and materialities that seem to present something unquestionably solid, as opposed to voice's fickleness. The nature of the voice (and of partial objects) affects them, but one cannot quite adopt the terms of cause and effect since they would subscribe to their temporal and ontological priority.

15. This may well be the point where Davies and I would perhaps disagree, despite the proximity.

16. To follow Lacan's list from the seminar on anxiety, the four basic forms of *objet a* would be the breast, the feces (the anal object), the gaze, and the voice. But Lacan also offered some other lists scattered throughout his writings, and the lists are symptomatically inconsistent, although all instances refer to the topology of an edge and of bodily orifices. See, for instance, *Écrits: A Selection*, trans. Alan Sheridan (London: Routledge, 2001), 349.

17. I have tried to explore this at more length in my essay "What's the Matter? On Matter and Related Matters," in the volume *Subject Lessons: Hegel, Lacan, and the Future of Materialism*, ed. Russell Sbriglia and Slavoj Žižek (Evanston, IL: Northwestern University Press, forthcoming).

18. Cf. Alain Badiou, *Logics of Worlds: Being and Event, 2*, trans. Alberto Toscano (London: Bloomsbury, 2009).

19. Roland Barthes, *The Grain of the Voice: Interviews 1962–1980* (New York: Vintage, 2010).

20. This is also where I have a number of reservations in regard to the admirable book by Adriana Cavarero, *For More Than One Voice: Toward a Philosophy of Vocal Expression*, trans. Paul A. Kottman (Stanford, CA: Stanford University Press, 2005). For my discussion of it, see "Sinn oder Präsenz?," *Zeitschrift für Kulturphilosophie* 3, no. 1 (2009): 17–34.

21. Many are deterred and put off by the term *castration*, the psychoanalytic name for this cut. It may seem outdated, or prey to phallocentric logic, or simply crude. Many would prefer to talk instead about human finitude, vulnerability, and frailty, which appears as the more generally acceptable and palatable vocabulary. But I think that insistence on the term *castration* is the insistence on the materialism of psychoanalysis, its "bodily anchorage" precisely at the point where it puts into question any simple extolling of the body.

22. Dolar, *A Voice*, 121.

23. As a philosopher, I may be too inclined to think in big oppositions. Sarah Nooter's essay lucidly explores all the complexities of *phone* in ancient Greece and gives a far more refined picture that in its implications may well complicate the supposedly neat opposition.

24. Dolar, *A Voice*, 40, 141–45, 160–61, respectively.

25. From *Papirer* III, B 2. I owe this reference to Denise Riley, *The Words of Selves: Identification, Solidarity, Irony* (Stanford, CA: Stanford University Press, 2000), 160, who quotes Lee M.

Capel's introduction to Kierkegaard's *The Concept of Irony with Constant Reference to Socrates*, trans. Lee M. Capel (New York: Collins, 1966), 23.

26. I guess my biggest disagreement with Shane Butler concerns this point. He writes: "The problem with Lacan's 'mirror stage' is not what it does to us, but what it does to its mirror, reducing it to a bare functionalism—a reflection, let us say, and nothing more." In my view, the central tenet of psychoanalysis is that there is more in the reflection, and the echo, than in the original. There can be no "reflection and nothing more"; it always bears heavy consequences. Perhaps the most conspicuous proof is the question of the doppelgänger that Freud addressed in his essay on the uncanny and to which Otto Rank devoted a classical study (1914, 1925, cf. *The Double: A Psychoanalytic Study* [London: Maresfield Library, 1989]). The doppelgänger is precisely "a reflection turned into flesh," the double that annihilates the subject, and in every reflection there is something of the same logic (of reflection striking back, as it were), including in the mirror stage.

27. Saussure himself couldn't quite sustain being a Saussurean. At the same time as he set up the new science of language built on the differentiality of the signifier, he was plagued by the obsessive search for anagrams. The moment he looked at any text (he confined himself to some classical Latin texts), the anagrams started swarming around, with no way to contain them. This was his own way of experiencing the "shimmering of the signifier" (to repeat Shane Butler's quoting of Barthes). Anagrams can be seen as "the voice in writing," the voice emerging from the combination of "dead letters." Michel Chion's intriguing essay mentions anagrams in this more restricted sense, but the larger picture he addresses centrally concerns "the voice in writing" as inherently linked to sexual difference. One is reminded of Lacan's adage that sexual difference is "what doesn't cease not to be written," a far-reaching formula that links sexual difference precisely to "the voice in writing."

Contributors

SETH BRODSKY is associate professor of music and the humanities at the University of Chicago. He is the author of *From 1989, or European Music and the Modernist Unconscious* (University of California Press, 2017), and has published on such topics as opera, influence, psychosis, and the music of Benjamin Britten, John Cage, and Wolfgang Rihm. He served in 2018–2019 as interim director of the University of Chicago's Gray Center for Arts and Inquiry, and is at work on a book about repetition, musical, historical, and psychoanalytic.

SHANE BUTLER is Nancy H. and Robert E. Hall Professor in the Humanities and professor and chair of Classics at Johns Hopkins University. His monographs include *The Matter of the Page* (University of Wisconsin Press, 2011) and *The Ancient Phonograph* (Zone Books, 2015), and he is the coeditor of both *Synaesthesia and the Ancient Senses* (Acumen, 2013) and *Sound and the Ancient Senses* (Routledge, 2018). He currently is working on the second volume of his edition and translation of the Latin *Letters* of Renaissance humanist Angelo Poliziano, as well as a new book on the Victorian writer and polymath John Addington Symonds.

MICHEL CHION, born in 1947 in Creil, France, is a composer of *musique concrète*, a writer, and a director of films and videos. He has written and taught extensively on sound, notably on the combination of sound, word, and image in films. Many of his works have been translated into English, including *Film: A Sound Art*, translated by Claudia Gorbman (Columbia University Press, 2009), which won the Richard Wall Memorial Award from the Theater Library Association; *The Voice in Cinema*, translated by Gorbman (Columbia University Press, 1999); *Sound: An Acoulogical Treatise*, translated by James Steintrager (Duke University Press, 2016); and *Words on Screen*, translated by Gorbman (Columbia University Press, 2017). He is married to the producer Anne-Marie Marsaguet, and lives in Paris. For more information, see his website, www.michelchion.com.

JAMES Q. DAVIES is associate professor of music at the University of California, Berkeley. He is author of *Romantic Anatomies of Performance* (University of California Press, 2014), and coeditor of *Sound Knowledge: Music and Science in London, 1789–1851* (University of Chicago Press, 2016). His current project is entitled *Creatures of the Air*, a project about aero-technologies and aero-techniques. The book will explore nineteenth-century ideas about breath control during singing, ideas for air-conditioning systems in buildings for sound, and ideas about how musical civilizations form in relation to the aerial effects of different climates. He has published extensively on voice.

MLADEN DOLAR is professor and senior research fellow at the Department of Philosophy, University of Ljubljana. His principal areas of research are psychoanalysis, modern French philosophy, German idealism, and art theory. He has lectured extensively at universities in the United States and across Europe and is the author of over a hundred and fifty papers in scholarly journals and collected volumes. Apart from twelve books in Slovene, his book publications include most notably *A Voice and Nothing More* (MIT Press, 2006, translated into eight languages) and *Opera's Second Death* (with Slavoj Žižek, Routledge, 2001, also translated into several languages). His new book, *The Riskiest Moment*, is forthcoming with Duke University Press. He is one of the founders of the Ljubljana Lacanian School.

MARTHA FELDMAN is the Mabel Greene Myers Professor of Music, Romance Languages and Literatures, and Theater and Performance Studies at the University of Chicago, and author of the award-winning books *City Culture and the Madrigal at Venice* (University of California Press, 1995), *Opera and Sovereignty: Transforming Myths in Eighteenth-Century Italy* (University of Chicago Press, 2007), *The Castrato: Reflections on Natures and Kinds* (University of California Press, 2015), and the co-edited *The Courtesan's Arts: Cross-Cultural Perspectives* (Oxford, 2006). Her current work explores racialized and trans* voices and includes an experimental book-in-progress *The Castrato Phantom*, which maps the aftermath of the castrato phenomenon in twentieth-century Rome. She is an associate producer on Patricia Barber's *Smash* (Concord Records, 2013) and *Higher* (ArtistShare, 2019).

TOM GUNNING is Edwin A. and Betty L. Bergman Distinguished Service Professor Emeritus in the Department of Cinema and Media Studies at the University of Chicago, and author of *D. W. Griffith and the Origins of American Narrative Film* (University of Illinois Press, 1991), *The Films of Fritz Lang: Allegories of Vision and Modernity* (British Film Institute, 2000), and over a hundred and fifty articles. He is currently working on a book on the invention of the moving image. His theater piece, created in collaboration with director Travis Preston, *Fantomas: The Revenge of the Image*, premiered in 2017 at the Wuzhen International Theater Festival in Wuzhen, China.

ANDREW F. JONES, professor and Louis B. Agassiz Chair in Chinese at the University of California, Berkeley, teaches modern Chinese literature and media culture.

He is the author of *Yellow Music: Media Culture and Colonial Modernity in the Chinese Jazz Age* (Duke University Press, 2001) and *Developmental Fairy Tales: Evolutionary Thinking and Modern Chinese Culture* (Harvard University Press, 2011). He has translated the fiction of Yu Hua and a volume of literary essays by Eileen Chang. His latest book, *Circuit Listening: Chinese Popular Music in the Transistor Era*, is forthcoming from the University of Minnesota Press.

DAVID J. LEVIN is the Addie Clark Harding Professor in Germanic Studies and Cinema and Media Studies and chair of Theater and Performance Studies at the University of Chicago. From 2005 to 2015, he served as executive editor of *Opera Quarterly*. He is the editor of *Opera through Other Eyes* (Stanford University Press, 1994) and the author of *Richard Wagner, Fritz Lang, and the Nibelungen: The Dramaturgy of Disavowal* (Princeton University Press, 1998) and *Unsettling Opera: Staging Mozart, Verdi, Wagner, and Zemlinsky* (University of Chicago Press, 2007). In addition to his academic work, he has also worked as a dramaturg and collaborator for various opera houses in Germany and the United States as well for the choreographers William Forsythe and Saar Magal.

SARAH NOOTER is associate professor at the University of Chicago in Classics and Theater and Performance Studies. She is the author of *When Heroes Sing: Sophocles and the Shifting Soundscape of Tragedy* (Cambridge University Press, 2012) and *The Mortal Voice in the Tragedies of Aeschylus* (Cambridge University Press, 2017) and is coeditor with Shane Butler of *Sound and the Ancient Senses* (Routledge, 2018). She has also published on the reception of Greek drama in twentieth-century Africa and is currently working on questions of embodiment and time in Greek poetry. She is the editor of the journal *Classical Philology*.

MARCELLE PIERSON is a musicologist and composer whose research focuses on postwar musical modernism and its intersections with voice, texture, timbre, noise, and compositional ethics. She is also interested in heavy metal. Marcelle holds a PhD in music history and theory from the University of Chicago, with a minor in composition. She also graduated from the Oberlin Conservatory of Music with a double major in composition and music theory. She has taught at the University of Pittsburgh, University of North Carolina, University of Notre Dame, and Harold Washington College in Chicago.

ROBERT POLITO is a poet, essayist, editor, and biographer. Polito received a National Book Critics Circle Award for *Savage Art: A Biography of Jim Thompson* (Knopf, 1996). He is also the author of the poetry collections *Doubles* (University of Chicago Press, 1995) and *Hollywood & God* (University of Chicago Press, 2009) as well as *Farber on Film: The Complete Film Writings of Manny Farber* (Library of America, 2009), *A Reader's Guide to James Merrill's* The Changing Light at Sandover (University of Michigan Press, 1994), and a study of Byron's poetry. The founding director of the

Graduate Writing Program at the New School, he served as President of the Poetry Foundation in Chicago (2013–2015) before returning to New York and the New School. He is working on a new collection of poems, as well as on a pair of nonfiction books—on noir and on Bob Dylan.

STEVEN RINGS is a music theorist whose research focuses on popular music, voice, and transformational theory. He has taught at the University of Chicago since 2005. His 2011 book *Tonality and Transformation* (Oxford, 2011) received the Society for Music Theory's 2012 Emerging Scholar Award. Rings's article "A Foreign Sound to Your Ear: Bob Dylan Performs 'It's Alright, Ma (I'm Only Bleeding),' 1964–2009," won the 2014 Outstanding Publication Award from the Society for Music Theory's Popular Music Interest Group. Rings is currently writing a book on Bob Dylan and is coediting *The Oxford Handbook of Critical Concepts in Music Theory* with Alexander Rehding.

LAURIE STRAS is research professor of music at the University of Huddersfield. Her performance, research, and teaching spans the fifteenth to twenty-first centuries, always with a focus on female musicians and the female voice. Her publications include a monograph, *Women and Music in Sixteenth-Century Ferrara* (Cambridge University Press, 2018), and two edited collections, *She's So Fine: Reflections on Whiteness, Femininity, Adolescence, and Class in 1960s Music* (Ashgate, 2010) and *Eroticism in Early Modern Music* (with Bonnie Blackburn; Ashgate 2015). She has received a number of prizes, including the ASCAP Deems-Taylor Award and the Noah Greenberg Award from the American Musicological Society.

NEIL VERMA is assistant professor of sound studies in radio/television/film at Northwestern University. He is author of *Theater of the Mind: Imagination, Aesthetics, and American Radio Drama* (University of Chicago Press, 2012) and coeditor of *Anatomy of Sound: Norman Corwin and Media Authorship* (University of California Press, 2016). His awards include the Best First Book Award from the Society for Cinema and Media Studies and the Best Moving Image Book Award from the Kraszna-Krausz Foundation. Verma is co–network director for the Radio Preservation Task Force at the Library of Congress, and founder of the Great Lakes Association for Sound Studies (GLASS).

JUDITH T. ZEITLIN is William R. Kenan, Jr. Professor of East Asian Languages and Civilizations and Theater and Performance Studies at the University of Chicago. She is the author of *Historian of the Strange: Pu Songling and the Chinese Classical Tale* (Stanford, 1993) and *The Phantom Heroine: Ghosts and Gender in Seventeenth-Century Chinese Literature* (University of Hawai'i Press, 2007), and coeditor of *Writing and Materiality in China* (Harvard Asia Center, 2003), *Thinking with Cases: Specialist Knowledge in Chinese Cultural History* (University of Hawai'i Press, 2007), a special issue of *Opera Quarterly* on *Chinese Opera Film* (2010), and *Performing Images: Opera in Chinese Visual Culture* (2014). She is collaborating with composer Yao Chen on the creation of a new opera for which she has written the libretto.

JONATHAN ZWICKER is associate professor of Japanese literature at the University of California, Berkeley. He is the author of *Practices of the Sentimental Imagination: Melodrama, the Novel, and the Social Imaginary in Nineteenth-Century Japan* (Harvard Asia Center, 2006), and his work on the Japanese novel has appeared in *The Novel: History, Geography, and Culture* (Princeton University Press, 2006) and *The Encyclopedia of the Novel* (Wiley-Blackwell, 2011). He is currently completing a book on the intersection of kabuki and print culture in nineteenth-century Japan.

Index